Television, Nation, and Culture
in Indonesia

This series of publications on Africa, Latin America, and Southeast Asia is designed to present significant research, translation, and opinion to area specialists and to a wide community of persons interested in world affairs. The editor seeks manuscripts of quality on any subject and can generally make a decision regarding publication within three months of receipt of the original work. Production methods generally permit a work to appear within one year of acceptance. The editor works closely with authors to produce a high-quality book. The series appears in a paperback format and is distributed worldwide. For more information, contact the executive editor at Ohio University Press, Scott Quadrangle, University Terrace, Athens, Ohio 45701.

Executive editor: Gillian Berchowitz
AREA CONSULTANTS
Africa: Diane Ciekawy
Latin America: Thomas Walker
Southeast Asia: William H. Frederick

The Ohio University Research in International Studies series is published for the Center for International Studies by the Ohio University Press. The views expressed in individual volumes are those of the authors and should not be considered to represent the policies or beliefs of the Center for International Studies, the Ohio University Press, or Ohio University.

Television, Nation, and Culture in Indonesia

Philip Kitley

OHIO UNIVERSITY CENTER FOR INTERNATIONAL STUDIES
RESEARCH IN INTERNATIONAL STUDIES
SOUTHEAST ASIA SERIES NO. 104
ATHENS

© 2000 by the Ohio University Center for International Studies

Printed in the United States of America
All rights reserved

The books in the Ohio University Center for International Studies Research in International Studies Series are printed on acid-free paper ∞™

08 07 06 05 04 03 02 01 00   5 4 3 2 1

Library of Congress Cataloging-in-Publication Data

Kitley, Philip, 1946–
    Television, nation, and culture in Indonesia / Philip Kitley.
      p. cm. — (Research in international studies. Southeast Asia series ; no. 104)
    Includes bibliographical references and index.
    ISBN 0-89680-212-4 (pbk. : alk. paper)
      1. Television broadcasting—Indonesia. 2. Television broadcasting policy—Indonesia. 3. Television programs—Indonesia. I. Title. II. Series.
HE8700.9.I6 K58 2000
384.55'09598—dc21

                                                                                     99-086405

for

Yvonne, Ben, and Clare

Contents

List of Figures	ix
List of Tables	xi
Preface	xiii
Spelling and Translations	xviii
Chapter 1. Introducing Indonesian Television	1
Part I. The First Phase of Television in Indonesia: Building a Monopoly	19
Chapter 2. State Monopoly Broadcasting, 1962–1981	21
Chapter 3. Television and Its Historical Audiences	73
Chapter 4. Serious Puppet Plays: Television Models the Child	112
Chapter 5. The Rahmat Family: Soap Opera Models the Community	146
Chapter 6. Good News: National Development and the Culture of News	178
Part II. The Second Phase of Television in Indonesia: Breaking Up the Monopoly	213
Chapter 7. The Monopoly Breaks Up: New Television Technologies	215
Chapter 8. Commercial Television News and the Culture of Diversity	250

Chapter 9. Regulating Ownership and Control	268
Chapter 10. Regulating Television Content and Policy	296
Chapter 11. Conclusions: The Cultural Politics of Television in Indonesia	330

Appendixes ... 345

    A. Significant Dates in the Development of Indonesian Television ... 347

    B. Exchange Rates for the Indonesian Rupiah, U.S. Dollar, and Australian Dollar, 1962–1996 ... 351

    C. *Si Unyil* Episodes Analyzed ... 353

    D. The Flow of *Si Unyil* and *Ria Jenaka* ... 356

    E. *Keluarga Rahmat*'s Setting and Characters ... 357

    F. The Corpus of *Keluarga Rahmat* Episodes Analyzed ... 360

    G. Recording Dates during December 1991 ... 362

    H. Categories of News Items ... 363

    I. Seminars on Television, 1993–1996 ... 365

Notes ... 369

Works Cited ... 385

Indonesian Legislation Cited ... 405

Figures

2.1. Number of Television Receivers Registered in Jakarta, on Java, and outside Java, 1967–1978   47

2.2. Television Receivers Registered, 1962–1981   58

2.3. Television Receivers Registered, 1962–1981 (Data Trend)   58

2.4. Domestic Manufacture of Television Receivers, 1971–1981   58

2.5. Domestic Manufacture of Television Antennae, 1971–1981   59

2.6. Imports of Television Receivers, 1975–1980   59

2.7. Cartoon: Indonesian greets Prime Minister Tanaka   65

2.8. Cartoon: Don't buy lipstick . . .   67

2.9. Cartoon: Man snoring   70

2.10. Cartoon Strip: Public television show   71

3.1. Cartoon: Television sponsorship   79

3.2. Cartoon Strip: Bung Joni   89

3.3. Cartoon: This Year's Festival   95

3.4. Cartoon: I'm still interesting, aren't I?   96

3.5. Cartoon: Public Taste   97

3.6. Cartoon: Oshin and Kartini   104

7.1. Cartoon: Globalization 237
7.2. Cartoon: Malay diplomacy 240
9.1. Cartoon: Advertisement 281
9.2. Ads for Categories of Goods and Services on
    TPI and RCTI, 1991 and 1993 283

Tables

2.1. Television Broadcast Stations Commissioned,
1962–1978 — 37

2.2. TVRI Program Categories as a Percentage of
Total Broadcast Hours, 1962–1972 — 39

2.3. TVRI Program Times, Weekdays and Weekends,
1963–1967 and 1971–1981 — 40

2.4. Distribution of Public Access Television Sets,
1978/79–1991/92 — 57

2.5. TVRI Broadcast Range and Population Covered,
1962–1981 — 60

2.6. Domestic and Foreign Productions as Percentage
of Total TVRI Programming, 1968–1981/82 — 68

5.1. Percentage of Domestic versus Foreign Productions
on TVRI Programming, 1983/84–1991/92 — 152

6.1. Frequency of Different Categories of News Items — 182

6.2. Frequency of Appearance of State Officials in
Key Roles in News Items — 184

6.3. Setting of News Items in Jakarta or Elsewhere — 185

10.1. Variables Affecting Media Impact on Television Policy
and Regulation — 318

Preface

Having me around the house in 1968 after I had completed my undergraduate studies was obviously too much for my mother. She encouraged me to take a summer course in Indonesian language offered by the University of New England. I was one of nine students lucky enough to be taught by that inspired teacher from Sydney University, the late Hedwig Emanuels. That course set me on a path of study, research, and involvement with Indonesia that has greatly enriched my life. At the conclusion of this project, a wholly unanticipated outcome of those early days, I thank both my late mother and father for nurturing in me a love of language and an interest in other cultures and people.

I never expected to write about television, for unlike most of my generation, I grew up in country New South Wales without television. Three "television moments" led me into this project. At Robb College, at the University of New England, I watched the events of the Vietnam War unfold on television and for the first time became impressed with the power of the medium. In 1969/70 I began research on modern batik art and spent some months in the house of Bambang Oetoro, one of the pioneer modern batik artists in Yogyakarta. Every Friday night, Mas Bambang placed his black and white television set on the verandah of his house in Babadan, Gedongkuning, for members of the village to enjoy. I watched with everyone else and enjoyed the national news, which enlarged my knowledge of the archipelago, and I remember how bizarre it seemed to be watching the American spy series *The Man from U.N.C.L.E.* in Central Java. I remember, too, that the villagers enjoyed the program greatly, though I don't know why. I did not think to ask—"reception analysis" was not part of my critical repertoire in those days. And then from 1986 to 1989 I was posted to the Australian Embassy in Jakarta as Cultural Attache, during which time my children, Ben and Clare, watched TVRI as uncomprehendingly, I often thought, as the villagers in Babadan had watched *The Man from U.N.C.L.E.* They enjoyed *Si Unyil*, as I did, and some of the other cartoon programs, but found everything else boring. For three years they alternated their consumption of TVRI with countless videos, which gave me a first-hand understanding of how televisual products, mostly imported, were booming "off screen."

These experiences were inflected further by the so-called Jenkins Affair in 1986, and the Australian Embassy's decision to use the popularity of the Australian prime-time soap *Return to Eden* as a way of mending fences after David Jenkins's *Sydney Morning Herald* article had plunged the Australia-Indonesia diplomatic relationship to an all-time low. The popularity of the Australian series, which had enjoyed only limited success at home, increased my interest in television in Indonesia and in the media relations between our two countries and led eventually to this research.

Much more directly, of course, my doctoral supervisors at Murdoch University have been a great encouragement, source of ideas, and constructive criticism during this research project. My principal supervisor, Krishna Sen, has been an enthusiastic, hospitable, and encouraging supervisor, tempering her insightful and uncompromisingly direct critique with a willingness to let me follow my own interests in mapping out the focus of the research. Her knowledge of Indonesian popular culture and sense of the ideological force of the media was very helpful to me in thinking through my conclusions. Cosupervisor Ien Ang's scholarship, her interest in Indonesia, which she had left as a young girl, and her careful critique, especially of the chapters concerned with soap opera and the children's program, were very helpful. When Ien Ang left to take up the Chair of Cultural Studies at the University of Western Sydney, I was extremely fortunate to have Tom O'Regan act as cosupervisor. Tom's knowledge of television studies, particularly in the area of policy studies, directed me to think about aspects of Indonesian television that I had previously given insufficient attention. His skill at editing has made this book much more readable than it would otherwise have been. The contributions Krishna, Ien, and Tom have made to my research and to this book are greatly appreciated, and I thank them most sincerely for all their help and time.

I am also very grateful to the Asia Research Centre at Murdoch University, which supported my candidacy as a postgraduate student and provided facilities and a stimulating, hospitable environment at Murdoch in 1993. David Hill and Ian and Ratna Chalmers were great friends and very kind and generous to me while I was living in Fremantle, and I thank them for making study leave so enjoyable.

The book could not have written without the help of my Indonesian informants, most of whom I can thank here, but some of whom I cannot, as they have asked that I keep their contributions confidential. For their time and their willingness to share their knowledge and memories, which have allowed me to write the story of television in Indonesia, I thank all my Indonesian colleagues and informants, especially the late Alex Leo Zulkarnain, Dr. Alwi Dahlan, Dr. Ariel Heryanto, Aziz Husain, Professor Astrid Susanto, Dr. Arief Sadiman, Awad Bahrosian, Bisri Hasanuddin, Chrys Kelana, Dr. Eduard Depari, Professor Emil Salim, Fahmi Alatas, Goenawan Soebagio, Ishadi SK, Professor Iskandar Alisjahbana, Kelly Saputro, Peter Langlois, Maladi, Suprapti Widarto, Rani Sutrisno, Philip Rich, Sjamsoe Soegito, Dr. Sumita Tobing, Suryanto, Sumartono, Suyadi, and Wahyudi.

In Jakarta, my host, Ibu Pujadi Aziz, and her family kindly allowed me to convert a portion of the house in Setiabudi into a small recording "studio" and welcomed me as part of the family. I am very grateful for the hospitality that helped make my period of fieldwork most enjoyable. Watie Syamsu and Bwee Sie, friends from my 1986 posting, have helped this project with all sorts of kindness and advice, and I thank them. John Milne and Kevin Evans, embassy colleagues, have also helped my research, and I thank them for their friendship and help.

I am grateful to the Faculty of Arts at the University of Southern Queensland for providing the conditions that allowed me to do fieldwork in Indonesia and take a period of residence at Murdoch University. My colleague and friend Professor Robert Dixon has been very generous with his time in reading chapters and in commenting on work in progress. I have valued his encouragement, stimulating conversation, and scholarship, and I thank him for helping to break down that sense of isolation I often felt so far away from Murdoch.

Finally, I thank my wife, Yvonne, for her unfailing support and encouragement during this drawn-out project, which had to be completed part-time, imposed extra burdens on her, and took me away from the family for extended periods. Ben and Clare have also been very tolerant of the time I had to spend away from them, and I thank them for their patience. All I can say is that it was through them that I got into this field, and I am very grateful, for it has been stimulating and, looking back, great fun!

I am grateful to Indonesian publishers for their permission to reproduce cartoons that originally appeared in the journals: *Berita Buana* (figs. 2.8 and 3.2), *Berita Yudha* (fig. 3.6), *Kompas* (figs. 2.7, 2.9, and 2.19), *Lensa* (figs. 3.3 and 7.1), *Surabaya Post* (figs. 3.1 and 3.5), *Suara Karya* (fig. 7.2), *Suara Merdeka* (fig. 9.1), and *Suara Pembaruan* (fig. 3.4).

Versions of some parts of this book have been published previously, and I acknowledge the publishers' permission to reprint:

"Tahun Bertambah, Zaman Berubah: Television and Its Audiences in Indonesia." *Review of Indonesian and Malaysian Affairs* 26 (1992): 71–109.

"The Indonesian Market for Educational Television." *Media Information Australia* 73 (1994): 97–103.

"Fine Tuning Control: Commercial Television in Indonesia." *Continuum* 8, no. 2 (1994): 103–23.

"Some Problems in the Cross-Cultural Criticism of Indonesian Television." *Southern Review* 28, no. 3 (1995): 321–31.

"Television News Rituals in New Order Indonesia." In *Images of Malay-Indonesian Identity,* ed. Michael Hitchcock and Victor T. King (Kuala Lumpur: Oxford University Press, 1997), 236–64.

"Shadow Language: Competition and the Television Sector in Indonesia." *Social Semiotics* 8, no. 1 (1998): 37–54. Published by Carfax Publishing Ltd., P.O. Box 25, Abingdon, Oxfordshire OX14 3UE, UK.

"Pancasila in the Minor Key: TVRI's *Si Unyil* Models the Child." *Indonesia* 68 (October 1999). *Indonesia* is published by the Southeast Asia Program of Cornell University.

Spelling and Translations

Spelling of Indonesian words follows the spelling reform of 1972, except where I have quoted from sources published prior to 1972. Names are spelled according to the preference of the individual in question and are listed alphabetically by first name. All translations are my own unless otherwise indicated.

Television, Nation, and Culture
in Indonesia

Chapter 1

INTRODUCING INDONESIAN TELEVISION

> For several decades, patterns made in a tube by fusillades of electrons have played an extraordinary role in our lives.... In living colour more real than life, the swirling dots represent the world; they tell us of the good, great, beautiful, and desirable—and their opposites. They have become the environment and context of our lives. (Barnouw 1977)

> The Asian challenge for Australia is not economic or commercial. It is intellectual, and the issues are political and cultural. (Fitzgerald 1997)

THIS BOOK IS THE FIRST EXTENDED STUDY of television in Indonesia and is intended as a contribution to understanding culture and politics in Indonesia from an Australian point of view. In the late twentieth century, television is truly a global phenomenon; all kinds of exchanges and mutualities mesh viewers into a global audiencehood. Indonesian and Australian viewers watch many of the same (imported) programs, and Indonesian viewers have watched Australian serials such as *Return to Eden* (screened Australia 1983; Indonesia 1986), *A Country Practice* (screened Australia 1981; Indonesia 1988), *Jack Thompson Down Under* (screened Australia 1988; Indonesia 1989), *Beyond 2000* (screened Australia 1985; Indonesia 1989–90), *The Flying Doctors* (screened Australia 1986;

Indonesia 1992), *The Henderson Kids* (screened Australia 1985; Indonesia 1992), and *Neighbours* (screened Australia 1985; Indonesia 1992, 93) (Isaac 1992; Moran 1993; Cunningham and Jacka 1996, 199). Australia's SBS television channel has screened Indonesian auteur films such as *Para Perintis Kemerdekaan* (1980, Asrul Sani), *Roro Mendut* (1983, Ami Priyono), *Doea Tanda Mata* (1984, Teguh Karya), and *Ibunda* (1986, Teguh Karya). Since 1993, the Australian Broadcasting Corporation's Australia Television (ATV) has used the Palapa satellite to broadcast Australian content to viewers in Indonesia, the Philippines, Brunei, Singapore, Malaysia, and Thailand.

More important than exchanges of programming, however, is the binding of Australia and Indonesia into a transnational public sphere by the television technology of the late twentieth century. Jurgen Habermas's concept of the bourgeois public sphere assumes face-to-face communicative relations between discussants in personalized, unmediated space (1989). It also presupposes forms of speech (discussion, debate) and print as the predominant modes of communication in the public sphere. Yet under conditions of globalized electronic communications, the public sphere simultaneously has a real and a virtual character. It may no longer be thought of as that space "*between* civil society and the nation-state" (Hirst 1995, 14; my emphasis), for state authorities, elite representatives, and other social groups are present and interact in a variety of ways across the same communicative space(s). Indeed, the public sphere is occupied not only by local actors but also by official and nonofficial voices from beyond the national territory, creating a *transnational* public sphere. As Miriam Hansen puts it, "the accelerated process of transnationalization makes it difficult to ground a concept of the public in any territorial entity, be it local, regional or national" (1993, 183). Events such as the worldwide screening of smuggled video images of East Timorese demonstrators fleeing from Indonesian soldiers in 1991, the diplomatic row between Australia and Malaysia over the Australian television serial *Embassy,* and the rift in diplomatic relations between Singapore and the Philippines following the intense media attention given to the execution in Singapore of the Filipina maid Flor Contemplacion in 1995 show how potent cross-cultural media relations are in managing contemporary diplomatic relations.

In the late twentieth century, Indonesian and Australian relations are increasingly inflected by television. Images of such scenes as the destruction caused by the earthquakes and tidal waves in Flores, Gareth Evans and Ali Alatas signing the Timor Gap treaty in an airplane high above the Arafura Sea, flag burning in Canberra and Jakarta, the batik shirts worn by APEC leaders at the Bogor meeting in 1994, Balinese dancers in temples well known to Australian tourists, and Democratic Party demonstrations in the streets of Jakarta in June 1996 are played and replayed on Australian television screens whenever the relationship gains attention. To paraphrase Barnouw (1977, iv), the flow of televised images across the transnational public sphere has become an important part of "the environment and context" of our relations with Indonesia, and the significance of television in Australia-Indonesia political and cultural relations can no longer be ignored.

Television and the Indonesian National Culture Project

This study is concerned with the development, role, and culture of television and television policy over the period from its establishment in Indonesia in 1962 as a public broadcasting service funded jointly by the public and private sectors through to deregulation of television broadcasting in 1990 and the rapid establishment of five national commercial channels. I argue that television in Indonesia can be understood as part of Indonesia's "national culture project," my shorthand expression for a range of state-sponsored and -directed activities designed to legitimate symbolically Indonesian national cultural identity. Under the "New Order" established following the coup attempt in 1965, television has three goals: (1) the promotion of national unity and integration; (2) the promotion of national stability;

and (3) the promotion of political stability (Alfian and Chu 1981, 23). But if television has contributed to the mediation of the national culture project, it has also, particularly in the period leading up to deregulation and since, become a site for contesting the elements of the New Order's cultural policies. Television, and press reporting and commentary on television, as well as seminars, workshops, and the like, have widened the public sphere. The public conversation over television has enabled audiences and interest groups in the community to focus their resistance to the state's dominant and dominating ideas of a unified and unitary national culture.

The national culture project takes its warrant from Article 32 of the 1945 constitution, which authorizes the government "to develop national culture" and clearly understands national culture as something to be constructed:

> National culture is an outcome of the thinking of all the Indonesian people. Ancient and original culture is taken as the height of regional cultures throughout Indonesia and added together as national culture. Cultural efforts must be directed toward the advancement of civilization, culture, and unity and should not reject new things from foreign cultures that can develop or enrich national culture itself and raise the humanity of the Indonesian people. (Muhammad Yamin 1959, 44)

Under the New Order, the national culture project can be understood as three entwined processes of cultural denial, affirmation, and invention, which together have attempted to map a unitary and unifying cultural identity across the territory taken over from the former colonial power in 1949. In this discussion I focus on the national cultural project of the New Order because it has the most relevance to the historical development of television in Indonesia. The national culture project has, however, been part of state practice from the earliest days of independence and has its roots in landmark events such as the "Youth Pledge" at the 1928 Youth Congress, the cultural polemic stimulated by Takdir Alisjahbana in the 1930s, and the activities of Japanese propagandists during the occupation.

The processes of denial, affirmation, and invention are not to be understood chronologically, as if they referred simply to the past (Guided Democracy period), the present, and the future (under the New Order). The New Order has affirmed some elements of Guided Democracy period culture as central to its national culture project, most obviously the foundational significance accorded the state ideology Pancasila.[1] It has equivocated, however, on the principle of *gotong royong* [communal cooperation] (which Sukarno represented as the essence of the Indonesian state), using it strategically in rural areas, where "it is an unremarkable fact of everyday life" (Sullivan 1992, 177), but otherwise giving it limited attention. Benedict Anderson has also shown that the New Order enthusiasm for the invention of tradition through monumental expressions of national culture relies on practices that Sukarno employed with great flair during the Guided Democracy period (1990, 173–93). The process of affirmation can also be understood as the selective acknowledgment and positive valorization of dimensions of national culture such as religion and institutions of family and community, which are understood as part of the general (indigenous) way of life of Indonesia and which may include cultural constructs of the Guided Democracy period. By processes of denial I mean the way the New Order has distanced itself from Sukarno's Guided Democracy by rejecting out of hand or by denigrating cultural values and practices that are believed to have contributed to the disorder and economic collapse of the early 1960s (Ramage 1995, 25f.).

The "invention of culture" is a phrase that signifies both the invention of cultural traditions (Hobsbawm 1983, 1–14), a process that has an eye fixed on the past and the representation of historical continuity, and the innovations in cultural policies, practices, and values introduced by the New Order, such as the preeminence given to "development" as an essential part of Indonesian identity, the expansion of elementary education, and the definition of women as wives and mothers through organizations such as Dharma Wanita, the organization of wives of civil servants (Sullivan 1991).

In some parts of the project, the processes of denial, affirmation, and invention overlap. The affirmation of Pancasila as the foundation of national development, for example, is imbricated with the denial of Sukarno's commitment to Pancasila and claims that he "deviated" from its principles (Ramage 1995, 25–27), the downgrading of *gotong royong,* the invention of intensive courses in Pancasila in the early 1980s, and the 1985 "Unifying Principle" legislation, which required all mass organizations to adopt Pancasila as their single basic principle. Similarly, the spread of universal, state-funded elementary education, begun during the Sukarno period and boosted substantially during the 1980s, can be understood as a rejection of the elitist and gendered educational traditions of the colonial regime, an affirmation of modernization, and the invention of tradition through the introduction of compulsory courses on Pancasila Moral Education in both elementary and secondary school curricula (Leigh 1991).

The impulse to affirm particular cultural values and practices may also involve a paradigmatic denial of other values. The affirmation of modernization and progress, for example, the key assumptions of the New Order strategy of development, involves a simultaneous denigration of "tradition," which is understood as a drag on progress (Dove 1988). Denial of some cultural values may also be inconsistent with values promoted in other parts of the culture project. For example, the rejection of Western culture as inimical to indigenous Indonesian culture, which is an aspect of the local content regulations for television, sits uneasily with acceptance of Western modernizing practices and knowledge, and in some circumstances, with the official status granted to Western religious beliefs (Christianity). Finally, I note that "culture" in the phrase "culture project" is understood in the anthropological sense as pertaining to "a whole way of life" and is not restricted to the arts. Under the New Order, "Indonesian culture" is a discourse of policy and power that interpellates its subjects across many aspects of their lives, such as religion, language, their roles as women or men, their involvement in development, their relationships with state authorities, their attitudes toward foreign culture, and their understanding of national history. In parts, therefore, the national culture project blurs into the national political project, but in Indonesia, where ideology penetrates so pervasively, this blurring is inescapable (Schlesinger 1991).

Fieldwork

Research for this book began with fieldwork in Jakarta from December 1991 to January 1992. I purchased two locally manufactured television receivers, two VHS video recorders, two antennae, and a supply of videotapes in Jakarta and set up a simple recording "studio" in my bedroom in Setiabudi. One antenna was angled to the west, toward Kebun Jeruk, and picked up TVRI (Televisi Republik Indonesia) and RCTI (Rajawali Citra Televisi Indonesia). The other antenna was directed to the southeast, toward Taman Mini, and picked up TPI's (Televisi Pendidikan Indonesia) afternoon programs. Reception was very poor because of the inadequate height of TPI's tower and the low power of the transmitter.

In 1991 there were four television channels on the air in Jakarta: Televisi Republik Indonesia (TVRI) with two channels, Rajawali Citra Televisi Indonesia (RCTI), and Televisi Pendidikan Indonesia (TPI). The only other channel on the air in 1991, Surya Citra Televisi (SCTV), broadcast to Surabaya in East Java and could not be received in Jakarta.

A random sampling technique (Jones and Carter 1959; Heidt 1984) was used to construct two "weeks" of television broadcasts during December. All material broadcast by the four Jakarta channels over the two constructed weeks was recorded. Recording occupied most of my time during December. In January I interviewed informants who had been involved in the establishment of television in Jakarta, and I began collecting print materials relevant to the history of television in Indonesia.

In 1993 I returned to Jakarta for about three months of fieldwork from March through June, when another two weeks of randomly sampled broadcasts by TVRI, RCTI, and TPI were recorded. I also met with informants and visited TVRI Yogyakarta and the SCTV studio in Surabaya.

In 1991 there was no collection of Indonesian television recordings in Australia. The recordings made in 1991 and 1993 provided me with an archive of programming, which I viewed to bring me up to date with Indonesian television. I had some familiarity with TVRI programming from an earlier period of research on Javanese textiles in 1969–70, during which I watched television over two months in a village setting in Yogyakarta. I saw a lot more of TVRI during my posting as cultural attaché in Jakarta in 1986–89, when I watched television at home as a casual, family viewer. But by 1991 the television scene had changed dramatically, and the tape archive was very useful for getting a feel for the flow of programming on each channel and for comparing scheduling. Chapter 6, which looks at the national news on TVRI, is based on an analysis of news bulletins broadcast during the period of my research. Chapter 8, a study of news programs on commercial television, is based on material recorded during 1991 and 1993. Chapter 4, a study of the children's series *Si Unyil,* refers to episodes broadcast during the fieldwork periods and is enriched by reference to episodes broadcast in the 1980s. Chapter 5, an analysis of the soap opera *Keluarga Rahmat,* screened in 1989–90, is based on a random sample of episodes supplied by the director of the series, Fritz Schadt.

My research also involved interviews with Indonesians involved in the establishment and development of Indonesian television. These interviews provided information that enabled me to situate the development of the television system, television policy, and even the development of specific programs in their historical and cultural context. The interviews I conducted were extended structured interviews (at least one hour long), framed by questions I prepared beforehand. Inevitably, interviews strayed from the questions and were often all the better for it. The interviews were conducted in Indonesian and English, depending on my own and my informants' linguistic abilities. Whenever possible, I recorded the interviews and transcribed the dialogue as soon as possible afterward. On those occasions when informants preferred not to have their comments recorded, I made notes during the interview and wrote up a fuller account of the discussion later.

Interviews of this kind present particular problems for the researcher. Questions may be framed in one language (English), asked in another (Indonesian), and the informants' responses noted in a mixture of hastily scrawled, abbreviated English and Indonesian. I wrote up the interviews in English, on occasions preserving in Indonesian an informant's exact words when they appeared to be particularly apt, idiomatic, or colorful. I kept copies of the original questions, the interview notes, and the transcript from each interview and have relied at times on all three in writing this text. Quotation marks around the words attributed to an informant generally mean that I have quoted directly from the transcript made from my tape of the interview. Whenever I have had to resort to indirect attributions such as "(the informant) believed that . . . ," I am relying on notes from a discussion.

The practicalities of fieldwork were difficult. Indonesian customs regulations prevented me from bringing in my own recording equipment and blank videotapes. And then I was unable to convince anyone in authority at TVRI to certify that the hundreds of videotapes I was taking out were part of an approved research project and had to obtain special, prior permission from customs before departure to take the boxes of tapes out of the country. Some informants, particularly public servants, were reluctant to speak frankly and on the record about television, which for so long had been closely tied to government business. As I explain in chapter 5, the soap opera *Keluarga Rahmat* came about because President Soeharto suggested it and lent archival material held in the State Secretariat to the State Film Centre to be used as props for some historical episodes. More recently, the first family associations of commercial stations' licensees made informants sometimes unwilling to speak frankly and provide basic information. In this sense, then, television in Indonesia is not like television in Australia, the United Kingdom, or the United States. It is a more highly charged field because of its close associations with government and first family elite business connections.²

It is not surprising, then, that there did not exist a lively critical context in which to situate my research. There were very few articles and very few postgraduate theses, let alone books on the subject. During my fieldwork the pioneer critic Arswendo Atmowiloto was serving a five-year sentence in Jakarta because he had made an error of editorial judgment in October 1990, when he published the results of a survey in *Monitor* that rated President Soeharto as more popular than the Prophet Muhammad. In 1992, the energetic and talented director of TVRI, Ishadi SK, fell out with Siti Hardiyanti, owner of TPI and daughter of President Soeharto, over TPI's use of TVRI's facilities and slowness in paying TVRI its share of advertising income. Ishadi was shifted sideways from TVRI to head the Department of Information's Research Section.³ In 1994, three influential Jakarta current affairs journals were banned by ministerial decree for supposedly jeopardizing national security by reporting critically on the business dealings of the presidential family and the purchase of warships from the former East German navy (Hill 1994, 41).

Access to press commentary on television was difficult to obtain. Documentation was derived mainly from the Centre for Strategic and Information Studies (CSIS), and Yayasan Idayu's library held back copies of clippings and newspapers in which I could search for background on the development of television. TVRI's own documentation was incomplete and unorganized.

Disciplinary Approach

This book takes its place among a relatively small number of books and chapter-length studies of popular culture in Indonesia, which I will survey very briefly. The earliest publication in the field was Judith Agassi's study of the mass media, published in 1969. Karl Jackson and Lucian Pye included a chapter called "The Mass Communications System in Indonesia" by Astrid Susanto and a chapter on the press by Nono Anwar Makarim in their book *Political Power and Communications in Indonesia,* published in 1978. Alfian and Chu published their study of satellite television in 1981 and followed in 1991 with their landmark longitudinal study on the impact of satellite television. These publications were concerned largely with the mass media as part of the communications infrastructure of Indonesia and with the effects of television on rural populations, rather than the political or cultural aspects of the media.

Arswendo Atmowiloto published an important first collection of newspaper articles on television in 1986. Arswendo's articles were the first to address the cultural politics of television in bright, elegantly written features with titles such as "Twenty Years of TVRI: Televising the Community," "Like Fish and Water: Television and Ads," and "Television and the Presidency: The Fatherly Touch." Arswendo's articles were often comparative, contrasting television in Indonesia with that in the United States, the United Kingdom, and, occasionally, Australia. In 1995 journalists Ashadi Siregar and Veven Sp. Wardhana followed Arswendo's lead and published collections of their newspaper articles on television. Andries Teeuw included a chapter on what he called "Fiction for Consumption" in his two-volume work *Modern Indonesian Literature.* Teeuw acknowledged the importance of popular fiction, noting that "pop novels" outsold all others. His analysis was largely formalist, and comments such as "[o]ne may perhaps deplore the fact that it is these books, rather than serious novels, which are captivating the minds of the reading public" negatively evaluated popular literature against the canonic standards of a corpus of high culture literature (1979, 157).

Studies of film and popular theater are rare. Salim Said's historical study *Shadows on the Silver Screen* was published in 1982.

Indonesian Cinema: National Culture on Screen (1991) presented a cultural analysis of Indonesian cinema by American anthropologist Karl Heider. In *Indonesian Cinema: Framing the New Order* (1994), Krishna Sen advanced the argument that "Indonesian cinema is political." James Peacock's ethnography on "proletarian drama" in 1968 and Barbara Hatley's (1990) chapter on popular drama in Budiman, *State and Civil Society in Indonesia,* are two important discussions of popular theater and its cultural significance. Hatley's wide-ranging essay on cultural expression under the New Order appeared in 1994 and expanded on themes she had outlined in the Budiman publication.

Virginia Matheson Hooker's valuable collection of essays published in 1993 on New Order culture and society ranged over literature, popular theater, film, television, literary institutions, architecture, public monuments, language, and book piracy. Most of the work is text-based and is concerned with aesthetic and critical judgments rather than linkages between signifying practices and social and political discourses and policies.

The approach of this study differs from most of the work cited above in its methodology, its assumptions about cross-cultural studies, and its disciplinary orientation. My assumption is that television overlaps with a range of other social and cultural phenomena happening around it. It cannot be understood as a closed semiotic system. As I have indicated in my comments on the role of television in the national culture project, television is integrated in complex processes of cultural socialization that affect the meanings that people make in, around, and beyond the immediate *content* of television. For that reason, I have chosen to consider a broad range of issues and have drawn evidence from a wide range of sources.

The critical apparatus I have relied upon has been equally eclectic. I have employed techniques familiar from the field of media research, such as content and textual analysis, and have supplemented them with historical research and theoretical concepts and approaches drawn from ethnography, political economy, and cultural studies, itself an interdisciplinary practice. To the best of my knowledge, my discussion of the construction of the idealized

Indonesian self in television discourses is the first analysis of its kind in the field of Indonesian studies and has been included for the insight it gives into how official cultural processes attempt to privilege specific identities for the public and private selves of viewers. In tracing shifts in representation of the model self, I draw attention to the constitution of the self in power relations and the possibility of resistance and reshaping of identity through political and cultural processes.

The approach in this book is thus part of the cultural studies tradition, which, in Tom O'Regan's words, is concerned with "a multilayered account of social practice in which the meaning of, say, a film or television program would be traced not in one analytical exercise but in a series of texts where textual analysis, political economy and ethnography would all play a part" (1993, 193).

Understood this way, this study shares affinities with the work of Indonesianists such as Herbert Feith (1963) in his comments on Sukarno's architectural "symbol wielding," Benedict Anderson (1978) in his innovative work on the "visual languages" of cartoons and monuments, which he understands as a mode of political communication, and James Siegel in his idiosyncratic study *Solo in the New Order* (1986), which took classroom language, a teenage fashion magazine, the neighbourhood security round, and the articulation of High Javanese with Low Javanese as texts from which ideas of social hierarchy and social stability could be read.

I have approached television in Indonesia as the "same but different," an orientation that disavows the a priori assumption of "otherness" when exploring the cultural practices of a "foreign" culture. As John Hartley says, "Neither television nor nations can be understood at all, in fact, except in relational terms. They have no pure, intrinsic properties, but only differences from each other" (1987, 123).

Overview of Chapters

This study of relations between television, nation, and culture traces developments in the use and reception of television in Indonesia from its earliest days to a time when it is poised on the edge of a global revolution in electronic communications that has implications for the regulation of television, its use as a normative influence in the fashioning of national culture, and the continued relevance of the idea of the nation as a territorially limited, sovereign, imagined community. Ac-cordingly, the book has been divided into two parts, which correspond to the period when television was largely under the control of the Indonesian state and the period of deregulation, when five national commercial channels were added to the two government channels.

Part 1 (chapters 2–6) examines historical processes of using television to fashion and shape the nation in line with official national development and cultural objectives. These processes are examined in five chapters that analyze the history of state involvement in television, changing conceptions of the audience, a popular children's program, a soap opera, and the national news. In each of these chapters I focus on the inscribed construct of the idealised Indonesian subject.

Part 2 (chapters 7–11) focuses on major changes that have occurred in the television sector since the first commercial channel began broadcasting in 1989. It looks at how globalization and deregulation have impacted the historical role of television as a medium for the construction of Indonesian national cultural identity. Parallel to the concerns of part 1, the chapters in part 2 show how the idealized Indonesian subject under the TVRI monopoly has shifted and is now fragmented and contested.

Individual Chapters

In chapter 2 I present a history of the establishment of television in Indonesia and trace its development from an emergent regional broadcasting system with a blend of nation-building and entertainment objectives, funded by the public and private sectors in the early 1960s, to a national network under the monopoly control of the state in 1981.

The launch of the domestic satellite Palapa and the ban on television advertising are identified as the crucial events that moved television in Indonesia firmly under the control of the state, positioning it to play a significant role in the New Order national culture project during the 1980s. I outline a tension in the culture of Indonesian television, which has been inflected and reinflected as television has changed over the last thirty years. The tension exists between an audience-centered, internationally informed television culture, congenial to both international and domestic culture, and a more culturally didactic television culture that puts questions of internal politics and the construction of a distinctive Indonesian national identity and culture as its main priority.

In chapter 3 the construction of television audiences is traced historically from 1962 to the early 1990s. I look at the TVRI audience imagined as nation, as family, and as childlike in official discourses. Journalistic and academic commentary challenged official discourses and constructed TVRI's audience as an audience of public citizens, aware of their diversity, realistic about the complexities of development, and interested in entertainment. In the final sections I turn to the audience constructs of the commercial channels RCTI and TPI and highlight differences in the idealized subjectivity imagined by TVRI and the commercial channels.

Chapter 4 is a detailed case study of the popular children's series *Si Unyil*. This program was the first local series produced for Indonesian children and aimed at naturalizing the government's role in directing the social and cultural affairs of the nation. The series is read as part of the normative development of children into model Indonesian (adult) subjects. The didactic content of the series is highlighted, and the role of parody and the marginalization of nonstandard language and accents are examined as devices that are intended to build and strengthen audience acceptance of the national language and the "national subject."

In chapter 5 I examine how TVRI has attempted to fashion and shape the adult subject in the context of the three inclusive settings: the family, the neighborhood, and the national community.

The argument is presented through a detailed study of a domestically produced soap opera: *Keluarga Rahmat*. I argue that TVRI's shift into soap opera was precipitated by the imminent arrival of commercial television and represented a desire to attract, entertain, and shape the audience by producing a local adaptation of a genre that had proved internationally popular. The process of adaptation of a transnational form is examined in detail, and reasons are advanced to explain why the series enjoyed only limited success. I argue that the series' ideological project overdetermined its dramatic potential and confused viewers by delivering a lumpy mix of documentary and soap opera, which strained viewers' interpretive competencies.

Chapter 6 outlines the distinctive culture of news programming in Indonesia. In a detailed study of national news bulletins, the ritual character of the news is emphasized. The national news is understood as a ritual that represents the nation as a unified community, a community that is peaceful, committed to development, and organized socially as a hierarchy in which state officials occupy dominant positions.

Chapters 4, 5, and 6 may be read together as an exploration of the idealization of the Indonesian subject in three progressively more inclusive "families": the domestic family of young children, the neighborhood family as a community of adults who share and cooperate in life, and the national family, a totalizing construct that imagines the great diversity of Indonesian social and cultural formations as an organic whole.

Chapter 7 examines the technological changes that have impacted the availability of televisual products and services through satellite delivery, circulation of videotapes, and for some viewers, spillover from neighboring countries. The state's inability to control these various sources made television into a site of cultural contestation. In a detailed discussion of discourses of competition and communalism, I examine the favorable response that greeted the introduction of commercial television. I read the enthusiasm for commercial television as community endorsement of the need for a more diverse and pluralist mediation of political and cultural affairs. I conclude the chapter by arguing that globalized television technologies challenge the continued theoretical adequacy of the idea of the nation as a territorially limited, sovereign, imagined community.

In chapter 8, tentative moves toward cultural and political pluralism are explored further in a study of news programs on commercial television channels. Although prevented by legislation from producing their own news broadcasts, commercial channels have developed "soft news" programs that differentiate their services from the national broadcaster. I argue that the different modes of address of the public and commercial news programs manifest a tension in the cultural construction of the Indonesian subject. On the commercial stations, the idealized subject is constructed as an embodied, (passive) sovereign consumer and appealed to using an apparatus of audience surveys and ratings. I conclude by arguing that, at the time of writing, news broadcasts on the two commercial channels studied do not offer any real alternative to the developmental priorities of the National News service.

Chapters 9 and 10 are both concerned with television policy and regulation. Taken together, they argue that deregulation has precipitated action in the public sphere on television policy and content and is contributing to the construction of a new Indonesian subjectivity that is enlarging the role and significance of civil society in Indonesia. In the deregulated television sector three different and conflictual ideas of Indonesian subjectivity are in play: the citizen-in-development, the sovereign consumer, and the viewer as consumer/active participant in "public conversation." Interaction between these three subjectivities has challenged the right of the state to regulate the television sector in line with a model of nation and culture that apparently ignores the increasing complexity of the globalized media environment and the resistance of audiences to a didactic and patronizing policy and programming regime.

In chapter 9, "Regulating Ownership and Control," I examine three issues: license fees, advertising on TPI, and the employment of expatriate workers at Indosiar. These three issues provoked public controversy over the regulation of the television sector and presented opportunities for the "political public" to influence television policy (Feith 1962, 109). In chapter 10, "Regulating Content," I focus on public debate over the content of television—specifically the volume and impact of sexually permissive and violent imported films—in relation to provisions of the Draft Broadcasting Law presented to parliament in June 1996.

Since deregulation, state authorities have equivocated over the regulation of issues that were previously their sole responsibility. The state's apparent reluctance to act decisively in some areas reflects the growing complexity of the media-policy environment since deregulation and under conditions of globalization. It is increasingly obvious that officials are pushed to manage and promote different normative prescriptions for the media that are necessarily in conflict. I argue that deregulation has provided both the need and the opportunity for the political public to use the institutions of the public sphere (the press, the parliament, seminars, nongovernment organizations) to urge the state to reregulate aspects of television. In examining processes of public debate over television in chapters 9 and 10, I look at the dynamics of the link between media and policy in Indonesia and describe a distinctive style of interaction between citizens, organizations, and the press.

The concluding chapter, chapter 11, draws together discussion of the relations between television, nation, and culture. I argue that the tension between the two cultures of television identified in 1962 remains significant, that the difference between the two cultures is becoming more marked, and that in the 1990s it is mapped over the public/private divide. The tension between the cultures produces competing ideas of subjectivity and will contribute to the reconstitution of the cultural content of citizenship and the dynamics of relations between television, culture, and nation in Indonesia as it approaches the twenty-first century.

Part I
The First Phase of Television in Indonesia: Building a Monopoly

Chapter 2

STATE MONOPOLY BROADCASTING, 1962–1981

INDONESIA'S FIRST TELEVISION BROADCASTS in August 1962, the seventeenth commemoration of the Declaration of Independence and the twelve-day coverage of the Asian Games, are televisual icons of two conflicting tendencies. The two broadcasts image a tension in the development and use of television in Indonesia over the last thirty years. One event was outward-looking, populist, and self-confident and positioned Indonesia as a modern nation, active in regional affairs. The second revealed a more narrowly constrained, inward-looking tendency to hold "the outside" at arm's length and construct a sense of identity predicated on assertions of a unique national culture and culture space. In this chapter I situate these two tendencies in the historical circumstances of the establishment of television in Indonesia, tracing a shift in the management, funding and programming of television from an emergent diversified, regional broadcasting system to a national broadcasting network under the monopoly control of the New Order government.

Early Days

On 23 October 1961 the Indonesian Minister for Information, Maladi,[1] received the instructions he had been pressing for since 1952. President Sukarno's cable from Vienna gave Maladi the go-ahead to establish television in Indonesia: "I have thought more about television and have come to the view that the order must be given to NEC [Nippon Electric Company] through Itoh [the trading company C-Itoh], reducing our outlay. NEC is even prepared to lower its price. End. President [Sukarno]" (Direktorat Televisi 1972, 34).

These brief instructions set in motion an intense period of planning, building, and training that culminated just ten months later on 17 August in a trial broadcast of the seventeenth anniversary of the Declaration of Independence from the *Istana Merdeka* (Freedom Palace) in Jakarta. A week later the newly established service broadcast the Fourth Asian Games live from the Senayan stadium, Jakarta, beginning on 24 August and continuing until 12 September, when broadcasting stopped because, as pioneer broadcaster Soemartono said, "no thought had been given to programming for after the Games" (personal interview, 23 January 1992).

After the Asian Games ended in early September, TVRI was integrated into the Spirit of Sukarno Foundation (*Yayasan Gelora Bung Karno*), a social welfare organization under the direct control of the president. On 19 September, broadcasts resumed but must have been anticlimactic for viewers, as the exciting live sports action gave way to reruns of films borrowed from the State Film Centre, introduced in voice-over by unseen presenters. Studio facilities at the new Senayan complex were not ready to broadcast visual signals until 11 October 1962. Although 24 August is accepted by TVRI as the beginning of television in Indonesia, 11 October was the start of continuous broadcasting by the Indonesian television service known first as *Televisi Republik Indonesia Jajasan Gelora Bung Karno* (Spirit of Sukarno Foundation Indonesian Television), later abbreviated as *Televisi Republik Indonesia*

(TVRI) (Indonesian Television), which has been on the air ever since as the official Indonesian broadcasting service (Menteri Penerangan 1961; Presiden Republik Indonesia 1963b).

Preparation

Sukarno's cable was the formal signal to begin preparation in earnest for the establishment of television in Indonesia. It was, however, just another step in a process that had begun when an interim committee to plan the introduction of television had its first meeting in Cipayung on 16 July 1961. The committee was formally convened by ministerial decree on 25 July 1961 (Direktorat Televisi 1972, 33; Menteri Penerangan 1961).

The driving force behind these arrangements was the (then) Minister for Information, Maladi, a keen sportsman, an experienced radio broadcaster, and head of the official radio broadcasting service *Radio Republik Indonesia* (RRI) from 1946 to 1959. As head of the first indigenous radio station, the *Solosche Radio Vereeniging* (SRV), and later as head of the *Hosu Kyoku* (broadcasting station) in Solo during the period of Japanese rule, Maladi had had extensive experience of well-organized political broadcasting. He understood how well suited television was to the spectacle of sports and how television could assist, both at home and abroad, the symbolic definition and construction of an Indonesian identity. Maladi's interests in education had developed when he worked as a schoolteacher and later school principal in Solo before the Second World War. He was convinced that television was an excellent means for rapidly developing mass access to formal and informal education.

Maladi first pressed Sukarno to introduce television in 1952, arguing that it would be politically beneficial for the government in the first national election campaign of 1955 (Maladi, personal interview, 30 January 1992). In 1952 Maladi prepared the ground for television by sending a team of broadcasters from the Department of Information to the University of Southern California at Los Angeles for a nondegree training program (Sjamsoe Soegito, personal interview, 7 May 1993). Maladi recalled that Sukarno had a keen appreciation of the political benefits of broadcasting "and never moved without a radio team." Sukarno's broadcasting experience had developed during the period of the Japanese invasion of Indonesia, when he and other nationalist leaders were permitted for the first time to use radio to address indigenous listeners. Prevented in the past by the Dutch colonial authorities from addressing the Indonesian community, Maladi remembered that "Sukarno took full advantage of the change in policy under the Japanese." Sukarno was keen to establish television, which he saw as more effective than radio in communicating with a largely illiterate population. But unfortunately for Maladi, "only the President supported my plan; the others [in Cabinet] thought it was too expensive, and so the introduction of television was deferred" (Maladi, personal interview, 30 January 1992).

Maladi's interest in sports and his association with the Indonesian soccer team took him to the 1952 Olympic Games in Helsinki, where the first Indonesian team competed. He traveled on to the United States, where over a two-month period he visited local, public, and national network (CBS) television and radio stations in New York, Los Angeles, and Seattle. He extended his knowledge of international sports management and presentation further when he attended the Olympic Games in Melbourne in 1956, the year Australian television began.

In 1959 Maladi pressed again for the introduction of television, linking its benefits on this occasion to the support television could give to education and to the desirability of providing television coverage of the forthcoming Asian Games as Japan had in 1958. These twin objectives were politically motivated. Maladi argued that television could play a vital role in forging national unity through a national education program. "How was it," he asked rhetorically, "that just seven million Dutch could rule so many [Indonesians]? Because [Indonesia] was not united. Radio reinforced nationalism," he said, and "television could do the same." His vision for a national education program on television was broader than the transmission of knowledge. He wanted the media to be used to "enlighten the life of the people of Indonesia. It wasn't only a matter of knowledge—but other aspects of life as well. The idea of moving to embrace *modern* life was important" (Maladi, personal interview, 30 January 1992).

Maladi believed that televising the Asian Games presented a prime opportunity to generate a sense of national pride and unity, which he felt had been "thrown into disarray" (*kacau balau*) by ideas of federalism in the early years of the republic. Maladi said that sports and politics in Indonesia "had always been linked" on what he called a "case by case basis." Sjamsoe Soegito recalled that when he was an RRI news reporter in Yogyakarta in 1946–48, "we used to monitor international news and events, and from time to time included news from the Olympic Games [London 1948] to give the people a sense of being in the world." Sjamsoe added that Maladi was head of the Indonesian Football Association, "and was keen to include reports of major championship games for the same reason" (personal interview, 7 May 1993). Maladi himself recalled that in 1962, as a way of diminishing tendencies of provinces to act individually or parochially (*sendiri sendiri*), forty-eight Peace Corps volunteers were brought from the United States and spread throughout twenty-three provinces to act as coaches for the Asian Games athletes. "They had a great impact," Maladi said, "even though the PKI [Indonesian Communist Party] said they were CIA!" (personal interview, 7 May 1993).

Maladi's eagerness to present Indonesia on the international stage complemented Sukarno's enthusiasm for what Herbert Feith (1963) called "symbol wielding," by which he meant Sukarno's passion for high-profile overseas trips accompanied by an entourage of from thirty to fifty men, the formulation of government ideology, speech making, ceremonial, ritual, and expenditure on the "insignia of national prestige and power" such as the building of an atomic reactor and a steel mill. Feith records that "immense resources were devoted for over two years to building stadia, hotels and highway projects in preparation for the Asian Games held in Djakarta in August 1962" (1963, 83). In 1959 Maladi's lobbying over television was timely and persuasive. Agreement was reached and the decision noted in the documentation of the Provisional People's Consultative Council session of 1960 (MPR 1960). In July 1961 Maladi obtained final approval to develop television as part of the Asian Games project and convened a working committee to plan its introduction. The next ten months were a period of intensive planning as most of the team had limited personal experience of television and certainly no specialized knowledge of television broadcasting.

Maladi formed a core team comprising broadcasters seconded from RRI and filmmakers borrowed from the State Film Centre (Pusat Perfilman Negara, PFN). Of the eighteen technicians and production staff sent early in 1962 for three months of intensive training with the national broadcaster NHK (Nippon Hoso Kyokai) in Japan, twelve were seconded from RRI, and four from PFN. Four other production staff from RRI were sent for training to the BBC in London. An early recruit to the planning committee was Sumartono Tjitrosidojo, a Colombo Plan–sponsored engineering student at the University of New South Wales in Sydney, whom Maladi urged to return to Indonesia as soon as possible after graduation. Sumartono, later to become director of TVRI in 1971–75, had worked as a technical operator and maintenance officer at the Hoso Kyoku (broadcasting station), Solo, where Maladi was Head of Station from 1943 to 1945. Sumartono had also provided occasional technical assistance to the underground Guerilla Radio (*Radio Pemberontakan*) active in the Gunung Balong district near Solo and to Maladi when he was in charge of communications for the People's Security Army (*Tentara Keamanan Rakyat*) (Sumartono, personal interview, 23 January 1992).

Sumartono turned his educational contacts to good effect and conducted a long-distance technical collaboration with Douglas Cole, one of Sumartono's former lecturers in radio engineering at the University of New South Wales. Cole volunteered his advice by mail and telephone and acted as a link between the Australian Broadcasting Commission (ABC) and the Indonesian project throughout the development phase (Sumartono 1991, 28). A team of eight Japanese engineers under the leadership of Tetsuo Imai from NEC also assisted in the design stages of the studio and technical facilities planned for the Senayan complex. During the games an NHK technician and reporter assisted the Indonesian team. NHK itself sent a mobile television and film production unit to the games, which shot its own material that was sent back to Japan by air for broadcast over NHK. Thailand and the Philippines also recorded material for rebroadcast in their own country (Alex Leo Zulkarnain,[2] telephone interview, 1 April 1997).

These aspects of the early days of TVRI, and the background of some of the decision makers involved, apart from their specific historical interest, demonstrate that television in Indonesia was established in full knowledge of advances in television broadcasting throughout the world. The various inputs, most significantly from Australia, England, and Japan but also from the United States and West Germany,[3] show that television was established in an entirely global context and meshed into a transnational context of production and exchange of hardware and software from its earliest days. After the Asian Games, for example, TVRI screened a press conference with Philippines parliamentarians, introduced a World News service (*Dunia Dalam Berita*) using film clips from CBS and ITN, and covered a soccer match between Indonesia and Sweden, which afforded the first occasion for an interview conducted in English on TVRI. It presented a live broadcast of an evening of German culture and in January 1963 screened an interview with Russian cosmonaut Adrian Nikolayev (Direktorat Televisi 1972, 46–51). By 1969, with the inauguration of the Intelsat ground station at Jatiluhur, West Java, TVRI was able to screen live broadcasts of international events, particularly sports, music, and current affairs, as well as send its own programs abroad (Direktorat Televisi 1972, 204–5).

Trial Broadcast

In the montage of images that TVRI presents as its opening signature each day, there is a sequence of shots that show the annual commemoration of the Declaration of Independence at the Freedom Palace (*Istana Merdeka*), Jakarta. It is a sequence that amounts to a multiple compression of time, daily representing and circulating the ghost image of more than one rite of passage important to Indonesia's construction of its national identity.

One week before the opening of the Asian Games, at President Sukarno's request, the TVRI broadcast team put their newly acquired skills on the line by covering the seventeenth commemoration of the Declaration of Independence at the Istana Merdeka. This three-and-a-half-hour live broadcast on 17 August 1962 was TVRI's initiation, a rite that overlaid the symbolic birth of the republic seventeen years earlier in the grounds of Sukarno's house in Jakarta. Symbolically, then, TVRI and the Indonesian nation share the same ritual beginnings, and it is this twinning that has linked TVRI since its first broadcast to the political processes of nation building and the construction and circulation of ideas of national culture.

The intimate link between the activities of the national broadcaster and the political, ideological, and cultural practices of the nation was very familiar to Indonesian broadcasters and audiences who had lived through the period of the Japanese invasion and occupation of the (then) Netherlands Indies from 1 March 1942 to 15 August 1945. "As soon as the Japanese occupied Java, the existing [radio] broadcasting stations were put under the control of *Sendenbu* [Propaganda Department] until the *Jawa Hoso Kanrikyoku* [Java Broadcasting Superintendent Bureau] was set up on October 1942" (Aiko Kurasawa 1987, 87). The bureau radically reorganized the existing radio broadcast system into a centralized, hierarchically administered network with a central broadcast station in Jakarta and a network of regional stations (Wild 1987, 28).

In Indonesia the Japanese discovered a richly developed, pluralist tradition of radio broadcasting, with indigenous-owned and -run stations spread throughout the main urban centers of the archipelago. The colonial community was served by a decentralized scatter of Dutch-owned and -run stations established since 1937 and a long tradition of short-wave radio broadcasting from Holland. Dutch stations in Batavia, Semarang, Bandung, Surabaya, Yogyakarta, and Solo broadcast in Dutch and Indonesian, and the indigenous stations, known collectively as *Radio Ketimuran* (East [Indies] Radio), broadcast in Indonesian. In reorganizing this babble of scattered voices, the Japanese looked more favorably in the first few months of their arrival on the Radio Ketimuran stations. In many cases, they kept the preinvasion Indonesian station managers and staff in place and attached experienced, highly professional Japanese broadcasters who made over the stations into Hoso Kyoku, or broadcast stations. The Dutch stations' staff were treated far less kindly, and by about June all Dutch stations were closed down and their staff interned (Wild 1987, 27).

Once the military had reorganized the broadcasting system, Indonesian broadcasters working alongside their Japanese supervisors were quickly introduced to the use of radio for overtly political and propagandist purposes. Loudspeakers, known as "singing trees," were set up in markets and on street corners to ensure that the invader's exhortations, Japanese language lessons, Western and indigenous music, and news of the war were always accessible (Kahin 1970, 108; Aiko Kurasawa 1987, 87). Privately owned radios (banned in many areas) were sealed so listeners could receive only Japanese broadcasts.

The Japanese programming was a potent mix for Indonesian broadcasters who had gained their first broadcasting experiences under the Dutch system of decentralized, privately funded radio societies. Under the Dutch authorities, programming on the Radio Ketimuran was required to be in the national interest, to contribute to public order, and to be politically neutral and culturally uplifting. Prewar broadcasting had thus presented an uncoordinated, differentiated blend of culturally assertive but politically bland programming to which the public had access on a "user pays" principle. In contrast, during the Japanese period, listeners' access to radio was strictly controlled, even to the extent of banning private sets and forcing people to listen to public sets that could not be turned off. Programming was highly political, overtly propagandist, and strident. Cultural programs, broadcast in local languages and Indonesian, were part of a systematic ideological process of influencing indigenous listeners in favor of the invader's plans. Historian and former BBC broadcaster Colin Wild argues that the Japanese created a revolution in Indonesian broadcasting:

> As the war continued Indonesians working in the various Hoso Kyoku, even if not particularly nationalistic to begin with, were radicalised by the stringency of the political control exercised by the Japanese, by an increasing awareness through surreptitious monitoring of Allied radio of the lies they were being asked to disseminate, and by a growing conviction that radio had a great potential for serving political ends after the war. (Wild 1987, 30)

Many of the radio broadcasters who later became decision makers in the establishment and organization of RRI and later TVRI, including Maladi, Sumartono, and Sukarno himself, had had firsthand experience of these two different systems of broadcasting organization, management, and programming. Wild argues that the prewar experience of radio in Indonesia, which was largely dependent for its development on local initiative and skills, coupled with the politicization of broadcasting, which the Japanese had introduced, provided the resistance movement with both the capability and the motivation for using radio as part of the nationalist struggle.

This history has also affected the development of television in Indonesia. The swift development of regional television stations, for example, initiated and funded by local interests (described below), was undoubtedly influenced by the Dutch broadcasting tradition. The two broadcasting traditions, mediated through the experiences of the individuals involved, the global nature of television technology, and the shifting political agendas of governments in Indonesia have contributed to the development of a tension between television as a medium of popular national culture and television as a means of privileging and legitimating a specific construct of national political culture, a claim that I explore extensively in part 1 of this book.

The Asian Games Broadcast

The broadcast of the Asian Games provided Indonesia with an international stage on which it could present itself to its regional neighbors as a modern, rapidly developing, technologically sophisticated nation. At that time, of the countries participating in the games, only Japan (in 1953), the Philippines (in 1953), and Thailand (in 1954) had established television broadcasting services. For a first broadcast made over thirty years ago, it was a remarkably modern television event. From 24 August until 12 September, the four frantic mobile broadcast crews maintained coverage of the events, broadcasting for a minimum of one and a half hours a day to a maximum of fifteen and a half hours on Saturday 1 September.[4] Well prepared in Japan, England, and America, the inexperienced broad-casters delivered a lively sports package to their audience. The immediacy of television was exploited in repeat broadcasts of the day's events using two-inch videotape, and the live access the medium afforded to the events was demonstrated on the public receivers at the "Information Counters" the Asian Games Municipal Committee set up in downtown Jakarta for the benefit of games visitors (*Bintang Timur*, 24 August 1962). The flexibility of the medium was evident in the daily "journal" segments, which gave details of events that had not been covered live. These segments used film and still photos of events as visual material. Television's ability to compress distance was also demonstated early on with relays of games events from Jakarta to Bandung, 180 kilometers away (*Indonesian Observer*, 29 August 1962).

Who was able to enjoy this remarkable television event is not clear. Just as Australians in 1956 left their lounge rooms and went downtown to watch the first television broadcasts through shop windows, thousands of Jakarta residents jostled to see the black and white images of the games on public access receivers, which the Jakarta Municipal government and the Gobel manufacturing company had erected in strategic locations in the city (Soemartono n.d., 13). Although for many Australian and Indonesian viewers their first access to television was in the streets, the experience was qualitatively different. In Australia, viewers watched television in shop windows where sets were for sale along with other electrical goods and "domestic appliances." Though the access was public, the viewing experience was bound into the private world of domestic consumption. In Indonesia, although the public access sets were sponsored by a manufacturing company, they were not displayed in the retail sector but were erected in the streets. Their location associated the sets and the viewing experience with the "singing trees" and government propaganda of the Japanese occupation. The distribution of 10,000 sets to public servants, and the projection of the games broadcast into the streets of the city constructed television as an official voice that was part of the government's elaborate public relations apparatus put in place for the Asian Games.

Newspapers of the day advertised smart looking 23½-inch Grundig and 14-inch Sharp sets that could be "immediately installed." Philips, Ralin, and Gobel between them imported about 5,000 sets (Sumartono n.d., 13). Sales picked up once the games got under way. Sumartono estimated that during the games there were between 10,000 and 15,000 sets in use.[5] The base figure is certain, as 10,000 sets had been purchased by government departments for distribution gratis to public servants to take home as a way of fostering interest and demand. Television sets were expensive, being twenty times the monthly salary of senior public servants (Sumartono n.d., 13). Set sharing would mean that perhaps four or five times this number of people actually saw something of the games on television, but even so, in its first months of operation television was by no means a mass medium, reaching no more than 80,000 viewers, or about 2 percent of Jakarta's total population, or 0.09 percent of the Indonesian population (*Indonesian Observer*, 28 August 1962; *Bintang Timur*, 23 August 1962; Direktorat Televisi 1972, 30, 59; Abeyasekere 1987, 171). Apart from the high cost of sets, TVRI's choice of Indonesian as the language of broadcast also limited its penetration. Indonesian, though widely spoken in Jakarta, was still not the first language of the majority in the 1960s and 1970s, although television was, along with radio, to be significant in familiarizing audiences with the language (see Hugo et al. 1987, 104).

The Institutional Setting of TVRI

TVRI was first established as a "special mass media project" as part of the Asian Games preparations and was coordinated by the newly created Bureau of Radio and Television under the direction of the Fourth Asian Games Organising Committee. In the way it was later incorporated into the bureaucratic structure of the government, TVRI has remained "special" ever since.

After the Asian Games ended in early September, Minister Maladi and Information Minister Mohamad Yamin clashed over the future disposition of TVRI (Soemartono, personal interview, 23 January 1992).[6] Following Mohamad Yamin's death in October 1962, Soemartono records that the Department of Information argued that TVRI should be part of its operations, as there were efficiencies in keeping radio and television operations together. General Suprayogi, who had been in charge of operations during the Asian Games and was also Minister for Public Works and Energy, argued against incorporating TVRI into the department, as "the state of the Indonesian economy at that time was a major concern, and it was beyond imagining that the government would be able to fund properly the operation and development of television" (Soemartono n.d., 15).

Suprayogi's view was shared by the Director of the Sukarno Foundation, Jusuf Muda Dalam, and by Maladi, whom Soemartono described as "very close to the president." As head of RRI, Maladi had built up a relationship with Sukarno through the president's extensive use of radio for political purposes. To resolve the crisis over funding for TVRI, Soemartono remembers Maladi "went straight to the president" and made sure that TVRI was not incorporated into the Department of Information. It became part of the Spirit of Sukarno Foundation (*Yayasan Gelora Bung Karno*) under the direct control of the president (Soemartono, personal interview, 23 January 1992). The sources of income available to the developing service were a subvention from the national budget, monthly fees paid by owners of television sets, and other income-generating activities such as sponsorships. After March 1963, this included earnings from sales of advertising time. The complexity of managing and allocating these sources of funds within the larger foundation budget led TVRI to establish itself as a foundation (*Yayasan*) in its own right on 20 October 1963 (Presiden Republik Indonesia 1963b). Although TVRI was in effect a government television service, its institutional affiliation put the use of TVRI's budget beyond the reach of government departments and gave it considerable day-to-day operational and creative autonomy.

As a foundation, TVRI has a curious status, sharing something with nongovernment, nonprofit organizations, and as a government agency, having a lot in common with other sections of the state bureaucracy.[7] As might be expected, its hybrid character has been a source of comment, bureaucratic irritation, and professional frustration since its inception (*Suara Pembaruan,* 19 February 1991). In 1966, the foundation was "brought within the environment" of the Directorate General of Radio, Television, and Film (RTF) in the Department of Information (Menteri Penerangan 1966). In 1975 TVRI's status as a directorate under the administrative supervision of the RTF Directorate was confirmed (Menteri Penerangan 1975) and then reconfirmed in April 1980 when TVRI staff were absorbed by the Department of Information (Presiden Republik Indonesia 1980). Despite these steps to bring TVRI under the bureaucratic control of the Department of Information, the foundation remained the legal body through which TVRI drew and expended its funds. Until December 1996, the foundation had sole, formal responsibility for the licensing of television services in Indonesia.

The foundation's licensing powers gained considerable significance in the late 1980s when commercial providers approached TVRI about establishing commercial television services. It was the TVRI Foundation that licensed the first commercial providers RCTI (in 1987) and SCTV (in 1990) to establish commercial television services in Jakarta and Surabaya respectively. TVRI also has the right to negotiate with each commercial provider for a share of gross advertising revenue (Menteri Penerangan 1990, part 4, clause 21). Fees from the commercial stations are reported to be lucrative (*Jakarta Post,* 9 November 1992). The legislative changes that cleared the way for commercial television, however, had been issued by the Minister for Information (Menteri Penerangan 1987).

This account of TVRI's structural position reveals a gradual shift in TVRI's perception of itself as a "professional media organisation" (Ishadi personal interview, 17 May, 1993) and in the financial and operational flexibility and independence of the service. When first established as an activity of the Presidential Foundation, TVRI's general policy, leadership, and operations were overseen by a lean but high-powered staff of eight appointed by the president.[8] The foundation's day-to-day operations and decisions were the responsibility of just four directors. The Director of Television became the Director of the Foundation. He was supported by Assistant Directors with responsibility for Technical Matters, Programming, and Commercial Relations and Finance (Presiden Republik Indonesia 1963c). These men were public servants, but most of the TVRI staff were employed directly by the foundation. The foundation status gave TVRI very considerable financial autonomy in its early years as it had the right to raise and expend revenue without reference to any government department. As the service developed and became more widely available, its value to the work of the Department of Information became more obvious, and the department looked more and more to TVRI for assistance. In the early 1970s, Minister for Information Boediarjo trod a careful line between acknowledging TVRI's necessary orientation to its audience and its responsibilities to the government.[9] The minister noted in his commemorative address in August 1972 that it was time to reconsider TVRI's status and give it a "more democratic character" by incorporating the service as a public corporation (*Perusahaan Umum,* abbr. *Perum,* the Indonesian expression and abbreviation for "public corporation") (Direktorat Televisi 1972, 17–19).

With a change of ministers in 1973, the Department of Information headed off moves for any greater independence for TVRI and slowly drew it under its auspices. This was effected in two important steps. First, in 1975 the executive authority of the director of TVRI was compromised when he was made responsible to two masters—the Director General of Radio, Television, and Film and the directors of the TVRI Foundation. In 1993 this issue still rankled with TVRI executives. The (then) Director of Television, Ishadi SK, raised with me his frustration over TVRI's hybrid status. Unlike previous directors, Ishadi was never formally appointed as director of the TVRI Foundation and consequently labored under even greater uncertainty than his predecessors had. Ishadi was convinced that TVRI could easily compete with the new commercial stations if only he could cut loose from "bureaucratic interference" by the Department of Information. Ishadi asserted that TVRI's association with the Department of Information cramped the "professionalism" of TVRI broadcasters and producers (personal interview, 17 May 1993).

The second major change in TVRI's status occurred in 1980 when the director of TVRI lost control over general staff. Information Minister Ali Murtopo unilaterally "improved the position" of approximately three thousand TVRI staff by registering them as public servants on the payroll of the Department of Information (Presiden Republik Indonesia 1980).[10] The final blow to TVRI's financial and operational autonomy was effected just a few months later when television advertising was banned. This decision denied TVRI its major source of discretionary funds, introduced a narrower "information" role for television, and emphatically asserted a much higher degree of state influence and control over TVRI's operations. I return to the ban on advertising in the final section of this chapter.

TVRI's Regional Broadcast Stations

TVRI's first studio complex was built in Jakarta on twelve hectares of swampy land in Senayan, purchased on its behalf by the Organising Committee for the Fourth Asian Games. Over the next sixteen years, eight regional broadcast stations were built in Java, Sumatra, and Sulawesi (table 2.1).

Table 2.1
Television Broadcast Stations Commissioned, 1962–1978

Location	Date Commissioned
Jakarta	14 November 1962
Yogyakarta	17 August 1965
Medan	28 December 1970
Ujung Pandang	7 December 1972
Balikpapan	22 January 1973
Palembang	31 January 1974
Surabaya	3 March 1978
Denpasar	16 July 1978
Manado	7 October 1978

Sources: Direktorat Televisi 1987, 8–12; Soemartono 1991.

When they were first established, these stations were not part of a TVRI network but more closely resembled the Radio Ketimuran stations established by indigenous broadcasters during the Dutch period. Until the domestic satellite Palapa linked the scattered television stations together, regional broadcasting stations produced their own programs supplemented with film or videotape sent from TVRI Jakarta. They were on the air for only one to two hours per day (see Direktorat Radio, Televisi dan Film 1983, 72).

The stations were developed on local initiative using diverse sources of funds (Alwi Dahlan 1981, 19; Direktorat Televisi 1972, 66, 229–33). Pioneer broadcaster and former Director General of Radio, Television, and Film Alex Leo Zulkarnain said that until the communications infrastructure linked them to Jakarta, the regional stations were in effect independent broadcasters servicing their immediate area, but they nevertheless saw themselves as part of TVRI (telephone interview, 1 April 1997). The first regional station at Yogyakarta, for example, was built by the Directorate of Radio, Department of Information, and not by the TVRI Foundation. R. M. Soenarto, former head of the Yogyakarta station, notes that when the station was first commissioned in August 1965 it saw itself as "the equal" (*tandingan*) of TVRI Jakarta (Direktorat Televisi 1972, 229). Potential rivalry between the two stations did not develop, however, as government activity after the coup attempt in October 1965 worked to suppress expressions of regional diversity:[11] "The effects [of the New Order restoration of control after 30 October] were felt by TVRI. There was no more talk of 'equals.' The Yogyakarta studio became a child of TVRI Jakarta and later grew into the Directorate of Television alongside the Directorate of Radio" (Direktorat Televisi 1972, 229).

The station in Medan was built using funds from the government of North Sumatra and the national oil company Pertamina, which was active in the region. Once facilities were in place, operational expenses were covered by a small contribution from TVRI, license fees were collected from local sources and from advertising revenue. The stations in Ujung Pandang, Balikpapan, and Palembang were established in much the same way.

TVRI Programming, 1962–1975

As early planning for television projected an exclusively educational role for the service, university cities were nominated as the sites for the first broadcast stations (Menteri Penerangan 1961, section 2). But by 1963 television's role had been informally and formally widened. In February 1963 TVRI decided that it would screen seven different categories of program: (1) education, (2) information, (3) religious affairs, (4) cultural affairs, (5) sports, (6) international affairs, and (7) political, social, and economic matters relevant to the process of nation building (Presiden Republik Indonesia 1963c, part 2, article 3). These program categories have remained the preferred mode of describing programming at TVRI ever since. Proportions of each different program type have been stipulated by decree, although the proportions have altered over time (table 2.2). The major change from 1972 through 1980/81 was in the allocation of hours to news and information and to advertisements. By 1980/81, news and information programming had risen to 28 percent of total broadcast hours. Advertisements, having risen to over 17 percent of total hours in 1971, accounted for just 6 percent of total hours from 1975 to 1977/78, and 8 percent from 1978/79 to 1979/80, and by 1981 had fallen away to zero (Direktorat Radio, Televisi dan Film 1983, 71).

Table 2.2
TVRI Program Categories as a Percentage of Total Broadcast Hours, 1962–1972

TVRI Program Category	1962	1963	1964–68	1969	1970	1971	1972
News/Information	20	30	30	20	20	25	19
Education/Religion	40	20	30	30	30	21	21
Entertainment, Culture	40	40	30	40	40	36.5	46
Advertisements	—	10	10	10	10	17.5	14
Total %	100	100	100	100	100	100	100

Source: Direktorat Televisi 1972, 223–24

Table 2.3
**TVRI Program Times, Weekdays and Weekends,
1963–1967 and 1971–1981**

Year	Weekdays	Saturday	Sunday
1963	1930–2130	1930–2300	1930–2130
1964	1900–2200	1930–2300	1930–2130
1965	1900–2200	1930–2300	1930 2130
1966	1900–2200	1930–2300	1930–2130
1967	1900–2200	1930–2300	1930–2130
1971	1800–2300	1800–2300	1800–2320
1972	1800–2217	1750–2217	1600–2217
1973	1750–2300	1655–2400	1555–2300
1974	1755–2300	1655–2400	1555–2300
1975	1755–2300	1655–2400	1555–2300
1976	1800–2220	1730–2400	1000–1330 1800–2300
1977	1730–2300	1730–2330	1000–1330 1730–2300
1978	1700–2300	1700–2300	1000–1300 1700–2300
1979	1630–2300	1630–2400	1000–1330 1630–2300
1980	1630–2300	1630–2300	0900–1400 1630–2400
1981	1630–2400	1630–2400	0900–1400 1630–2320

Sources: Direktorat Televisi 1972; *Sinar Harapan, Indonesia Times,* various years.

In line with the gradual increase in weekend broadcasts (see table 2.3), the main changes during the period under review have been an increase in news from 20 to 28 percent of programming (1962–1980/81) and a reduction in educational programming from 40 percent of all programs in 1962 to 23 percent in 1980/81. Entertainment and culture programs increased from 40 percent to almost half of total programming (47 percent) over the same period. This category of programs was not even mentioned in the somewhat stern, social engineering language of Presidential decree number 27 of 1963 (Presiden Republik Indonesia 1963a).

The government's perception that television was part of the national development apparatus led to strict policy guidelines that governed the selection of suitable programs for TVRI. These guidelines articulate the normative relationship between programs and the state ideology of Pancasila and the national constitution, human rights, moral values, culture and worldview, religion, lifestyle, customary norms and practices, major differences of opinion and belief, and matters of legality (Direktorat Televisi 1972, 83–84; Alfian and Chu 1981, 177–78). Two points need to be made about these guidelines. First, they are culturally and politically conservative, but in the spirit of principles of development media theory (McQuail 1994, 131), they acknowledge the value of "two-way traffic" of information between the government and community in the development process. In their conservatism, and the intention to use television for nation-building purposes, they echo the authoritarian theory of the media (McQuail 1994, 127), which Japanese practice exemplified during the occupation. In response to my question whether there had been any consideration given to developing private television in Indonesia in the 1960s, Maladi said "no, because private television was too open for manipulation by antigovernment or disruptive forces. We thought we would wait until the intellectual awareness of the public was sufficiently high—about ten years." He added that when RRI was first established shortly after the Proclamation of Independence, it was a private broadcaster. "But when the power of radio became evident, the private funding arrangement, which had lasted for one year, was abandoned, and RRI became wholly government-owned and -run" (Maladi, personal interview, 30 January 1992). These statements reveal an assumption that the private sector or sphere is associated (almost by definition) with disruption and antigovernment sentiment. The conflation of private dynamics with the disruption of government can be understood as part of the motivation for the gradual absorption of TVRI into a departmental framework and was certainly a factor in the ban on commercial advertising on TVRI in 1981. Apprehension about the political reliability of the private sector may also explain the allocation of commercial licenses in 1989 to licensees with impeccable New Order political credentials. I return to this issue in chapter 7.

Second, the model of communication implicit in the guidelines requires comment. Television programs are assumed to influence their audiences directly and en masse. The assumption is that television is a powerful instrument of social development. In the early documentation that authorized television, it was described as a "tool" for nation building, revolution, and the formation of Indonesian socialist humanity (Presiden Republik Indonesia 1963c, part 1, article 1). In later documentation the same assumption persists, although the language has changed: "In the context of assuring a successful completion of national development, . . . the duty of the mass media is to inflame the spirit of dedication and struggle of the nation, consolidate the national unity and cohesion, enhance the sense of national culture and identity, and stimulate participation of the community in development" (Soeharto, 1982).

In later chapters I explore a tension between the government's normative theory of TVRI's role and divergent expectations of the national broadcaster expressed by TVRI's audiences.

Review of Programs

It is difficult sum up thirteen years of (unseen) programming, and whatever is said by way of brief comment must inevitably be partial and impressionistic.[12] The difficulty of describing what was on screen is compounded by the fact that there are very few sources that comment on television programming. Indeed, the prominent critic D. H. Assegaff (*Indonesia Raya,* 28 September 1972) observed that publications on the mass media in Indonesia were almost entirely lacking and that those that had been published (including the publication the first part of this chapter has relied upon) were largely commemorative volumes whose main virtue was that they pulled all sorts of scattered statistics together. Arswendo Atmowiloto, author of the first book on Indonesian television, notes that in 1974 neither the leading daily *Kompas* nor any other newspaper published anything about television apart from the scheduled program, "which you could never be certain would coincide with what was shown." Arswendo's own column began in *Kompas* in 1982 (Arswendo Atmowiloto 1986, xiii).

Despite Assegaff's enthusiasm for critical comment, TVRI was probably relieved that critics such as M. L. W., who published his comments in *Bintang Timur* on 2 September 1962, did not maintain his interest over the next ten years. His comments, made just a week after television had been on the air, reveal a sophisticated appreciation of the new medium and a tantalizing glimpse of what we might have seen in the games coverage. M. L. W. compares gymnastic displays by elementary and junior high school students with performances of the traditional dances *Tari Pendet* and *Saudati*. He argues that the traditional dances, usually so brilliant, were disappointing on television because they were not choreographed with the camera in mind, whereas the gymnastic displays had been especially designed for the stadium and the cameras. The traditional dancers were unable to adjust to the scale of the stadium and performed their dances as if they were on their usual small stage. He went on to comment on some of the coverage of the sports events and argued that action events such as boxing, soccer, table tennis, and badminton lent themselves to television very well. The javelin, 100-meter sprint, and long jump, however, were static and dull, despite the commentators' best efforts to fill the yawning spaces, for their comments were equally monotonous!

Some expatriate viewers were also unimpressed with TVRI in its early years. The American historian Harry Benda recalled how distressed the eminent linguist Louis Damais felt about the extent to which the medium had been appropriated for political purposes: Louis Damais "winced as we watched uniformed Gerwani [Communist Women's Organization] women go through 'political callisthenics' on TV in Bandung" (Benda 1967, 221). And Judith Agassi quotes from an early study of the Jakarta press by journalism student Andrew Crawford: "Programming on the Djakarta television station was only two hours each evening, plus extended coverage of mass rallies, presidential speeches, or other special events. About half of the total content was live speeches, or other events of a political nature, and the other half was mostly documentary films" (Agassi 1969, 67).

Indonesian viewers were also concerned about the political content on television. One viewer complained in *Harian Kami* that the constant repetition of the Pancasila symbol was "not funny" (28 August 1968). Agassi refers to symbol wielding as well and reports that the Pancasila symbol was taken off screen during 1968 in response to audience complaints (Agassi 1969, 105). She sums up TVRI programming in 1968 in these words:

> The Government-owned and controlled Indonesian television was by 1968 overwhelmingly a politically neutral educational and entertainment medium, giving some access to educators, university professors and students' organizations and sports clubs as well as to ABRI [the Armed Forces]. Political news and comment took up on regular days between ⅛ to ⅕ of its broadcasting time. While the contents of newscasts themselves are obviously government controlled, there is a limited space reserved for some independent political comment and press criticism. Patriotism and ideology play a rather minor role in its program. (Agassi 1969, 105)

The amount of foreign content on TVRI received comment over the years, and many viewers were frustrated by TVRI's lack of capacity in subtitling imported films (*Sinar Harapan*, 26 August 1970). Other critics were more concerned with issues of the media's role in the construction of cultural identity, succinctly expressed in the *Tempo* headline (26 August 1972) "Indonesian Television: Not Enough Indonesia" (*"TVRI: Kurang 'RI'?"*), pre-figuring another headline nearly twenty years later, when it was suggested that RCTI actually meant "Rajawali Citra Televisi Impor" (Imports), not "Indonesia" (*RCTI Diartikan Rajawali Citra Televisi Impor*) (*Jayakarta*, 21 February 1990).

The term *film* is used generically in Indonesian television and refers to features, serials, documentaries, news clips, commercials, and trailers (Direktorat Televisi 1972, 220). In an article commemorating TVRI's tenth anniversary, *Tempo* (26 August 1972) noted that just over one-third of all programming was film and that almost all of these films were imported and used foreign-language dialogue. The 1972–73 TVRI Program Planner shows that between 6 and 7 P.M., seven days a week, child viewers could look forward to a year-long engagement with *Daktari, Bozo the Clown, Jungle Jim, Popeye the Sailor, Bat-Man, Gentle Ben, Sinbad Junior,* and *Lost in Space*. Between 9 and 10 P.M., Sunday to Friday, adult viewers were offered a similar diet of mainly American programs, most of them equally familiar to Australian viewers: *The Untouchables, Bonanza, Mission Impossible, Dr. Kildare, The Avengers, Ironside,* and *Echo* (Direktorat Televisi 1972, 140).

TVRI also adapted American and British television formats and screened locally made variety shows; religious programs; plays; cooking programs; popular, folk, and classical music and dance; and current affairs. After the construction of the Intelsat ground station at Jatiluhur in West Java, TVRI had the capacity to send and receive television signals to and from international destinations. A varied mix of cultural, sports, and current affairs programs emerged, and Indonesian audiences saw the launch of Apollo 12 in November 1969, the popular music program *Bandstand* from Sydney, a preview of the Munich Olympics, the meeting between President Soeharto and President Nixon at the White House, the World Cup final live from Mexico, and live coverage of the Muhammad Ali–Joe Frazier fight in New York. TVRI itself began sending a series of film reports to Nederland Omroep Stichting in August 1971.

Drawing these various threads concerning hardware, software, training, policy, and programming together, the first thirteen years of Indonesian television were years that saw the rapid development of a decentralized television system, a system predicated on a production role for regional stations guided by a national station under the control of a high-profile, politically influential foundation, funded largely by advertising revenue and license fees. The television audience became used to a mix of programming that included ceremonial nation-building material; regular screenings of imported, particularly American-produced, fictional material; and after November 1969, live access to cultural and current affairs programs from around the world. It was an entertaining, outward-looking service, which, within available production resources, seems to have balanced the interests of its audiences with its responsibilities as a public service broadcaster. It was this secure foundation that became the platform for the dramatic take-off in television services after the launch of the domestic satellite Palapa in 1976.

1976—TVRI Goes National

In the mid 1970s, TVRI broadcasts were largely restricted to Java, where about 62 percent of Indonesians lived. Figure 2.1 shows that in 1974, 90.81 percent of all television sets were registered on Java, and about half of these were registered in Jakarta. The launch of the Palapa satellite in 1976 brought the Outer Islands, home to about 38 percent of Indonesia's population, within TVRI's reach. In the space of just a few years, television took on a truly national scope. Sales of television sets rose dramatically. Figure 2.1 shows that from 1975 to 1978, the total number of receivers registered almost tripled (269 percent). The number of receivers registered outside Java rose by at least 133 percent in North Sumatra, by 257 percent in West Sumatra, 235 percent in Sulawesi, and 165 percent in Kalimantan (Alfian and Chu 1981, 25).[13]

There is an irony about the impact of Palapa on television in Indonesia. In many ways the Palapa launch was the single most

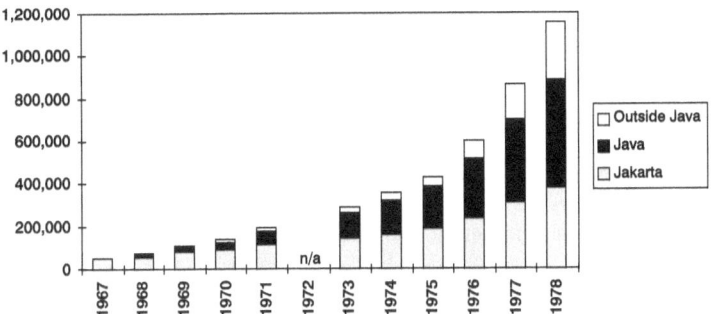

Figure 2.1. Number of Television Receivers Registered in Jakarta, on Java, and outside Java, 1967–1978

important decision about television in Indonesia. It promoted television as a means of unifying the country, and constructed the television set and television viewing as a key cultural experience. Palapa turned television into a service that was the right of all citizens, as much a part of being Indonesian as the other key cultural symbols that were shared nationally: the language, the flag, and the national anthem. Like radio, only more vividly because of its visualizing power and its high-tech cachet, television was devised to be both the channel and the manifestation, the nightly dramatization of a shared cultural identity. After Palapa, no viewer was unaware that she or he was taking part in a process that effortlessly embraced Sabang in the West and Merauke in the East.

The very efficiency of Palapa in the distribution of signals reinforced centralist tendencies in Indonesian television at odds with TVRI's own original plan to develop a system of regional production stations, which began in 1965 and continued through the First and Second Five-Year Plans. What is most interesting about the development of regional stations is that they were established using local funding (Alwi Dahlan 1981, 19). After the advent of Palapa, private sector interest in developing regional stations diminished, as control of the television system and signal shifted more decisively to Jakarta. Undoubtedly the 1981 decision to ban television advertising also caused private investors to lose interest in expanding access to television by building local stations. Here, then, the tension between the centralizing tendencies of the state, intent upon improving the efficiency of its reach throughout the nation for political and ideological purposes, and a culturally diversified system that envisaged an important role for regional production and local initiative, is again apparent. In chapter 6 I will show that during the 1980s the strain in the system became increasingly intense, until 1987 when TVRI's almost thirty-year monopoly of television broadcasting came to an end.

In 1981 Alfian and Godwin Chu commented in their monograph *Satellite Television in Indonesia* that

> The decision to launch the Palapa satellite was reached with the full awareness of its cost.... The expenditures for constructing television facilities in Indonesia were low from 1969 to 1974, but began to increase in 1975, and peaked in 1976 when Palapa was finally decided upon. The total expenditure for that year was nearly one hundred times that for 1974 because of the foreign currency payments amounting to US$73 million for Palapa. For 1977, expenditures were still high because of the construction of ground stations for Palapa. (26)

The attribution of the total cost of the Palapa project to the costs of constructing television facilities in 1976 suggests that Palapa was primarily a television project funded by the Department of Information. The truth is quite different and requires that we return to 1969 and the personalities and considerations that led to the construction of the Intelsat earth station at Jatiluhur, West Java. Alfian and Chu's comments can be understood as part of a process of myth making and celebration that has grown up around the launch of Indonesia's domestic satellite. Different sections of the bureaucracy publicized the bravura of the decision to develop satellite communications, perhaps as a way of justifying the sudden and huge additional outlays on communications infrastructure.

Former Minister for Communications Emil Salim argued that Indonesia had isolated itself internationally by its "confrontation" with Malaysia in 1963/64 and by withdrawing from the United

Nations in January 1965.[14] In 1965/66 it had been traumatized by the alleged communist coup and the terror that followed throughout the archipelago. Following these events Emil Salim said two interests came together: an interest in developing a more efficient communications system for security and political purposes, and an interest in signaling to the international political and investment community that the extremism and upheaval of the late Sukarno years were past (Emil Salim, personal interview, 21 April 1993).

The individual who did the most to progress Indonesia's move into satellite communications was the late Soehardjono, Director General of Post and Telecommunications, 1966–78. Soehardjono developed an early interest in radio communications, working at the Radio Laboratorium Luchtbeschermingdienst company in Bandung from 1940 to 1941 and later as a technical officer in the Bondowoso and Yogyakarta Hoso Kyokyu from 1942 to 1944. He joined the People's Security Army as a sergeant in 1945 and served in Surabaya, West Java, Central Java, Sulawesi, and Jakarta. From 1965 until July 1966, Soehardjono, now Brigadier General, was director of communications with additional responsibility for RRI and TVRI under security arrangements established over the period of the coup (Direktorat Jenderal Pos dan Telekomunikasi 1985, 614).

Soehardjono had had extensive day-to-day experience of planning and developing communications systems for security and civil purposes. Working closely with Emil Salim, then Deputy Head of the National Development Planning Board (*Bappenas*), Soehardjono proposed that Indonesia join the Intelsat consortium, which involved building a satellite earth station at Jatiluhur in West Java. Cabinet agreement was reached and a contract signed on 9 June 1967 between the International Telephone and Telegraph Corporation (USA) and the government of Indonesia represented by Emil Salim. The earth station was commissioned by President Soeharto on 29 September 1969. During the inauguration ceremonies Soehardjono proposed to the president that Indonesia should consider launching its own domestic satellite to obtain the same communication benefits domestically that it had now achieved internationally (Directorate General of Posts and Telecommunications 1983, 5:174). Within seven years, and in the midst of difficult economic circumstances, Indonesia became the third country in the world to deploy a domestic satellite.

Emil Salim considered that, given Indonesia's geography, the development of a domestic satellite communications system was "entirely logical, the only alternative" (personal interview, 21 April 1993). The extensive development of microwave transmission, linking Bali to Sumatra during the period of the First Five-Year Development Plan (1969/70–1973/74), while successful, had taken many years to construct, and the development of link stations every eighty kilometers or so had been very expensive. The geography of Indonesia ruled out further development of terrestrial microwave links to Kalimantan, Sulawesi, and Eastern Indonesia. For these regions, tropposcatter technology or submarine cable links seemed the only solution, although neither was regarded as ideal for both technical and financial reasons. Indonesia also felt under considerable pressure from the international community to demonstrate its good intentions in fully integrating West Irian into the national life and culture of Indonesia following the Act of Free Choice in 1969, which sought the opinion of over one thousand tribal leaders concerning the integration of West Irian into Indonesia, but did not involve a vote on the issue. "The eyes of the world were on us," as Emil Salim put it. The development of efficient communications between all parts of Indonesia, but especially between the central government and Eastern Indonesia, was regarded as a high priority.

The idea of developing a domestic satellite system, while it may have been "the only possibility" from a technocratic perspective, was an ambitious and imaginative plan. At that time, only the United States and Canada had domestic satellites. In the United States, the satellite did not provide a nationally integrated service, so it was really only Canada that had developed the kind of national system contemplated for Indonesia. Skeptics focused on these facts and argued that the technology was really untried and that as a developing country Indonesia was moving too far, too fast. Critics described the project as a *"mercu suar"* (white elephant), using language that had been used to attack the grandiose schemes of the late Sukarno period (*Kompas*, 29 May 1975). But as Emil Salim put it,

> We knew that Canada had used a domestic satellite system, and we knew that distances in Canada were about the same as in Indonesia. We knew that the United States used the system and that it linked New York with San Francisco. And we knew that New York to San Francisco was about the same distance as Sabang [in Sumatra] to Merauke [in Irian Jaya]. That appealed to us; that sunk in. (Emil Salim, personal interview, 21 April 1993)

To the planners, the satellite had the appeal of solving with one bold decision the intractable mix of technical and development problems that extending communications throughout the archipelago presented. Realizing the goal, however, meant overcoming considerable opposition and in the end required the president's intervention. Public finance was not available as the government was under great stress following the collapse of its oil company, Pertamina, which had borrowed funds short term for long-term development. Although the project had been signaled in the Second Five-Year Plan budget, the Pertamina financial crisis put the project in doubt as department budgets were cut to pay Pertamina's debts (Republik Indonesia 1974, 375).[15] Commercial funding was not available either, as the Pertamina affair had scared off private funding for other government projects (Winters 1996, 54–74), and telecommunications were regarded as a low priority for aid funding. If Palapa was to get off the ground, the project needed backing at the highest level.

It was the political and strategic benefits of the system that were finally persuasive. In the late 1960s it was easier for Indonesia to communicate with overseas countries than within its own borders, and the security implications of this situation were keenly felt by the government (Iskandar Alisjahbana, personal interview, 19 April 1993).[16] Emil Salim's personal experience supported Iskandar Alisjahbana's comments. Twenty years later he still remembered his frustrations as Minister for Communications in traveling in Eastern Indonesia. "It was a black hole. I had to wait for nine days for a boat in Kupang and had great difficulty in contacting Jakarta [from there]" (personal Interview, 21 April 1993). Emil Salim and other planners believed the satellite could make a major contribution to the realization of national unity, which had been a long-term goal that had in reality been only weakly developed. At that time, he said, "Indonesian unity amounted to little more than one flag, one language, the national anthem, and a national leader." He went on to say that

> The overriding issue which eventually led to the decision to develop the satellite system was the political issue of unifying the nation—all other aspects or benefits were secondary. The political and technical needs pulled the others along. In fact we had to convince the Department of Information and TVRI to become involved. Television was pulled along by this project, it did not pull the project. At that time, television was distributed more or less only in Java. The idea of a "national" system was hardly contemplated. Politically the development of the system had the additional benefit of being a high-profile, national development, which it was believed would boost the government's electoral success in elections planned for the mid-1970s.[17] The Armed Forces, and the Directorate General of Posts and Telecommunications were very supportive. (Emil Salim, personal interview, 21 April 1993)

The Directorate General of Posts and Telecommunications created some antagonism toward the satellite project by displaying a technocratic smugness and an impatience with reservations expressed by other departments.[18] In September 1974 the directorate convened a seminar in Jakarta ostensibly to solicit input from other departments and institutions in the development of a domestic satellite system. Some reservations about the project were expressed by academics and members of the National Development Planning Board. In response to further discussion, "mostly negative," Soehardjono impatiently and imprudently declared that delegates' concerns were irrelevant, as the project was certain to go ahead! (Astrid Susanto,[19] personal interview, 10 May 1993). But Sjamsoe Soegito, then Director of Radio, Television, and Film in the Department of Information and a member of the organizing committee (Direktorat Jenderal Pos Dan Telekomunikasi 1984, 20), while freely acknowledging that the initiative for development of the system had come from the Directorate of Posts and Telecommunications and that the Department of Information was uninformed about the technology, recalled that Information Minister Mashuri was supportive of the plan as he believed it would expand the Department's operations and contribute greatly to the development of educational services on television (Sjamsoe Soegito, personal interview, 7 May 1993).[20]

Two other implications of satellite technology were raised at the seminar. These discussions can be read as expressions of an urban elite's concern over its rural Others and over the infiltration of the margins of the Indonesian national space by foreign Others. More generally, they are expressions of planners coming to grips with the implications of developing for the first time a communications capability that would unite the nation. First, there was concern that advertising and images of "metropolitan culture" mediated through television would set up wants beyond rural viewers' capacity to pay. This consideration led to a discussion of how to limit what was broadcast to the regions, and it also resulted in the government-sponsored longitudinal study of the social and economic impact of satellite television by Godwin Chu, Alfian, and Wilbur Schramm (1991). Second, concerns over the security aspects of spillover were raised in terms of the likelihood of Palapa being used by non-Indonesian providers. These questions reflected a concern over control of the national culture space. The view of speakers whom communications specialist Alwi Dahlan described as "social scientists" (personal interview, 12 April 1993) was that the satellite might amount to a technological threat to the unity and union (*persatuan dan kesatuan*) of the nation. It was argued that it was simplistic to take the view that the domestic satellite system would of itself create unity, for it might contribute to disunity. No wonder that Soehardjono was impatient with the discussion, as these concerns addressed the very heart of his case for developing the satellite, namely that it would be an integrating force, not a divisive one.

In the end, President Soeharto was crucial to the development of the system. He ensured that the Export Import Bank funded the project—on commercial terms, but not at peak rates. Soeharto named the satellite "Palapa" (Direktorat Jenderal Pos dan Telekomunikasi 1984, 36; Emil Salim, personal interview, 21 April 1993; Soeharto 1985, 19), a reference to the vow taken in 1334 by Gajah Mada, Prime Minister of the fourteenth-century Kingdom of Majapahit, not to rest until the kingdom was united: "When I have unified the archipelago, then I will rest. When Gurun, Seran, Tanjungpura, Haru, Pahang, Dompo, Bali, Sunda, Palembang, and Tumasik are united, only then will I rest" (Direktorat Jenderal Pos dan Telekomunikasi 1984, 36).[21]

Six hundred years later, on 16 August 1976, the political intent of the ancient oath was echoed in Soeharto's telephone calls to the governors of Ache and Irian Jaya, calls that linked the most western and the most eastern provinces to the national capital, Jakarta (*Sinar Harapan,* 16 August 1976).

But while the prime motivation for developing the domestic satellite communications system in the 1970s was, as Emil Salim emphasized, primarily internal political and security considerations, the value of the technology in opening up regional commercial and political links was not overlooked. From 1979 Palapa was leased by Indonesia's Asean partners Thailand, Malaysia, and the Philippines for their communications purposes (Directorate General of Posts and Telecommunications 1983, 5:233; 237–43).

The Impact of Palapa on Television Services

The impact of the satellite on the delivery of television services was immediate and dramatic. The Palapa A1 satellite, launched on 9 July 1976 and commissioned 16 August 1976, was a twelve-transponder geostationary telecommunications satellite manufactured by the Hughes Aircraft Company of the United States. Its tandem backup satellite, Palapa A2, was launched on 11 July 1977.

Palapa was designed to receive radio signals from ground (uplink) stations and direct those signals to other ground (downlink) stations within its geographical range, which is best described as the Asean region including Papua New Guinea.

Use of Palapa for television distribution required the development of a network of downlink stations and relay stations to distribute the signal over a wider area using terrestrial microwave links. The Department of Information has been responsible for developing the terrestrial links, while the construction of downlink stations has been performed by the state telecommunications company, Perumtel. Forty downlink stations were built from 1975 through 1976, with further downlink stations planned for construction during the Third Five-Year Plan (Republik Indonesia 1979, 203).

When Minister Widjoyo Nitisastro appointed communications specialist Astrid Susanto as Adviser to the National Planning Board in 1974, one of the first tasks she was given was the extension of television services. Susanto recalled that her brief involved balancing technical requirements with the political considerations of national unity and security: the distribution of the transmitters was to reflect national military security priorities and the government's interest in marking out the national culture space to counter spillover from foreign broadcasts in border regions. Susanto developed a plan for a "transmission belt" around Indonesia. Sites were selected literally from Sabang to Merauke. Tenders for the supply of transmitters were called and received from Thompson (France), Philips and Marconi (United Kingdom), Siemens (West Germany), and Harris (United States). The government did not invite tenders from Japan because of sensitivities following demonstrations against Japanese investment in Indonesia in 1974. These tenders were seen as a chance "to balance" Japanese penetration of the economy (Astrid Susanto, personal interview, 4 May 1993).[22] In the end, the board played it safe and divided Indonesia into regions and awarded contracts to all tenderers. On Manado, Sulawesi, and East Kalimantan, all implicated in mutinies against the government in the late 1950s, transmitters were erected as "beacons" to signal the regions' attachment to the central government. The transmitter on Bali was set up with an eye to the benefits it would bring to the tourist industry (Astrid Susanto, personal interview, 10 May 1993).

Further development of the transmission belt brought the Department of Information into conflict with Perumtel. As signal strength dropped away over distance, repeater stations had to be built every eighty kilometers or so. After three repeating stations, another transmitter was required. Despite the government's security priorities, Perumtel was not prepared to build repeaters or transmitters in sites where the demand for telecommunications was not likely to cover costs. Astrid Susanto recalled that the Department of Information argued that it had a responsibility to deliver television services throughout the archipelago and that it was prepared to take over responsibility for the construction of repeaters and transmitters in isolated areas. In this way the Department of Information, a software department, gained control over transmission facilities, and arguments over maintenance have continued for years (Astrid Susanto, personal interview, 10 May 1993).

After the launch of Palapa in 1976, the Department of Information distributed thousands of public access receivers (*televisi umum*) in rural areas now within the satellite footprint. The distribution rose rapidly from 7,866 receivers in 1978/79 to 11,145 in 1979/80, and to 21,303 in 1980/81 (table 2.4). The program was proposed by Astrid Susanto, who saw it as a "have/have not issue":

> To escape the charge that the government was only looking after the rich and the educated [with Palapa], Minister Widjoyo agreed with my suggestion to distribute public sets. As a Javanese, I suggested that the sets should be in the *alun alun* [village square]. But when I toured, I found that the sets were mostly in the *Bupati's* [Regent's] houses—their argument was that they needed access to information from Jakarta! (personal interview, 4 May 1993)

Table 2.4
Distribution of Public Access Television Sets, 1978/79–1991/92

Year	Number of Sets	Year	Number of Sets
1978/79	7,866	1985/86	54,000
1979/80	11,145	1986/87	54,000
1980/81	21,303	1987/88	54,318
1981/82	21,543	1988/89	54,318
1982/83	29,866	1989/90	54,318
1983/84	38,072	1090/91	54,400
1984/85	54,000	1991/92	54,156
Source: Pidato Kenegaraan, various years			

Astrid Susanto told me that her idea for the public sets was based in part on the wartime experience of the Japanese, "who had radio everywhere" (personal interview, 4 May 1993). It may also have owed something to Japan's own experience with television: Indonesia purchased its broadcasting equipment from NEC, and NHK had trained many of the pioneer TVRI broadcasters. When Japan introduced television in 1953, large television sets were erected on "busy street corners, parks, railway termini, and other places of public gathering" in Tokyo (Kato 1995, 290).

The most immediate effect of Palapa was greatly to expand the reach of the service. The period from 1976 to 1980 was one of rapid development of broadcast "hardware" facilities. Three more regional broadcast stations were commissioned, bringing the total number of regional stations to nine at the end of the Second Five-Year Plan in 1978/79. This configuration remained stable for ten years and then rose when another station was commissioned in 1990. Table 2.5 shows that as soon as the satellite came on line, it

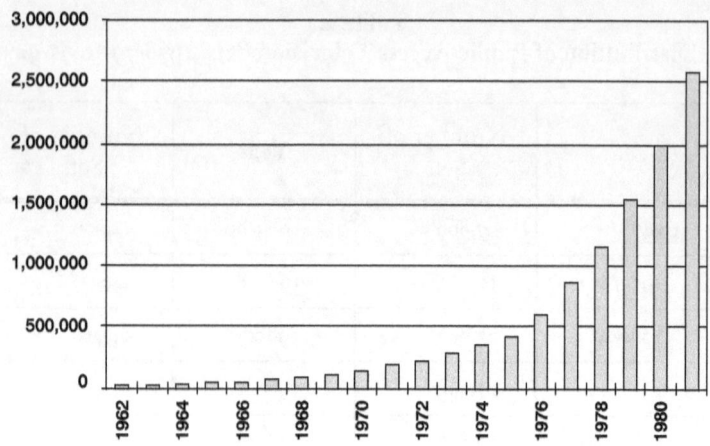

Figure 2.2. Television Receivers Registered, 1962–1981

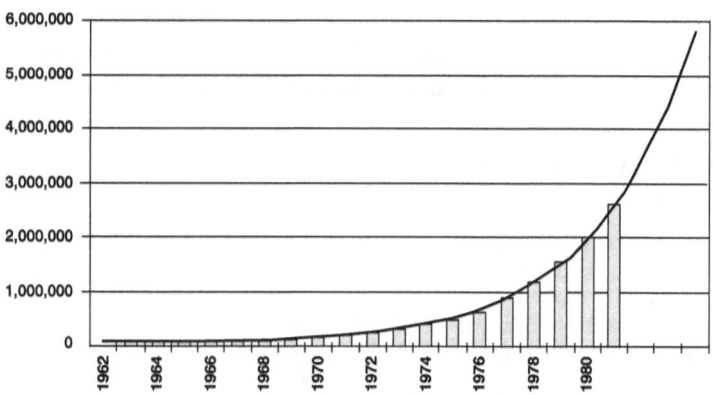

Figure 2.3. Television Receivers Registered, 1962–1981 (Data Trend)

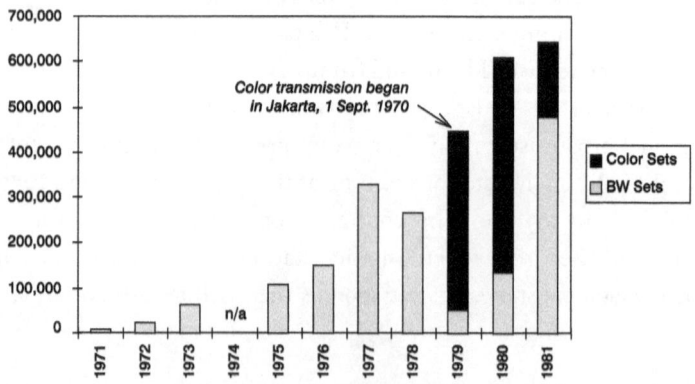

Figure 2.4. Domestic Manufacture of Television Receivers, 1971–1981

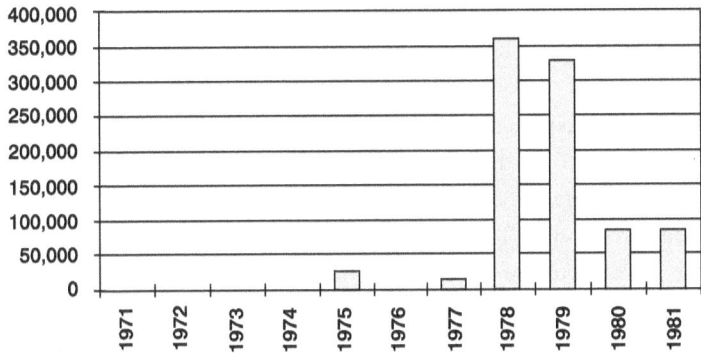

Figure 2.5. Domestic Manufacture of Television Antennae, 1971–1981

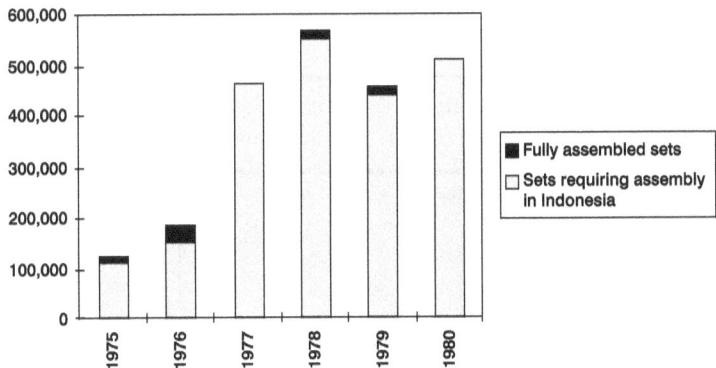

Figure 2.6. Imports of Television Receivers, 1975–1980

Note: For the years 1962 to 1967, the statistical records do not list television receivers separately. They are bundled in with "Machinery: Telegraph, Telephone, TV Appliances." The same is true for 1971 to 1974. In the years 1968 to 1970, the statistical records do not indicate whether the receivers imported were knocked down (for domestic assembly) or fully assembled.

doubled its reach. Within four years, Palapa had extended television services over nearly five times the area covered by TVRI in 1975/76. The potential audience more than doubled over this period. The exponential growth in the number of television receivers registered over the years 1976–81 (figs. 2.2 and 2.3) indicates that there were many people who were able to take advantage of the increased service. The manufacture of locally produced receivers rose by a factor of six during that period, another indicator of increased demand for television services stimulated by Palapa (figs. 2.4 and 2.5). Imports of television receivers also rose dramatically over the years 1976–80, boosting the hardware on sale to Indonesian viewers (fig. 2.6).

Table 2.5
TVRI Broadcast Range and Population Covered, 1962–1981

Year	Broadcast Area (km²)	Population (in millions)	Note
1962	5,000	7.5	0.24 of total land area of Indonesia; 3.78% of Java and Madura
1963	6,000	9	
1964	6,000	9	
1965	9,000	13	Yogyakarta Stn. commissioned; 39,913 TV sets registered
1966	13,000	17.5	
1967	17,000	20.5	
1968	18,200	22	
1969	18,500	22.5	

Table 2.5 (cont.)

Year	Broadcast Area (km²)	Population (in millions)	Note
1970	24,500	26.5	Medan Stn. Commissioned; 133,095 TV sets registered
1971	34,500	36.5	Est. 1.725% of total land area of Indonesia; reached 36% of total population
1972	36,500	37.5	1.3% of total population owned TV sets; Ujung Pandang Stn. commissioned
1973	72,100	40	Balikpapan Stn. commissioned
1974	72,900	40.5	Est. coverage 29% of area of Java, 3.6% of Indonesia; 93% of all TV sets registered in Java
1975	75,600	42	
1976	212,000	78	Palapa satellite launched; 511,490 TV sets registered
1977	229,000	80.9	

Table 2.5 (cont.)

Year	Broadcast Area (km²)	Population (in millions)	Note
1978/79	400,000	82	Suarabaya, Denpasar, Manado Stns. commissioned
1979/80	406,000	85	
1980/81	419,000	87	24% of national space, 60% of total population; 2,126,000 TV sets registered

Sources: Direktorat Televisi 1972, 58–59; Pidato Kenegaraan 1973, 552; 1980, 942; 1981, 18; 1984, 1208; Drake 1989, 119.

These figures provide clear evidence that the claimed benefits of the satellite were achieved more or less immediately. The gains that the improvements in hardware brought, however, were not matched by an expansion of programming services, which depended on human skills and time. Investment in hardware had left few funds for increased programming expenditure. The dramatic improvements in coverage and audience reach (table 2.5) were not accompanied by a similar expansion in programming. While the total hours of television broadcast rose, as shown in table 2.2, daily hours of programming showed very little change, and Sunday schedules contracted slightly (table 2.3).

One might have expected that Palapa would facilitate exchange of programs between stations and that in this way programming could be quickly and easily expanded. That this did not happen is a reflection of the way the satellite was integrated into the television system. I have noted that the Palapa project was largely an initiative of the Directorate General of Posts and Telecommunications and that it benefited from presidential patronage. The Department of Information and the Department of Education and Culture were not involved in the development of the system in the way that the Directorate of Posts and Telecommunications was. These differences are reflected, for example, in the way the Palapa project is described by the different departments in Five-Year Plan documents, in the Department of Information's long-harbored feelings of resentment at being trifled with during the development of the project, and in ongoing interdepartmental rivalries persisting into the present (Sjamsoe Soegito, Astrid Susanto, personal interviews, May 1993; Alwi Dahlan, personal interview, April 1993).[23]

Palapa was never well integrated into TVRI's planning. The friction between the Department of Information and Perumtel can be understood as reflecting a tension between technology-led policy making and programming-led policy making. After Palapa was launched, the scope for increased regional production with programs that were sensitive to local interests was reduced under the pressure of a more powerful Jakarta-centred national system. The early justification for the satellite placed emphasis on the boost it would give to educational television, but no additional funds were allocated for training educational broadcasters, and there is no evidence of a coordinated approach to educational television by the departments most affected.[24]

The Ban on Advertising

In the early 1970s, Sjamsoe Soegito, then Director General for Radio, Television, and Film, ruled that advertising must be presented before and after programs so the commercials would not interrupt the programs. In part this reflected a Javanese programming aesthetic that considered commercials demeaning to program content. In recalling the decisions about advertising, Sjamsoe Soegito said that he just "did not think it felt right" (*rasanya tidak enak*) to interrupt programs with commercials. The decision also reflected a view that rural audiences were especially vulnerable to the seductive appeals of advertising. Bunching up commercials made it easier for regional stations and viewers to edit them out. The launch of Palapa, and the potential for advertising to be relayed nationally, led to even more drastic steps. On 5 January 1981, President Soeharto announced that advertising on television would be banned after 1 April. He had taken this step, he said, "to focus television more on facilitating the [national] development program and to avoid the detrimental effects [of advertising], which do not promote the spirit of development" (*Tempo*, 17 January 1981, 20).

Discussion of this drastic step usually takes it in isolation and fails to see the decision as a reverberation of a process that had begun in the early 1970s. The ban on advertising can be understood as another expression of the protection of the uniqueness of Indonesian national culture against the corrupting and aggressive penetration of the Indonesian economy by transnational corporations and investors, particularly Japan, former invader and now major overseas investor. Frustration and anger over inequalities in the distribution of wealth and resentment at what was perceived to be an excessive degree of foreign investment and control of the Indonesian economy erupted in rioting during the visit of Prime Minister Tanaka of Japan in January 1974 and became known as "the Malari affair."[25] G. M. Sudarta's cartoon was published just a day before the riots (see fig. 2.7). It points to the historical shifts in relations between Indonesia and Japan. The crossed-out expression "older brother" may be understood as a strategy of putting signifiers "under erasure" to draw attention to the shift in political, economic, and cultural relations between the two countries. The Asian big brother/ colonizer is now a much less political business partner.[26]

In the previous year, students had raised the Indonesian flag over large billboards advertising Japanese products and had been praised in the press for their actions in words very similar in intent and tone to those used by the president seven years later:

> We ourselves view the two Japanese billboards as being in conflict with our own advertising ethics. Advertisements must be construc-

Figure 2.7. In this cartoon by G. M. Sudarta, the Indonesian on the left smilingly greets his one-time colonial master as "Friend." (*Kompas*, 14 January 1974)

tive, conforming with the Indonesian identity and the norms prevailing in the Indonesian society. Advertisements must not do damage to society and cause psychological effects which are harmful to the nation's identity. (*Abadi*, 12 December 1973, cited in Anderson 1980, 1265)

In the 1970s the advertising industry was dominated by transnational advertising agencies. Prominent journalist Mochtar Lubis criticized the advertising industry for contributing to rising levels of frustration by circulating images of a "foreign" materialist lifestyle: "We are shuddering under the impact of international consumerism. Every night on the TV and in the cinemas, the commercials entice our people to join the great bandwagon of wasteful consumerism" (cited in Anderson 1980, 1255).

Television commercials of luxury goods were banned in 1975 in an effort to meet community criticism (Direktur Jenderal Radio, Telvisi Film 1975), and by 1978 all transnational advertising agencies had established joint ventures with Indonesian partners as a way of reducing their "foreignness" (Anderson 1980, 1266). In 1980, advertising was still a matter of public concern. The National Press Council introduced regulations that limited newspapers to a maximum of twelve pages and ruled that advertising should not exceed 30 percent of space (Anderson 1980, 1269).

The ban on television advertising cost TVRI between Rp 17 billion and Rp 20 billion per year (*Tempo,* 24 January 1981; 18 April 1981). Alfian and Chu (1981, 97) report that advertising contributed 34 percent of the national television budget in 1975/76. In 1976/77, however, the Jakarta station financed 91.58 percent of its production and operating costs from advertising and in this way substantially subsidized television services in other urban and rural areas. Anderson (1980, 1261) shows that in 1977, 28 percent of all advertising expenditures across all media was spent on television and amounted to 10.8 million U.S. dollars. Alfian and Chu (1981, 110) suggest that the findings of the LEKNAS/LIPI (LEKNAS: National Institute for Economic Research; LIPI: Indonesian Institute of Sciences) study (1980) of the effects of television commercials in rural villages lent weight to the decision to ban advertising (see also *Tempo,* 17 January 1981). That study showed that imported and joint-venture goods accounted for nearly 75 percent of all goods advertised (Alfian and Chu 1981, 103). The study itself recommended retaining advertisements on television (LEKNAS/LIPI 1980, 28–30). Thus, while the TVRI ban was more drastic than these other measures, it should be seen as part of an extended process of scaling down public representation of what was usually referred to as a "*konsumtif*" (consumerist) lifestyle (*Suara Merdeka,* 2 April 1981).

The reason the government took the step of cutting television advertising completely may also have been linked to internal political rivalries and deserves further comment. A source whose identity must remain confidential claimed that President Soeharto had called both the Minister for Information and the Director General for Radio, Television, and Film to ask them how much revenue TVRI received from advertising. The two men deflated the figure, hoping for more funds for TVRI from the national budget. The president said that he was surprised that it was so low, but being so

Figure 2.8. On screen: "Don't buy lipstick. Instead, buy vegetable and fruit seedlings, fish fry, and rabbit kittens." (*Berita Buana,* 8 January 1981)

low, it wouldn't be missed, as he was concerned about consumerism and planned to cut advertising.[27]

The same source claimed the recommendation to ban advertising came from the State Secretary, Sudharmono, while he was Acting Minister for Information, standing in for Minister Ali Murtopo, who was in the United States for medical treatment.[28] The advertising ban cut funds flowing to the TVRI Foundation, sharply reducing funds available for Ali Murtopo's covert political activities, which had earned the president's displeasure after the Malari riots of 1974 (confidential interview, 1993; see also Bourchier 1990, 193).

Another consideration apparently taken into account was the national election planned for 1982 (*Sinar Harapan,* 6 January 1981; *Kompas,* 7 January 1981). The government believed that banning advertising would be politically beneficial. The ban cleared away an issue over which it felt vulnerable to attack by rival political groups, particularly conservative Muslim groups (confidential interview, 1993; *Pelita,* 7 January 1981). Though often cited as a reason for the ban, the religious factor may be exaggerated. My search of the pro-Muslim papers *Berita Buana* and *Pelita* for the months of January and April through June 1981 showed a lack of interest in the ban. The *Berita Buana* editorial (9 January 1981) published after the ban was announced discusses TVRI's future funding rather than the issue of consumerism and advertising. *Berita Buana* even poked fun at the ban in a cartoon, which shows a rural family supposedly delighted with advertising messages urging them to buy vegetable and fruit seedlings, fish fry, and rabbit kittens (fig. 2.8).

Banning advertising from TVRI had three lasting effects. First, it made TVRI much more a government and national/political voice. Table 2.6 shows the increased proportion of domestic productions after 1981, part of the Department of Information's plan to boost TVRI's role in fashioning and representing an idealized national culture. In chapters 4 and 5, I explore this process in depth. Second, it removed the incentive for private enterprise to take further interest in television (at least in the short term). Third, it made TVRI programming duller (fig. 2.9) by deleting commercials that many people enjoyed, by making programming less audience-centered and more development-oriented (fig. 2.10), and by reducing the funds for production.

Table 2.6
Domestic and Foreign Productions as a Percentage of Total TVRI Programming, 1968–1981/82

Year	TVRI Productions (%)	Imported Productions (%)
1968	40	60
1968/69	47	3
1969/70	NA	NA

Year	TVRI Productions (%)	Imported Productions (%)
1970/71	NA	NA
1971/72	NA	NA
1972/73	NA	NA
1973	48.1	51.9
1973/74	54	46
1974/75	61	39
1975/76	63	37
1976/77	73	27
1977/78	76	24
1978/79	65	35
1979/80	78.5	21.5
1980/81	80	20
1981/82	88	12

Source: Soeharto, *Pidato Kenegaraan*, various years

The advertising ban was linked to a polemic that constructed foreign capitalism as materialistic and based on assumptions and a way of life inimical to idealized principles of Indonesian national culture. The ban can be understood as part of a process that helped to shift the culture of television more to the center of the government's ideological apparatus. Director General Subrata stated that the ban legitimated TVRI as a public broadcaster (*Kompas*, 6 January 1981). He said that in stable, mature countries such as England, government television was noncommercial. Subrata's ingenuous comment ignored that public service broadcast services such as the BBC were founded on a tradition of independence

oom pasikom

Figure 2.9. TVRI has become boring since ads were banned. (*Kompas*, 4 April 1981)

Figure 2.10. The banner reads "Public [TV] Show." A village group is watching public TV. An old man says, "The program yonder that led people astray has been banned. And now the [license] fees have gone up. And, would you believe it, the programs are becoming more boring. We're forced to watch; this is the only entertainment available." A second man says, "Pailul, for the sake of development, don't grumble." Pailul: "I have paid my license fee. Why can't I grumble? It seems the natural thing to do." (*Kompas,* 5 April 1981)

from government. In Indonesia, as advertising was cut from TVRI, the service became more closely aligned with government cultural and development priorities. The ban reinforced television's role in defining the sovereign cultural space of the nation and in defining differences between the Indonesian nation and culture and others beyond. The decision reflected the tension I referred to at the beginning of this chapter between an audience-centered, public/private funded "professional" television system that mediated and circulated a mix of domestic and transnational values, attitudes, and televisual products and a system more narrowly concerned with internal political and ideological values, and characterized by top-down policy making. This time, the change in funding arrangements decisively shifted control of TVRI into government hands and established it as a government monopoly, a monopoly that was to last until August 1990, when the first two commercial stations began broadcasting free-to-air.

Chapter 3

TELEVISION AND ITS HISTORICAL AUDIENCES

Television, Culture, and Audiences

THIS CHAPTER IS AN INVESTIGATION into how television discourses have developed in Indonesia over the last thirty years, the way the television audience has been constructed by different social institutions, and the ideological work that the constructions of the audience perform. In this analysis of television's audiences in Indonesia I start from the position, outlined by John Hartley (1987), that the television audience is an imaginary construct of discourses that surround and institutionalize broadcast practice in particular settings. The discourse is carried on by all those who have vested interests in television and may include the following: the television industry, political and legal institutions, critical institutions (academic and journalistic), and voluntary groups with special interests that function as pressure or lobby groups. In chapters 9 and 10 I explore the growing significance of nongovernment organizations in the regulation of television in Indonesia since deregulation.

In this discursive sense, the television audience is a projection by an institution over the infinite diversity of the actual viewing practices of individuals and groups. Hartley acknowledges the empirical nature of viewing practice but argues that the categorization of the particularity of viewing practices into an imagined audience represents the need of the institutions implicated in television to construct a fictional audience. Institutions then endeavor to control this audience as a way of taking charge of their own survival. In so far as the survival strategies are likely to be different for different institutions, it follows that the imaginary audience each constructs will also be different.

Hartley's general point about the way institutions construct television's audiences has been extended by Ien Ang (1991). Ang brings into sharp focus the way institutions imagine their audience through a detailed analysis of the role of audience measurement, or ratings, in both commercial and public service broadcasting. For Ang, the institutions that plan, produce, and broadcast television messages, and the institutions that shape and regulate their flow, work with a construct of the "invisible mass" of the television audience, "onto which large-scale economic and cultural aspirations and expectations, policies, and planning schemes are projected, allowing these institutions to realise their ambitions to govern and control the formal frameworks of television's place in contemporary life" (Ang 1991, 2).

Relying on published documentation such as Indonesian government policy and legislation and critical commentary in the press and (more rarely) in monographs, this chapter examines historical shifts in ideas of the ideal-typical Indonesian television audience since the service first began in 1962. In brief, there was a move from TVRI's normative construct of the audience as a "national family" to a construct of the audience inflected by values of commercial television and imagined as an audience of globally informed, critical consumer/citizens.[1] The different constructions of the audience, developed by the government, the television industry, television critics, and very occasionally members of the audience through self-representation, are examined for the contribution they make to our understanding of the imbrication of television in the ideology of nation and culture in contemporary

Indonesia. First I discuss TVRI's audience constructed by official government discourses, commercial interests, and critics from 1962 to 1989, a period that begins with the establishment of television and ends with the introduction of the first commercial broadcaster. The next section of the chapter looks at shifts in TVRI's audience construct after the introduction of commercial television, referring again to official and critical discourses concerning TVRI. The concluding sections of the chapter look at the audience constructs of the two commercial channels, Rajawali Citra Televisi Indonesia (RCTI) and Televisi Pendidikan Indonesia (TPI), from 1989 to 1991, when they first began broadcasting. The analysis in these sections parallels the discussion of TVRI's audience, taking up licensees' and journalistic discourses of the commercial television audience.

TVRI-A (Commercial) Public Service Broadcaster

In *Desperately Seeking the Audience* (1991) Ang distinguishes between commercial and public service broadcasting systems and argues that the two systems "differ fundamentally as regards assumptions about the cultural and political purpose of broadcasting, and this difference is inextricably linked to a marked distinction in how each system prefers to define the institution-audience relationship" (27).

While there are weaker and stronger forms of the public broadcasting model (McQuail 1994, 172), public broadcasting systems such as the ABC (Australian Broadcasting Corporation) in Australia, the BBC in the United Kingdom, and NHK in Japan are based on the assumption that the broadcaster is there to serve the whole national community through programming that is comprehensive, educational, informative, culturally sensitive and appropriate, entertaining, and of high quality. As Ang says, public broadcasting systems are characterized by a "pervasive sense of cultural responsibility and social accountability, which is emphatically opposed to the easy-going commercial dictum of 'giving the audience what it wants'" (1991, 28).

Models of funding public broadcasting differ throughout the world. The ABC in Australia is funded by the whole community through allocation of tax revenues to a broadcaster that is independent of the state and private sectors. The BBC and NHK are even more independent of government, being funded out of license fee receipts. Public broadcasting in Denmark, Norway, and Sweden is funded similarly (Siune 1986, 46). Some public broadcasters rely on mixed funding. Finland, Germany, Greece, Ireland, Italy, the Netherlands, and Switzerland raise up to 50 percent of public broadcasting revenue through advertising. In France, FR3 raises 94 percent of its budget from license fees, but the public broadcast channels A2 and TF1 raise between 53 and 61 percent of their funds from advertising. In Luxembourg, public broadcasting is funded completely by advertising, as is the IBA/ITV Channel 4 in Britain. In Spain the advertising contribution is 79 percent (Siune 1986, 46–54). The Broadcasting Corporation of New Zealand (BCNZ) relied on mixed funding from 1961 to 1989. In 1985, four years before television in New Zealand was deregulated, license fees contributed 13 percent and advertising 87 percent of the BCNZ budget. In 1989 the Broadcasting Corporation was restructured as a state enterprise. The 1989 Broadcasting Act requires BCNZ to "return a profit on all divisions" (Wilson, cited in Moran 1996, 170).

A commercial broadcasting system is typically concerned with segments rather than the whole of the national audience and pitches its programming to attract and hold its "target" audiences. The broadcaster's objective is to deliver a predictable (demographically segmented) audience to advertisers, which are the main source of funding for commercial broadcasting. Commercial broadcasters construct their audience as a market and as spectators. Given that commercial broadcasters' prime aim is to deliver audiences to advertisers, simply gaining audience attention satisfies (minimally) their prime economic goal.

In terms of the distinction between public and commercial broadcasting, TVRI was from its beginning a hybrid, in practice, if not always by intention or desire. TVRI began broadcasting in 1962 with clear public service "paternalist" aims (Williams 1976, 131) formalized in Presidential Decree #27 (Presiden Republik Indonesia 1963a), which I discussed in chapter 2. But TVRI quickly developed a commercial character as well. Advertisements appeared on TVRI for the first time in March 1963, when poster cards and slides, accompanied by music, were screened for ten-second intervals between scheduled programs (Agassi 1969, 67; Direktorat Televisi 1972, 49). A "commercial section" was created within TVRI to handle commercials and sponsorship arrangements. Official guidelines stated that only 10 percent of broadcast time should be taken up by commercials, but in 1978, 14.58 percent of broadcast time was taken by commercial messages at the Jakarta station (Alfian and Chu 1981, 81, 98; Direktorat Televisi 1972, 148).

While the mixed funding model in public broadcasting is widespread, the different objectives of those contributing funds are a source of tension wherever the model applies (McQuail 1986, 152–78). In Indonesia, the paternalist values of the government sat uneasily with the commercial values of the sponsors and companies that contributed so significantly to TVRI revenue. Alfian and Chu (1981, 97), for example, describe commercials as "a necessary evil," a view reflected in TVRI's *Televisi Republik Indonesia* (1983, 30), where the prime role played by commercial funding in the broadcasting system is acknowledged but at the same time considered inappropriate for TVRI's future growth. The then director of TVRI, Subrata, regarded advertising income as a sign of the immature nature of broadcasting in Indonesia. He claimed that in "stable countries" (*yang sudah mantap keadaannya*) where public television was government-owned, it was completely government-funded (*Kompas,* 6 January 1981).[2] Alfian and Chu and Subrata's remarks reveal an inherently teleological view of the development of television broadcasting. Commercial television is understood as a kind of early stage through which it must move before achieving maturity. The "stain" of commercialism is tolerated only because it helps get the system off the ground and only because the state has the authority to remove the disfiguring influence of the private sector later.

It is this mixed government broadcaster mission, combined with substantial (in some stations, such as Jakarta, almost complete) commercial funding that led me to describe TVRI as a "hybrid" in which paternalist values and commercial values were blended in what seems to have been an uneasy truce. Thus the assertion that commercial and public service broadcast systems have a markedly different perception of the audience-institution relationship and that there are two alternative paradigms of audience as public and audience as market has to be modified to suit Indonesian circumstances before 1981. TVRI's audience was simultaneously its public and its market, though the tolerance with which each of the broadcast parties accepted the other's vision and priorities refracted in what was screened is difficult to assess.

This hybrid (tele)vision continued until 1 April 1981, when advertisements on television were banned on the order of President Soeharto. The justification given for banning advertisements was a textbook example of the duty of a paternalistic public broadcast system to "protect and guide" its audience, as Williams puts it (1976, 131). After 1981 TVRI was "truer to type" as a public broadcaster funded from government subsidy and license fees. But the impact on TVRI of such a substantial and sudden loss of revenue was considerable. TVRI had difficulty covering its costs and resorted to what the critic Arswendo Atmowiloto described as covert advertising (Arswendo 1986, 83). In Gatot's cartoon in the *Surabaya Post* (14 April 1981), a television presenter whispers to the audience, "Psst! This program is sponsored by...," suggesting that TVRI will be unable to continue without advertising and will be forced into the most obvious contortions both to acknowledge and to conceal its sources of funds (fig. 3.1).

Figure 3.1. [Man on screen]: "Pssst! This program is sponsored by ..." (*Surabaya Post,* 14 April 1981)

TVRI's Audiences, 1962–1989

Official Discourses

As noted in chapter 2, at the introduction of television, it was not an Indonesian audience for which the service was rushed through, as few Indonesians owned television sets and only a very limited Jakarta audience would have been able to benefit from coverage of the games. Indeed, in its first month TVRI's imagined audience was Indonesia's Asian neighbors, or more specifically, their official representatives, whom the Indonesian government sought to impress with the sophistication of its conduct and mediation of the international event.

The Audience as Nation

After the games the government's focus shifted back to domestic circumstances. The Indonesian audience was imagined as a revolutionary mass that needed to be guided and shaped into model citizens of a "socialist humanity." Presidential Decrees #27 and #215 (Presiden Republik Indonesia 1963a and 1963b), described television as a mass communications tool (*alat komunikasi massa*) that could be used in molding and reforming the masses. But by 1962–63, the Indonesian revolution in the narrow sense of the term was over. What sense did "revolution" carry at this time? It was a revolution of physical and spiritual transformation, a planned development of skills and attributes that would contribute to the process of "nation building." In this early statement, the ethnic and cultural diversity of the Indonesian population is not considered. Proffered instead is the vision of an undifferentiated mass that was to be comprehensively transformed into members of a nation in the making. Education was to play a crucial role in this transformation, and for that reason TVRI was initially designed to broadcast to educational institutions. High priority was to be given to instruction in Indonesian language and to establishing the values of *persatuan dan kesatuan* (union and unity).

By 1972, while the function of TVRI as a medium of mass communication remained, the imagined audience had shifted from an amorphous mass to a mass that had something to offer the process of national development and whose views were worthy of consideration. This view was consonant with the "great optimism and rejuvenation of Indonesia's social, cultural and educational life" in the 1970s after the polarized cultural politics of the late Sukarno period and the years immediately following the coup in 1965 (Mackie and Macintyre, 1994, 12; Hatley, 1994). The Minister for Information then described TVRI as "audience-centered" and acknowledged the challenge facing a single channel to meet the varied needs and interests of a population as vast and varied as Indonesia's (Boediardjo 1972, 17–19). As discussed in chapter 2, Minister Boediardjo's more progressive view of TVRI's role was clawed back after popular activism erupted into street riots in 1974. Thereafter the government pursued a more centralist, state-centered role for television. Once again, this reflected the politics of the day. Mackie and Macintyre argue that "Malari marked a decisive shift from the relatively open, pluralistic phase of political life under the New Order toward one in which society-based forces were to be largely excluded and rendered almost powerless to influence state policies" (1994, 14).

In 1981, with Ali Murtopo, the faction leader who led the crackdown on student dissent after Malari, as Minister for Information, the early 1970s view of the audience gave way to a construct of a differentiated mass (*lapisan masyarakat*) that needed to be informed, educated, and enlightened for the good of the national development process (Menteri Penerangan 1981). The rhetoric of the decree signaled a return to a one-way process of didactic communication, which had been part of the original understanding of television as a means of continuing the Indonesian Revolution through mass public education.

State Power, the "Cone of Light," and the Palapa Satellite

It was the launch of the Palapa satellite in 1976 that revealed most tellingly the construct of the nation(al) audience. In Benedict Anderson's well-known essay on power in Javanese culture, he introduces the image of a cone of light, shining down from the central power, embracing, ordering, and unifying the state as a model of center-periphery relations and of territorial sovereignty (Anderson 1972, 22). He makes two additional points about the center of power that are instructive in analyzing the significance of satellite broadcasting in Indonesia. He notes first that Javanese rulers typically linked their rule with past centers of power and greatness, and second that the traditional state was defined by its center, not by its perimeter (Anderson 1972, 25–28).

These three points gain a special cogency when related to the introduction of domestic satellite broadcasting and the imagining of a national audience in Indonesia. The naming of the satellite as

"Palapa" signifies historical continuity of Indonesia as a nation with an ancient and glorious past, which the present government is determined to preserve and enhance. The satellite, immobile above the territory of Indonesia, effortlessly in touch with the farthest corners of the archipelago, is a contemporary manifestation of the central power of the government and updates Anderson's image of the cone of light. The fragmented, far-flung archipelago is unified in a seamless electronic net that annihilates space and imposes its own time, drawing the vastness and diversity of Indonesia into a whole, structuring for the periphery a clear and constant fix on the center.

Nationhood and national audiencehood can also be articulated through a process of disengagement from wider sociopolitical constructs in which the nation defines itself as different from its Others. This process is evident in two interrelated perspectives in television discourse. First, there is a tendency to be critical of foreign programs as "too Western" or otherwise incompatible with indigenous values and traditions (*Suara Merdeka,* 24 August 1982; *Editor,* 23 February 1991; 6 April 1991; *Kompas,* 12 September 1991; *Tempo,* 26 October 1991). Second, there is a tendency to idealize the value of "national" films and programs, to reify a national Indonesian culture, and press for greater representation of national programs on local television, which, it is assumed, will be enjoyed by the imagined national audience (*Tempo,* 9 February 1972; 26 August 1972; 9 August 1980; *Kompas,* 25 November 1987; *Suara Pembaruan,* 8 January 1991).

The Audience as Family

The nation(al) audience becomes more than a spatial entity and takes on the character of a national family through TVRI announcers' customary form of address to viewers as *"saudara,"* an inclusive kinship term that hails viewers as members of a family.[3] In chapter 5 I explore the idea of the "national family" and "familyism" (*kekeluargaan*) as central elements in the national culture project through a case study of the TVRI soap opera *Keluarga Rahmat*. The commercial channels have not followed TVRI's lead in addressing their viewers as family. The different mode of address crystallizes the different audience constructs of public and commercial broadcasters. On commercial channels, TVRI's somewhat formal but always inclusive "saudara" was passed up for the less personal term *"pemirsa"* (viewer), especially by RCTI announcers. *Pemirsa* has been used for many years to describe viewers (not only of television but of *wayang* as well) (*Kompas*, 23 August 1971), but my impression is that as a form of address it is more recent. *Pemirsa* hails the viewer as a spectator rather than as family, bringing to the foreground an *individuated viewing experience* rather than a fictional extended family audience. Ariel Heryanto notes that *pemirsa* is just one of many recently coined words in contemporary Indonesian deriving from Old and High Javanese or Sanskrit that are part of an attempt to craft a new, grander lifestyle among the New Order's rich by way of "aristocratization" (personal correspondence, 1997).

The Audience as Childlike

I turn now to examine TVRI policies and decisions that illustrate what Hartley (1987, 127, 130) has called the "paedocratised regime" of television production, by which he means an institutional perspective that imagines its audience as childlike. There are two aspects of the childlike image of the audience in Hartley's analysis. The second has more salience for Indonesian television in the period under discussion. The second aspect of the "retarded child" model of audiencehood is the construction of the audience as requiring guidance and protection. In this model, it is the broadcasting authority that exhibits the parental attributes of wisdom, balance, order, mature judgment, and responsibility and that claims to know what is best for the audience. The disjunction between the maturity of the ruling (urban) elite and the audience as childlike, "unenlightened" (*masih bodoh*), and requiring firm guidance, echoes traditional Javanese power relations and cultural dispositions explored by Anderson in his essay "The Idea of Power in Javanese Culture" cited above.

I have already commented on TVRI's almost aristocratic disdain for the necessity of commercial funding. It has also demonstrated an elitist tendency in its attitude toward advertising. As in other (European) public broadcasting systems that rely on public sector and advertising revenue, strict rules governed the presentation and content of advertising (McQuail 1986, 152–78). Advertisements were expected to contribute to and promote government development goals and were not to challenge government priorities. A strict code of ethics was developed to guide advertising on television (Direktorat Televisi 1972, 150). The timing and presentation of commercials was under the control of TVRI and was heavily influenced by the government's paternalist value system. In the early 1970s commercials were presented before scheduled programs so they would not interrupt them. By 1981, as in European systems (Smith 1995, 80), commercials were scheduled into two thirty-minute segments known as "commercial broadcast" (*siaran niaga*) to make it easy for viewers to avoid them and for TVRI to delete them from satellite transmissions to rural areas, "so the products are not shown to persons who cannot obtain them" (Alfian and Chu 1981, 98).

As a public broadcaster, TVRI clearly differentiated between the worldly audience it constructed in urban areas and the rural audience that needed protection and shielding from the seductive messages of consumerism. The government's elitist construct was based on the belief that the center was robust enough to resist the seductive appeal of advertising and would not be diverted from approved national goals implied in the general rubric "development" (*pembangunan*). It was equally convinced that the rural majority was not similarly committed. When Palapa was launched, the center/rural opposition was in some senses erased.

What the center had access to, Palapa also delivered to rural audiences. Satellite technology made the ban on advertising inevitable, given the government's paternalistic attitudes concerning the rural mass. In 1981 President Soeharto's government was certain that the pleasure principles promoted through advertising represented a threat to the development ethos of national policies and programs and outlawed it, and this time even worldly Jakarta was not exempt.

Journalistic and Academic Discourses: The Audience as Public Citizens

Journalistic discourse represents TVRI's audience as a public, though its construction of the public is different from the public the government sees itself addressing. I have tried to summarize the difference in the subheading for this section, as over the years what emerges most strikingly in the critical discourse is the construction of an audience that is resistant to being interpellated simply as the subject of an improving regime of state-directed policies and programs. The basis for the resistance is complex, being an amalgam of different attitudes and rights. There is, first, the assertion of rights of ownership, based on the assumption that as viewers/consumers, the audience has a stake in programming because they contribute directly to the service by paying for it; TVRI is "their television" (*Indonesian Observer*, 21 August 1987; *Suara Pembaruan*, 24 August 1990). Second, there is a view that the public's television service should be professionally managed and presented. Third, the service should be socially responsible and not simply available for exploitation by commercial interests for their own gain. Finally, there is a rejection of any demeaning assumption that the audience is immature or lacking in judgment, and the audience is accepting and self-confident about its diversity and resistant to any attempt to position it as a uniform mass.

Here the audience is not an amorphous mass; it is a differentiated audience with rights, tastes, critical standards, and special interests. It is not an audience that sees itself split into an urban and rural mass. It is an audience that rejects ceremonialism and government monopolization of the medium for reasons of self-interest and self-congratulation. It is also an audience interested in the pleasure television offers. Television critic Eduard Depari identifies TVRI's (mis)understanding of its audience as crucial for future success: "It will be very ironic, if at the age of a quarter of a century, the crucial problem for TVRI still turns on the issue of *not knowing who its audience is*" (*Suara Pembaruan,* 24 August 1987, emphasis in original).

TVRI's paternalist model of television broadcasting fits a transmission model of communication (McQuail 1994), where the audience is seen to be a more or less passive receiver of messages, and the intended consequence of the whole process of communication is an ordered transference of meaning (Ang 1991, 29). The audience imagined in Indonesian journalistic discourse rejects these assumptions. It is instead a mature, complex public that has a right to be informed but not dominated. The resistance to domination is expressed in a variety of ways. If early government decrees concerning television referred to television as an *alat kommunikasi*, a communication tool, or instrument with which to perform a task, journalistic discourse invariably refers to television as a *medium* of mass communication, a phrase which still objectifies the mass but acknowledges the possibility of a two-way flow of information (Presiden Republik Indonesia 1963a; 1963b; *Kompas,* 25 August 1985; *Suara Merdeka,* 24 August 1987; *Suara Pembaruan,* 24 August 1987).

I have already noted the close link anticipated between TVRI and education in the 1961 planning documents. While the mapping of TVRI onto universities was not proceeded with, in subsequent policy statements of 1963 the idea that TVRI should perform an entertainment function was not even mentioned (Presiden Republik Indonesia 1963a; 1963b). But right from the very early days of television, viewers had different ideas. An impatient, disgruntled pioneer viewer in Jakarta complained in October 1962 about the lack of interesting programming and suggested that there were plenty of films that could be screened, adding that cartoons were "not uninteresting" for parents with families (Direktorat Televisi 1972, 46). Five years later, "entertainment" programs had become part of the standard program schedule and accounted for 30 percent of screen time up to 1967. The percentage continued to rise from then on. TVRI developed a detailed code of what constituted "healthy" family entertainment to ensure that the entertainment function of television would not distract the audience from its development priorities (Direktorat Televisi 1972, 85, 91).

A *Kompas* editorial of 26 August 1975 urged the government not to be didactic but to construct a dialogue between viewers and TVRI: "There is only one television channel. Like it or not, the community must tune in to it, if they want to watch. Viewers can accept its sole status. But even so, the relation between TV as a medium and viewers as audience will be closer if the basic principle of communication between television and viewers is observed."

One aspect of dialogue, it was suggested, was TVRI's willingness to accept criticism. Criticism may be directed at aspects of programming, or to the standard of presentation, a point of view usually expressed in terms of demands for a "professional" service. Another *Kompas* editorial from 27 August 1973, criticized censorship on TVRI and made a case for more contemporary drama on television, saying gently that it was unlikely to "upset public safety." A similar view can be found in another *Kompas* editorial of 26 August 1975, which stated that more trenchant communication on social issues was required and that television should extend its role in this field. Finally, it recommended that TVRI should present more balanced interview programs and feature community as well as government views on issues of daily concern.

Criticism of the professionalism of TVRI broadcasting has been a long-term concern. In what must be a very early example of an open-line complaint service, a *Harian Kami* (28 August 1968) reader rang the paper to complain about subtitles being off-screen, programs ending before time, overly frequent display of the Pancasila symbols, and the poor quality of a recently featured singer! In 1972, *Harian Kami* maintained this criticism of the technical proficiency of TVRI, noting in an editorial of 24 August that programs were frequently canceled or altered without adequate notice to viewers, that overseas-trained staff were being placed in administrative positions where their recent training could not be utilized, that programs were frequently slapped together without scripts, and that TVRI was guilty of hiding behind the excuse of lack of funds for inadequacies in its service. For its part, in an article headlined *"Masih Ada Yang Berkerja Asal Jadi"* (There are Still Workers Who Just Do the Bare Minimum), *Suara Pembaruan* (23 August 1987) suggested fifteen years later that the casual attitude toward programming was still an issue and that many staff took a "she'll be right, mate" attitude to their work.

Stressing the need for a greater degree of openness between TVRI and its public, critic Eduard Depari suggested that development issues should be handled differently. He argued that there was no objection to a focus on national development but that there were objections to programming that failed to acknowledge real difficulties in the development process and simply presented a continuous flow of "good news":

> Dialogue about development will be hampered by information about development presented always from the success story perspective. From an empirical point of view, there are plenty of difficulties about development that must be communicated to the public. Community awareness about problems in development grows with the information they utilize and will contribute to the development of more spontaneous cooperation and not forced cooperation. (*Suara Pembaruan,* 24 August 1987)

The critical discourse also rejects TVRI's tendency to create a normative construct of the audience that erases its diversity. The public should be acknowledged in all its complexity and range of tastes, interests, and background and not imposed upon as if it were one particular ethnic group or just an amorphous mass

(*Suara Karya,* 24 August 1975; *Kompas,* 24 August 1985; *Suara Pembaruan,* 24 August 1987; *Indonesian Observer,* 21 August 1987). Rusli Desa, chair of the Parliamentary Commission on Information, Defense, and Foreign Affairs, on the twenty-fifth anniversary of TVRI, said that "TVRI broadcasts should therefore reflect the complexity of the Indonesian nation in reporting, as well as art, and should not be dominated by certain ethnical [sic] cultures, because TVRI is [the] Indonesian people's property and is not owned by individuals, groups or certain ethnical [sic] group[s]" (*Indonesian Observer,* 21 August 1987).

President Soeharto, taking the view that as a public broadcaster TVRI should "protect" its audience from the undesirable aspects of advertising, authorized the advertising ban. The duty of care TVRI owes its audience is also asserted in the journalistic discourse, but from a different perspective, highlighting the different normative construct of the public between state authorities' paedocratic view and the audience-as-public-citizens view. Critical discourse expresses concern, for example, over unethical advertising of drugs that have not been approved for consumption by national authorities. In this case, the audience is imagined as sufficiently responsible to make everyday choices as consumers, but as nonspecialists, not equipped to make decisions concerning the benefits or otherwise of commercially manufactured drugs. Even so, Johnny Hidayat's cartoon strip (fig. 3.2) suggested that the ad ban removed

Figure 3.2. *Left to right:* TV no longer has ads . . . ; And if radio and the papers have no ads, what then?! Bung Joni: "Plenty of people will be tricked into buying dodgy goods." (*Berita Buana,* 14 April 1981)

information from the public sphere and disempowered consumers by depriving them of one way to judge the worth of the goods they might want to buy. Speaking from a small flat high up in (probably) Jakarta, a woman reading of the ad ban in the newspaper asks, "What if ads on radio and in the newspapers are banned?" In the third frame Djon Domino says that if that happened, many ordinary people would be tricked into buying dodgy goods.[4]

The audience-as-citizens construct acknowledges the duty a public service broadcaster has in carefully monitoring advertising content and protecting viewers from unethical products, but it implicitly rejects the view that the broadcaster has the right to make comprehensive restrictions on programming and advertising in the name of protecting the mass from itself (*Harian Kami*, 24 August 1972).

Despite TVRI's efforts to determine what the audience ought to find entertaining, viewers continued to criticize what the *Suara Karya* editorial of 26 August 1975 saw as "a lack of balance or harmony" between educational and entertainment programs. Ten years later, *Sinar Harapan* conducted a straw poll of young viewers about how TVRI could be improved, and they responded that more entertainment was needed but that it should be of good quality and have a "Pancasila spirit." Their solemn interest in Pancasila-spirited programs is not entirely convincing, however, as later in the same poll they complained that when there was poetry on television, it was only about Pancasila and was narrated in the declamatory style of primary school kids (*Suara Karya*, 25 August 1985).

Eduard Depari was not as coy when he argued on TVRI's twenty-fifth anniversary that it had tended to cater too much to the needs of those in power who should realize that the majority of viewers saw television as a source of entertainment, not of information (*Suara Pembaruan*, 24 August 1987). Finally, the choices available to viewers in the late 1980s sharpened the issue of the content and balance of public service programming. Journalistic discourse presented an image of an audience that frankly acknowledged its interest, right and, expectation to be entertained by television. Critics pointed to the overly formal, dull educational programming as the reason for the burgeoning video industry, and the reason some sections of the TVRI audience tuned out to watch the more entertaining Malaysian TV3 (*Suara Pembaruan,* 24 August 1987; *Suara Merdeka,* 24 August 1987).

TVRI's Audiences, 1989–1991

Official Discourses: Enlightened Paternalism

The satellite technology that was integral to TVRI's construct of its audience as identical with the nation brought that construct into question after 1989. The borders that Palapa so early, so distinctively, and so clearly reached and defined are now electronically porous and diffused by television signals from Malaysia, Thailand, Singapore, the United States, Taiwan, the Philippines, and Australia. The signals not only are a function of spillover on the borders but also may be tuned in by individuals and groups who have access to satellite dishes (*Tempo,* 14 June 1986).

In response to this subtle invasion of its territorial integrity, TVRI's response has shifted from electronic isolationism to resigned acceptance of the impossibility of deflecting the intrusive signals. On 20 August 1986 the Minister for Information decreed (Ministerial Decree #167B, 1986) that individuals were permitted to own and use satellite dishes to receive television signals from Palapa without licenses. The legislation inscribed the fiction that the Indonesian audience, particularly the segments living in cities such as Jakarta and Surabaya, where access to TVRI was perfectly adequate, was under the control of TVRI and sufficiently loyal to use the sophisticated, expensive equipment only to improve and maintain their access to TVRI. It also chose to ignore that even if village cable systems were tuned to Palapa they would also be tuned to Malaysian and Thai services, as both used Palapa for their own domestic purposes. The fiction was reinforced in the decree issued by the Minister for Tourism, Post, and Telecommunications, which authorized hotels and tourist venues to install satellite dishes for "general television broadcasts and in this way help extend the range of national television." No restrictions were placed on what broadcasts could be received (Menteri Pariwisata, Pos dan Telekomunikasi 1986, article 2).

In 1990 the privileged access to global television enjoyed by tourists and wealthy Indonesians was extended to all Indonesian citizens. The legislation began on a regretful note, saying that "satellite dishes introduced new horizons that could not easily be rejected." It went on more positively to give the audience the right to take advantage of the technology for its own purposes, trusting that it would use the opportunity wisely and would select programs that would not contribute to any weakening of national security (Menteri Penerangan 1990, article 32). This legislation records an important shift in TVRI's construction of its audience. Now it imagined the ideal-typical TVRI audience as an audience that had a broad general right and interest in television as a source of information and entertainment, that was largely beyond the control of TVRI, that had "grown up," and that could be trusted to make its own viewing choices. The trust was not complete, however, as cable distribution facilities set up by local authorities or individuals in areas of poor TVRI reception were required to be licensed and were still only permitted to be tuned to TVRI.

The liberalization of choice and the trust placed in the maturity of the audience was, however, more illusory than real. The government still tightly regulated situations it had a greater chance of controlling, and freedom of choice was still largely limited to better-off individuals and tourists. In 1986, for example, the Director General of Radio, Television, and Film commented that it was unnecessary at that time to ban satellite dishes because their cost put them beyond the reach of most people (*Kompas,* 13 February 1986). In practice the government still works with the segmented, discriminatory view of the audience I outlined above in connection with exposure to advertising. The new rules allowed the economic elite access to information and entertainment denied to general viewers and contributed to a new class structure based on wealth and information. The policy recreated the defacto two-tiered information system that existed in TVRI's earliest years when Jakarta (and by 1965, Yogyakarta) viewers had access to a commercially inflected, entertaining programming regime including national and international news, while regional viewers had to put up with just a few hours a day of local programming, which, by regulation, could not include locally produced news or current affairs.

Journalistic Discourse

For all its insistence on cooperation, TVRI is keenly aware of the need to be informed about audience interests and preferences in a competitive environment (Departemen Penerangan 1989/90). Critical discourse interprets the situation as competitive, and there is a lot of comment about the unfairness of TVRI having to compete with the other two channels without having access to advertising revenue (*Kompas,* 24 July 1988; *Tempo,* 25 August 1990; 13 October 1990; *Prospek,* 19 January 1991; *Kompas,* 24 August 1991). Cartoons in TVRI's in-house publication *Lensa* and in the Jakarta press expressed doubt about TVRI's ability to compete with its up-market commercial "partners" (figs. 3.3 and 3.4). In the *Lensa* cartoon, RCTI and TPI parade like models down a catwalk. Out front is the eroticized image of RCTI, provocatively moving her thighs, which have dollar signs inscribed on them. All eyes are on RCTI. TPI and TVRI may as well not be present. After all, TPI is in school uniform with her hair in schoolgirl plaits. Flat-chested and immature, TPI holds little appeal for the audience. Last of all, and yet to mount the catwalk, TVRI is represented wearing the costume of a classical Javanese dancer, refined and aloof. The implicit suggestion that the only way TVRI can meet the challenge from the skies and commercial broadcasters at home is to promote and develop its special expertise and feel for "national" cultural programs maintains the public broadcasting construct of TVRI as a distinctively Indonesian cultural conduit (*Suara Pembaruan,* 24 August 1990).

The image of public broadcasting left behind by the sexualized, imported (dollar signs) programming of "new" television represents the television sector as bound up in the competitive marketing apparatus of consumer culture and accurately images the emerging division of labor and audience constructs among the television channels. *Suara Pembaruan*'s cartoon relies on the same metaphor of eroticism to point up the fading attraction of TVRI. Middle-aged Mrs. TVRI, wearing a sensible (modern) dress, holds little appeal for her audience, represented as a man who, with bulging eyes and tongue hanging out, lusts after Miss Commercial TV's sexy strut.

The highly sexualized imagery of these cartoons is unusual in "respectable" journals. It can be understood as a representation and denunciation of the competitive (whoring) for audiences that deregulation has introduced, reflecting perhaps the "great emphasis President Soeharto has put on the notion that Indonesia is not and should not be a 'capitalist' society, despite abundant evidence that his policies are steadily making it so" (Mackie and Macintyre 1994, 27). In chapter 7 I explore the impact of economic competition on the television sector and record the contortions state authorities perform in denying its impact.

RCTI's Audiences, 1989–1991

Licensee's Discourse:
The Audience as Market

In the Ministerial Decree (Menteri Penerangan 1987) that authorized commercial (pay) television, the government acknowledged the desirability of providing alternative television services for an audience increasingly interested in video and satellite sourced programs. It was an "alternative" for those who already had an alternative—

Figure 3.3. Banner reads: "This Year's Festival." (*Lensa,* 1 May 1991, inside back cover)

Figure 3.4. The TV screen on the left reads, "27th [Anniversary] of TVRI," and the TV screen on the right reads, "Commercial Television." The woman on the left says, "I'm still interesting, aren't I?" (*Suara Pembaruan,* 24 August 1989)

those who owned videocassette recorders or satellite dishes or who lived in range of foreign broadcasters. It was an alternative, moreover, for only limited segments of the national audience. The decree determined that commercial services would be established as "restricted broadcast channels" (*Siaran Saluran Terbatas*, SST), available only to those in Jakarta and its environs who modified their receivers with a decoding device costing approximately Rp 131,000 and paid a monthly rental of Rp 30,000 (*Suara Pembaruan,* 3 June 1988; *Kompas,* 12 July 1990).

From the outset RCTI's audience appears to have been an evolving creature of commerce more than policy. The demographics of the audience were initially defined by the limitation imposed by the requirement for decoders and the limited broadcast range. Nevertheless, station management was very conscious of the need to attract subscribers and keep them by delivering what they wanted. This attitude persists today. The president director of RCTI made the channel's commercial orientation absolutely clear: "Private TV is a commercial enterprise, you know, which must be *profitable*" (*Prospek,* 19 January 1991, emphasis in original). RCTI imagines its audience as something to be won and held. Management was clear that it had to draw segments of TVRI's audience away and deliver them to RCTI so advertisers would be prepared to use the channel.

To win its audience, RCTI uses the familiar strategies of commercial television. It seeks to attract and hold its audience with predictable scheduling and frequent announcement of "coming attractions" presented in fast-paced, up-market address by female presenters. The more traditional approach of TVRI is replaced with an intimate, international style, and the audience is invariably addressed as "viewers" (*pemirsa*), never as *bapak, ibu,* or *saudara*. It makes no attempt to broadcast programs "for the audience's good" but instead schedules programs "the audience wants." Management has said that they are very responsive to audience opinion and popular taste (*Prospek,* 19 January 1991). The *Surabaya Post*

Figure 3.5. The sign reads, "Public Taste." The runner on the right is commercial TV, and the fetter breaking loose is labeled "Decoder." (*Surabaya Post,* 16 July 1990)

cartoon suggests that the commercial channels will quickly overtake TVRI in the race to satisfy audience tastes (fig. 3.5).

RCTI also relies upon weekly research and ratings information supplied by Survey Research Indonesia (SRI) in targeting its audience. Philip Rich from SRI commented that RCTI had been surprised "how far off-beam they had been with some of the high-rating U.S. shows they had bought." He mentioned *Golden Girls*, *Cheers*, and *Family Ties* as disappointments. SRI's diary research with 750 households in Jakarta and Surabaya targets households whose average monthly expenditure (excluding durables) is between Rp 500,000 and Rp 700,000 or more. These "A1" and "A2" households represent just 12 percent of all Jakarta households and 16 percent of all "TV households." RCTI discovered that "kung-fu type shows" rated better than many American programs and that "the David Carradine *Kung-fu* show" [1972–75, American Broadcasting Company] had been a "sleeper" and was becoming increasingly popular (personal interview, 5 April 1993).

RCTI's SST status (theoretically) limits its audience geographically, and one might think that this would be reflected in the construction of a "local" audience. And indeed there are a few RCTI programs that have a local cultural reference, such as *Lenong Rumpi*. In general, however, RCTI constructs an audience that is national and even international. The audience is imagined as a sophisticated elite with time and resources for abundant leisure, a materialistic lifestyle, and an interest in world events, particularly sporting and financial events. The audience is addressed as an "Indonesian" audience, not a metropolitan audience. The channel logo, a stylized eagle, is visually similar to the *garuda*, which is part of the national emblem. The channel identification signature is a sweeping pass through the whole of the Indonesian landscape accompanied by the national anthem and makes no particular reference to its designated broadcast region. In contrast, TVRI's Second Program also opens its broadcast with the national anthem, but the images that accompany the anthem make explicit and frequent reference to Jakarta and the surrounding region.

RCTI is linked to commercial broadcasters that have been established in Bandung, Surabaya, and Denpasar, and while prevented by its license from networking, it does purchase and make programs for its associated broadcasters (Isaac 1992, 7). It is possible, then, that RCTI's imaging of itself as a national rather than local broadcaster may be a reflection of its wider links, or it may reflect a desire to position itself for a national networking role in the future.[5]

Another dimension of the commercial discourse about television is the expanding range of print media publications that promote commercial programs. *Vista, Hai, Monitor* (banned in 1990), and *Citra* are slick, glossy publications that provide weekly programs listings, features on stars and forthcoming films, and industry gossip about the film, music, and television world. Their style and content differentiate them sharply from the high-road, quality journalism and commentary that papers such as *Suara Pembaruan* and *Kompas* have traditionally presented on TVRI. The audience-as-consumer construct of the industry publications reinforces the commercial construct of the commercial channels.

Journalistic Discourse:
The Audience as Global Citizens

The critical discourse that speaks on behalf of RCTI's audience is not extensive, and much of the comment in the early '90s was taken up with keeping track of changes in the provision and regulation of commercial television. The discourse was well informed, but not particularly critical, which is surprising given that much of what had happened occurred almost overnight.

Although the public values the alternative RCTI provides to TVRI programming, there is a perception that it is not enough of an alternative. The view is that advantages have been provided to RCTI and TPI that should also be extended to TVRI. The advantage most discussed is the opportunity to accept paid advertising and sponsored programs. So the audience constructed in this discourse is one that is open to commercial broadcasting and readily acknowledges the benefits of commercial television, but it wants the benefits to be extended to all providers. It is constructed as an audience that believes "its" television is not getting a fair go and that powerful business interests are being specially favored (*Kompas*, 24 August 1989; 7 April 1991; *Tempo*, 6 July 1991; 31 August 1991). The government's decision in April 1991, for example, to reduce the percentage of foreign films screened on TVRI by 35 percent was vigorously protested. Noting that TVRI had recently been screening foreign films in an endeavor to hold its audience against the flood of imports on RCTI, the writers complained that the arbitrary and unexplained decision restricted the audience's access to films they enjoyed (*Suara Pembaruan*, 7 April 1991; *Kompas*, 10 April 1991; *Bisnis Indonesia*, 24 August 1991). One headline stated the issue succinctly by asking "What Crime Is There in Foreign films on TVRI?" (*Apa Dosanya Film Asing Di TVRI?*) (*Suara Pembaruan*, 10 April 1991).

The weight of the critical discourse about RCTI in particular, and commercial television more generally, is, however, concerned with two audience constructs: one an internationalist and the other a nationalist construct of RCTI's viewers. The internationalist construct of the RCTI audience presents a view of the audience as internationally or globally oriented, an audience that tunes to RCTI because of the alternative it offers and because it provides access to plenty of foreign sourced entertainment that is enjoyable and of high quality. One source noted appreciatively, for example, that RCTI had recently decided to record and screen later the compulsory government news program *Dunia Dalam Berita* (World News) so it could bring the Italian soccer league live to viewers. The same writer also noted that RCTI was fortunate that it was not required, like TVRI, to broadcast national ceremonies and that it had recently screened the movie *Max Havelaar* instead of covering the 30 September ceremony at the Pancasila monument (*Tempo*, 13 October 1990). Another critic praised RCTI's technical presentation, saying that the camera work, settings, and dynamic visuals were "international style" (*Kompas*, 24 August 1990).

In a survey conducted in May 1991 by Survey Research Indonesia, Jakarta and Surabaya viewers rated their favorite programs as *MacGyver, Knight Rider, Airwolf, Miami Vice, The Incredible Hulk, Wonder Woman, My Secret Identity, Old Mission Impossible,* and *Tour of Duty* (*Tempo,* 6 April 1991). This audience segment does not consider that the imported programs represent any kind of threat to indigenous values or standards and looks on RCTI as a source of entertaining and informative television. It is secure and self-confident about the business orientation and consumerist values of commercial television and accepts that economics dictates to a large extent the scope the channel has to screen particular kinds of programs (*Suara Pembaruan,* 8 January 1989; *Kompas,* 24 August 1990; *Kompas,* 7 April 1991; *Tempo,* 26 October 1991). It is an audience that appreciates "quality" or professional presentation, predictable scheduling, and the chance to tune in to world events such as World Cup soccer, international tennis tournaments, and Mike Tyson championship bouts.

The Audience as Public Citizens

Finding an apt shorthand description for the second major audience construct in the critical discourse concerned with RCTI is difficult. It is an audience that foregrounds "Indonesian" cultural values, but not in the highly self-conscious, nationalist way that official discourse does when discussing the role of TVRI. The audience is self-confident and assertive in claiming that it has a right to alternative sources of information and entertainment apart from TVRI, but it is also sufficiently self-confident culturally to be highly critical of the inscribed values of much of the imported programming screened on RCTI.

For these reasons, the most apt description of the second audience construct is probably again the idea of the audience as public citizens, recalling that a key element in that construct as outlined above was the construction of an audience resistant to being imposed upon. Commercial television has introduced an additional element into the audience's mix of concerns, namely the perceived domination of commercial programming by Western, materialist values that are not consonant with what are described as "Indonesian" values. There is a need here to use quotation marks, for as I have already shown, there is an audience, also Indonesian, that does not appear to object to the values of imported programs.

Communications analyst Yuniman T. Nurdin put the point this way: RCTI was appreciated as an alternative to the previous monopoly of TVRI, which had become monotonous and lackadaisical in its standards of presentation. RCTI was especially valuable, however, because it provided an alternative to the permissiveness of the open sky policy, which allowed viewers to see programs that were not reflective of general community standards. Even though RCTI screened imported programs, the writer argued that the programs shown had all been approved by official censors and were thus more in line with community standards (*Bintang,* 21 July 1991; *Bisnis Indonesia,* 24 August 1991). Unfortunately, this process is not infallible, as the notorious case involving SCTV showed. In this case, the audience in Surabaya was outraged when the Canadian program *Wok with Yan* presented a segment that demonstrated a recipe using pork fat at the beginning of Ramadan in 1991. The audience was also highly critical of *Wonder Woman,* whose revealing costume they found sexist, offensive, and unsuitable for children (*Tempo,* 6 April 1991). These events led President Commissioner M. Noer, the high-profile former governor of East Java, to resign his position in support of the protest.

Other critics took the view that whether the imported films had passed the censor was not the main issue, pointing out that there were many Indonesian films that were sadistic and violent (*Suara Pembaruan,* 10 April 1991). The main concern was that much of the far greater volume of imported entertainment now available generally through the commercial channels was "too Western" and threatened indigenous values (*Editor,* 26 February 1991; *Kompas,* 12 September 1991; *Tempo,* 21 September 1991; 26 October 1991).

These concerns about "Westernization" and the degradation of indigenous culture on RCTI echo a long-running concern about the undesirable influence of imported films, music, style, and values, which was most strident in the Sukarno years, when rock music, jeans, and long hair were banned. Thirty years later, legislators have found it impossible to maintain their rage, and foreign commodities dominate the recorded music, film, video, and television industries. The audience that is opposed to the Western cultural style and values of RCTI programming is frustrated and feels it lacks power in the face of the production conditions of globalized television, which mean the cost of high-rating, internationally produced programs such as *MacGyver* are available at prices far below the cost of locally produced programs (*Tempo,* 6 April 1991; *Kompas,* 7 April 1991; *Prospek,* 19 January 1991). While the criticism about Westernization was part of the critical discourse surrounding TVRI when it was the sole television broadcaster, it has sharpened and become more insistent given the sheer volume of imported programs on RCTI. It is now recognized that the rule that required TVRI to produce 80 percent of its own programming has meant that indigenous cultural values were much better represented before television was deregulated than they are in the 1990s (*Suara Pembaruan,* 24 August 1990). The alternative offered by commercial television has for some become a kind of cultural parasite. It lives off the local audience but has devalued indigenous culture in its own programming and has put pressure on TVRI to go the same way in an endeavor to hold its audience against the lure of consumerist hype and global values (*Suara Pembaruan,* 8 January 1989; *Kompas,* 16 July 1990; 26 August 1990; *Suara Pembaruan,* 24 August 1990; *Kompas,* 24 August 1991; *Editor,* 6 April 1991; *Suara Pembaruan,* 10 April 1991; *Tempo,* 21 September 1991; 26 October 1991). The *Berita Yudha* cartoon (fig. 3.6) shows a family glued to the very popular Japanese serial *Oshin* (screened on TVRI in 1989). A little figure at right (whom I assume is a kind of cultural conscience) asks rhetorically, "Do we know Oshin better than [the Indonesian feminist icon] Kartini?"

Figure 3.6. Figure at right: "Do we know Oshin better than we know Kartini?" (*Berita Yudha*, 10 July 1990)

These issues are implicated in the discourse about local production and the growing interest in *sinetron*, or "electronic cinema," a form that is cheaper to produce than film and has become a perceived strength of TVRI in the face of RCTI's challenge. The abbreviation *sinetron* was coined by Ishadi SK in 1985 (*Vista* #121 1991, 33), and although the word was new, it referred to an activity TVRI had been involved in since its foundation, when *Sebuah Jendela*, written by Alex Leo Zulkarnain and directed by M. E. Zainuddin, was screened in December 1962. In those early days, the locally written and directed plays were called "TV-Play" in station documentation (Direktorat Televisi 1972, 48). TVRI's long interest and support for local production has taken on a special significance in recent years. Management, particularly the then director Ishadi SK, identified sinetron as TVRI's special strength and expertise with which the channel could meet the challenge presented by high-rating foreign films on RCTI. Critical comment on sinetron thus frequently goes beyond the merits of individual productions and links the development of sinetron to the perceived negative impacts of imported films and programming on commercial television and the desirability of meeting this challenge with locally made productions (*Tempo*, 7 January 1989; *Kompas*, 31 December 1989; *Vista* #121 1991; *Suara Karya Minggu* Week 2, November

1991; *Tempo,* 14 September 1991; *Surya Televisi,* 22 November 1991; 24 December 1991; *Sarinah,* 23 March 1992).

In chapter 10 I return to the these debates over television content and argue that since deregulation, program content has become a site for contestation of Indonesian cultural identity and has contributed to a reconstitution of the idea of the citizen in Indonesia.

TPI's Audiences, 1991

Licensee's Discourse:
A National (Commercial) Audience

Televisi Pendidikan Indonesia (TPI) was approved as a commercial broadcaster with a general educational mission on 16 August 1990. It went on the air on 23 January 1991, just five months later, without a clear working arrangement with the Department of Education and without a feasibility study, pilot project, or its own studio facilities. TPI has not articulated its role or plans in any detail, and it is difficult to obtain a detailed understanding of how it constructs its audience. In part, this is because the audience is a "lack." The audience is abstracted even more than the usual normative abstractions of audiencehood, because the channel defines its mission as filling in the gaps, or adding to, the general educational services of the government. The audience addressed is thus an educational gap and has not been fleshed out much more than that.

The channel constructs its mission as a national service and sees itself as a public service broadcaster with clear paternalist goals. In that way, it is a historical revival of the educational mission of TVRI as first conceived. Its public service associations are strengthened by the close relationship it has with TVRI and the Department of Education. The channel's public service role was reinforced on the occasion of its first broadcast when the president officially inaugurated the channel and conducted a dialogue with students and teachers in Aceh in the west and Dili in the east (*Suara Pembaruan,* 23 January 1991; *Media Indonesia,* 24 January 1991). The signification of the ceremony reflects once again the notion of territoriality and nationhood that I examined in my discussion of TVRI's construct of the audience as nation, and it suggests that TPI shares a similar construct of its audience.

Like TVRI, TPI sees itself as part of a paedocratic regime. It positions itself as a powerful, centrally organized broadcaster with superior knowledge, abilities, and right to address perceived inadequacies in the audience. The process of communication is one-way, and the audience is not differentiated; it is a mass audience, flung far and wide throughout the vastness of Indonesia. It is an audience that is constructed as lacking skills, knowledge, and motivation, which TPI aims to supply in tandem with the teachers and educational facilities put in place by the government. To fund this complex and specialized mission, TPI charges fees for advertising time during its broadcasts. The human face of TPI's audience is broad and includes students in formal educational settings, specifically junior high school and senior high school students, children in nonformal educational settings such as play groups, students who have dropped out of school, and beyond that, adult men and women in domestic roles (*Tempo,* 26 January 1991).

Journalistic and Professional Discourses: The Audience as Informed Consumers

While the industry and official discourse surrounding TPI is lacking, critical commentary has been lively since the proposal for an educational service took almost everyone by surprise in 1990. This is understandable in a country where education is a valued and respected process, especially because the introduction of the new service was perceived to be too hasty. In contrast to the critical discourse concerning TVRI and RCTI, which has been conducted largely by journalists and industry professionals, critical discussion of TPI has been produced by educators and public servants. These critics draw on their own professional expertise, experience, and knowledge in critiquing TPI.

The idealized TPI audience constructed by the critical discourse is an audience that values education, recognizes the desirability of complementing formal education with educational television, and is concerned that the educational programming presented on TPI is high quality and meets the needs of the target audience. It is this last phrase that has been the focus of considerable discussion, as many critics consider that TPI's educational objectives have been neither thought through nor clearly described (*Kompas*, 3 August 1991; 20 November 1991; *Suara Merdeka*, 21 January 1991; *Kompas*, 23 January 1991; *Tempo*, 26 January 1991; *Suara Pembaruan*, 1 February 1991).

Critics argue that TPI should address three audiences: pupils and students, teachers, and the community (*Kompas*, 3 February 1991). Programs should be developed to meet the educational needs of each group, and broadcasts should be scheduled to suit the circumstances of the audience segments. The issue of the timing of the broadcasts has been the focus of the most intensive criticism. Many critics have pointed out that the early morning to noon timetable is totally inappropriate for the channel's mission, as during those hours, most of the target audience is at school or otherwise engaged and not available to watch the programs. Education Minister Fuad Hassan suggested when the channel's plans were first announced that evening broadcasts would be of most value. But lacking independent production facilities, TPI has been forced (or better, chose) to broadcast their programs during TVRI's downtime, a decision that has puzzled many critics and made others suspicious of the channel's real motivation. Some writers, for example, have questioned the channel's priorities, pointing out that the programming plan allocates about 51 percent of time to entertainment and commercials and just 33 percent to educational programs (*Kompas*, 18 August 1990; *Suara Merdeka*, 19 January 1991; *Kompas*, 21 January 1991; *Suara Pembaruan*, 2 February

1991; *Kompas,* 3 February 1991; 6 February 1991; *Suara Pembaruan,* 17 February 1991). I return to these criticisms of TPI in chapter 9, relating them to increased activism over television since deregulation.

The inappropriate timetable of TPI broadcasts has caused some critics to question whether TPI's target audience is an educational audience or simply a general audience that might be turned to commercial advantage. The television critic Eduard Depari, for example, suggested that TPI was unique in the world as an educational broadcaster in accepting paid advertising as a way to fund an educational service (*Suara Pembaruan,* 19 August 1990). Many other critics have focused on the same issue and have been highly skeptical in their comments about TPI's assertion that only "educational advertising" will be permitted. The concept of educational advertising has given scope for a wide range of humorous as well as more jaundiced comments, with the majority taking the view that there is some degree of conflict of interest in a broadcaster presenting itself in a public service role and also seeking to profit from that role.

The final range of concerns that contribute to the critical construct of TPI's audience are, once again, matters of wider social equity and commitment to policy. Many critics have raised the question of the access that the general public will have to the education service. Scheduling aside, writers have pointed out that not all schools have television sets and that the service discriminates against schools in poorer communities (*Kompas,* 6 February 1991). This criticism has been addressed by the Department of Education, which has undertaken to equip all schools (*Kompas,* 21 January 1991; *Tempo,* 26 January 1991). The fairness issue is addressed again in articles that question whether it is reasonable that a commercial broadcaster should be able to impose itself on government resources and facilities in the way TPI has imposed itself on TVRI. Questions have also been raised about whether a Rp 7 billion allocation from government funds to TPI was justified (*Kompas,* 19 September 1990; 2 February 1991; *Tempo,* 2 March 1991).

Drawing these threads together, the critical discourse constructs an audience for TPI's educational initiative that is generally positive about the additional alternative that TPI presents and is enthusiastic about the opportunity to use the special qualities of television as an audiovisual medium in furthering education. But it wants the programming to be of high quality, to be produced under expert and professional guidance, and to be presented by a broadcaster that genuinely has the educational ideals and needs of the audience as its highest priority. It is a national audience, an audience intent on improving its life chances through the benefits of linking modern technology with education, and an audience that above all wants a genuine, long-term commitment to the educational and social demands that educational television presents (*Suara Merdeka*, 21 January 1991).

Conclusion

As a broadcasting medium television depends on its audience. The way the institutions involved in providing television services imagine that audience helps shape the form and content of television broadcasts and the way the industry acts. Drawing on discourses surrounding television in Indonesia from 1961 to 1991, I have examined different visions of the audience imagined by the institutions involved in producing television. I have also shown the distinctive character of public broadcasting in Indonesia and the recent emergence of a national system of television services that organizationally is more like a nationally coordinated package of television options than a system of rival, independent broadcasters. This model matches the original relations between the BBC and (a heavily regulated) Channel Four, where complementarity, not competition, was emphasized (Smith 1995, 85).

If the audience construct is a fiction that serves the needs institutions have to take charge of their own survival, then the crucial needs TVRI has to meet on behalf of the government are as follows:

(1) reinforcement of the ideological construct of the sovereign territory of Indonesia, (2) preservation of national identity and unity in a geographically, historically, and culturally very diversified young nation, and (3) maintenance of the momentum of national growth and development. Given these imperatives, the construction of the audience has changed from an undifferentiated mass whose needs, tastes, and judgments were patronized by a monopoly broadcaster to a more complex contemporary situation. Here there is a greater acknowledgment of the diverse needs and interests of the audience, the value of wider distribution of the benefits of national growth and technological and economic development, and the desirability of access to alternative services. Even so, a hegemonic nationalist ideology has continued to perpetuate the fiction of the cultural unity of the Indonesian audience, has insisted on greater Indonesian content on TVRI, and has reified and promoted the ideal of an essentialist Indonesian national culture—at least at the level of public discourse.

By contrast, RCTI has been driven by the more straightforward and limited motivation of "profit making," to use Joni P. Soebandono's words. RCTI's audience is seen as a collection of well-off consumers who enjoy a materialistic lifestyle increasingly influenced by international styles and values. This suits a broadcaster dependent on advertising revenue for the continued profitability of the channel, and the logic of the global market sanctions the importing of programs without any feelings of guilt about their impact on national cultural ideals.

In between these is the hybrid creature TPI. It is a throwback to the early days of TVRI when it functioned as a public broadcaster and also accepted advertising. TPI's construction of its audience is based on the vision of an audience characterized by crucial deficiencies in knowledge, information, and education, which TPI presents itself on hand to make good. It also interpellates the same audience as its market and promotes goods and services that it claims are of educational value. It appears to have a straightforward but immensely demanding mission. However, its programming, scheduling, and commercial orientation are not, in the view of many critics, entirely compatible with this audience construct.

In concluding this chapter, I wish to link this discussion about audiences to the idea of the two cultures of television in Indonesia introduced in chapter 2. The different, shifting, and increasingly complex audience constructs of TVRI and the commercial channels display the tension between the different cultures of television in Indonesia. Policy changes that introduced commercial television to Indonesia acknowledged the value of alternatives and choices. The SST structure was introduced to enhance and preserve regional diversity in television services, and commercial television itself was established as a way of improving the public's access to high-quality information and entertainment services. However, powerful economic and political influences involved in the delivery of the new commercial services seem bent on a unitary construct of the audience that would serve their needs of maximizing audience share. At a time when state authorities have shown an increasing understanding and tolerance of the value of diversity in the audience, commercial broadcasters are attempting to reduce diversity and impose their own constructs on the audience. These constructs are primarily driven by economic motivations and depend on consumerist values, products, and services and economic and political relations that are potentially inimical to the public broadcasting values and practices of TVRI.

Chapter 4

SERIOUS PUPPET PLAYS: TELEVISION MODELS THE CHILD

THE BAN ON TELEVISION ADVERTISING IN 1981 shifted the state to center screen and changed the way TVRI constructed its audience. After 1981, untrammeled by market considerations and with a vastly expanded national audience within its reach, TVRI interpellated its audience as a public and a national family. One segment of the family singled out as subjects for specific national address was the audience of young children. This chapter presents a case study of how television asserted its role in the Indonesian government's national culture project as an important agency of political and cultural socialization through the development of the children's puppet series *Si Unyil* ([The Boy] Unyil), screened for the first time in April 1981. *Si Unyil* is perhaps the best-known television program in Indonesia. The first episode was screened on 5 April 1981, and the series has been broadcast continuously ever since, making it the longest-running fictional program on Indonesian television. A total of 603 episodes were screened between 1981 and 1993.

The series modeled the child in three ways. The puppet characters and sets modeled a village community, creating an Indonesian playscape where children's lives and games were foregrounded. *Si Unyil* delivered to children throughout the archipelago what Bourdieu (1980) has called "the pleasure of recognition." In the scaled-down, fictional village of Suka Maju, children recognized with delight their own (national) language and rhythms of speech, familiar stories from their indigenous oral tradition, and elements of folk tradition such as games and pastimes. The ups and downs of the children's relations with each other and the adult community were intended to socialize children into preferred ways of behaving, and the desired effect of the program was to produce model Indonesian children.

In chapter 3 I noted that TVRI addressed its audience as a national family. In this chapter I argue that the *Si Unyil* series can be understood as a translation of the policy emphasis on the family into an actual program that explores the dynamics of family relations. Individual families in Suka Maju are represented as the bone and marrow of a village-as-family, which in turn is understood as one of innumerable other communities that are members of the great, inclusive national family. All members of the national family are united in an organic whole and share the responsibility of national development. The deferential, dependent subject position inscribed for children in the series and the didactic style of the episodes mean that the series can also be understood as an instance of the paedocratic character of television generally. And third, the series may be linked to the concern outlined in chapter 3 that Indonesian television was dominated by imported content. *Si Unyil*, the first series ever produced for Indonesian children, was developed specifically to redress the imbalance.

In Indonesia, as in most countries, "the state assumes that its inhabitants are not necessarily born as good citizens; children must be taught and socialised by the state to become good citizens" (Parker 1992, 42). In the politics of state television, so-called children's television becomes part of the machinery of state hegemony. The weekly episodes of *Si Unyil* were crafted by a talented production team to contribute to the managed development of children into good Indonesian citizens who would be knowledgeable about and committed to national development. In this chapter

I begin by situating the series in the discourses of Pancasila citizenship and national development. Official statements of the objectives of the series and the top-down directives that initiated it are noted. The series is also shown to be part of a flow of programming focused on national development and the modeling of preferred center-periphery relations. In the section "Narrative Form and Generic Characteristics" I turn to textual analysis and discuss the ideological work of the series in modeling the desired child social subject. I argue that the adaptation of the conventional structure of the situation comedy in *Si Unyil* models dependent, paternalistic political relations between village communities and the national center.

Following a discussion of character in which the hierarchical relations between children and adults, community and state-center are noted, I move on to consider the role of parody in the series in the characters of Pak Raden and Ogah and Ableh. Here I argue that parody performs the paedocratic function of turning unacceptable adult behavior into derisory comedy to delineate and reinforce preferred values and behavior. The final sections of the chapter examine the modeling of cultural differences and the role of the national language in the construction of an idealized national family. I show that the series acknowledges cultural differences but erases their range, specificity and potential political significance to produce a unitary, homogenous national family.

This chapter and the next can be read together as an extended study of the way state authorities have used television to represent and foster official Indonesian culture across generations. The target audience of the *Si Unyil* series was children (its loyal adult following notwithstanding), while the target audience for the soap opera *Keluarga Rahmat,* discussed in chapter 5, was adults. It assumed its viewers possessed cultural competencies in dealing with conflicts in interpersonal relations far beyond the experience of children. It is remarkable, however, that in both series, the appropriation of popular entertainment genres for social and cultural instruction infantilized the audience and became a site of resistance and struggle over control of the preferred meanings encoded in the series.

Si Unyil and Metaphors of Shaping and Guiding

The ideological goals of the *Si Unyil* series were made clear by its first producer, the late Gufron Dwipayana:

> The puppet serial was put together [*dikerjakan*] as an entertainment for children. Government messages were incorporated into the narrative. "So it is a kind of lesson [*pelajaran*] in the 'Guide to Realising and Experiencing the Principles of Pancasila' [*Pedoman Penghayatan dan Pengamalan Pancasila*] for children.... But, nevertheless, I don't want *Si Unyil* to carry government messages (propaganda) in an obviously crude manner." (*Tempo*, 31 October 1981)

The state reaffirmed these goals three years later in a national five-Year Plan (*Repelita IV*) document:

> The mass media will be utilized to distribute information that promotes the political education of the people and the development [*pengembangan*] of Indonesian identity based on Pancasila. This recognizes the geography of Indonesia, which makes mass media essential for education and [the need to deliver] Pancasila education (P4) broadcasts using role play and other means that are appealing [*menarik*] but effective [*efektif*] primarily for school-age children and young people.[1] Children's films such as *Si Unyil* and *Huma* will be continued and used to greater advantage to plant P4 values [*nilai nilai P4*] in the young generation. In planting these values as early as possible, it is hoped that the young generation will grow into citizens with high levels of national tenacity. (Republik Indonesia 1984, 519)

The metaphoric contours of these two statements reveal the state's instrumentalist communication model and politico-cultural strategy for television. The teleological organic metaphor in the second passage imagines the *managed* development of children into competent adulthood and citizenship. The organic metaphor is interestingly linked to television technology. The generality implicit in the concept of broadcasting acknowledges the inherent crudity of the technique. The risk of failure in social nurturing through broadcasting is implicit in the suggestion by Indonesian planners that P4 values should be implanted "as early as possible." For subjects left without the benefit of P4 values for even a short time, let alone until later in their lives, may grow in ways that reflect individual preferences and choices rather than state priorities. Development outside regimes of state guidance may produce a subject different from the desired ideal citizen. But if the state catches its subjects in time it can reap the harvest of a generation of adults who are model national citizens.

The organic metaphor signifies processes of shaping and guiding and of nurturing in potentially unpredictable subjects truths that will function as built-in regulators and producers of desired social and cultural behavior. The model of communication implicit in the metaphor is the sender-message-receiver model, which assumes an effortless, transparent, and successful transfer of meaning from the state as sender to generations of children as receivers. It ignores the specificity of individual subjectivity and the possibility of the *un*successful transfer of meaning through negotiated decodings (Hall 1980).

The policy position outlined for Indonesia is not fundamentally different from children's television policy in Western countries such as the United States and Australia. Dwipayana's statement represents a difference of degree rather than fundamentals. The internationally famous *Sesame Street* and the renowned Australian *Play School* are both concerned with the socialization of children in socially approved ways. In recent years, for example, *Sesame Street* has presented a "race relations" curriculum that emphasizes that "diversity is good" (Graves 1996, 71). The Indonesian series differs from the American and Australian programs only in the rather closed subject position inscribed for the child and the relative lack of explicit instruction in preschool skills such as numeracy, literacy, and classification. To an Australian viewer, at least, *Si Unyil* is much more about the ideal-typical place and role for children in the family, community, and nation than Australian children's programming. In comparison, Australian standards for preschool programming seem more child-centered:

> Children should have access to a variety of quality television programs made specifically for them, including Australian drama and non-drama.... Children are entitled to a viewing choice of a diversity of ideas and information. [Programs should be] conceived, developed and produced with a specific age group in mind. (Australian Broadcasting Tribunal 1991, 1:71)

The Australian Broadcasting Tribunal places great importance on the entertainment values of children's programs, which it rates far higher than the "worthiness" of programs. That said, the Australian standard does require children's programs to "show Australia to Australians," enshrining an idea of *national* cultural content that Indonesian regulators would find completely acceptable and understandable (Australian Broadcasting Tribunal 1991, 1:71).

Dwipayana's statement describes the series as a mixed pedagogic and entertainment practice. It goes beyond the second in suggesting that the practice should efface its mode and telos. State objectives should desirably be achieved without the subjects being consciously aware that they are being guided toward a specified subject position. The reason for effacing the directive motivation of the series is suggested by the paradigmatic distinction struck between the series as entertainment and the series as a lesson. The distinction signifies a difference between a series that accepts the textual pleasuring of children as an end in itself and a series that uses pleasure as a means to a predetermined end. One is audience-centered in its recognition and valorization of children's enjoyment of play; the other subordinates children's pleasure in entertainment and uses it as a means in the construction of desired social subjects. The intersection of two discourses, one that seeks to entertain the subject and the other to direct and shape the subject, produced contested readings and inscribed fractured and sometimes contradictory representations of the desired social subject. These tensions between subject positions are traced in a discussion of selected episodes (appendix C) and by reference to critical discourse in the Indonesian press.

Development of the Series

The *Si Unyil* series is a production of the State Film Production Center of Indonesia (Pusat Produksi Perfilman Negara, PPFN).[2] An outline for the series was prepared in 1979 by screenwriter and well-known children's author Kurnain Suhardiman in response to a request from the foundation director of the center, Gufron Dwipayana.[3] Kurnain's brief was to write a scenario for a children's television series that was "authentically Indonesian." For artistic director Suyadi, Dwipayana's invitation reflected the perception that Indonesian culture needed to figure more assertively on television (Suyadi, personal interview, 3 May 1993).

The decision to set the series in a rural village reflected an intersection of ideological and aesthetic factors. For Suyadi, an urban environment presented a more difficult design problem because of the complexities of including traffic and crowds. The village setting was preferred because of the belief that a rural way of life reflected the circumstances of the majority of Indonesian people, about 78 percent of whom lived in rural areas. It was also a better vehicle for the representation of a modest way of life (Suyadi, personal interview, 5 May 1993).

The idealization of village life as a harmonious idyll was overdone in the first few episodes.[4] Suyadi reported that in those episodes all the characters were uniformly "good." The episodes were saccharine (*terlalu manis*), unconvincing, and lacking in dramatic intensity. Accordingly, in subsequent episodes, Kurnain and Suyadi introduced antagonistic characters into the village community. "Pak Raden," for example, was "someone you could hate, someone who was lazy, who was stingy, who had no community spirit [*gotong royong*] at all. He was someone who annoyed and irritated people." A second character, "Engkong," (Chinese: Grandfather) was also introduced. Suyadi described Kong as "someone who was not evil but who had a one-track mind, focused on money. Kong was always dreaming about his glorious homeland [*tanah luhur*], which showed that he was not fully assimilated into Indonesian society."[5]

Two other Chinese characters, the children Mei Lan (Melani) and Bunbun, are, like all the children, positive characters. However, the stereotyped representation of ethnic Chinese as flush with money is maintained with Bunbun, who occasionally helps the indigent Ogah and Ableh by lending them money so they can join in village activities (Suyadi, personal interview, 5 May 1993).

Unyil and his puppet friends in the village Suka Maju captured the imagination of children throughout Indonesia from the earliest episodes. The immediate popularity of the series prompted PPFN to produce a dramatized feature film, *Unyil Becomes Human*, using live actors in all roles.[6] The film was well received by children's audiences around the nation (*Berita Buana*, 21 October 1981).

Funding for the series drew from three sources: PPFN, TVRI, and funds raised by PPFN from government departments such as the Department of Health, the Department of Population and Environment, and the armed forces (*Angkatan Bersenjata Republik Indonesia*, ABRI). Departmental funds were advanced on the understanding that particular episodes would focus on issues nominated by the sponsoring department. Consequently the Department of Health underwrote episodes promoting village cleanliness, the role of community health centers, the need for care in taking drugs and the like. The Department of the Environment supported episodes encouraging children to care for the natural environment. The armed forces underwrote episodes such as "ABRI Comes to the Village" (1982/83), "Long Live ABRI" (1988/89), "Victory ABRI" (1989/90), and "Our ABRI" (1991/92). Some funds were raised from approved community groups, who used the series to broadcast information about their activities.

Si Unyil—Part of a Bigger Picture

Raymond Williams's observation that television is characteristically organized as an associative sequence or "flow" of programming suggests that part of any examination of *Si Unyil* episodes should locate them in the larger context of TVRI programming.[7] A weekly regimen of programs with a rural emphasis framed the appearance of the *Si Unyil* series on Sundays, enriching the inscription of the fictional village and community in Suka Maju. The flow of programs structures a mutual transfer of content and generic characteristics and is intended to reinforce development values and the (adult) roles modeled for children.

Si Unyil was first broadcast in a Sunday morning time slot and has retained this slot ever since. Between 1984 and 1987 it was also broadcast on Wednesday afternoons. Over many years, a range of nonfictional programs about rural and village life have been broadcast in the late afternoons. In five episodes of *Siaran Pedesaan* (Village Broadcast) screened in December 1991 and six episodes screened in April 1993, I discovered significant intertextual associations between *Si Unyil* and *Siaran Pedesaan*. The tone of these episodes, the idealization of villages as cooperative, friendly places, and the incorporation of children and adolescents engaged in social welfare activities in the narratives are strong links with the portrait of life in the fictional village of Suka Maju. In *Siaran Pedesaan* the audience is frequently informed about institutions such as village health centers and programs such as family planning, immunizations, and clean village campaigns. These topics, and others like them, regularly feature in the fictional world of Suka Maju. Although *Siaran Pedesaan* is a nonfictional program, it included fictional segments in some episodes. In 1991, for example, an episode concerned with accident insurance explored the consequences of a traffic accident in a short drama set in a village. Another episode used role-play methods with villagers to explore the implications of a change in land tenure rules.

Si Unyil also shares a complex intertextual association with *Ria Jenaka* (Great Comedy).[8] Scheduled on Fridays and Mondays when it was first introduced in 1981, since 1984 the series was screened on Sunday mornings (see appendix D). The program is performed by four male actors who take the roles of the clowns from the shadow puppet (*wayang kulit*) repertoire. The program was devised by TVRI as a way of promoting national development, and it addresses an audience of children and adults (*Tempo*, 20 June 1981). The extempore antics of the clowns have been popular with children. Adults, particularly those familiar with *wayang*, enjoy the verbal texts that blend Indonesian and Javanese expressions in amusing ways. *Ria Jenaka* has dealt with many of the same issues covered in both *Si Unyil* and *Siaran Pedesaan*.

Across these three different series, each produced to build consent for the national development program, there is a blurring of generic characteristics and a sameness of content. The predominantly informational/educational *Siaran Pedesaan* incorporates fictional strategies in addressing its audience. *Ria Jenaka* turns humans into puppets so it can communicate about development issues in a humorous way. In *Si Unyil,* puppets are human, meshed in a mundane world of school and homework, national celebrations, village cleanups, literacy drives, and energy conservation.

Suka Maju—a Model Village

The events of *Si Unyil* are set in the fictional village of Suka Maju, "somewhere in Indonesia." The village functions metonymically as the space of governance, where proper relations between the center and the periphery are modeled. Quite deliberately producers have created an ideal-typical space that can not easily be identified with a specific province or even island. Suka Maju reflects the modest ideal of the *"cukupan"* (just enough, subsistence) lifestyle (Geertz 1963, 97). There appears to be enough food for everyone, most people enjoy good health, most adults appear to be self-employed as farmers, and many women maintain minor trading enterprises such as selling food and hawking.

The name of the village is an emblem of its support for the

dominant development ethos of the New Order state. "*Suka* (be willing/ready/enjoy) *Maju* (to improve/ progress/ go forward)" is a phrase that can be translated as "ready or willing to advance."⁹ However, these dictionary references fail to capture the ideological force of the phrase that paradigmatically opposes *maju* (progressive) to *kuno* (old fashioned, conservative).

James Peacock explored the connotations of the *maju/kuno* distinction in a study of Javanese folk drama that is particularly relevant to this discussion (1968). Peacock understands the basic distinction as being between "objects or actions that symbolize a progressive stance toward modernization and objects or actions that symbolize a conservative attitude" (1968, 8). He expands our understanding of the paradigm in the following set of signifiers that prefigure a number of important themes in the *Si Unyil* episodes analyzed below:

> Madju is opposed to kuna to contrast: ... use of Indonesian language with the use of Javanese or other provincial language; playing volley ball with gambling on pigeon races; wearing tight slacks, skirts, and lipstick with wearing sarong and jacket; employing medically trained midwives with employing animistic midwives; feminists with gentle wives of yore; movies with puppet plays; choosing one's own spouse with status-based, parent arranged marriage; neighborhood cleanups and communal feasts on national holidays with neighborhood purification rites and communal feasts on non-national holidays; being educated with being illiterate; youths with elders. (Peacock 1968, 8)

Suka Maju is a small, self-contained community where "everyone knows everyone else," where people are tolerant of each other and ready to help each other. It is a rural idyll. Suka Maju is everywhere and nowhere, a setting that permits a majority of viewers throughout the archipelago to find themselves fictionally in Suka Maju. In its very formlessness the village contributes to the representation of a homogenous national culture-space, where differences between places and lifestyles are not as important as the similarities. The economic linkages that Suka Maju shares with other spaces are not articulated. Many details of the social life of the village community are also unknown. It is a place without history. Together these silences contribute to the self-sufficiency of the village. It is a place, as the name of the village suggests, fixed on the future, and it almost effortlessly manages its own affairs.

But Suka Maju is not completely self-contained. Its progressive disposition waits upon and is directed to goals determined by the national capital. The rural rhythms of Suka Maju are intersected by larger rhythms that fictionally link Suka Maju and villages like it throughout Indonesia in a unity of space, time, and culture. A progression of national days such as Education Day, Environment Day, and Independence Day punctuate Suka Maju's calendar. These events are observed in the village, but they are not of the village. They are aspects of official culture imposed from outside the village. Suka Maju reacts to these events; it does not initiate them, and it is dependent on the national capital for their timing and content (Teruo Sekimoto 1990). The dependency relation is, however, constructed as a positive, beneficial one. National days and village cleanup days create opportunities for Unyil and his friends to get together and show how responsible they are. Their contributions to the celebrations demonstrate the skills and competencies their presidentially sponsored (Inpres) school has provided them with.[10] The events provide opportunities for them to enjoy themselves in entertaining the village community. In this way producers merge national priorities with local pleasures and forge a shared set of interests.

The model citizen inscribed is the subject who is communally minded—one who accepts the regime of improvement determined by the state and energetically and enthusiastically contributes to its implementation. Unyil himself is frequently inscribed in this way. Often Unyil takes it on himself to suggest how he and his group can celebrate a particular event or carry out a nationally directed program. In performing these socially beneficial roles, the children seek approval and are usually guided and directed by village authorities such as parents, their teacher, or the village head. These intravillage relations can be read another way. The dependent relationship between children and adults may be read as an analogue of the paedocratic relationship between center and periphery.

Relying on a representational, mimetic logic, Suka Maju is

inscribed as an Indonesian microcosm. It is ethnically and linguistically diverse; it is culturally pluralist. Like much of Indonesia, its people are rural workers. This fictional, scaled-down space is designed to enable Indonesian children to find themselves reflected in the Suka Maju environment and see it as if it were their own. But the microcosm crucially lacks a center, the center of governance. The village as self-directing, where subjects take part in village activities ostensibly on their own initiative, masks the reality of a highly directive center and the inscription of the model citizen as a compliant supporter of state priorities.

Narrative Form and Generic Characteristics

Si Unyil is structured as an episodic series in which narrative closure or resolution is achieved by the end of each episode.[11] The narrative form and comic elements of the series resemble the situation comedies of 1970s American television, which dealt with families confronted from the outside by a variety of socially derived problems and issues (Feuer 1986).[12] In the *Si Unyil* series it is not the nuclear family that is the boundary situation but rather the village community as family (Neale and Krutnik 1990, 239, 241). The village is idealized as a stable, harmonious community motivated by a spirit of mutual cooperation and self-help.

David Reeve (1985, 43) has traced the collectivist family construct as a model for social relations in Indonesia to early nationalist philosophy and the idealization of primordial relations:

> There was an enthusiasm for the idea of society as a totality, an interdependent whole, an "organic" collectivity, an idea that seemed at once modern and socialist and yet in accordance with "the family principle," the "unity of *kawula* and *gusti* [servant and master]," the "law of nature," *adat* [customary] law and original village practice.

It is striking that in the *Si Unyil* series the outside disruptions are not threats or "problems" (Feuer 1986, 107) but are perceived to be beneficial. This represents a major departure from the generic characteristics of sitcoms as described by Eaton and Feuer and deserves further comment. Mick Eaton (1978/79, 70) has argued that the plot of the typical British sitcom is structured as an intersection of discourses of the "inside/outside" that disrupt the harmony of the opening situation (family, workplace), which has then to be restored by the end of the episode. In British and American sitcoms, agency is ascribed to the members of the inside to expel the threats from the outside. Whatever the conflict, whatever the threat, the dynamics of the sitcom require that the resources of the family are capable of resolving the disruption so that next week a new upset can be introduced (Feuer 1995, 125).

In the *Si Unyil* series discourses of the outside are disruptive, but rather than being rejected or challenged, they are accepted. Village programs such as adult literacy, the "clean village" campaign (*Operasi Bersih*), courtesy and friendliness campaign, environmental protection, and celebration of national days are all discourses of the national government addressed (respectively) to a range of incompetencies and inadequacies: illiteracy, lack of hygiene, poor cross-cultural skills (in interacting with foreign tourists), lack of environmental awareness and knowledge, and parochialism (a tendency to put local concerns ahead of national priorities).

In contrast to the British and American sitcoms, where the family resists the destabilizing outside discourse, in the *Si Unyil* series the outside compensates the village community for what it lacks. The community absorbs and acts on external interventions and in doing so remakes and enhances its communal life. The outside (the state) plays a pedagogic, even therapeutic and pastoral role, addressing perceived lacks in its citizens as individuals and as a community. This shift in generic conventions in *Si Unyil* displays the fundamental political assumptions and objectives of the series. To maintain its role as guide and mentor in life, the state through the agency of the *Si Unyil* series empties out the agency of the village and its children, positioning them as dependent subjects.

The generic convention in both the domestic and workplace or "surrogate family" (Neale and Krutnik 1990, 241) sitcom of resistance and triumph over disruption from the outside hails the members of the inside group as possessing the resources that will enable them to work through the threat of fragmentation to restore harmony. In the *Si Unyil* series, the shift from resistance to *acceptance* of external disruption signals a different set of implied power relations. The village is disempowered by the pastoral relationship. It hails the village and its subjects as inadequate and in need of improvement. Although the village community appears to enjoy its involvement in the programs introduced from the outside, it does not do so on its own terms but in terms that have been determined for it.

The narrative structure of equilibrium-disruption-restoration is also typical of nontelevisual oral forms such as legends and folktales (*dongeng*) (Danandjaja 1984). The *Si Unyil* series appropriated elements of indigenous oral culture by retelling traditional folktales and legends, by producing episodes written in folk style, and by making references to folk beliefs in the course of general episodes.[13] This has a twofold effect. First, it familiarizes (in multiple senses of the term) the television series and increases its appeal through a process of indigenization. Second, it displaces and disempowers traditional storytellers such as parents, village elders, and puppet masters (*dalang*). By absorbing elements of folk culture the series performed the hegemonic role of reproducer, processor, packager, and circulator of folk culture. In appropriating the discourse of the private, domestic sphere of the home and neighborhood, the *Si Unyil* series performed a political function in the way it merged the private sphere with the sphere of official, public culture. The articulation of the private sphere with the public sphere here created the nation as family, and the family as nation, in line with government policy as noted in chapter 3. Series such as *Si Unyil* and *Keluarga Rahmat* reach deep into the social lives of viewers to attempt a thorough transformation of the lived experience of Indonesian citizens from childhood through adulthood.

The cloying familyism (*kekeluargaan*) and the dominant and

dominating roles of *Ibu* and *Bapak,* which Saya Shiraishi describes in her insightful studies of Indonesian children's literature, are not, however, as obvious in the *Si Unyil* series. This deserves a brief comment, for it may account for the popularity of the series and the audience's sense that *Si Unyil,* while familiar, represented something new.[14] In the Unyil series, it is the children who are center screen most of the time, who initiate most of the action, and who at times get the better of adult characters, even if it is only Ogah, Ableh, and Pak Raden. The children are not represented as tied to their own homes. Episodes generally open with Unyil and his friends out and about, already engaged in making something or going somewhere. The children's activities are not constrained by parents' or teachers' say-so. Unyil and his friends are not, then, helplessly dependent in the way that Shiraishi describes. For much of the time, they are represented as independent and capable. At times, too, Unyil and his friends are found engaged in generally innocent but clearly unsanctioned escapades such as playing in the forest when they had been told not to, or challenging each other to walk by the scary cemetery. And while it is true, as discussed below, that often the children fail in their endeavors and need the guidance of their parents and teachers, this is not inevitable. The series gives the children space to be adventurous, to be successful, and to enjoy themselves. Perhaps this is why *Si Unyil* was so popular with Indonesian children in its early years and became less popular as adult messages began to overtake the children's initiatives.

The Characters

The pivotal character in the series is Unyil, but he is never presented alone.[15] In the title sequence, Unyil is shown with his friends Usroh and Ucrit. The inseparability of these three, signified not only by their constant interaction but also by the symmetry of their names, inscribes Unyil not as an individual but as a member of a group. The village community is represented as a stratified set of age groups divided into two major divisions—

adults and children. The protocols of age structure a number of different subject positions within the village. Relative age and the expectations of different age groups are the focus of numerous episodes. I will argue below that age and expectations as to what is "proper behavior" by individuals in specific age groups are salient in understanding the subject position structured for the marginalized characters Ogah and Ableh.

Unyil's group includes the boys and girls who attend elementary school (*Sekolah Dasar*, SD) together. Another group, formed around Endut, Cuplis, and Pesek, provides opportunities for the writers to introduce variety into the children's activities.[16] Children of kindergarten (*Taman kanak-kanak*, TK) age form another stratum of characters. The adults in the community are in turn divided into two groups, the first of which is a group of adults of indeterminate age who are the bearers of most of the key adult roles. This group includes characters such as parents, the village schoolteacher, the food seller Ibu Bariah, Ogah and Ableh, and Pak Raden and his wife. Elderly adults (*manusia usia lanjut*), fewer in number, complete the village population pyramid.

Parodic Subjects

If Unyil, along with his friends, is the very model of a modern (minor) citizen, Pak Raden and Ogah and Ableh are not, and this is what makes them funny. While Bu Bariah and Engkong are comic in their "funny voice" routines, the other three are comic because they systematically transgress the role and expected behavior of model adult citizens. It is significant that the humor in *Si Unyil* primarily comes not from jokes or events initiated by the children but from adults. The role of the parodic adult characters can be linked to the paedocratic objectives of the series. Stallybrass and White have argued (1986, 13) that transgressive characters can be understood as a *licensed* inversion of established order, which serves the interests of official culture. Recall that the authors of the fourth Five-Year Plan had their eyes fixed firmly on the desired *adult* citizen (Republik Indonesia 1984). Parody is funny because it is founded on the transgression of decorum and verisimilitude, "on deviations from any social or aesthetic rule, norm, model, convention or law. Such deviations are the basis of comic surprise" (Neale and Krutnik 1990, 86). Transgression of what is expected and familiar simultaneously draws attention to and reinforces social conventions. This process functions through the creation of an "inside" (we who share the joke) and an "outside," which creates a relationship of power, of inclusion and exclusion (Neale and Krutnik 1990, 242). Children in Suka Maju are empowered by this process. In laughing at deviant adult behavior, they signal acceptance of the idealized norms and expectations of conventional adult behavior in the village. In this way, parody performs a paedocratic function. Its teleological fix is on the desired adult subject. It creates a regime of complicity in providing the audience with opportunities to join in laughing at those who do not subscribe to the normative discourse and roles of official culture.

Pak Raden is a cultural anachronism. His aristocratic title and sense of superiority mark him as a relic of Java's feudal past.[17] His Dutch language and the pride he takes in his role as a former Dutch civil servant mark him as out of touch with the social changes introduced through the Indonesian revolution. His title, costume, tastes, and hobbies are all signifiers of the idealized refined (*alus*) Javanese character.

When Unyil suggests a painting competition, and the judges from Jakarta declare all participants' paintings as good as each other's, the episode closes on an apoplectic Pak Raden, loudly complaining that his work is much better than anyone else's. When Pak Raden arrives late for the celebrations in "Hardiknas" and finds no time left for his speech, he jumps to his feet and complains furiously. Late again in "Anak Masa Depan," Pak Raden protests loudly that he has not been given any time to deliver the two-hour speech he had prepared.

The trope of an angry, loudly complaining Pak Raden is frequently used to close episodes. These images emphatically signify Pak Raden's inability to adhere to his own values. More generally, his tantrums mark him as a selfish person, whose frustration comes from his egoistical and elitist desire to be recognized as a superior individual, deserving of special consideration. Pak Raden's customary behavior and values transgress those of the ideal subject, who is modest, self-disciplined, egalitarian, and motivated by a spirit of communalism (*gotong royong*).

Pak Raden is a contradictory character. He is funny not because he is Javanese but because he is not Javanese *enough*. As Clifford Geertz (1960, 240) writes, "Emotional equanimity ... is the mark of the truly *alus* [Javanese] character." Conversely, "spontaneity or naturalness of gesture or speech is fitting only for those 'not yet Javanese'—i.e., the mad, the simple-minded, and children" (Geertz 1960, 247). If Pak Raden managed to maintain the refined politeness that is the Javanese cultural ideal (as his long-suffering wife indeed does), his parodic value would be significantly reduced. Recalling Neale and Krutnik's (1990, 94) point that "comic pleasure is ... inextricably linked to a replacement of transgression in relation to ideology, a re-setting of the boundaries," Pak Raden's parody of Javanese norms suggests that Javanese cultural values (the ideal Javanese subject) remain valid in modern Indonesia. Clifford Geertz asserts that there is indeed "an attempt to revitalize traditional Javanese beliefs and expressive forms, to return them to public favor by demonstrating their continued relevance to the modern world" (1990, 80). Keith Foulcher holds a similar view and notes that "there is ... an increasing tendency to align 'Indonesia' with a redefined *priyayi* [upper class] Java," which he understands as "the most visible and tangible way in which the state seeks to balance the 'modern' attitudes of a national culture with the awareness of an indigenous basis to cultural identity" (1990, 303). One unexpected outcome of "Javanization" has been a renewed pride in regional culture, a counter-hegemonic tendency that contests the unitary cultural construct of the New Order cultural project (Lindsey 1993). The contemporary legitimation of Javanese cultural traditions is discussed further in chapter 6.

Ogah (reluctant, unwilling) and Ableh/Enyeng are two adult male characters who perform a complex parodic function in the *Si Unyil* series.[18] Ogah and Ableh are unmarried and unemployed. They have no home of their own but sleep in the village security post (*Pos Siskamling*),[19] which Ogah sometimes describes as "his office." As comic characters, they function as a classic double act—Ableh as straight man setting up Ogah as fall guy. In terms of the organic metaphor, they are socially stunted child-adults whose inadequacies go to the heart of the model adult subject.

Unemployed and owning no land, Ogah and Ableh are chronically short of money and food. They spend a lot of time (though not much energy) in trying to scrounge from passers by. Like children, they are dependent on others for their subsistence. Their insistent "gimme gimme" as the village children pass by reinforces their inscription as dependents. The village children rarely give money or food to Ogah and Ableh, mainly because the two men usually try to trick them out of their money, and are unwilling to do anything to earn the money. It is their unwillingness to take part in productive work which makes Ogah and Ableh sinister as well as comic characters. The Security Post, at the center of the village, might be read as the center of a web, where Ogah and Ableh wait, ready to prey on passersby. Read this way, Ogah and Ableh are feral, potentially destructive forces.[20] Their comic parody of the self-sufficient, productive villager has a sharp edge. The inverse logic of their parody suggests that citizens who do not grow up to play a productive role are destructive and incompatible with the well-being of the community.

In most episodes Ogah and Ableh/Enyeng are presented as incompetent, irresponsible, immature, dependent, and selfish. This list paradigmatically substitutes valued adult attributes with qualities usually associated with children rather than adults. The comic pleasure Ogah and Ableh/Enyeng provide derives from the way their behavior and attitudes parodically invert our expectations of acceptable adult behavior in Suka Maju. Ogah and Ableh are models of all that children growing up should strive *not* to be.

They are the negative case, and they help to delineate more clearly the positive attributes of the model Indonesian villager.

Si Unyil *Models Cultural Differences*

The religious faith of families in Suka Maju is varied and draws attention to three "world religions" that the state has "officially recognized" and promoted as part of the national culture project. Unyil and his family are Muslims, Ucrit is a Catholic, and Meilani is a Protestant. Although Muslims are obliged by their faith to pray five times a day, the *Si Unyil* series rarely makes reference to the practices of prayer, and Unyil is not shown at prayer. Very occasionally Ucrit's family is shown saying grace before eating. The major religious festival of Christmas, the Islamic fasting month (*Ramadan*), and the end-of-fast festival **Idul Fitri** are acknowledged in *Si Unyil* episodes around the time of their actual occurrence. Producers link the fictional representation of religious events in the series with religious practice in real life by scheduling screenings in this way (Suyadi, personal interview, 5 May 1993).

In Indonesia the media are not permitted to publish or broadcast any material that is likely to incite ill will or conflict between people and communities on the basis of race, religion, or ethnicity. "TVRI avoids anything in its programming that may cause the slightest uneasiness for any ethnic or religious groups" (Chu and Alfian 1980, 53). The MISS SARA code (Hill 1994, 45) has contributed to the structure of complex televisual texts in episodes that touch on religious themes in the fictional lives of Unyil and friends.[21]

The *Si Unyil* program has regularly presented episodes that focus on aspects of religious belief and practice. In the episodes available to me, a structure of what may be called embedded narrative is used when dealing with the highly sensitive topics of religion and moral guidance. I read this strategy and the subject positions it constructs as a practice that distances discussion of religion as faith and foregrounds religion as a discourse of teaching and learning.

The first few minutes of "Perjalanan Kakek Abror" (Grandfather Abror's Journey) illustrate the practice of embedding one narrative within another. The episode opens in Ucrit's home, where "O Come All Ye Faithful" is playing on the radio. Ucrit's mother reminds her husband that he had promised to read the children a Christmas story (*dongeng*—legend) from the book he had just bought. Mr. Ucrit yields to his children's eager pleas and begins to read. As viewers, we share the children's point of view. We see the black and white illustrations in the book, which show a town in the ancient Middle East in the time of Roman occupation. As Mr. Ucrit reads, the storybook comes to life. The illustrations become puppets, and we and the fictional readers in Suka Maju are transported to a set representing a town near Bethlehem. For the remainder of the episode we remain in the storybook setting.

This story within a story performs two functions. First, it unites us as viewers with the Ucrit family and offers us the opportunity to enjoy the Christmas story along with Christians. Second, the storytelling interpellates us as observers, not participants or believers. Listening to the story involves no devotional practice or commitment from the implied audience in the way that a scene that showed the family praying together might. Third, the story distances the audience from Christian faith and practice; it takes Christianity out of Indonesia and sets it in a faraway place in the distant past. These devices enhance the "legendary" characteristics of the story. It is not a biblical story. It is a story about children and their parents risking their freedom to help an old man achieve his life's ambition to travel to Bethlehem after misfortune has made him a pauper. It is the story, as the title of the episode signifies, of a journey or pilgrimage, a metaphor that resonates beyond Christianity in Muslim Indonesia. The story is told more to reveal what religious traditions *share* than what makes them distinctively, doctrinally different. It is another instance of the practice of acknowledging cultural differences while erasing their specificity, which, as I noted in chapter 1, is an important process in the national culture project.

Serious Puppet Plays

A similar distancing strategy is evident in the episode "Hijrah" (Migration), which is concerned with key events in the life of the Prophet. As in the "Perjalanan Kakek Abror" episode, the retelling of events in Muhammad's life is distanced from an overtly religious context. First, the exclusively religious connotation of the signifier *hijrah* is broken down by linking Muhammad's migration to Medina with events during the Indonesian revolution in 1945. Archival footage at the beginning of the episode shows Surabaya citizens fleeing from military action in Surabaya in November 1945. Pak Raden describes this event to Unyil and his friends as a "*hijrah*." Second, Muhammad's migration to Medina is framed as a school history lesson introduced by the village schoolteacher (presumably in response to a question from Unyil about the meaning of *hijrah*). Once introduced, the story is continued by puppets, who dramatize the story. The episode ends in the schoolroom with a question from Unyil that provides the motivation for the teacher to round off the account of events.

The use of black and white archival footage and the framing of the *hijrah* within a school history lesson together function to suppress the exclusively religious connotations of *hijrah* and foreground the political and historical narrative. This device positions Unyil and friends as students of religion. They are not inscribed as protagonists of any particular faith. Framing religion as "history" signifies that it is something to be studied and learned in the same way that many other topics are in the village. Viewers, together with Unyil and friends, are drawn into learning, studying, and enjoying each other's beliefs.

In the episode described above, the mixing of codes and artifacts of official culture (history of the Indonesian Revolution and archival footage) with codes of legendary and religious tales produces a complex intersection between religion, fiction, and history. The *hijrah* story may be read as a somewhat bookish exegesis of events in the history of Islam, much in the way Lynette Parker described Balinese religion being treated in lessons on "Religion" in a Balinese primary school (Parker 1992, 111). It may, however, be read as ascribing an almost sacred character to the events in Surabaya. Read this way, the episode ascribes an epochal significance and aura to the events of 1945–49 and reinforces the official valorization of the unifying power of the struggle against the colonial Dutch government, which features prominently in primary school texts as "The History of the National Struggle" (Leigh 1991).

Language, Consent, and Hegemony

The constraints on the expression of emotion and on other dynamics of interaction imposed by using puppet characters in the series are considerable and raise the verbal text to an importance it would not usually hold in a televisual or filmic medium, where gesture, facial expression, spatial relations, and other subtleties of nonverbal communication "speak volumes." In *Si Unyil,* language is the prime channel of expressive communication. Language performs a hegemonic function in the series, functioning as a prime strategy of building and strengthening audience acceptance for the national language and the "national subject."

The language used by all of the *Si Unyil* characters for most of the time is Indonesian, the official, national language of Indonesia and the prime language for education and television broadcasting (Menteri Penerangan 1990). Indonesian has made the series intelligible to children throughout the archipelago. Even though for many Indonesian children Indonesian may not be the language of primary, familial orientation, it is the language of primary socialization beyond the home, at school, and in most "public" situations (Anderson 1991, 134).

The Indonesian that Unyil and his friends speak is instantly recognizable in its expressiveness, its abbreviated forms and elisions, its syntax and vocabulary, as the language of an in-group, a group of friends whose close social relations make it unnecessary to "spell everything out." The appreciation and acceptance of children's language is signaled in the first few moments of the title sequence when Unyil, Usroh, and Ucrit play a game, chanting out the nonsense syllables "Om Pim Pah, Unyil Kucing!"[22] The language of Unyil and his friends, and of many of the adults in Suka Maju (with notable exceptions that will be discussed later), is an example of a "restricted linguistic code" that reinforces "the *form* of the social relationship (a warm and inclusive relationship) by restricting the verbal signaling of individuated responses" (Bernstein 1971, 78; emphasis in original). The representation in *Si Unyil* of the restricted code so common among peer groups of children makes the language of the series accessible and familiar and encourages the audience to identify and empathize with the characters, drawing viewers imaginatively into the unfolding of the narrative.

Language is also a source of humor. An episode concerned with national education day foregrounds literacy. It opens on Ogah laboriously sounding out letters in a newspaper. Ableh gently points out that the paper is upside down. Ogah airily dismisses his friend's remark, saying that his action is quite deliberate, for if one is a clever reader, one can read upside down just as easily as right way up! Later in the same episode, Ogah is again a figure of fun as he tries to cover up his inability to read by memorizing the words on a banner. Caught out, Ogah protests that his substitution of "stir up" (*galakkan*) for "raise" (*tingkatkan*) in the text means the same, sending the children into peals of laughter, as they insist that that is not what reading is all about. In "Tua Muda Belajar Baca," Unyil takes over from a flustered and frustrated Pak Raden in tutoring an adult literacy class. Before doing so, he obtains his father's agreement that he will be let off a punishment he had imposed on him. This kind of humor, involving inversions of child-adult relations mediated through language, attributes power and prestige to the children because of their language competence and is a site of children's pleasure in the series.

Making fun of characters who have only a restricted code at their command, who have "deviant" accents, or speak a regional dialect, is another strategy that legitimates the dominance of Indonesian and makes competence in Indonesian an attribute of the model citizen. The Bu Bariah and Engkong characters are striking in this regard. Their speech habits constitute their whole dramatic (and ideological) impact, particularly Bu Bariah, who often appears on screen without any motivation from the plot. Ibu Bariah is little more than a source of linguistic pleasure for the viewer. Her entry is usually heralded off-screen by her hawker's cry, "*Rujak, Rujak petis!*"[23] readying the audience for the rushing tumult of her idiosyncratic Indonesian mixed with Madurese and Surabaya-inflected Javanese words and phrases.[24] Once on screen, Bu Bariah's statements are delivered with what we might think of as Cockney verve and are greatly enjoyed by the audience. But Bu Bariah's speeches frequently end by simply trailing off. She rarely gives any closure to her comments and is not used to provide narrative development. She is a sideshow in which her dialect is the freak. Similarly, Engkong's stereotypical singsong Chinese accent is a major part of his comic impact (Suyadi, personal interview, 3 May 1993).

This play with accents and dialect makes "nonstandard" Indonesian laughable. Nonstandard speakers are constructed as deficient subjects, lacking competency in the national language. The validation of a geographically and ethnically unmarked Indonesian signifies a preference for a national, homogenous culture over an ethnically and regionally differentiated culture. The play with language illustrates Jackson Lears's argument that "the essence of the concept of hegemony is not manipulation but legitimation. The ideas, values and experiences of the dominant groups are validated in public discourse" (1985, 574).

Yet the ideal subject created by this discourse is a fractured subject. The national motto of Indonesia (*Bhinneka Tunggal Ika:* They are Many, They are One, or Unity in Diversity) legitimates diversity, but as we have seen, the subject position provided for regionally and ethnically inflected Indonesian accords "standard" Indonesian high prestige and denigrates other languages and ways of speaking.

Much of the dialogue between children, and between children and adults, is conducted in a restricted linguistic code, signifying the close, shared relationships enjoyed by the Suka Maju village community. There are however, some adults and, on occasions, children, who use an elaborated linguistic code. The elaborated code is associated with "standard" Indonesian (*Bahasa baku*) and is typified by the use of complete sentences, inflected verb forms, an expanded vocabulary of unabbreviated words, and less expressive and more deliberate delivery compared with restricted code utterances.[25] An elaborated code is usually associated with valued roles and statuses in the society (Bernstein 1971, 78). In Suka Maju the village head, schoolteacher, and visitors habitually use an elaborated code. When a Jakarta-based journalist visits Suka Maju, his conversation with the village headman focuses on the journalist's experience in writing about life in widely scattered parts of the nation. Their conversation makes it clear that it is the journalist's Indonesian language (and the institution of the press) that are crucial in representing the nation to itself. The key role of Indonesian is reinforced when Unyil and his friends crowd around the journalist, asking how they too might become journalists. The visitor impresses upon them that an ability to use "good Indonesian" is essential.

Children are represented using an elaborated code on those occasions when they perform individualized, public roles, such as acting as announcer, narrator, or chairperson for a villagewide event. The code shifting involved in performing these roles is highlighted in two ways. As viewers we are sometimes given access to the children "behind the scenes" as they prepare nervously for a performance. The children's language is in restricted code and is highly expressive, with a lot of teasing about who should do the announcements, protestations about being shy, and the like. But when the young master or mistress of ceremonies takes the stage to welcome guests and announce the program, he or she usually speaks in fluent, well-formed Indonesian. Sometimes, however, the difficulty of using an elaborated code is foregrounded. In "Saya Anak Indonesia" the normally fluent Unyil, acting as master of ceremonies, stumbles over the word *hadirin* (guests or people attending), mispronouncing it as *haridin* and drawing attention to the rather more formal vocabulary and constructions required on such occasions. But this is an exception, and on most occasions children are shown to be competent in using an elaborated linguistic code in public.

Standard Indonesian is therefore systematically associated with socially and culturally prestigious roles in the case of adults, and with those occasions when a child performs a representative or beneficial public role such as providing others with information. The elaborated code of Indonesian is thus associated with cultural and social success. The literate, educated, Indonesian-speaking subject is preferred over citizens who have only a restricted code, a dialect, or a regional language at their command. But producers faced the problem that the elaborated Indonesian is usually spoken by the least funny and entertaining characters. It tends to appear bookish or bureaucratic and removed from everyday life. In this event the producer's desire to build consent for Indonesian, and "good" Indonesian at that, may be undermined. Indeed letters from viewers urged producers to represent a wider range of provinces in the series. One viewer noted that while the range of dialects present in the series did reflect the diversity of Indonesia, more regional dialects should be represented.[26] Gramsci has reflected on this issue in the Italian context, noting that dialect may become a source of pride and self-defense or resistance by subordinate classes against the hegemonic power of a ruling elite and a caste language (Hall, Lumley, and McLennan 1978, 50).

A wider vocabulary and more complex syntactical structures provide users of an elaborated code with the linguistic means for distancing themselves from the dynamics of a context-dependent, particularistic restricted code. Such a capability is important for individuals who perform social roles requiring exercise of individual judgment and leadership. Professional roles will almost invariably require such competencies. But in many *Si Unyil* episodes, it appears that communalism, or collectivism, characterized by a high degree of mutuality, is highly valued, and individual initiative relatively devalued. An elaborated code introduces a degree of social distance and individuation that in some measure is antithetical to communalism and the maintenance of superordinate-subordinate power relations characteristic of the village world inscribed in Suka Maju.

In "Anak Masa Depan," a story about how Unyil and friends commemorate National Children's Day, Unyil suggests to his friends that they ask Pak Raden to be their adviser in preparing for the show they have decided to present to the village. Endut objects, saying that he is sure they can do everything themselves, and lists what they have already accomplished. Unyil isolates Endut, asking for a show of hands from those who think Pak Raden should not be their adviser. Endut raises his hand and tries to get Cuplis to join him. Cuplis declines, saying he would rather go along with the majority. On another occasion in the same episode, in resolving a quarrel with another group of children, Pak Raden urges them to seek mutual agreement through discussion, which he expresses as *musyawarah dan mufakat,* a reference to the Pancasila principle "Popular sovereignty governed by wise policies arrived at through deliberation and representation" (*Kerakyatan yang dipimpin oleh hikmat kebijaksanaan dalam permusyawaratan/ perwakilan*). The theme of consensual decision making is explored in a number of other incidents in the narrative that need not detain us here. The main point is that the narrative legitimates decision making processes that are consensual and that apparently find it difficult to accommodate individual points of view.

Another illustration of this tension appears in the episode "Saya Anak Indonesia." The village children decide to present a performance of songs and a play for the adult community. Throughout the narrative, there are many affirmations of the children's sense of independence, responsibility, and commitment. One woman, for example, sitting in the audience, waiting for the show to begin, says to a friend, "It's marvelous, isn't it, children putting on a show like this without adult help." There are also many instances that remind us that these are "children" after all: some players arrive late, others have a scuffle going across stage, and one nervous boy threatens to go home. Eventually, the children begin their play. Set in a schoolroom, it concerns the visit of an official from the Department of Education and Culture. The fictional teacher drills the class in how to greet the official from "Dep Dik Bud" (*Dep*artemen Pendi*dik*an dan K*ebud*ayaan), which provides a lot of scope for jokes about the Indonesian custom of developing acronyms. The children get confused, and thinking that the official's name is DepDikBud, chant that out, sending the audience into fits of laughter. Then the official arrives, and one of the class makes a formal speech of welcome and thanks. Halfway through, he forgets his lines, and despite Unyil hissing the final phrases for him, he loses his nerve and begins to cry. At that, his friends seated on the stage all begin to jeer and tease him about being a crybaby, and the episode ends with the (fictional) teacher and the visiting official saying over and over that everything is "Chaos, chaos!" (*Kacau! kacau!*)

Two aspects of this entertaining, multilayered televisual text are of interest for my argument. In the schoolroom scene, the children of Suka Maju, for a few delicious moments, send up officials and teachers, turning the officialese of the national bureaucracy into a set of nonsense syllables, something to play with, like the "*Om Pim Pah*" that introduces each episode. It is a ritual of reversal (of roles and social categories), a licensed period of rebellion and mockery that draws attention to the normal state of affairs and affirms accepted power relations (Gluckman 1965; Peacock 1968; White 1982). But the narrative steals the children's fun. They are not able to bring off their send-up of the education system. Their parents' pride in them as capable, independent organizers is dashed as the play falls apart because one of the players fails to carry off the joke. The hints we were given of the cracks in the performance are gathered up in the final scene, where it becomes obvious that these were, after all, only children playing at being adults. Thus the narrative restores normal relations of deference and power, of organization and control between adults and children. It is as if even the *fiction* of such a change in village dynamics was beyond imagining. It is clear from these extracts that it is adult supervision, knowledge, and judgment that ultimately bring order out of chaos. The subordinate role of children (even educated children) is reaffirmed along with the suggestion that innovation and individual initiative have the potential to be disruptive and may lead to chaos.

The idea that the usurpation of adult roles leads to chaos is taken up by Saya Shiraishi in her discussion of children's literature (1997, chap. 4). Shiraishi contrasts stories in which mothers neglect their duties and children demand their rights with the "family basis" educational models proposed by influential nationalist intellectuals such as Soetatmo Soeriokoesomo, first president of the Taman Siswa movement. Shiraishi notes that Soetatmo described democracy, in language and imagery remarkably similar to the "Saya Anak Indonesia" episode, as a chaotic state in which roles are reversed: "If the mother persistently neglects her duties, collision is unavoidable. And when it—this collision—comes, the children will triumph. The roles will be turned upside down and the father and mother will have to obey. And we will here see the picture of the democratic state."[27]

In these narratives, then, it is possible to identify a tension that produces a fractured subject. The discourse of education encourages initiative, independent action, and judgment in children, mediated through an elaborated linguistic code. The discourse of communalism, and conventional expectations of proper relations between children and adults, however, offer a subject position that does not acknowledge children's independence and valorizes the group over the individual. If the development of an elaborated linguistic code is intimately related to the development of individual judgment and expression of ideas, narrative closures that offer negative rewards to individual achievement will produce a subject split by a disposition to articulate his or her individuality and a desire to conform to conventional (paternalistic) power relations and norms of communalism.

Conclusion

When Kurnain Suhardiman died on 26 February 1991 (*Kompas,* 26 February 1991), artistic director Suyadi and Agust Suprapto, long-term director of the series, took over Kurnain's role as script writers, but given their dual roles they have been unable to maintain the momentum of the series. In 1990/91, fifty-two episodes were screened. In 1991/2 and 1992/3, the series was screened once every two weeks. When I interviewed Suyadi at PPFN in May 1993, the series was not in production. Unyil and his friends rested on dusty shelves in the workroom at PPFN, and the adjacent studio was locked. Suyadi himself seemed uncertain of Unyil's future.

The loss of Kurnain is not the only factor, however, nor even the main factor that has put Unyil on the shelf. Apart from a natural waning of audience interest after such a long run, critics such as Hannoeng Sumanthadiredja and Eduard Depari have argued that the program "lost its way" (*Suara Karya,* 24 January 1988; *Pos Film,* 15 January 1989; *Suara Pembaruan,* 13 August 1989) as the balance tipped too much toward modeling the ideal child subject as part of national development and away from the entertainment of children (*Kompas,* 31 March 1985; *Angkatan Bersenjata,* 12 January 1988; *Suara Pembaruan,* 13 August 1989). For *Pos Film*'s critic EV, the episode in which *Si Unyil* moved outside the studio to visit the largest steel factory in Indonesia, was definitive: "since *Si Unyil* has been mixed up with instructional films like this one, it is no longer a puppet film but is headed toward being a documentary (*Pos Film,* 4 February 1990).

Pos Film reported in November of the same year that from its observations, the Sunday film on RCTI was more popular than *Si Unyil,* which had lost touch with its folk content and lively characters (11 November 1990).

The insertion of *Si Unyil* in a flow that aligned it with nonfictional and heavily didactic comedy added to problems of reception. Rather than unifying the sequence, as Raymond Williams's (1974, 95) theory might seem to predict, the intersection of development discourse across *Ria Jenaka, Siaran Pedesaan,* and *Si Unyil* became a focus for audience dissatisfaction and even confusion in the case of *Si Unyil*. Critical comment in the press and letters to the editor suggest that the unsubtle and inappropriate use of the program for instructional purposes insulted and confused its audience. The dramatist Ikranegara, for example, comparing *Sesame Street* with *Si Unyil*, argued that the American program was "one hundred percent" better than *Si Unyil* because it did not make fools of the audience. He noted further that the program was enjoyed by adults as well as children for that reason (*Zaman*, 23 August 1981). Eight years later, critic Hannoeng Sumanthadiredja made a similar point: "It is no longer clear to whom this puppet film is targeted. To children who are forced to think like adults, or to adults who have the minds of children" (*Pos Film*, 15 January 1989). Kurnain Suhardiman himself complained that government departments restricted his freedom to write in a way that appealed to children (*Kompas*, 31 March 1985; 18 February 1990). Suyadi said this became especially trying after TVRI learned that *Si Unyil* was watched by families, not just by children. He reported that it prompted government departments and other interest groups to seek access to the program as a way of extending information about their role and programs to adults as well as children (personal interview, 3 May 1993).

For a decade, *Si Unyil* was TVRI's most popular children's (and possibly adult) series. The familiarity and charm of the scaled-down Indonesian world communicated to audiences across Indonesia in the same way that the highly successful series *Skippy* did for Australian audiences (Moran 1993, 419). But the desire to create an "authentic" or "identifiably Indonesian" series by drawing on indigenous aesthetic content and the decision to use a children's series to popularize and build consent for national development priorities have been problematic for producers. Overly didactic episodes foregrounded the production conditions of the series and contributed to a perception that the series sought to manipulate its audience. The central problem of balancing the intersection of entertainment and instructional voices in *Si Unyil* opened the text to criticisms that threatened the consensus position the state intended to create. The co-option of Unyil and the inappropriate adult voice with which he often spoke made the text vulnerable to readings that interpreted development as a heavy-handed, coercive process. The insistent lecturing of village friends that Unyil was pushed into, far from constructing a world of mutuality and self-help, drew attention to the one-way, dependent relationship between the state and village communities it interpellated as subjects needing "development."

Chapter 5

THE RAHMAT FAMILY: SOAP OPERA MODELS THE COMMUNITY

IN THIS CHAPTER I examine processes of fashioning and guiding the adult subject as member of three ever more inclusive families: the domestic family, the neighborhood, and the national family through the television series *Keluarga Rahmat*. The series went on the air at a significant moment in Indonesia's television culture—the moment when for the first time Jakarta viewers had the opportunity to tune to a nongovernment pay-TV, and later, free-to-air commercial service, which at that time screened largely imported entertainment. The moment is significant for a number of reasons, first because RCTI broke the government monopoly on television broadcasting, and second because the establishment of RCTI ushered in a rapid and comprehensive deregulation of television over a five-year period. Third, and most important for the argument of this chapter, the moment was significant because it can be seen as part of a reappraisal of the significance of the audience and forms of popular culture in TVRI programming.

Keluarga Rahmat was screened at the same time TVRI launched its second channel, "Programa Dua," a service that hailed the Jakarta audience as different from other segments of the national audience and set out to deliver to the metropolitan audience programming that was more in tune with their experiences, tastes, and interests.[1] The emphasis on meeting audience demands, which became more insistent with the introduction of commercial television, influenced the production of *Keluarga Rahmat*. The series producers appropriated an American prime-time serial form, adapted it, and used it as part of the national culture project. This chapter uses the study of *Keluarga Rahmat* as a way of examining the intersection of complex processes of modernization, transnationalization, and nation building in public television in Indonesia.

Keluarga Rahmat—*Mediating the (National) Community*

Fritz Schadt differentiated the *Keluarga Rahmat* series from foreign, particularly American, serials screened on TVRI and RCTI on the grounds that American serials tend to focus on the individual. *Keluarga Rahmat,* by contrast, was an attempt to represent the authentic color of Indonesia (*"warna" khas Indonesia*), where life as part of a community is the fundamental condition of social existence (press release PPFN, 20 April 1989, Jakarta). The televisual community that *Keluarga Rahmat* imagines is represented in four normative discourses, which together transcode "the *political idea* of nationhood into the daily experience and feeling of nation" (Martin-Barbero 1993, 165; my emphasis). These discourses are (1) the central value of "familyism" (*kekeluargaan*), (2) the ideal of social harmony or neighborliness (*kerukunan*), (3) the ideal of living within one's means (*hidup sederhana*), and (4) the necessity of a national perspective (*wawasan nusantara*). These four discourses, with different emphases, are recurrent and intersecting themes throughout the *Keluarga Rahmat* series, which is structured on the experiences and interactions between four neighboring families who live in suburban Jakarta.

The first three discourses sit comfortably in the (female) gendered, private, informal sphere of the urban neighborhood community. In many parts of Indonesia the private world is focused on home and family but extends beyond to include a spatially limited "neighborhood" of relatives and friends (Guiness 1986, 143; Sullivan 1992, 102; see also Murray 1991, 81–82).² Krishna Sen (1994, 114f) has discussed the representation of the ethos of communalism in popular film in her discussion of *Perawan Desa* (The Village Virgin) and argues that communalism is associated with the majority and lower classes. The rich and powerful live protected, individualized lives behind the walls of their "mansions." The modernist discourse of a national perspective for national development is not part of the private sphere, neither of the *orang kampung* (the people of the home community) nor of the *orang gedongan* ("streetsiders" [Guiness 1986, 4]). It is part of the official ideology of development, mapped over the private spaces of lower and privileged classes alike and belongs to the public, male sphere. "National perspective" discourse imagines a scalar, progressively more inclusive movement between the preoccupations of families in local communities and the nation writ large. It is a movement intended to personalize otherwise abstract relations between families and communities across the dispersed but encompassing wholeness of the nation, to establish what Benedict Anderson called the "deep horizontal comradeship" of the imagined *national* community (1991, 7). This fiction of the national family turns the private into public and the public into private. It subsumes the distinction between the female/private and male/public spheres. Yet mapping the public sphere onto the private, informal sphere ruptured viewers' generic expectations of the series. It muddled the cultural competencies required to interpret episodes and became the site of viewer dissatisfaction and resistance, as I explain below.

Keluarga Rahmat—*The Series*

Preparation for the *Keluarga Rahmat* series began in January 1987 following a suggestion by President Soeharto to the former director of PPFN, Gufron Dwipayana (Pak Dipo), that a series that addressed aspects of the lives of Indonesia's public servants (*pegawai negeri*) should be produced (Fritz Schadt,[3] personal interview, 22 May 1993; *Monitor,* 2 May 1989).[4] The president's suggestion was developed into a fifty-two episode series, with episodes of fifty minutes. Shooting began on 31 August 1987, and the first ten episodes were in the can by 19 December 1987. President Soeharto himself took part in the series and was shown shaking hands with the veteran Pak Sadikin. It was the first time the president had ever agreed to take part in a television series (Iskandar Nugroho, telephone interview, 2 February 1995).

The terminology of PPFN's early planning documents suggests that there was some confusion over the generic characteristics of *Keluarga Rahmat.* In various documents *Keluarga Rahmat* is described as a film series, a film serial (in one case as both on the same page), a serial "sinetronik," and a video serial (PPFN 1987). But while the terminology might have been confused, producers were clear from the beginning that *Keluarga Rahmat* would be based on an analysis of interactions between characters and of the conflicts that arise out of interpersonal relations (PPFN 1987).

In a paper prepared for the script writers after the first ten episodes were finished, director and producer Fritz Schadt expanded on earlier statements about the nature of the series. He emphasized at the outset that the team was in the business of producing entertainment and that viewers could not be forced to watch television. He urged the team to work hard and to help make the series appeal (*memikat*) to viewers. He noted that *Keluarga Rahmat* was "not intricate or complex" like *Dynasty* or *Return to Eden* but was fundamentally about human relationships. It was crucial, he said, in a long-running series to ensure that viewers became psychologically involved with the characters and developed an interest in the unfolding of events so they would continue to tune in. Schadt went on to say that episodes should not work toward a climax in the way that a feature film does. Each episode should include a very brief anticlimax so that the events appear to be just a moment in the lives of the characters. Leaving some parts of the story unresolved from one episode to the next would also contribute to the impression that "life goes on" (*bahwa hidup dan kehidupan berkisar terus*) (Schadt 1988). The producers were not prepared to leave too much to viewers' interpretation, however. The openness and suspension of the serial narrative is counterproductive if your interest as a producer is to prefer a particular reading and model of community. Consequently, Fritz Schadt advised writers to "come back [at the end of each episode] to inform the viewers just what message [*misi:* ideological message, theme] we have presented over the last fifty minutes or so. Of course, this will have to be done through dialogue" (Schadt 1988).

The emphasis on popular entertainment, the variability of human character, relations between individuals in a family setting, and the maintenance of (some) story lines from episode to episode (seriality) suggest that the generic form of *Keluarga Rahmat* is closest to soap opera, which Ien Ang describes as "characterised by an accent on human relations, domesticity and daily life" (Ang 1985, 54). Robert Allen (1985, 137–38) is more specific in listing the features that, combined, make "any given text legible to its readers as soap opera": absolute resistance to closure, contemporary setting, emphasis on domestic concerns, didacticism, and a clear orientation toward women as the target audience. Allen has recently (1995, 17–18) extended his definition and has stressed the "seriality" of soaps, rather than resistance to closure as the distinctive characteristic of soaps, which is "recognised by their viewers around the world" (1995, 17). This shift embraces differences between the narrative "openness" (the absolute resistance to closure) of soaps in the United States, England, and Australia and the "closed" narratives of the Latin American *telenovelas,* which evolved from American soaps (Ang 1996, 155) and have been spectacularly successful both domestically and internationally (Lopez 1995). The shift recognizes the intense transnationalization of the trade in television products in the late 1980s and '90s, when productions from the "south" (including Australia, with its exports of *Neighbours* and *Good Times, Bad Times*) attracted huge audiences and revenues in Europe, East Asia, and the United States. What Allen acknowledges in redefining soap opera is that the critical apparatus needs to take into account the diversity of global television programming and the hybrid nature of transnational forms.

The American daytime soap opera form and its variant, the prime-time soap, is well known and popular in Indonesia. The American soap *Peyton Place* was broadcast in 1973 in the days of black and white television. In 1986 the Australian prime-time soap/melodrama *Return to Eden* was enormously popular and "stopped" Jakarta on Thursday nights. When the star of the serial, Rebecca Gilling, visited Jakarta in January 1987 as part of the Australian Embassy's so-called glamour diplomacy, she was mobbed at the airport, and fans climbed over cars to catch a glimpse of her.[5] In 1987 TVRI screened the American soap *Falcon Crest* and followed it in 1988 with *Dynasty* and the Australian "quality soap" *A Country Practice*. RCTI screened the hybrid courtroom drama/ "workplace soap" *L.A. Law* (Gripsrud 1995, 165) in 1989. In 1990 TVRI's Second Channel screened the high-gloss American soap *Santa Barbara*. What these data show is that just before the launch of commercial television in Indonesia, and for its first year of operation, TVRI and the Second Channel turned to high-rating imported soaps as a way of building a kind of credit balance as providers of popular entertainment in anticipation of the competition expected from RCTI.

Fritz Schadt's appropriation of the narrative form and emotional appeal of transnational television serials suggests that a similar motivation was at work in the production of *Keluarga Rahmat*. Implicit in the appropriation of the transnational form and in the programming of high-rating soaps is the belief that these narratives meet audience needs. The further assumption, that borrowing and adapting the *form* of the imported serials would of itself allow a locally produced show to establish a similar relation with the audience, was more problematic and will be examined throughout this chapter.

TVRI's embrace of transnational television products and forms

The Rahmat Family 151

occurred during a period when the national broadcaster was also determined to enhance its credentials as a producer of programming that was authentically Indonesian and non-, or even anti-"commercial." The *Si Unyil* series was one (very successful) outcome of the push to boost local programming. Its form owed a lot to American sitcoms, but its setting, content, and incorporation of indigenous oral narratives was highly original. In the early 1980s, the percentage of local productions compared with imported programming rose to an almost unsustainable 88 percent for five years, until it settled at 80 percent in 1987 (see table 5.1).

Table 5.1
Percentage of Domestic versus Foreign Productions on TVRI, 1983/84–1991/92

Year	TVRI Production (%)	Imported Production (%)
1983/84	88	12
1984/85	88	12
1985/86	88	12
1986/87	80	20
1987/88	NA	NA
1988/89	80	20
1989/90	80	20
1990/91	80	20
1991/92	80	20

Source: *Pidato Kenegaraan*, various years.

The construction of TVRI as producer of authentic Indonesian programs was accompanied by a perception that much imported programming was inimical to Indonesian culture and values. The appropriation of the *form* of high-rating transnational serials, which would then be "Indonesianized," was a strategy that sought to achieve three objectives through the production of a single program: (1) to deliver audiences the kind of popular entertainment they enjoyed, (2) to hold TVRI's audience share in the face of commercial competition, and (3) to produce programs that were informed by and sensitive to Indonesian culture and contributed to the discourse of "nation."

The *Keluarga Rahmat* series can be understood as a site of what Jesus Martin-Barbero (1993) calls "mediations" between the forces of production and reception. The two-way movement between the expectations, interests, demands, and needs of spectators, and the nation building and cultural objectives of the producers created a tension in the production process. PPFN producers felt a need to acknowledge and satisfy audience interest in popular transnational products. Simultaneously they felt a need to distance their own productions from culturally inappropriate imported content and to produce an essentialized "authentic" series that would displace its transnational "Others." This delicate balancing act imposes very considerable strains on the producers of hybrid products, and as might be expected, results may be more or less successful. In Chile, for example, the Catholic Church, which owned and operated channel 13, adapted a "racy" Brazilian novela "to suit not only the specificity of the Chilean 'national characters,' but the station's commitment to the Catholic Church's values and standards of decency" (Lopez 1995, 263). As Lopez explains, the "stratagem" was very successful. The telenovela earned 60 percent of audience share, with some episodes rating as high as 90 percent.

The reception of *Keluarga Rahmat* was not as positive. The series never achieved the transparency of communication or the popularity the producers wished for. What popularity it did enjoy was in part at the expense of the series' ideological project. Indonesian viewers complained that the acting was amateurish, that the series was didactic, and that it was not sufficiently entertaining. The public fallout between freelance writer Tatiek Maliyati and the producers arose because Tatiek was keen to boost the entertainment values of the series, while director Fritz Schadt made the ideological thrust of the series his main priority (Iskandar Nugroho, telephone interview, 2 February 1995). Some observers have celebrated the appropriation and adaptation of global televisual forms by those at "the peripheries of the world" (Ang 1996, 157) as economically and culturally liberating (Straubhaar 1991; Rogers and Antola 1985). Yet the cases that illustrate these euphoric accounts tend to be the success stories. We rarely hear of the failures. *Keluarga Rahmat* was not a complete failure, but neither was it a great success. The *Keluarga Rahmat* story is worth telling, however, for the light it sheds on the complexities the transnational trade in television products presents for producers who are put in the position of mediating between their audience's "horizon of expectations" (Gripsrud 1995, 130–31) and their own ideological and political projects.

Familyism in *Keluarga Rahmat*

Keluarga Rahmat centers its ideological preoccupations in the realm of the personal. As Charlotte Brunsdon says, "it is through the concerns and values of the personal sphere that the public sphere is represented in soap opera" (1983, 78). In the episode "Ulang Tahun" (Birthday), for example, Pak Rahmat urges his neighbor, Sadikin, to stay during his meeting with two unemployed young men who wish to join his department. Rahmat draws out the suspense in this scene by letting the men stumble on, not saying what he and the viewer suspect they want to say. He finally cuts the tension and gives voice to the unsaid and unsanctioned when he says, "so, you want to give me money to guarantee you a position." As if relieved by Rahmat's excellent grasp of their unspoken request, the men eagerly assent, only to be crushed by Rahmat's next statement, that "there's no need to go on with this conversation." After the men depart, Sadikin praises Rahmat for his principled decision, resolving any doubts the viewer might have had about the "right" thing to do under these circumstances.

The scene presents a situation in which openness, sharing in the family, and principles of fairness and merit are opposed to underhand practices and a preference for advancement through connections. More abstractly, the men's attempt to corrupt Rahmat opposes an economic system run on principles of fairness to one where individuals with sufficient resources can obtain their own ends, as Rahmat says, by "preying on the weaknesses of others." Unfortunately the opportunity to hold viewers' interest by playing with the question of whether Rahmat will accept the bribe or not is passed up when Rahmat identifies himself at the outset as someone who has no secrets and who is not afraid to conduct his affairs under the scrutiny of friends and neighbors.

The subject position constructed for the viewer in this scene works to support the preferred reading, which valorizes modest living and a national perspective. Rahmat's directness in dealing with the two men, and his disinclination to enrich himself dishonestly is contrasted with the evasiveness of the petitioners. His concern for fair practice and due process are clear from the way he dismisses the bribe and from the fact that he has not advanced his own son by using his connections. When Rahmat, Sadikin, and his children later laugh at the way the men were disconcerted by Rahmat's refusal even to hear how much was being offered, the viewer is intended to side with Rahmat and enjoy the embarrassment the men feel over offering a bribe. One of the difficulties viewers had with the series, however, was the unsubtle way preferred readings and reader positions were inscribed. By not exploring the perspective of the unemployed young men, for example, the series tended to lose viewers' interest: "The story that turns on the lives of public servants, ... is just as you would expect. Don't forget [the series] is made by PPFN. . . . It's not surprising then that out of the fifty-two episodes produced, the proportion about the lives of the oldies is greater than stories about young people" (*Suara Pembaruan,* 11 February 1990).

The all-too-obvious signaling of Rahmat's likely response to the visitors closed off opportunities for rethinking the values Rahmat and Sadikin champion within a wider frame of reference. While the scene acknowledges bribery as a practice, it does not go any further than condemning it. There is no shift within the episode that might problematize relations between the ethical actions of individuals acting within a family or close neighborhood and the impact of such actions on a (national) economy in which bribery and a range of other corrupt practices have become institutionalized (Schwarz 1994, chap. 6; Antlov 1995, 150–54). The opportunity to explore the continued relevance and validity of preferred values and consider other actions that individuals might take as a way of addressing entrenched malpractice is not taken. The episode keeps the focus in the scene on the two individuals who sought favors from Rahmat, and it passes up the opportunity to see the men's problem within a wider frame of social reference. Indeed, Krishna Sen has noted that in state-sponsored discourses such as popular film there is a persistent tendency to attribute responsibility or fault for social problems to individuals and their particular problems or "fate," rather than to institutionalized disadvantage or inequalities (Sen 1994, 118).

The problematic historical transition between a system in which family relations and connections have been the preferred path to privilege and power (patrimonialism) and a system based on modernist principles of advancement on merit as espoused by Rahmat was not addressed. Of course, in the context of widespread resentment of the privileges extended to presidential family members, it is not unsurprising that a possible conflict between familyism and modernism was left out of consideration in this government-sponsored series. The scene forgoes the opportunity to narrate Rahmat and Sadikin's values into and out of crisis, to explore the tensions between the values of the young men and the idealized system Rahmat espouses. The *Keluarga Rahmat* scripts constrain and contain the subject positions for viewers, prompting comments such as "Why are the stories always so "black and white"? You know, Deddy Soetomo's [Rahmat's] performance is like he's just going through the motions. He always turns out to be a ministering angel; it feels as if he isn't human anymore, and it feels boring and preachifying" (*Monitor,* 28 May 1989) and "Since the first episode of this series, Pak Sadikin has been painted as a wise old man.... In daily life, perhaps there are figures like Sadikin. But when a person with this kind of character appears on our TV screens, he seems awkward. The character appears foreign in our eyes" (*Monitor,* 14 February 1990).

The obvious difference in material circumstances between the Subangun family and the Rahmats, both of whom hold similar government positions, is not explored by the producers. The impression is that Subangun's position is open to opportunities for corruption, or "wet" (*jabatan basah*), and that he has taken advantage of his position. Rahmat's position is also wet, but he has resisted temptation, as is made clear in the first episode. In the later episode "Air Tuba Dibalas Air Susu" (good for evil, literally "poison answered with mother's milk"),[6] Ibu Rahmat shows herself to be just as ethical as her husband when she turns down Ibu Subangun's offer of a bribe to have Untung accepted into a state high school despite his low marks.

While the series raised issues and explored tensions that crucially affect the lives of ordinary Indonesians, unlike the open narratives on which it was modeled, *Keluarga Rahmat* tended to close them off, leaving little room for viewers to read their own endings and resolutions to problems such as the Rahmats faced. Even in making the series, its official ideological project was invoked to shape interpersonal relations among the cast. Iskandar Nugroho, "Pratomo" in the series, reported that on those occasions when there was friction between members of the cast—"it was a competitive situation"—the friction was resolved by Fritz Schadt and Pak Dipo, who told the young actors that they were not just actors; they were taking part in something that was "a state duty" (*tugas negara*) (telephone interview, 2 February 1995).

The tension between the screen families structures a tension in the imaginary orderings of real family relations. The text positions the viewer as a subject-in-ideology between the open, sharing, harmonious relations of the Rahmat and Tambayong families, for example, and the materialistic, conflictual Subangun family. The intersection of the family principle with a wider fan of ideological referents, such as communalism in political organizations, the administration of the neighborhood and hamlet level of urban and rural settlement,[7] and the Cooperatives movement, also positions the viewer as a subject-in-ideology between models of the economy as a collective enterprise, informed by principles of familyism, and the competitive, individualistic capitalist economy.

The *Keluarga Rahmat* narrative thus reaches beyond itself in its articulation with a range of discourses. Stephen Neale has argued that in the narrative process of disruption, dispersal, and refiguration of elements, the restructuration and modification that discourses undergo as a result of their interaction mean that the ideologies inscribed in the discourses are never simply passed on unmodified, nor are the tensions between them simply retold (Neale 1981, 6–7). In a particular narrative, viewers' interest is dependent in part on the way ideologies are narrated into and out of tension, to be finally reordered into a new equilibrium. As a consequence, the subject positions structured for viewers shift. The direction of the movement, and its degree, is not simply a matter of narrative or intratextual processes. Intertextual discourses will play their part as well in creating movement within the ideological field. It is precisely the *lack* of movement in ideology in the *Keluarga Rahmat* series that left viewer expectations largely unmet and prompted criticism that the series was unentertaining because it was too predictable and the characters lacked complexity.

The Reception of *Keluarga Rahmat*

Having looked briefly at the encoding of preferred meanings through normative discourses of nation and community, in this section I consider aspects of the reception of the series. My focus is on what viewers enjoyed in the series and on sites of resistance and struggle for control over meaning. The data that inform this discussion consist of fan letters and critical commentary published in Indonesian newspapers and magazines, supplemented by information obtained in interviews with Fritz Schadt and Iskandar Nugroho ("Pratomo").[8]

> It is as if the scenes that you play are real (*nyata*), and not scenes from a television drama. (fan letter #6)

> I really do enjoy family dramas like *Keluarga Rahmat*. Because in the story line they examine issues that have a strong link with the community. (fan letter #16)

> The reason [*Keluarga Rahmat*] is successful in grabbing the viewers' attention is that the story line is about everyday matters that are not too remote for ordinary people. Like Pak Rahmat, who washes his own car. Or Ibu Rahmat, who cooks dinner after returning from the office. And Ibu Sadikin, too, who sells clothing and material on credit, and opens a small stall to boost her housekeeping money. All the kinds of things that are done by housewives whose husbands are middle-level public servants and who don't have a position they can exploit.

> A modest way of life like that is like a mirror of the daily life of the community. The feeling of closeness to a world like that [means that] it is possible to develop feelings of empathy toward Pak Rahmat and the family of the veteran Pak Sadikin (*Swadesi*, 4 March 1990).

In these quotations viewers signify their approval of the naturalism of the *Keluarga Rahmat* series. The first viewer applauds the series for its verisimilitude, for the way it accurately represents the specificity of everyday life in Indonesia. The second and third writers approve of the way *Keluarga Rahmat* plots address issues that have parallels in real life. It is obvious from the letters that viewers find pleasure in narratives marked by local specificity. Following Bourdieu (1980), we can say that the pleasure Indonesian viewers find in the series is the pleasure of recognition—the pleasure of being able to integrate what is screened into everyday life. This sense of identification with the series confirms for Indonesia the pleasure that researchers have discovered domestic audiences worldwide find in indigenous programming (Larsen 1990). Of course, not everyone found it realistic. Some fans pointed to discontinuities in the plot and complained that they made the stories implausible (fan letters #17, #16). These comments, however, condemn the series for not being realistic enough, rather than criticizing the attempt at realism.

If viewers enjoyed the sense of finding themselves and their way of life in the series, a different kind of realism threatened the identification with the program that they had established. Five episodes of the series, all written by Fritz Schadt, were shot away from Jakarta. Producers justified the decision to include provincial locations in the series by an appeal to realism. "Indonesia is not only Jakarta," Fritz Schadt told *Majalah Film* (#28, 1989). In a press interview Schadt explained that the series, especially through the regional episodes, was intended to acquaint viewers better with Indonesia and to "plant the feeling of love for one's country and the perspective of a unified archipelago." The culture of a number of different provinces had been selected, he said, "to develop the value of Indonesian culture and to strengthen Indonesian identity and national pride" (*Suara Pembaruan Minggu,* 20 August 1989). Location shooting was intended to showcase the diversity of the Indonesian landscape and to perform and display the idea of community through regional voices, languages, and faces on screen. Local people, most with very little acting experience, were recruited to lend "authenticity" to the episodes shot on location.

Yet the location shoots strained the realist appeal and entertainment values of the series in three ways: first, they ruptured the close identification between characters and their (fictional) community, which Fiske and Brunsdon consider crucial to the way the personal is played out in family or close community settings in soap opera (Brunsdon 1984, 86; Fiske 1987, 149). Second, because they were set apart from the rest of the series, the episodes understandably failed to generate a similar level of intensity as the episodes set at "home." Third, the episodes' generic characteristics differed from those of the main narrative. The dynamic of the main narrative, holding close to its generic origins, was inward, an intense focus on personal relations between a restricted range of characters in a Jakarta suburb. The fictional community, a metonym for the national community, was brought to life over the weeks by the naturalistic style of interaction between a restricted set of characters.

The representation of Indonesia in the way Fritz Schadt described it, however, involved an outward dynamic. Its narrative logic was premised on an inventory of peoples and places. In the location episodes, the reality of Indonesia was made coherent and brought to life not through the interaction of the people represented but through a narrator (usually a local official) who organized viewers' seeing and appreciation. The regional cultures represented had no life of their own but were refracted through the homogenizing, hegemonic lens of official mass culture. This is the conventional mode of the documentary and the travelogue, where the creation of a fictional world is displaced by an ostensibly objective and analytical examination of the *real* world:

> Evaluating this film [series], it seems similar to *Paket Nusantara* [Archipelago Package], which is usually broadcast together with the *National News* about development in a particular region and takes up matters of tourism, the arts, culture, farming, fishing, or other aspects of social living. There are elements of this kind of thing in this film. . . . Shots, editing, and sound are pretty good. It's a shame there is too much dialogue and that it tends toward a documentary style. (*Pos Film,* 26 November 1989)

The irruption of the reality of the national space inside the fictional space of the series intruded the public sphere into the private sphere, shattering the fictional compact between the series and its viewers. As viewers said, the round-the-islands episodes caused generic confusion in their reception of the program. The spatial shift transcoded a shift from the private, fictional sphere of the soap opera to the public discourses of nation building. Rather than engendering a sense of identification with the national community, however, the spatial shift became a site of resistance in reception. The political objective of showing that "Indonesia was not just Jakarta" led to the criticism that the series had lost direction and had become more like a documentary or a travelogue.

Ibu Subangun—Model Bitch

> I enjoy your role. Mrs. Subangun is just like my mother when she's angry. Truly! If Mum starts grumbling, it's like she won't stop. (fan letter #3)

If confusion over the realist character of *Keluarga Rahmat* became a site of resistance, the "emotional realism" (Ang 1985, 45) of the Ibu Subangun character was an important, though controversial, element in the popularity of the series. Moel Rose, who described herself as "a great fan of *Keluarga Rahmat*," drew attention to her pleasure in the role of Ibu Subangun:

> I think that a family such as the Rahmat's is a picture of a family that has been successful in educating their children, but it is nothing more than a [puppet] show. The impression is that there is nothing interesting or excessive (*berlebihan*) about the family, and it just comes across as quite proper (*kewajaran*). Different from the Subangun family, which is frequently taken up with a range of complex problems because of the conflict between the mother and her children. But truly, you know, it is such matters that create the perfect atmosphere for watching [television]. (fan letter #23)

Her comments help us to understand the irony that it was Ibu Subangun who became the most popular character in the series, at once deplored and enjoyed, and eagerly looked forward to. Audience reactions to the Ibu Subangun character are complex, ranging from uncertainty, possibly even fear, through rejection to the enjoyment of a character viewers "loved to hate." For some viewers, the Ibu Subangun character was the site of feelings of intimacy that were liberating, even therapeutic. Many fan letters and press articles express the enjoyment that viewers find in the nastiest character in the series:

> Strangely, if the villain Bu Subangun doesn't appear in an episode, many fans get upset. While they might hate to death the characteristics of Pak Subangun's wife, if she doesn't appear, the show becomes insipid, tasteless, like vegetables without salt. (*Swadesi*, 4 March 1990)

> This drama series has now become the favorite of housewives, thanks to the presence of Ibu Subangun. A vicious wife. One who always wants to win. One who dominates the family. Who has a

superiority complex. Who enjoys showing off. Who belittles her husband. We may indeed be amazed that it is an antagonistic character like her whose appearance on screen people go crazy over. (*Sarinah,* 31 July 1989, 7)

In these letters and articles it is clear that Ibu Subangun's confrontational style, dominance, and selfish relations within her own family and in the neighborhood were greatly enjoyed. There is no doubt, however, that viewers recognize that Ibu Subangun is the villain of the piece. They are equally certain that her antics have great entertainment value. Through their enjoyment of the Ibu Subangun character, viewers turned the producer's serious attempt to produce a sensitive and uplifting window on Indonesian life into a comedy, if not a farce. Viewers confessed that they were surprised at themselves for enjoying the nasty (*yang judes, dominan dalam keluarga, ingin menang sendiri, menyepelekan suami, tokoh antagonis*) character. This suggests that the generally flat characters, the intrusion of public discourses into the private sphere in the sermonizing quality of Rahmat and Sadikin's speeches, and the occasional representation of President Soeharto on Rahmat's television screen, or posters on the walls of the Tambayong's waiting room, led viewers into an ironic appreciation of Ibu Subangun. Producers responded to the audience's pleasure in the Ibu Subangun character and wrote her up, revealing a conflictual tension between satisfying audience demands in the way commercial producers typically do and their nation-building cultural priorities.

The popularity of Ibu Subangun can be understood by reading her role as an inversion of the stereotyped roles of women in Indonesian film. Krishna Sen has examined aspects of the representation of women in New Order cinema (1994, chap. 6). Sen notes that while it is difficult to generalize about gender representation in Indonesia, the idealized female role of a passive, unexpressive, dependent mother is inscribed in many contemporary films. Saraswati Sunindyo confirms the appearance of this stereotype in contemporary television drama (1993). This model of Indonesian womanhood closely resembles the subject of soap opera described by Tania Modleski. Modleski argued that the female subject was "constituted as a sort of ideal mother ... who has no claims of her own" (1984, 92). Perfectly represented in the tumult of Ibu Subangun's emotion and scheming is all that Indonesian women have been socialized *not* to be. To find the negative model so explicitly and entertainingly represented on screen is disturbing for some women—and for some men. Even her screen husband found her role a problem: "Haryo Sungkono, 40 [years], in fact does not like his role as Pak Subangun. 'What I hate most is a husband who is bested [*kalah*] by his wife' was his reason" (*Monitor,* 8 August 1989).

For some other women the role of Ibu Subangun, played by Thenzara Zaidt, was liberating, even therapeutic, for it acknowledged behavior that was part of their own home life. These writers address Thenzara Zaidt in a familiar way, without any of the formal and formulaic language customary when writing letters. It is as if they feel they have something in common with Ibu Subangun:

> Hallo! How are you, Ibu Thenzara "Subangun" Zaidt? When I see you on television, you are just like my mother, sometimes fine, sometimes really mean. (fan letter #2)

> Greetings from Nanda from N.

> My situation will probably make you laugh, but the fact is my mother is mean like "Ibu Subangun." But each time my mother sees *Keluarga Rahmat* she becomes less mean and doesn't press her demands on her children. (fan letter #21)

> When I see and comprehend fully the performance of Ibu [Su]'Bangun, it seems exactly like the daily behavior of my mother. My mama acts mean and cruel just like [Ibu] Subangun. So, you know, when *Keluarga Rahmat* is on screen, and Mama is in the work room, I quickly turn up the volume, so Mama may happen to hear the characteristic hard voice of Ibu Subangun, which is so like her's when she is griping.... Because of your performance, Mama has changed drastically. (fan letter #24)

For these viewers Ibu Subangun's role confirms that the female subject who does not conform to the passive, compliant model of feminine behavior is not beyond imagining. It speaks a reality they live with every day and introduces greater complexity into the representation of women. Of all the *Keluarga Rahmat* characters, Ibu Subangun proved to be the most entertaining, and she was the only character to stimulate a complex range of reactions from the audience.

The strain between performing the ideological project of the series while maintaining the production and international appeal typical of American prime-time soaps was evident in the resolution of the series. In the final episode, Purnomo's band performs a rock concert for the community. Purnomo announces at the end of the concert that a rich promoter (*cukong*) is interested in taking the band on. As part of the evening's performance, the Rahmat's foster child, Nastiti, presents her first fashion collection to an appreciative audience and announces that she has persuaded Ibu Subangun to finance her new fashion label. The young stars of the community are thus bound into the fashion and pop music industries, two exemplary sites of the excess of globalized, mass-mediated consumerism. Their future careers displace the modest lifestyle that Rahmat and Sadikin had enjoined on their families throughout the series. For the younger generation of Indonesians, real success lies in the competitive individualism of consumer culture. The focus on Ibu Subangun and the identification of Purnomo and Nastiti's success with consumer culture reveals the strain producers experienced in creating episodes that would mediate their priorities and at the same time be popular. The shift toward complicity with the values of transnational capitalism sits uneasily with the objectives of the series to promote indigenous values and a modest lifestyle.

Conflict, Harmony, and Form in *Keluarga Rahmat*

In this section I turn to textual analysis to examine aspects of the appropriation of the soap form in *Keluarga Rahmat* and reflect on the "fit" between the form of the series, viewers' cultural competencies in the reception of series and serials, and the cultural setting in which the series was produced. In a letter to his production team early in 1987, Fritz Schadt emphasized that the series would foreground aspects of the character of those involved in particular episodes and that the narrative "would develop from the interaction between characters and conflict derived from differences between characters" (PPFN 1987). The emphasis on conflict is most developed in the Subangun family, which is in a constant turmoil of confrontation.

In *"Rumah Itu Masih Ada"* (The House Is Still There for You),[9] Purnomo is criticized by his elder brother Pratomo for not taking his university studies seriously. Purnomo angrily tells the self-righteous Pratomo that he has dropped out of university. When Pratomo asks what was wrong with the course, Purnomo says he hated law. The only reason he had enrolled was because his mother wanted him to do it for the associated prestige. Pratomo rejects Purnomo's explanation, siding with his mother. Purnomo explodes, shouting that of course Pratomo would not accept his explanation because he was his mother's golden boy. The conflict between the two brothers is not resolved by the end of the episode, but neither is it developed in this or later episodes.

In the episode *"Sebuah Harmoni"* (Harmony), Ibu Subangun and her daughter Lestari become involved in a blazing row when Lestari tells her mother that she wants to divorce her husband. Ibu Subangun says Lestari's husband has money and position, "everything," and that Lestari has a privileged life. "That's all you ever think of," says Lestari, "I don't love him, I only married him because you insisted I should." Gossip from Ninuk at the neighborhood stall lets viewers know that Lestari is still in love with Franky, whom her mother would not let her marry because he was from a different (Indonesian) ethnic and cultural background.

Lestari rushes out of the house to the Tambayongs, who have taken temporary care of her children. Talking with her friends and neighbors gives her some relief from her mother's ranting. Late in the evening, Lestari returns home with the children, saying to the Tambayongs that they "have given me peace in my heart."

The next morning Lestari apologizes to her mother and pleads with her to see the situation from her point of view. The final moments are intended to be, as the title suggests, a harmonious resolution of the conflict. Yet the harmony at the end of the episode is a simplistic and unsatisfying rush to resolution, overdetermined by an idealized valorization of harmony in family relations that has been allowed to distort the dynamics of the relationships. The reconciliation between Lestari and her mother is represented as a restoration of harmony within the family. But it completely denies the root of the falling out between mother and daughter. The closure suggests that the exercise of individual judgment creates strife and that submission to the wishes of one's parents will preserve family and communal harmony. The preferred reading endorses authoritarian parental values and the suppression of individual desire. It equivocates on the wider issue of relations between different ethnic groups in the national community and denies viewers opportunities to narrate the characters out of crisis.

A third conflict, this time at the village community level, is explored in the episode "*Bila Wader Makan Manggar*" (When the Fish Eat Coconut Blossoms).[10] The story, the locations involved, and the conflict over land compensation between villagers and the government all indicate that this episode is a fictional representation of aspects of the controversial World Bank Kedung Ombo dam project in East Java (Patterson 1987; van Klinken 1991; *Surabaya Post*, 15 November 1989; Stanley 1994).

The main interest in the episode is the conflict between the headman, who has been urging the villagers whose lands will be inundated by the dam to accept the government's offer of transmigration, and the villagers, who are uncertain of their future in a far-off, frontier settlement.[11] They are also confused about their rights. One of the villagers, Pak Bondo, has stirred up the community by arguing that as the government is forcing them out of their ancestral homes and lands, they should claim compensation and should not move before it is paid.

Old Pak Wiyono, a former resident of the village and now a transmigrant in Bengkulu (Sumatra), returns to the village. Hearing of the strife and confusion, he meets with the headman and with great deference offers his services as an honest broker. Wiyono explains to his village friends that transmigration is an opportunity for additional experience and for developing a better knowledge of the country. Pak Bondo bursts in on the session, claiming that Wiyono is in the pay of the headman. For a moment it looks as if a brawl is likely to develop. Old Wiyono calms down the hotheads, saying that no one has paid him, that he just feels for his people, who are likely to lose their inheritance and their landholdings.

In the end it is the advice of Wiyono and the process of talking things through that prevail. We can read the meeting between Wiyono and the headman as a nostalgic and idealized representation of a golden age in Java when order and harmony were an outcome of selfless service, "proper" (deferential, hierarchical) relations between people, and institutionalized, formal processes of talking things through (*musyawarah*) and consensus decision making (*mufakat*). These images evoke a counterpoint to the present strife in the village and implicitly suggest that if only the community would listen to the headman and trust that the government has their best interest at heart, then all would be resolved. The whole issue of the way state-directed modernization disturbs family relations and communal harmony in the name of national development remains suppressed. The issue of the village being drowned, the rights villagers have to refer their case to the courts, and the question of proper compensation are trivialized through their association with an evil, scheming individual who is represented as fighting for compensation just so he can sell his own land for a higher price.

The issue of transmigration, for all its impacts on women, is an official, public policy, "male" issue. The shift away from Jakarta, and the focus on a public policy, political issue displaced the cultural competencies viewers had relied upon in their enjoyment of the series before the "*Bila Wader*" episode was screened.[12] The lead characters in the episode are all men, and the formal process of *musyawarah* is part of the state's invented tradition of community, rather than a practice of the domestic sphere (Sullivan 1992, 4). The conflict in *"Bila Wader,"* and its mode of resolution, is another example of the way the public sphere irrupts inside the private sphere of the *Keluarga Rahmat* series. The focus on an issue of the public sphere, and the producer's reluctance to leave room for viewers to resolve the conflict from their reading positions, reveals the producers' lack of understanding of viewers' generic expectations. If an issue of the public sphere figures in the fictional text, and there is nothing unusual or "wrong" with that, viewers' competency in resolving the crises as an issue in their *private* sphere, must be recognized and provided for. Denying this opportunity shatters the conventions of fictional texts, and displaces the imaginary world of the private sphere with a public sphere where decisions are matters of policy rather than conjecture.

Conflict, Culture, and Domestic Production

For some observers, the tumult of emotion, the dense play of conflict between characters, and the unfolding of endless crises are a central characteristic of the soap opera genre (Ang 1985, 9, 62; Tulloch and Moran 1986, 24–25; Fiske 1987, 57; Cranny-Francis 1988, 176–77; Gripsrud 1995, 239–40). Fritz Schadt also emphasized that the dramatization of conflict was central to the *Keluarga Rahmat* series. But for all the stress placed on conflict in the production brief for the series, the conflict inscribed in the narratives is contained and end-of-episode resolutions often work to mask these contradictions. It is contained first in the sense that it is rarely developed. Conflict in one episode does not continue into the next. Conflict between families never develops into anything approaching a feud and is never allowed to spill over and generate division within the neighborhood.

Conflict is not only narratively inhibited, it is also structurally contained. In serial narratives such as *Dallas* or *Dynasty*, endless crises within the family allow for readings that interpret the disintegration as a critique of the family itself (Feuer 1995, 128). In a series in which the ideological potency of the harmonious family is a given, however, this possibility must not arise. In this sense *Keluarga Rahmat* is more of a sitcom than a serial. Almost all conflict is generated by just one family in the neighborhood. The Subanguns are demonized, with almost all strife being traced back to the overbearing, materialistic Ibu Subangun. The Subanguns are the "Outside" that typically threatens harmony and order in the sitcom. The Rahmats and the other families are never allowed to become a site of conflict that threatens the disintegration of the community. As local critics observed, all characters and families lack depth and are painted simplistically as either "black or white," leaving little room for any complexity in interpersonal relations (*Majalah Monitor* #28 May 1989; *Monitor,* 17 January 1990).

Second, the episodic structure, unlike the serial form, inhibits narrative development and works against the exploration and development of the narratively interesting friction such as that opened up between Pratomo and his brother. The unconvincing reconciliation between Lestari and her mother at the end of "*Sebuah Harmoni*" is another example of the way the producer's desire to *perform* harmony is achieved at the expense of exploration of the personal complexity of character and conflictual relations.

At first sight, the elements of the series do appear to have been put together to maximize their dramatic potential. The four families have some things in common but differ importantly in ethnicity, religion, and material resources. Elements that in other cultures' soaps are fertile ground for conflict and drama must be handled quite differently in Indonesian productions. Issues such as religion, ethnicity, and official corruption (raised in the first episode) must all be treated so carefully, even in fictional texts, that their dramatic potential is heavily compromised. A postscript added at the foot of the document describing the *dramatis personae,* for example, reveals something of the sensitivities with which producers must contend and the continuing tendency under the New Order to represent Java as the microcosm of Indonesia: "The Subangun and Rahmat families have been given Javanese ethnicity deliberately so that no other ethnic group will consider that what has been done is unfair. If there is a good Java[nese family] and a bad Java[nese family], then that seems fair" (PPFN Kerangka Cerita: Film Seri "Manusia KORPRI" nd).

The structure of the series opens up the possibility of confrontation and conflict between characters based on religion, ethnicity, and class. The MISS SARA code, however, inhibits the melodramatic celebration of sensation that has traditionally been a characteristic of the soap genre. In *"Sebuah Harmoni,"* ethnicity is implicated in the quarrel between Lestari and her mother, but the issue is not pursued. Recall that it is raised by the Subangun's servant, a distancing device that shifts the issue into the realm of gossip and rumor. And while the prejudice against mixed marriage is incidentally raised by Ninuk, the happy home life of the Tambayongs, where a Tapanuli Batak is married to a man from Manado, is a constant and continuing idealization of interethnic harmony the MISS SARA code is designed to protect.

The possibility of religious conflict is not addressed in the series. First, the range of religions represented in the neighborhood is very restricted. Monotheistic Islam and Christianity are represented, but the other "offically recognized" religions—Hinduism, Buddhism, and Confucianism—are not, and thus the potential in the series for communal strife to erupt over religious issues is deliberately minimized.

Harmonious relations between families of different faiths are emphasized in the episode *"Menyambut Hari Natal"* (Christmas Celebration), which foregrounds the Rahmats and the Sadikins calling on the Tambayong family to reciprocate the Christmas gifts they had taken around the neighborhood. To make sure no one misses the point, Ibu Rahmat reminds her husband that "they [the Tambayong family] always call on us at Idul Fitri." Pak Rahmat labors the point further when he agrees with his wife, saying,

The Rahmat Family 171

"yes, we must make sure we visit our neighbors; we live in one environment." And leaving no one in any doubt about religious harmony, Ibu Rahmat takes the chance to bring up an occasion when they had visited their (Balinese) friend Made during Hari Raya Galungan.[13] Earlier in the episode, Ibu Sadikin applauds Ibu Rahmat's decision to make a cake for the Tambayongs, saying that "as neighbors, we have to care for and nurture the harmony between us."

The denial of religious conflict, and the didactic style in which religious tolerance is emphasized (more like a Pancasila lesson from a school text than the way people ordinarily talk), opens the series to resistant readings prompted both by the absence of some religious faiths (particularly Confucianism, which has traditionally been a target in communal strife) and by the intrusion of public discourse into the private sphere. The repeated references to harmony seem to beg questions about lack of harmony and speak to a troubled field of religious relations in Indonesia.

A similar tendency to deny ethnic conflict rather than explore its dynamics is evident in the episode *"Loro Sae Selalu Dalam Hatiku"* (Loro Sae [Tetum: East Timor] Will Stay in My Heart Forever). This episode, like *"Bila Wader,"* is a fictional representation of a contemporary political issue. Its links with the Jakarta setting are extremely tenuous. With its unacknowledged subtext of communal violence, the episode sits uneasily with the much more innocuous domestic themes that engage the Jakarta community.

"Loro Sae" concerns Indonesia's annexation of East Timor. Pratomo decides to pursue a class research project in East Timor, saying that he does not want to do something like everyone else. His (Timorese) friend Espirito applauds Pratomo's decision, saying that his expatriate brother refuses to accept his objective assessment of the favorable situation in the province. Espirito says that Miguel will not change his views and will not come to visit the province to see for himself how things are. Espirito says, "It's hard to change the perceptions of others, especially if their views have been influenced by people from overseas." And later he suggests that only an objective, scientific approach will defeat the negativism of ill-informed and prejudiced opinions. "Negative views like this are everywhere. What's important is that we fight with science, with knowledge." "That's right," says Pratomo, "one view can only be challenged with another view." These opening scenes acknowledge the long-running dispute between Indonesia and the indigenous people of East Timor. They do so, however, in vague, nonspecific terms. Opposing views are attributed to people who are out of touch and lacking in knowledge, who have closed minds, and who have been influenced by presumably hostile foreigners.

Having acknowledged (and at the same time disparaged) conflicting views concerning East Timor's status, the narrative pays no further attention to the opposition view. The discourse of objectivity, of disinterested research, of weighing one perspective against another, is completely denied, as Pratomo follows his own limited exploration guided by regional officials. He does not initiate any discussion concerning local resistance to Indonesian rule with his informants, nor do his guides and newfound friends take up any issue that reflects on the politics of the annexation of the province.

On the contrary, seemingly every opportunity for praising the development of the province is relished. Passing soldiers wave cheerily to Pratomo, local officials assure him expansively that he is free to visit whatever village he chooses, and staff in the Dili library eagerly help him collect data on the province. Stopping at a tourist spot, Pratomo comments, "it seems that everything is peaceful and quiet here." In a letter home, he assures his family that the people are friendly, that their fears about the dangers of the province were groundless, and that provincial development is going well.

Helping his host family's daughter Cisca with her homework, Pratomo points out similarities between some local words and words in the Tapanuli language of Sumatra. He asks Cisca to count to ten and underlines similarities with Indonesian, implicitly suggesting that East Timor has close historical and cultural relations with Indonesia and that it is truly part of Indonesia. It is precisely this issue that is denied by those who oppose the incorporation of the territory into Indonesia.

What is obvious in this episode is the culturally and politically conditioned reluctance to engage with and exploit the dramatic potential of conflict for its entertainment value. As I showed in reference to ethnicity and religion in *"Sebuah Harmoni"* and *"Menyambut Hari Natal,"* the *"Loro Sae"* narrative is compromised by the denial of its own ideological premise. It opens up the possibility of a frank exchange of views on a controversial topic and then closes it off, consistently and insistently choosing instead to present a simplistic and idealized picture of a harmonious and prosperous community entirely comfortable with Indonesian administration.

The episode builds its idealization of East Timor as part of Indonesia on a highly ambiguous foundation. The production of Indonesia as a united, harmonious, developing nation requires the constant manufacture of Others, both within development ("backward provinces") and beyond it (foreign and "primitive" races and cultures). In this episode, Pratomo's nightmare before going to Timor, in which he finds himself at the edge of a cliff, staring down into the abyss, and his family's and friends' repeated expressions of fears for his safety in going to such a "dangerous place," reveal an anxiety about Timor's incorporation within the national cultural space. Pratomo's eager reports in letters home about the "rapid development" of Timor after "five hundred years of nothing" represent Timor as an emergent province, a province delivered from its primordial backwardness by Indonesia's modernizing national culture project. The annexation of Timor disturbed the boundaries of the nation by making visible their fluidity and arbitrariness. Annexation required the suppression of the fear of incorporation of the marginal, the primitive, and the backward into the national cultural space (Heider 1991, 108f; Anderson 1987, 73f). As Barbara Babcock says, "What is socially peripheral is often symbolically central" (cited in Stallybrass and White 1986, 20). Pratomo's nightmare transcodes fears of the introduction of heterogeneity and backwardness into the idealized unity of the nation onto the body of Pratomo. The intense anxiety produced by the desire to annex a marginal space and people is similarly transcoded into a narrative of Pratomo's desire for the Timorese Cisca, whose face had appeared in his nightmare. In the final scene, the transcoding shifts between the cultural categories of nation(al) space and body, center and margin, when Pratomo says to Cisca that "she and Loro Sae will stay in his heart forever."

Conclusion—The Model's Limits

Soap opera, as a genre of the personal and domestic sphere, is well known and popular in Indonesia. Soap opera is enjoyed because it speaks across the transnational cultural space to the conflictual nature of the personal sphere, which in Indonesia tends to be masked by an official ideology of interpersonal and communal harmony (Guiness 1986, 139f). Put another way, soap opera can be understood in part as compensatory entertainment, opening up the private sphere for public enjoyment through the mass media.

Todd Gitlin (1983, 75–76) has described television as a "recombinant form," drawing attention to adaptation as common practice in the American commercial television industry. Adaptation, and the integration of elements from different generic forms into a "new" hybrid form is not unusual and should not be understood as offending against the purity of any reified generic form. The adaptation of televisual forms cross-culturally does, however, complicate the process of production, given that producers work with different conceptions of the implied audience and assume different cultural competencies in their implied audiences.

Like its American models, *Keluarga Rahmat* speaks to the private, personal sphere and presumes that viewers will have the cultural competence necessary for reading the genre. Producers included in *Keluarga Rahmat* a number of episodes that assumed a different interpretive competence from the original American form and from the episodes set in the Jakarta suburbs. The episodes set in provincial locations and the episodes that focused on political issues such as transmigration and development in East Timor assumed viewers who were competent in the generic codes of information giving and current affairs. In the Indonesian setting, the intersection of codes of official, public culture with the codes of personal relations and the domestic sphere created generic instability, a blurring of soap and documentary genres, pulling viewers across a distinction in the Indonesian lifeworld that is fundamental. The resistance expressed by viewers, which I discussed above, can be understood as resistance to the colonization of the private sphere by official, state-driven culture.

The irruption of the public sphere inside the private sphere also occurred within episodes ostensibly framed by the codes of personal relations and the domestic sphere. Viewers objected to the sermonizing speeches of the (male) characters Rahmat and Sadikin. The lack of complexity in characters, the insertion of recorded segments of President Soeharto speaking as if he were part of the fictional text, and the inclusion of real events within the fictional text all challenged viewers' cultural and generic expectations of the series. The decision to produce *Keluarga Rahmat* as an episodic series while retaining just a few story lines as ongoing impelled episodes toward the containment or resolution of interpersonal and community conflict rather than its suspension, a characteristic of soap opera that offers viewers space to become involved in the unfolding of the narrative.

Keluarga Rahmat modeled New Order community too successfully. People didn't like what they saw. The Jakarta community was read not as exemplary but as a feudalization of their lifeworld. While individuals and communities may find it difficult in the real world to object to the intrusion of official culture into the private sphere, they can object to its representation on television by not watching, by complaining about the show, or by extracting their own pleasures in resistant reading of characters and episodes. Viewers felt patronized by an overly simplistic and idealized portrait of daily life, and they were frustrated by a series that promised the pleasures of popular entertainment but delivered instead a confusing and aesthetically lumpy package of domestic drama interlaced with documentary segments and "stifling advice."

Chapter 6

GOOD NEWS: NATIONAL DEVELOPMENT AND THE CULTURE OF NEWS

NEWS PROGRAMS IN WESTERN COUNTRIES tend to foreground their presenters and reporters as stars and to concentrate on the activities of elite institutions and the activities of newsmakers—a disparate group composed of politicians from home and related "elite" nations, the rich and famous, international sports and pop stars, and, occasionally, the ordinary person. Western news programs overwhelmingly present news that is in some ways "bad news" (Hartley 1982; Glasgow Media Group 1976, 1980, 1982). To anyone familiar with this kind of news programming, the *National News* (Berita Nasional) on TVRI from 1962 to 1991 appeared very different. There were many items concerning newsmakers, but the newsmaker group was far more restricted. It generally consisted of the president, vice president, ministers, high-ranking military officers, and state bureaucrats. With the exception of official visitors, it was very rare for a person from a foreign country to feature in a national news bulletin.

TVRI news is based on what Denis McQuail (1994, 131) has called "development media theory," which emphasizes the following goals: (1) the primacy of the national development task (economic, social, cultural, and political), (2) the pursuit of cultural and informational autonomy, (3) support for democracy, and (4) solidarity with other developing countries.

While the idea of supporting democracy as such is not part of TVRI's brief, the other goals are clearly part of TVRI's news culture.[1] The way TVRI's news contributes to the achievement of the first two goals will be explored throughout this chapter. The objective of forging solidarity with other developing countries is pursued formally in the television context in part through the mechanism of Asia Vision News (AVN), a news exchange program sponsored by the Asia Pacific Broadcasting Union. TVRI's *World News* is an edited assembly of items sourced from overseas and accessed through Intelsat. TVRI's coordinator of news teleconferencing said, however, that AVN items were mostly unsuitable for the *World News* as "they are too much like our news—ribbon cutting and the like!" (Kelly Saputrohamijoyo, personal interview, 8 April 1993).

In the period under investigation, TVRI news presenters remained modestly in the background and were usually not identified by name during the bulletin. News reporters were shadowy figures, disembodied voices most of the time, and they very rarely spoke straight to camera on location, forgoing the hallmark practice of Western television reporters whose direct-to-camera reports are designed to validate that they are "on-the-spot." In this respect Indonesian news recalls older forms of television news presentation from the 1950s and 1960s, before news became a pivotal component of the prime-time schedule.

But while Indonesian bulletins share something with Western news bulletins in their emphasis on elite figures, it is the ceremonial content of the news, the very high representation of state officials in news items, and the convention of giving equal or more than equal time on screen to nonelite people involved in ceremonial events that clearly indicate that a distinctive news culture operates in Indonesia. This chapter explores that culture of news, examines the ideological work performed by *Berita Nasional* on TVRI, and assesses the legacy of this practice for an emerging paradigm of news that is closer to the so-called Western model, bringing Indonesian television into line with news values of the print media and print journalism.

TVRI's news broadcasts have been consistently criticized within Indonesia over the past thirty years, but they still score well when viewers are asked about the program they watch most or most enjoy.[2] The *National News* and *World News* programs were rated as the two "most watched" programs across all demographics in Chu, Alfian, and Schramm's 1982 study (1991, 60). The Department of Information's national survey in 1989/90 showed that *World News* was the most popular program in the "News and Information" program classification. The *National News* rated third after *Dari Desa Ke Desa,* a program about village life (Departemen Penerangan 1989/90, 41, 49). Survey Research Indonesia's news tracking analysis shows that about 60 percent of households apparently prefer to watch *Berita Nasional* on TVRI rather than on RCTI (about 32 percent) or the Second Channel (SRI 1992). We might interpret this as an indication of the authoritative position TVRI has built for itself as a news provider, noting that both RCTI and the Second Channel show exactly the same bulletin at exactly the same time.

While *World News,* with its largely imported content and information style of journalism has been consistently preferred to the *National News,* TVRI has ignored the criticisms and has continued with the kind of bulletins I have described above. The following critical comments, made almost twenty years apart, are revealing:

> There are more than enough news stories about development. For example, Minister A or B or even Director General A or B opens a bridge, harvests the first head of rice—essentially any official ceremony attended by high status figures is covered.

> Eventually people become bored watching these items over and over again. The reason being that often what is emphasized is not the development project itself, its function, its orientation, its significance for the local community and so on, but instead the Minister or the Director General. (*Kompas,* 25 August 1970)

> The most obvious weakness [in TVRI's programs] is the regional and national news broadcasts. They are not far from being simply ribbon-cutting ceremonies or marketing ceremonies to launch

something, export goods, for example. Perhaps themes like this can be covered, but because their presentation is unprofessional, they become uninteresting. (*Media Indonesia,* 18 August 1991)

Here Is the News in December 1991

This chapter is a case study of a particular news practice that dominated Indonesian television for many years but is now being eclipsed as the commercial channels develop their own "soft news" programs. While aspects of the old news style remain, TVRI has modified its news-gathering practices and style in response to the success of programs such as RCTI's *Seputar Indonesia* (Around Indonesia), which I discuss in detail in chapter 8. In 1991 TVRI broadcasted four news bulletins a day: (1) *Berita Nusantara* (Local and Regional News, at 5 P.M.), *Berita Nasional* (National News, at 7 P.M.), *Dunia Dalam Berita* (World News, at 9 P.M.) and *Berita Terakhir* (Late News, at about 11 P.M.). The second TVRI channel, Programa Dua, presents a half-hour English-language news service at 6:30 P.M. for Jakarta metropolitan viewers. Commercial channels and the Second Channel are obliged to schedule *Berita Nasional* and *Dunia Dalam Berita* in line with TVRI's scheduling, but they have more leeway in fitting the other bulletins into their own schedules.

The analysis in this chapter focuses on *Berita Nasional* bulletins, with some reference to *Dunia Dalam Berita* bulletins. The analysis is based on a random sample of two "constructed weeks" (Heidt 1984; Jones and Carter 1959) of news bulletins broadcast during December 1991.[3] A total of 205 news items were broadcast during the fourteen days sampled. If the daily weather report, program identification, and reading of lead story headlines are excluded from consideration, there remained 177 news items for close study. Each item was timed, its shot sequence plotted, and items were categorized in terms of the kind of event reported on. The content of items was categorized following the categorization used by Alfian and Chu in an earlier study (1981, 89–90). Where no ceremonial event was featured, and "actuality" footage dominated, the item was categorized as a "film report."

An outline of the categories used and the tally of the frequency of each category broadcast are presented in appendix H and tables 6.1 and 6.2. To summarize those data, 54.7 percent of news items involved a report on a ceremonial event, and state officials played key roles in 53.52 percent of all news items; 41 percent of all items were concerned with development activities.[4] A tally was taken of who it was who played "key roles" in news items.[5] If a government minister, another cabinet-rank officer, and a provincial government official all played key roles in a particular item, for example, it was given a value of only one in the tally. This slightly deflated the role played by state officials, but not significantly. State officials played key roles in just over half of all news items.

Table 6.1
Frequency of Different Categories of News Items

News Item	Week A		Week B	
	No.	%	No.	%
Film report	40	40.40	28	26.66
Report	3	3.03	1	0.95
Visit	5	5.05	11	10.47
Meeting	9	9.09	18	17.14
Speech	14	14.14	11	10.47
Signing	3	3.03	8	7.61
Press conference	0	0	6	5.71

	Week A		Week B	
News Item	No.	%	No.	%
Courtesy call	1	1.01	2	1.90
Award presentation	4	4.04	3	2.85
Vox pop	2	2.02	1	0.95
TVRI	18	18.18	16	15.23
Total	99	100*	105	100*
* rounded				

Although the wives of the president and vice president are not strictly state officials, they are considered to hold First and Second Lady status in Indonesia. The presence of the president's or vice president's wife at a function was not sufficient grounds for including them as playing a key role. They were only counted when they performed a key role in their own right. On all occasions, they performed this role in the absence of their husbands.

Finally, the setting of news items was examined and presented in two robust categories: Jakarta or elsewhere (see table 6.3). Overall, 64.49 percent of items shot outside the studio were set in Jakarta. On 10 of the 14 days surveyed, news items set in Jakarta accounted for at least 60 percent of all items not set in the studio. On one day of the eleven, the figure reached 100 percent, and on another, 85 percent. On the three days when the figure was less than 50 percent, the figures were 20, 38, and 46 percent, meaning that Jakarta was the setting for at least one out of every five items. These figures reveal a clear bias in the setting of news items and reflect the dominant role of the center of political and administrative power in what makes "news" in Indonesia. The figures are consistent with the findings of Alfian, Nnaemeka, and Pabottinggi (Alfian and Chu 1981, 91–92), who surveyed TVRI news bulletins thirteen years earlier during April 1978. They found that urban settings accounted for 49.1 percent of news items and that 63.1 percent of those "urban" items were set in Jakarta and West Java.

Table 6.2
Frequency of Appearance of State Officials in Key Roles in News Items

Week A	Day 1	2	3	4	5	6	7	Total
Frequency	1	9	4	6	6	8	7	41
No. of items	13	16	12	13	15	16	14	99
Week B	Day 1	2	3	4	5	6	7	Total
Frequency	6	7	10	8	8	8	3	50
No. of items	13	14	17	15	16	14	16	105

Notes: For week A, 41/99 = 41.41%. If station identification and weather reports (18) are deducted from the total number of news items broadcast, then state officials performed key roles in 41 out of 81 items, or in 50.61% of items.

For week B, 51/105 = 48.57%. If station identification and weather reports (16) are deducted from the total number of news items broadcast, then state officials performed key roles in 50 out of 89 items, or in 56.17% of items.

State officials in key roles: week A + week B: 41 + 50 / 170 = 53.52%.

* State officials may include any of the following: president, vice president, wife of the president or vice president, minister, cabinet-rank officer, chief of the armed forces, provincial government officer.

Table 6.3
Setting of News Items in Jakarta or Elsewhere

Date (Dec. 1991)	Total No. of Items	No. of Items Set in the Studio	No. of Items Set in Jakarta	Jakarta Items as Percentage of Total
4	13	2	8	72.7
5	16	2	10	71.4
6	16	3	5	38.4
7	17	2	10	66.6
11	15	2	8	61.5
13	14	3	7	63.6
14	14	2	9	75
16	16	4	7	58.3
17	16	3	12	85.7
22	13	3	2	20
26	15	2	6	46.1
29	13	3	7	70
30	14	2	12	100
31	12	2	6	60
Total	204	35	109	64.49

My findings confirm a long-term emphasis on state officials and ceremonial events in the news. There are some signs, however, that the emphasis on ceremonialism, which built up over the 1980s, has declined slightly in recent years. This may be related to the more competitive news environment of the 1990s, where ceremonialism in TVRI news has come under pressure from the more instrumental, information-focused news programs of the commercial channels. I return to this issue in chapter 8.

The 1991 figures on news items about development activities (41 percent) were significantly higher than the figure of 27.5 percent cited in Alfian and Chu (1981, 90) for news broadcasts in

April 1978. However, Sumita Tobing's study (1991) of "development news" content in *Berita Nusantara, Berita Nasional,* and *Dunia Dalam Berita* bulletins over fourteen days in 1990 is much closer to the 1991 results. Tobing showed that development news items accounted for 54.7 percent of all news items and that government officials were "prominent actors" in 55.7 percent of development and nondevelopment news items (1991, 98, 102).

My findings are also generally consistent with data presented in a 1982 study. Arswendo Atmowiloto noted that of the total of 909 news items broadcast on TVRI's five news programs during April 1982, 68 percent were items concerning "official openings" of development projects (1986, 35–41).

The viewer who complained in 1970 about seeing too much of Minister A and Director General B, the quantitative study here, and those by Alfian and Chu, Arswendo Atmowiloto, and Tobing all show that for the last twenty years the national news on TVRI has persisted with a ceremonial form and content focused largely on ritual celebration of the development activities and ethos of the government. The national news has been a prime vehicle for the symbolic representation of the central significance of development in the national culture project. A passage in the twenty-second anniversary commemorative booklet underlines the development news values the various empirical studies have revealed: "News and features aimed at encouraging development and the spirit of unity are considered high priority, while sensationalism and exploitation of violent, destructive or negative incidents are discouraged" (TVRI 1984, 61).

Ritual Forms and Structures in Television News

James Carey introduced the idea of ritual in communication in an influential article in 1975.[6]

A ritual view of communication is not directed toward the extension of messages in space but the maintenance of society in time; not the act of imparting information but the representation of shared beliefs. It does not see the original or highest manifestation of communication in the transmission of intelligent information but in the construction and maintenance of an ordered, meaningful cultural world which can serve as a control and container for human action. (Carey 1989, 18)

These comments are very useful in thinking about news programming. Each night, news bulletins strive to present "new" facts, names, and events, but while the details change from day to day, "the news" is framed within an enduring conventional format (Bird and Dardenne 1988). My argument is that it is the form and structure of the news as a program and the visual practices that are characteristically used in the presentation of news stories that symbolically transcend the instrumental functions of reporting and information giving. Together they construct the news as a ritual reinforcement of central social, cultural, and political values.

This kind of approach, however, has not been applied in the analysis of news programs in Indonesia, nor has a multilevel analysis of the visual syntagms of television news and news programming been attempted previously. In the analysis of TVRI news that follows, I show how the dominant ideologies of state hierarchy and national development are discursively constructed as rituals in a variety of visual forms. I also show how the rituals are articulated together with second-order significations of (particularly) Javanese culture. In this way they "take on additional, more active ideological dimensions" (Hall 1980, 133). The encoding of preferred meanings in codes that privilege Javanese culture and institutions may, however, be a source of slippage in the decoding of preferred meanings, as many non-Javanese, and even many contemporary Javanese, may not share or accept codes that idealize a golden age of Javanese culture and social relations.

On the reception side, David Morley suggests that "for many viewers, ... watching and engaging in a joint ritual with millions of others can be argued to be at least as important as any informational content gained from the broadcast" (1992, 268). Benedict Anderson makes the same point, writing about the power of the daily newspaper to merge public and private concerns in an "extraordinary *mass ceremony*" of reading that becomes the means of imagining the national community (1991, 350; my emphasis). Antlov, in one of the very few reports of the reception of television in Indonesia, affirms Morley's proposition:

> The formal—to an outsider even tedious—character of television programmes ... could perhaps hamper the dissemination of the government's messages. But the formality and orchestrated repetitiveness of the cultural indoctrination have their own powers. Residents of Sariendah can recognise and identify themselves with the peasants who attended the meeting on television. The Jakarta celebrations of major national events are broadcast on television, often with tens of thousands of people participating. Because it is shared by a larger community, loyalty towards the rulers takes on a deeper meaning. (Antlov 1995, 60)

Antlov's comments suggest that we can understand Indonesian television news as both like and unlike television news in the United States, the United Kingdom, and Australia. Indonesia has taken one element of the television repertoire—royal weddings, presidential inaugurations, state funerals, America's Cup triumphs, and the like—and turned these spectacles into something more routine rather than regular but intermittent. It has also sought to render them quotidian, thereby taking the place of other "news" stories that also bind the community together, or organize its dissent.

The value in looking at the news as ritual is that it draws attention away from the informational content of the news, which has been a long-term and almost overriding concern in research on television news (Griffin 1992). "News as ritual" directs attention to the visual form and structure of news bulletins, interpreting the news as a symbolic construct that performs an ideological and political function. In the words of historians Cannadine and Price, "Politics and ceremonial are not separate subjects, the one serious, the other superficial. Ritual is not the mask of force but is itself a type of power" (cited in Schulte Nordholt 1991, 5).

Visual Syntagms in News Bulletins

The customary visual structure of TVRI ceremonial news items is as follows:
- Introduction by studio presenter
- Video footage that establishes the scene or location
- Establishing shots, zooms, and pans that present the actors to the viewers
- Voice-over throughout by studio presenter
- Occasional sound bites of the key figure speaking
- Occasional sound bites from "door stop" interviews (a live interview conducted as the speaker is caught leaving a building) with key actor

This structure is less dynamic than the characteristic visual form of American or Australian news stories. Interaction between the reporter on the spot and the studio is not part of the everyday grammar of TVRI news. TVRI news reporters do not generally work with satellite hookups that enable the "live" exchanges of American broadcasts to take place. But it is not just technological or financial considerations that make the grammar of TVRI bulletins different. The different symbolic value of one format compared with another has to be understood in order to develop a more nuanced understanding of the different news conventions operating.

Michael Griffin has shown that American news broadcasts have a characteristic visual structure that puts control of the news firmly in the hands of the network and its reporters, projecting the news institution as the source of action (1992, 133). Griffin argues that the visual structure serves the promotional needs of the networks, rather than an information function (139). Daniel Hallin has shown in his analysis of television reporting of election campaigns that the length of "sound-bites" (recorded words of candidates or other key actors) declined from an average of 60 seconds in 1968 to 8.5 seconds in 1988. He relates the change not to any practice or desire to include more sound bites in news reports but to the increasingly intrusive role of the journalist and network in "packaging" news: "Modern TV news is much more *mediated* than the TV news of the 1960's and 1970's. During the earlier period the journalist's role as a communicator was relatively passive.... Today [candidates'] words ... are treated as raw material to be taken apart, combined with other sounds and images, and reintegrated into another narrative" (Hallin 1992, 9–10, emphasis in original).

TVRI news in the early 1990s is much more like the American news of the 1960s and '70s. Rather than simply being "out-of-date," however, the TVRI structure keeps the control and mediation of the news as much in the hands, voices, and presence of the newsmakers as possible (over half of whom were state officials). News is part of the public relations activities of state officials and departments, who use it to promote aspects of the national culture project for which they are responsible. News bulletins are rituals of power. The television institution is positioned as a servant of, or a publicity vehicle for, government priorities. The ideological work performed by the emphasis on hierarchy and development is significant and powerful, and in Indonesia it is achieved almost through a denial of the journalist's role, rather than with their explicit or obvious assistance.

To understand how the mythology of hierarchy is ritually constructed and naturalized on TVRI news, it is necessary to shuffle systematically the scale of analysis (the order in which this is done is unimportant). I begin, for example, with an analysis of the micro-practices of the news stories embedded in the bulletin and then examine the shape of the bulletin as Griffen has done. I then pull focus so as to understand that *Berita Nasional* is part of a more extended programming syntagm (flow). The flow structures viewers' frame of news reference in a kind of cyclic news journey or pilgrimage, sweeping the audience's point of reference from the local, to the national, to the international, before finally bringing it back home again in the *Late News*. For practical reasons these different levels of analysis have to be performed separately but need to be shuffled together so that the significations embedded in one level of the television flow can be seen as contributing to the signification of others. For, as Roland Barthes says, "To understand a narrative is not only to follow the process of the story, it is also to recognise in it certain 'stages,' to project the horizontal concatenations of the narrative 'thread' on an implicitly vertical axis; to read (to hear) a narrative is not only to pass from one word to the next, but also to pass from one level to the next" (1988, 102).

One example of the layered density of the significations in TVRI's news programming is the contribution that the *World News* program, with its far higher quantum of "bad news," makes toward reinforcing the *National News* construct of Indonesia as a peaceful, progressive, developing country where the state has everything in control, compared with the rest of the world, which appears constantly chaotic. Taken together, these two different bulletins may be read as ritualizing, night after night, a basic opposition between Indonesia and its Others. The return to domestic news in the *Late News* bulletin rescues the viewers from the disturbing images of chaos characteristic of the *World News* and incorporates them in a social order in which everyone has a clearly defined place, and where the state's key role is the betterment of the people's welfare. Through this structure Indonesian state authorities attempt to reinforce ideas of Indonesia's identity and uniqueness in an increasingly globalized television environment. In the final sections of the chapter I show how the construction of Indonesia's uniqueness is reinforced through visual references that resonate with idealized images and memories of "traditional culture."

One point of slippage in the TVRI news strategy is that the regular production of another news model within the TVRI schedule socializes editors, presenters, and audience into a different set of news values, making them dissatisfied with a domestic television news coverage, which cannot match that of the press. The popularity of the *World News* bulletin and the long-running criticism of the ceremonial content and style of *Berita Nasional* suggests that the desire to create a sense of cultural identity and uniqueness in this way has not been wholly successful.

Social Hierarchy and Bulletin Structure

In both Western and Indonesian news programs bulletins are introduced in such a way as to cue the audience that the first few items in the bulletin have a particular significance, or are more important. In Indonesia this is typically done by the female news presenter announcing the "main stories" or "lead stories" immediately following the program identification, and then handing the lead story to her male colleague to present in full. *Berita Nasional* bulletins are presented by two readers, one male and one female. The female presenter introduced the bulletin on all occasions, and the male presenter always carried the lead story. The two readers alternate their reading throughout the bulletin. Despite the conscientious and consistent gender balance displayed over presentation of the news, not one of the items surveyed over the fourteen-day period featured a woman in a key role, and no female voices were accessed on screen.

While Indonesia shares with Western nations the conventional practice of structuring bulletins with a number of "lead" stories, it does not use the same criteria in determining what items will lead a bulletin. John Hartley suggests that in the "north-western corner of the world" news items are prioritized within bulletins by reference to the general news values of the different items (1982, 76–79). In Indonesia the organizing principle is simpler and less ambiguous. Generally it is the relative political and bureaucratic status of the key figures involved in an item that determines its position in the order of presentation. This order of items naturalizes the mythology of state hierarchy and patriarchy in the way reports involving high-status officials are given priority in order of presentation and in the way that the male presenter always reads the items that are considered "most important." In this way, as

Clifford Geertz puts it, news ritual provides both a "model of" and a "model for" social relations (1968, 7).

The forms and language of the national news in Indonesia are an amalgam of historically and culturally specific signifiers, codes, and practices. TVRI producers discursively construct news bulletins that can be fully understood only in terms of the policies and values of the New Order state in Indonesia. For, as Virginia Nightingale says, "A television programme holds within its structure signs of the history and culture which produced it" (1996, 125). In the section that follows I describe the visual grammar of elements of news bulletins, preparing the way to link these ritual forms to the history and culture of their production in the section on cultural resonances.

Ritual Forms in TVRI News: Report, Meeting, Visit, and the Missing Journalist

In this section I describe three examples of visual rituals in TVRI news—the report, the meeting, and the visit forms and then relate these forms to the missing journalist in TVRI news. I describe these visual structures as rituals first because they are conventional forms that are habitually repeated. An audience may retain little in terms of specific information from the forms I describe below, but as David Morley argues, an audience "may well retain general definitions of the order of things—ideological categories embedded in the structure of the specific content" (1992, 80). In the two weeks of broadcasts, the three forms accounted for 21 percent (week A) and 33 percent (week B) of news items excluding TVRI announcements (see table 6.1). Second, the forms are rituals because of the symbolic work they perform in circulating cultural meanings. They are channeled spectacles of the pervasive mythology and development priorities of the New Order state, expressing and reexpressing a fixed set of hierarchical relations. They perform and display proper relations between the state and its citizens. The rituals naturalize the unequal distribution of power and influence within society while still suggesting that no one, however humble, is overlooked or without a place in the overall system of social relations.

In the report (Laporan) form one or more individuals are shown making a verbal report to a high-status figure, usually the president or vice president, or occasionally the wife of the president or vice president. In the case of reports to the president or vice president, it is only ministers of state, or especially commissioned groups such as the Commission of Enquiry set up to report on the Dili massacre, who are shown making reports. On 12 November 1991 Indonesian troops opened fire on Timorese demonstrators who had gathered at the Santa Cruz Cemetary. Between 18 and 100 people were killed. (See Schwarz 1994, 211–29). These rituals clearly construct the president as the highest-ranking officer of state, someone to whom all others report. Viewers are given vicarious access to a privilege that it is obvious only the highest-ranking officers of state are normally granted.

The report ritual is visually the simplest of the three forms. The ritual usually begins in either one of two ways. In the first, in a wide shot we see the person who is to make the report ushered into the presence of the higher-status actor through a cluster of aides. The point of view is that of the higher-status actor. The aides, their deferential demeanor, and the wide shot of the reception area with its huge doors all combine richly to inscribe ideas of power and high status. In the second case, we intrude as it were into the thick of the reporting session without any of the orienting shots described above. The camera angles tend to take the point of view of the subordinate actor, looking toward his superior, who is listening intently. This constructs a more intense, almost intimidating situation.

As the reporting proceeds, alternating shots of both actors are shown in medium close-up, rarely in close-up. The viewer, however, has no access to the actual words spoken, as all details of the event are relayed in voice-over by the news presenter. On one occasion, this practice of holding the audience at arm's length from the event was taken one step further. No footage of the reporting session was screened, but two ministers who had just reported to the president sat outside the audience hall and described to journalists the matters they had reported on to the president. In this case the viewers were given an even more abstract, vicarious quality of access to the president, a practice that clearly signifies the unequal access that different members of the state have to its highest officers. It can also be read, paradoxically, in line with Javanese ideas of power, as an image of the formlessness, the invisibility of power, and the unseen, inner-derived center of control over the external world exercised by legitimate authority (Anderson 1972, 7).

Status differences are also signified in the characteristic way each person involved in the ritual behaves. An active/passive dualism is constructed. The person reporting is deferential, sitting well forward in his chair, and usually has with him a sheaf of notes. He is seen to present his case briefly and seriously. The superior remains almost silent, listening intently. He carries no notes, and his whole demeanor expresses a capacity to calmly absorb what is presented to him, a perfect embodiment of the figure Geertz, quoting Elliott, describes as the "still point of the turning world" (Geertz 1980, 130).

In the meeting (Rapat) form, two groups of actors are shown spatially separated but in close interaction. One group, "the audience," is usually much more numerous than the other. The audience is shown seated, never standing, facing the smaller group, shown facing them, frequently raised above the level of the audience on a dais.

TVRI's usual practice in visualizing these events is to begin the item with a wide shot of the auditorium or meeting venue, one or two very brief shots of the audience, and then go closer in for a medium close-up or pan along what we might call the "status group" seated on the dais. The camera will then pick out the actor who is to play the key role during the event. The view then shifts to the audience, and anything up to twelve different shots of the audience present will be screened. These shots are often pans across the rows of seated participants, but the camera operator takes care to make the faces picked out clear and personal. Some coverage of the audience will be in close-up, making members present immediately recognizable. This is the kind of visual practice with which we have become familiar from events such as the Australian Film Awards, the Oscars, and even international tennis tournaments. On those occasions, there are many roving shots of the audience as the camera looks for "celebrities" to pick out.

The shot will then return to the status group or key actor if he or she is presenting a speech. The speaker is often identified or "nominated" on screen by a superimposed title that gives his or her name and affiliation. Voice-over throughout the item informs the viewer as to what is going on, and sometimes a sound bite will be taken from the key actor's speech. In meeting rituals, the audience is the passive group, the status group is clearly in control of the event. The camera, however, is more active and devotes more time to visualizing the audience, rather than the status group. The audience is shown sitting patiently and passively, attentive but not particularly so. There was no indication in any of the items analyzed that the audience ever interacts directly with the status group.

Venues that do not allow clear spatial separation of the status group from the audience or others participating in the meeting cause confusion. In the parliamentary commission working sessions, for example, seating for the four factions of the parliament is usually arranged so that they face each other on four sides of a square. Reports of these meetings often appear confused as the camera attempts to provide a balanced representation of the factions. But this is not done in such a way that the viewer can get a clear understanding of the distribution of the factions. While these DPR meetings are obviously different from the kind of meetings described above, the visual confusion in these scenes is evidence of a certain feeling of unease with nonhierarchical, representative structures. It is as if there is no common agreement, no visual language, as to how more egalitarian social relations can or should be encoded.

A variant of the meeting form is the speech (Sambutan) form, where a high-status (usually government) figure delivers a speech to a seated audience. The inscription of hierarchy on these occasions is often more diffused than in the meeting form, as the speech form is one that often involves the private sector more than the government sector. The speech form is visualized in ways similar to the meeting form.

In the visit (Kunjungan) form, the viewer is presented with images of a group of about fifteen to twenty people accompanying a high-status individual who visits a particular location "in the field" such as a rural village or project site or some other location such as a factory or customs warehouse. The visual shape of the group resolves invariably into a "spearhead," with the high-status figure shown leading the group in an active manner. The attendant group trails behind the status figure, and only the few close to the leader can communicate directly with him (most ministers are men). The majority of the group usually appears to have no other objective in mind apart from simply following the leader. The size of the entourage and its aimlessness signify its dependent relationship with the group leader.

The visit group is usually shown in medium shot from a vantage point in front of the group as it moves around the field site. This practice constructs the visit group as a spearhead, with the high-status figure positioned at the head of the group, signifying his leadership qualities and his active, practical, energetic approach in monitoring and encouraging national development. At other times the camera positions itself in order to show the minister asking questions of the people from the visit site. In medium close-up, the key figure is presented asking questions and taking a keen interest in what he is being shown.

The visual trademark of the visit ritual is the close focus on the key actor in the midst of what is often a visually exciting location. The viewer is held back from enjoying the visualization of all sorts of craft activities, manufacturing processes, and the like by the camera's insistent swing onto the key actor and his apparent interest and enthusiasm for what he is inspecting.

In some visit rituals, the high status of the visitor and his entourage is expressed by including shots of people from the field site performing welcoming rituals such as dances and presentations.

Such rituals break the flow of visit rituals as they turn the active group leader into a passive observer. The symbolic and elaborate expression of status differences seems, however, to outweigh the benefits to be gained from editing out these rites of deference. They create what Victor Turner (1969, 48) called "multi-vocal" symbols, where the visit, which may be read as a rite of responsible government, becomes at the same time a rite that draws attention to rural-urban differences and the status differences between ordinary folk in the field and visiting dignitaries from the center of power.

One aspect of the visual style of the three ritual forms I have described is that television journalists and cameras "look on" rather than take part in actively structuring what happens. In one sense this is more illusory than real, as the coverage of the events and the editing of footage afterward are in the hands of the television team. Even so, we might say that news is "covered" in Indonesia, it is not "made." The insistent thrust of microphones and cameras, an unmistakable visual reminder of the mediation of "news events" in competitive media environments, is absent in Indonesia. Until recently there was only one crew covering events. In part the passive visual style of the news is a reflection of the monopoly TVRI enjoys. More significantly, it is an indication that the power in the news rituals lies with the performers and not with the news institution.

Unmediated News: The Missing Journalist in TVRI News

In this section I look very briefly at the visual representation of the interaction between the "on-the-spot" reporter and key subjects in TVRI news items. Attention will be restricted to meeting and speech events. In seventeen of the fifty two (33 percent) meeting and speech items analyzed, the TVRI journalist successfully gained a brief "door stop" or "grab" interview with the key actor. Interviews occurred in about 43 percent of film reports, and 50 percent of visit items. In these items, the interview style is very similar to that described below.

The visual format of TVRI's grab interviews foregrounds the key actor and not the journalist. There is no shot-reverse-shot sequence to visualize the question and answer session between the journalist and the subject. Apart from a very brief establishing shot that shows the journalist with the interviewee (and occasionally other journalists from the print media), the journalist is hardly visualized at all. Even the hand-held microphone the journalist uses is kept as much out of the frame as possible. The questions the journalist asks are not included in the news item, not even in voice-over. The viewer hears only the subject's response and is therefore unaware whether the reply is appropriate or not. Viewers are not able to judge what kinds of questions, or how many questions, on what topic, the journalist asked.

It is for these reasons that I have described TVRI news reporters as shadowy, disembodied figures. The position constructed for the reporter is that of a gap, an absence, a nonintrusive, literally self-effacing nonpresence whose questions, it appears, are not as important as the subject's response. The exception to this practice is the press conference, where print, radio, and TVRI journalists are shown interviewing a key figure. On these occasions, the exchange of questions and answers is presented in the final edit, and the dialogic process more familiar from *World News* bulletins is incorporated into the national news. But press conferences are the exception. In the present sample, there were just six press conference items out of the total of 177. Three of the six were focused on one topic, with questions put to three different key actors one after the other.

The TVRI reporter's role appears to be almost entirely that of information gatherer. The reporter never speaks directly to camera to hand back an item to the studio at the end of a report. Nor do reporters ever contribute their own opinions on a subject as part of the news item. TVRI journalists are not built up into "personalities" in the way that Australian journalists such as Jana Wendt, Indira Naidu, or George Negus are. TVRI journalists do not feature on the covers of popular magazines, nor do they join chat shows or perform as "celebrities" on popular occasions. Both inside and outside their news roles, TVRI journalists are largely absent.

The conventional form of the door-stop interview as practiced in Indonesia, then, is another ritual that expresses hierarchical and deferential relations. The effacement of the reporter performs three symbolic closures. It contributes, first, to the impression that TVRI news is unmediated, that it is a transparent visualization of "what actually happened." Second, it constructs the illusion that the ordinary person (viewer) has access to "their" president or minister. The figure of power is both majestic (and distant), but also immediately available or present to all. The president can be imagined as speaking "to me." Third, the effacement of the reporter is a sign of a nonconfrontational, nonadversarial system, a system in which key actors are shown to be subject only minimally to the scrutiny of the media. A hint of accountability is retained in the door-stop format, but the dynamics of the interview are not preserved in the final edit. The absence of the reporter's questions constructs whatever response the key actor makes as an additional contribution to discussion, generously given in the midst of a busy schedule, out of consideration for a wider audience, rather than an answer motivated by a question. The format denies an acceptance of a general right to question high-status actors. While paradoxically making the high-status actor seem available in a direct way to the viewer, the reporter's door-stop interview may be read as the site of a struggle in TVRI news, a struggle to determine which kinds of interactions between high-status figures and citizens are proper and which are intrusive cases of *lèse majesté*.

Cultural Resonances of the Television Rituals

The ideological work TVRI news performs through the visual forms described can be examined by looking at ways in which news producers select and appropriate particular cultural codes as part of their encoding practice to reinforce the inscription of hierarchy and positively affirm the value of national development. The intertextual references in news to an idealized classical (Gesick 1983), (particularly) Javanese society and culture aim at naturalizing hierarchical structures and state involvement and control of national development. In this section I show that this ideological work is articulated by inscribing in the news formal parallels between valued indigenous traditions and contemporary practices and social relations.

In *Islam Observed* (1968), and twelve years later more extensively in *Negara* (1980), Clifford Geertz used the phrase "theatre state" to describe the way the Javanese Indic state and the nineteenth-century Balinese state displayed their understanding of the ultimate nature of reality through an "endless re-expression of a fixed set of symbolic relations" (1980, 113). State rituals were expressions of the fundamental belief that spirituality was unequally distributed throughout the material world and that the king was the most spiritual of all men, a mediator between this world and the world of the gods. The lofty superiority, spiritual grace, and knowledge of the king were defined contrastively by the lowliness and spiritual backwardness of the peasants. Geertz's work on the "theatre state" has been criticized in anthropological literature for overemphasizing the religious aspect of the rites and for giving insufficient attention to the politics of state ritual in Bali in the nineteenth century (Tambiah 1985; Schulte Nordholt 1991, 9). In my analysis of contemporary ritual, the focus is on the imbrication of secular politics in ceremony and the appropriation by state authorities of familiar ritual forms as a way of endowing television news bulletins with symbolic power and reinforcing their political and cultural goals.

Geertz was undoubtedly aware of this link. He suggested very briefly that there were signs that the theater state had been re-created in recent Indonesian history, particularly in the Guided Democracy period. He noted further that even "the so-called 'New Order' in Indonesia is already beginning to evince some of the traits of Sukarno-like theatricalism" (1968, 89). The ethnographic work of Teruo Sekimoto (1990) and Hans Antlov (1995, 60–67) confirms

Geertz's apprehensions. Anthropologist Henk Schulte Nordholt comes to a similar conclusion: "The paradox of the New Order is that the state emerges as a modern state aimed at economic development, and simultaneously creates 'timeless,' traditional means to assert its authority" (1991, 41).

A second point of interest for this discussion is Geertz's idea of "sinking status"—his observation that rituals of hierarchy had a conventional form and were repeated not only in court centers but on a lesser scale by others at different points on the hierarchy in "a piling up of mirrorings upon mirrorings upon mirrorings" (1980, 107). Arswendo Atmowiloto's evidence from 1982 that state officials dominated *all* news bulletins, not just the national news, supports Geertz's point (1986, 35–41). Schulte Nordholt provides evidence that this also occurs in contemporary Bali:

> Although the Eka Dasa Rudra [ritual] was definitely a unique event, the role of the state at the provincial level is regularly reinforced in smaller rituals as well. . . . Moreover, during the preparations of the rituals, time and time again the important connections between religious well-being, social stability and national development were emphasised, as if these were elements of a timeless and divine triangular order. (1991, 35–36)

It is this focus on hierarchy and its relation to state ceremonial that I wish to explore further with particular reference to television. As I have argued above, it is possible to identify recurring visual motifs and forms in TVRI news that function to naturalize hierarchy and the controlling knowledge, authority, and social commitment of state officials. In TVRI news this "model and copy hierarchy" (Geertz 1980, 136) is evident in the consistent practice of giving prominence to state officers whatever the content of the item happens to be. It is understandable that news reports should give prominence to the president if he visits a rural area or inspects a development project, but it is not obvious that news reports concerned with agricultural practices, flooding, or pollution should necessarily feature state officials.[7] But invariably in such reports, it is the state officials who are interviewed, whose names appear superimposed on the screen, and who become the center of visual gravity in the way the item is shot. Alternative ways of shooting the reports, with more emphasis on the impact of the situation on ordinary people's lives, are not pursued. When farmers are interviewed, they are not identified by name or title. Almost all reports are mediated through the perspective of the state officials who are seen to be "in charge." Up and down the bureaucratic scale then, in a stylized form, the central organizing role of state officials is constructed by TVRI, reinventing traditional relations of hierarchy.

Geertz also made the observation that the state rituals that celebrated "status pride" involved all strata of society in the performance. "It was a theater state in which the kings were the impresarios, the priests the directors, and the peasants the supporting cast, stage crew and audience" (1980, 13). All levels of the social and political order had to be involved, for as Louis Dumont (on whom Geertz relies for his understanding of spiritual status) has shown, the top requires the bottom; the Brahmin is defined in terms of the Untouchable (Dumont 1970).

In the modern, secular context of the contemporary state, where television increasingly mediates state ritual, there remains in many TVRI news items an echo of the political and cultural value of addressing all levels of hierarchy as part of an inclusive structure. A hierarchical social order may be legitimized by demonstrating that the hierarchical differences have an instrumental value for the whole social order and do not simply privilege the few. News items that link high-status figures with the management and oversight of community development projects perform this ideological work, showing the higher levels of the state as necessary in the promotion and management of the common good. Indeed, Schulte Nordholt suggests that the New Order's successful "revival" of "all-Bali" rituals has "confirmed that under the New Order, conflict and chaos have been replaced with order and development" (1991, 34). It is against this background that I suggest we interpret the emphatic care TVRI takes in including the audience of nonelite people in news items. Recall the quotation from Antlov, who notes that the news reports function to bind the community together from bottom to top: "Residents of Sariendah can *recognise and identify themselves with the peasants* who attended the meeting on television (Antlov 1995, 60; my emphasis). The representation of nonelite members of the community becomes a rite of incorporation, endlessly reinforcing the view that development is for all, while still maintaining the position that there is a complex, graded hierarchy of state officials whose job it is to control and manage, not on their own behalf, but *pro bono publico.*

In the vox pop category of news items, the persons selected to be interviewed were persons in the most humble occupations: a street sweeper, a street musician, and a parking attendant. In a question about hopes and plans for the new year, it was not the manager of a branch office, a bank clerk, or a student who were interviewed. It was the "little people" who were brought for a few awkward moments onto the screen, which, for the rest of the year would feature, for at least 50 percent of the time, high-status state officials. This is an example of a rite of "status reversal," where the structure of the normal order is reinforced by being turned on its head for a brief moment (Stallybrass and White 1986, 13; Turner 1969, chap. 5).

Further Cultural Resonances: The Intertextuality of Television News Forms

In this section I draw attention to the expression of hierarchy and state ceremony, not in ritual but in textual sources, and suggest that the form of television news is intertextually related to particular literary genres and performance traditions such as *wayang.* Hierarchical social formations were the norm in the classical states of Southeast Asia. As Tony Reid notes, "the great texts of the high cultures of Southeast Asia" celebrate cooperative unity between different levels of the hierarchy (Reid 1983, 7). In Indonesia, hierarchical relations were definitive of the structure of classical states at least in Java, Bali, and South Sulawesi (Errington 1983; Moertono 1968; Reid 1983, 7). These relations provide a historical and cultural background that assists contemporary audiences in decoding hierarchical relations inscribed in news bulletins. The metacommunicative codes of the cultural traditions explored below will not work for all viewers. For some, including those familiar only with modern *wayang* styles and those who have no knowledge of high cultural texts, they may be a site of resistance. Nevertheless, the older styles of *wayang* are still part of the cultural capital of many Javanese. And for non-Javanese, transformation of the *wayang* in comics, on radio, in cassettes, and in epic Indian television serials (*The Mahabharata,* TPI 1992, '93; *Ramayana,* TPI 1993) maintains the story-realms in Indonesian symbolic life, contributing new, though vaguely familiar, symbolic images that play a part in the discourses of contemporary popular culture.

Contemporary audiences might find in the visit form an echo of royal progressions. In classical Javanese literary texts such as the *Nagarakertagama,* descriptions of royal tours through the countryside are a common organizing theme. These texts record occasions when the king, accompanied by a large entourage, traveled from his palace city through his realm and along the way distributed funds, blessed irrigation works, and the like. The texts usually provide fascinating and detailed descriptions of the entourage that accompanied the king on his travels.[8] As Benedict Anderson has noted, one index of power in Java and Southeast Asia was control over people (1972, 30). The size of the retinue, then, was a sign of power. This can provide a way of reading what seems at times the unnecessarily large groups that accompany ministers into the field.

The king's interest and support for "infrastructure development" helped to construct him as a just and beneficent king. The classical texts record close involvement of high-status rulers in the development of the material welfare of the state, not only its spiritual welfare, and provide a historical background that helps contemporary viewers in decoding the presentation of contemporary news reports of the government's development activities.

The dominance of Jakarta-centered news items resonates with the special status of the court center as the locus of power, knowledge, and wealth in classical times. The character of the court center, and the idea of center-periphery relations, have been well described by Anderson and Geertz and will not be expanded on here. The royal progressions noted above also emphasize the centrality of the *negara* in the structure of the pilgrimage: the court is both the beginning and the end of the royal tour.

Related to the idea of the *negara* as exemplary center is the dichotomy of the *negara* (here meaning a more encompassing territory, not just the court city) and the *mancanegara* (foreign lands). In shadow puppet (*wayang*) narratives (*lakon*), the home state is an idealized realm of peace and order, while foreign states are characterized as the kingdoms of ogres. W. S. Rendra, in *The Struggle of the Naga Tribe*, used this *wayang* trope to differentiate the agriculturally rich Astinam from the industrial "ogre" nations of Europe, America, and Japan. There is a parallel here in the way *World News*, with its emphasis on "bad news," is articulated with the national news, where the emphasis is on stability and development (Rendra 1979, 5).

And it is to the *wayang* that I turn finally to consider some aspects of the ordering of narrative form. In Javanese culture (and in Sundanese and Balinese cultures) the puppet theater (*wayang*) has traditionally been a most influential and highly developed art form (Holt 1967). The contemporary American scholar Laurie Sears has recently shown that the *wayang* has been a dynamic element in Javanese political and cultural life, and comments that "as a theatrical medium with the potential to absorb and reinterpret political allegories, *wayang* has served the purposes of many governments, not least that of the New Order" (1996, 232). Sears notes that President Soeharto has fostered the use of *wayang* as a means of mediating state development projects:

> Certainly it would not be appropriate for us to change the artistic role of the dhalang [puppeteer] into that of a mouthpiece for development, for if we did *wayang*'s artistic coherence would be destroyed. This would harm all of us, harm the artistic culture which we should develop. But I believe you dhalang understand what needs to be done. The development message can be conveyed

while preserving the artistic level and coherence of the *wayang*. (Soeharto, cited in Sears 1996, 233)

In *wayang* narratives, there are three major divisions, each of which is divided in turn into a prescribed internal structure of audience, journey, and battle scenes (Becker 1979, 220).[9] This hierarchical structure of divisions and scenes is intensified in the order of performance. Audience scenes (in front of a ruler or holy man) are always performed first in each division, and *wayang* plots always begin and end in a court, a structure that emphatically figures the centrality of the ruler in both a spatial and sociopolitical sense (Becker 1979, 225). The movement from local affairs to international affairs and back to local affairs in the schedule of evening news bulletins, which I described above, replicates the familiar structure of *wayang* narratives. A more direct appropriation of the *wayang* occurs in the television comedy program *Ria Jenaka* (see chapter 4), which uses the familiar conventions of *wayang* performance to mediate development programs. The direct and indirect reference to these conventions assists contemporary audiences in finding meaning in the internal order of news bulletins and visual structures such as the report form.

Television and the Possibility of Communitas

TVRI news is one site of the discursive construction of *communitas* in Indonesia, one mode no doubt among many (Amrih Widodo 1995; Acciaioli 1985) that contributes to a political process of creating within a dispersed and culturally very diverse nation a sense of shared community, of nationhood, a sense of the unity transcending the diversity. TVRI news circulates among its audience, dispersed widely throughout the archipelago, endlessly reiterated images of the state's interest and role in national development. In many of these items audiences of "ordinary people" are shown to be involved (though not as equals). Metonymically, on a national scale, the part stands for the whole. The vast audience of people watching the news imaginatively participates in all these different projects and events throughout the archipelago.

Victor Turner's concept of *communitas* is useful here, as it can deepen our understanding of the two questions raised in the introduction concerning the incorporation of nonelite or "ordinary people" in television news items and the persistence of "ceremonial" in news for the past thirty years. For Turner,

> It is as though there are ... two major "models" for human interrelatedness, juxtaposed and alternating. The first is of a society as a structured, differentiated, and often hierarchical system of politico-legal-economic positions with many types of evaluation, separating men in terms of "more" or "less." The second, which emerges recognizably in the liminal period, is of society as an unstructured or rudimentarily structured and relatively undifferentiated *comitatus*,[10] community, or even communion of equal individuals who submit together to the general authority of the ritual elders. (Turner 1969, 82)[11]

The set of oppositions that, following Turner, might be considered in exploring aspects of TVRI news are these: high status/low status; named people/unnamed people; state/civil society; actors/audience; Jakarta/rural areas; center/periphery; Indonesia/the world (beyond Indonesia). This set of dichotomies has not been randomly derived—it is an outcome of the previous analysis of news bulletins and items, where the oppositions above were present in different guises—as statistics, in the settings of news items, shot sequences, and the structure of TVRI news programming.

The news program signature and the weather report also reinforce the spatial unity of Indonesia. The map over which the "*Berita Nasional*" identification is superimposed is a synoptic representation of the shape of the national territory. The TVRI logo circulates around the map, signifying the channel's reach and involvement in all parts of the nation. The simultaneous screening of the national news bulletin at 7 P.M. (West Indonesia Time) across Indonesia's three time zones creates a single time-space zone, contributing to the construction of a unified, national community as a *lived* experience, a part of domestic routine and time. And finally, the weather report also expresses a unity, not only because the weather seems to be virtually the same everywhere but also in the way the report, like a boundary rider, checks off the names of cities and places throughout the archipelago, identifying and making familiar places that might otherwise remain far away and strange. These more formal, or more procedural, aspects of the news, then, can also be read as nightly expressions of an integrating impulse.

In these many ways, the national news bulletin is a structure and discursive process that suspends the idea of the cleavages in the social order through emphasis on the community or nationwide scope of the process of national development, introducing a sense of shared purpose, shared effort, shared benefit, and shared involvement. At the same time, the bond of *communitas* involves the recognition that the state and its pervasive hierarchy is a necessary part of the creation, through endless performance, of the national community. In Turner's evocative phrase, the "perennially tensed opposition" between structure and antistructure is never obliterated; it is there for all to see in the frequency with which state officials feature in news items and in the dominance of Jakarta as a preeminent site and source of news, the center of planning and organization of national development.

If these points about the opportunity the rituals of TVRI news create to perform *communitas* in Indonesia are granted, we can more easily understand the general popularity of the news as a television program. Anderson has identified the feelings of "profound emotional legitimacy" that nationalism generates as one of its most distinctive characteristics. He speaks of the nation as an imagined *"community,"* "because, regardless of the actual inequality and exploitation that may prevail in each, the nation is always conceived as a deep, horizontal comradeship" (Anderson 1991, 7; emphasis in original). What Anderson understood about the role of the print media in the history of Indonesian nationalism can be extended to the role of television. His comments provide a path toward understanding how and why TVRI news programs, which appear so formulaic and repetitious, can generate positive associations among viewers. It is the discursive (audio and visual) imagining of the nation that the news performs, and the imaginary experience of taking part in the life and development of the nation, that is the foundation of the allegiance the audience has to the program. That the news is usually "good news" assists the audience to maintain their commitment, even though, as Anderson and Turner have both shown, the feelings of *communitas* do not deny or ignore the "bad news" but integrate it into a more inclusive, comprehensive understanding of the nature of society.

Some empirical evidence of television's contribution to the promotion of the kinds of knowledge, values, and attitudes that might contribute to the creation of *communitas* is found in Chu, Alfian, and Schramm's survey of rural communities before and after the introduction of television. Television showed a marked propensity to intensify the following: knowledge of the national language, especially among viewers with little or no formal education; knowledge of national development programs; and the discussion of national development programs (Chu, Alfian, and Schramm 1991, 224–55).

In concluding this section, the limits of my analysis of news as ritual requires comment. Although the analysis above has focused attention on distinctive processes of building cultural identity and unity through television news, there has not been scope to address a range of concerns that would round out a more extensive study of TVRI news. The news-as-ritual model suppresses attention on news gathering and the institutional production of news. In its focus on news as (ritual) performance, little attention is given to audience feedback. The focus on performance also tends to distract attention from the presence or absence of other voices in the news and from questions about the scope the political public has to gain access to news bulletins as a way of publicizing issues of public concern. These various issues could be opened up by adopting other interpretative models such as the transmission, publicity, and reception models for the analysis of news (McQuail 1994, 55), but this is beyond the scope of this book.

The Winds of Change: New Paradigms

One of the assumptions of news producers working with a linear transmission communications model is that audiences will by and large produce the "preferred" reading or meaning when they watch the news bulletin. But encoding strategies, however nuanced and however carefully they draw on what are believed to be shared meanings and values, can never determine the readings produced by historically situated audiences. Encodings that rely on Javanese cultural traditions, for example, may not be effective with non-Javanese audiences because of the lack of shared significations and evaluations of those significations. But even among Javanese, encodings that draw on classical values and traditions may be considered out of date or more seriously out of place in the modern Republic of Indonesia, with its multicultural base and more representative (at least in theory) structures of government.

For these reasons, critics of the ceremonialism of TVRI news have suggested that more emphasis should be placed on the nature of development projects and their likely impact on the lives of ordinary people rather than on the individual government representative performing a ceremonial role in relation to the project. The critics do not object to the government's role in broadcasting its development work; they simply would prefer the items to be less concerned with the inscription and reinforcement of hierarchical relations in society and more concerned with the lively representation of the benefits of development for all sectors of society.

For nearly thirty years TVRI has been able to shrug off this kind of criticism and persist in its monotonous attempts to represent a unitary view of society because it has had a monopoly on television news broadcasts. But there are signs that it will not be able to do so for much longer. A two-order culture of information-rich and information-poor (Murdock and Golding 1989) is developing in Indonesia. Those who can afford them have satellite dishes that provide access to news broadcasts from CNN, France, the BBC, Australia, Thailand, the Philippines, and Malaysia. Without additional expenditure, residents in border areas in northern Sumatra and parts of Kalimantan gain access to Malaysian television news through spillover effects. In the newer transmigration sites in Kalimantan, satellite dishes are a normal part of the infrastructure provided by the Department of Transmigration. These dishes are tuned to Palapa, but even so, they willy-nilly provide access to foreign sourced news, as Malaysia, Thailand, and since February 1993, Australia, use Palapa to distribute their signals. In addition to news broadcasts that are available in these different ways to sections of the Indonesian population, the commercial television stations have begun to urge their way into news broadcasting, even though TVRI remains strictly the only authorized source of television news.

These alternative sources of news present a major challenge for TVRI. If it chooses to quit the production strategies described above and join the increasingly mediated, more informal news style made popular worldwide by CNN, then it risks losing the *communitas* it has been able to structure.[12] The appeal of the alternative services has already prompted TVRI to take the significant step of changing the name of its *Berita Nasional* (National News) bulletin to *Berita Malam* (Evening News) and incorporating international items in what had always been a bulletin about the Indonesian nation.[13] TVRI news will have to fight for its audience in the future. TVRI may find that the ritual performance of national unity needs to yield to a more information-focused tradition of news that can mediate and interrogate social and political processes but, like news in most Western nations, ultimately support state power. As the TVRI news service changes, we will be in an excellent position to track the discursive reconstruction of the Indonesian nation, which satellite technology once helped create as a sovereign unity. Now, ironically, this technology increasingly fragments and challenges the very idea of territorial and cultural sovereignty, an issue I take up in the following chapter.

Part II
The Second Phase of Television in Indonesia: Breaking Up the Monopoly

Chapter 7

THE MONOPOLY BREAKS UP: NEW TELEVISION TECHNOLOGIES

IN THE 1980s, new television technologies presented Indonesian policy makers with a series of challenges. The government's television monopoly, developed since 1962 as a prime engine of national union and unity, came under threat. The threat derived from television products and services that expanded the scope for private consumption, where time and content were managed by individuals and not by the state. Some of these challenges were inherently easier to control than others. Advertising and video were dealt with firmly. But spillover and transnational satellite broadcasts were elusive, and regulators found they could not be met head on. Many regional communities had access to television services that the Indonesian state found it virtually impossible to control, and some of these—particularly the international satellite feeds—were rooted in political, social, and cultural assumptions that challenged the unitary values of the national culture project that had been central to the New Order's development of television. Transnational satellite television brought the Indonesian government face-to-face with the fact that the Indonesian nation space could not be sealed off from exogenous cultural processes, pressures, and influences. Elite and middle-class segments of the community were prepared to pay for alternative media services. The state had to develop a mode of living with transnational culture.

The problem facing the Indonesian state, and more particularly those who directed its television services, was how to extend its hegemony across two different cultural arenas—one driven by political and ideological imperatives concerned with nation building and circulation of ideas of national culture and the other, more audience-centered and driven by the dynamics of demand, concerned with the consumption of popular local and international cultural goods and services. In this context, introducing commercial television became an attractive option for the government as it appeared to have the capacity to bring together nation building and popular audience-centered dynamics.

The 1980s: Push Comes to Shove

Changes in technology and subtle intrusions into the national culture space proved difficult for the state to come to terms with in the 1980s. These changes were not part of any grand conspiracy but were the outcome of people looking for new ways to enjoy themselves and of local and transnational businesses alike trying to make profits. As the decade drew to a close, these pressures forced the state to look for new ways to manage its monopoly and to reassert its hegemony over the national culture space. It reversed its 1981 decision and reintroduced advertising, opened up commercial broadcasting, and introduced competition. These decisions opened the way for different constructions of the audience as the commercial channels imagined their audience as a market. The political public resisted its interpellation as passive consumers and constructed itself as an audience of sovereign consumers and active citizens. These questions of shifting cultural identity are discussed extensively in chapters 8, 9, and 10. On the face of it, the 1987 policy decisions radically altered the system. But these measures were also designed to allow the state to maintain its monopolistic control of television and to pursue its major cultural objectives, although in a new way.

My discussion here is structured as follows. First, the challenge video, spillover transmissions, and transnational satellite broadcasts posed to the sovereign unity of the Indonesian culture space will be discussed. Second, the state's response to the challenges is described, and reasons for different policy and legislative responses in each case are analyzed. Third, I argue that it was the state's experience in dealing with the complexities of these encroachments on its mediascape, and its realization that the encroachments could not be resisted, that was the proximate cause of the decision to authorize the development of commercial television. Finally, I examine an emerging tension between the state's interests in commercial television as a means of modifying and mediating international influences and capitalist interests in developing commercial television into a profitable broadcasting system. This discussion focuses on the discourse of "competition," which framed the debate over the introduction of commercial television.

The Video Boom

Following the introduction of color television to Indonesia in 1979, the potential that video technology offered for private consumption and popular entertainment led to a so-called video fever, particularly in the urban centers of Medan, Surabaya, and Jakarta (Arswendo Atmowiloto 1986, 158; *Jurnal Ekuin,* 7 December 1981). In a country that had recently banned television advertising and emphasized the national development role of television, video represented a threat in the state's eyes. Clearly, if people were watching videos at home, they were not watching TVRI (Ishadi 1984, 49). But for many people video was cheap entertainment. The cassettes could be rented for Rp 1,000 to Rp 1,500, watched a few times, and then shared or swapped with friends. If it was still cheaper to go to the movies (where a film could be seen for as little as Rp 150 in the cheapest seats and cinemas), videotapes had the advantage that they could be watched over and over again, and if shared with just one friend, in real terms cost only Rp 500. But video's principal attraction was that it offered a bill of fare TVRI could never match. The video underground offered customers copies of the latest international movies sometimes only days after their release in overseas cinemas and offered films banned in Indonesia— a category that included Chinese- language films, propaganda from foreign sources, and pornography (*Jurnal Ekuin,* 30 December 1981). Many of the illegally produced videos in circulation also included advertisements.

Video was therefore a medium that threatened the restrictive media policies and services managed by Indonesian state authorities. It was able to be consumed in private, and it gave the consumer control over what was on the screen. Unlike the "center-out" model of broadcasting, it was a dispersed, differentiated practice enjoyed by many different people throughout the community. The government initially took the view that home video promoted hedonistic, individualist media consumption and ran contrary to the corporatist and developmental ethos of national television. Many of the tapes in circulation had not been passed by the Board of Censors and were, in the government's view, likely to damage what is usually referred to as "national resilience" by maintaining ethnic differences within society, promoting individualism, and undermining community moral standards.

Beyond this, the burgeoning video industry was especially feared because it thrived on *exogenous* culture. The video sector enthusiastically circulated this culture within the Indonesian cultural space and challenged the government's construct of a distinct, and self-sufficient national culture. The legal challenges presented by the rapid growth of a home video industry were also complex, involving issues of international copyright. In 1982, an international report ranked Indonesia third behind Taiwan and Hong Kong as worst offenders in video piracy and counterfeiting (Boyd and Straubhaar 1989, 120). The video industry, which grew largely outside legal frameworks, also threatened the cinema industry and the legally incorporated video producers and hirers.

These last interests lobbied the government to move against the black marketeers, pirates, and smugglers.

The government acted. Pirate copying studios were closed down and illegal videotapes were searched for, seized, and burned. Although smuggling still represented a threat, customs officers made spectacular seizures duly trumpeted in the press. To complement this active policing, the government published a comprehensive series of decrees and regulations to control the industry, which Ganley and Ganley describe as "one of the most strenuous and sweeping efforts of any country to control videocassettes" (Ganley and Ganley 1986, 144).

A total of twenty-one separate decrees and regulations were brought down from 1983 to 1987. The regulations were all concerned with developing and managing a closely regulated home video entertainment industry. All matters concerning the import, production, copying, distribution, and public screening of videotapes were declared the responsibility of the Minister for Information. Videos could not be imported in bulk. Only master copies for which the importer had an import license could be imported. Once in the country, the videos had to be submitted to the official censor, and the importer was required to demonstrate that they legally owned the video and had rights of reproduction. Once a video was approved by the censor, it could be reproduced only by one of three state-owned institutions, and the copies had to be loaded into specially manufactured and identified cassettes. These stipulations describe only a few of the conditions and procedures importers were required to observe in importing video material.

The overall impact of these regulations is difficult to evaluate because of a lack of data. Consumers are now aware that the only legal videos are the red (for viewers 18 years or older), blue (for viewers 13 years or older), and green (unrestricted) cassettes produced by government agencies. But piracy still goes on. In 1988, 425,145 illegal cassettes were destroyed (*Jakarta Jakarta* #270 1991), and it was estimated that even greater numbers of illegal cassettes were in circulation in 1991. There are data that suggest that the regulations have perhaps had their major impact on the legal industry. In 1983/84, 1,920 foreign titles were legally imported for reproduction as videos (*Kompas,* 13 February 1986). In 1985 the number had fallen to seven hundred, and in 1991 stood at just one hundred. In the same year, only ninety-six titles of Indonesian-produced films were released on video (*Jakarta Jakarta* #270 1991).

Spillover Transmission

Unlike videos, which can be controlled, spillover transmissions are far more elusive and difficult to control. In border areas, and in areas of the archipelago that lie close to neighboring countries, Indonesian citizens have access to non-Indonesian television without modifying their receiving equipment. Indonesian policy makers have expressed concern about the national perimeter in regular statements in major planning documents (Republik Indonesia 1983, 25-20; 1988, 517; 198?, 510). They have taken care to extend cultural and information programs right up to the border areas, which are described as "strategic and sensitive" (Republik Indonesia 1983, 25-20), and where it is feared modern media both from within and from beyond the borders may circulate information not in accord with national objectives and policies. Indonesian advertisers, on the other hand, took advantage of spillover to promote Indonesian products on Malaysia's TV3, targeting Indonesian audiences. The newly appointed director of TVRI, Ishadi SK, commented that this situation was highly undesirable and "posed a threat to national security." He had to bear the brunt of a stiff diplomatic note from the Malaysian government, which resented the notion that their good-neighbor status should be questioned (Ishadi, personal interview, 24 January 1992).

The strategies employed to resist the transmissions, however, do not always reveal an understanding of the nature of spillover effects. Alwi Dahlan reports, for example, that to counter television spillover from Singapore and Malaysia in parts of Sumatra, the Department of Information attempted to meet the challenge by strengthening Indonesian broadcast signals to these areas (personal interview, 12 April 1993). The Minister for Information advised a parliamentary commission that he would take similar action in West Kalimantan province, where Indonesian citizens appeared to enjoy Malaysian television more than TVRI (1991, 13–15). Alwi Dahlan pointed out that the minister and the department had failed to understand that signal strength was not at issue but rather viewers' boredom with TVRI's programming.

Satellite Television and Dishes

Dish receivers for radio and television transmission became familiar technology in Indonesia following the installation of the Intelsat ground station at Jatiluhur in 1969, and with the erection of nearly two hundred ground stations throughout the archipelago after Palapa's launch. But only in the early 1980s did satellite dishes mushroom on the roofs of houses and offices in the larger urban centers of Indonesia.

In the mid-1980s, dishes were expensive, a three-meter dish with horizontal and vertical adjustment costing between Rp 15 million and Rp 17 million (approximately U.S.$9,000–10,000). These prices put dishes out of the reach of the working class and made them very expensive for middle-class Indonesians. Given these costs, the equipment was mostly restricted to the social and economic elite. These dishes were tuned to transnational television signals transmitted by regional satellites, and they delivered television programs from Malaysia (RTM, TV3), the Philippines (ABS-CBN, PTV4), Thailand (ARMY, BBTV), Taiwan (FO7), the Soviet Union (USSR-TV), and the United States (World Net America) (*Bursa Konsumen,* July 1988, 17; *Suara Karya,* 8 December 1989; *Bintang* #21 July 1991).

It is instructive to compare state authorities' different legislative responses to the home use of satellite dishes and video. Indonesian policy makers acted quickly, comprehensively, and with strict resolve to control home video. Unlike the twenty-one decrees for video, however, there have been only five decrees issued between 1986 and 1990 to control home satellite dishes. The difference between the bureaucratic relish with which the video situation was addressed and the minimalist approach to satellite transmissions is revealing. In the case of video, the authorities were dealing with something that could be stopped at the gates. Alert customs officials could and did make sure that videocassettes and recorders were not smuggled in, and the police were instructed to root out pirate studios engaged in illegal reproduction of films. Once the illegal entry of cassettes was in hand, the Board of Censors made sure that what was available met government guidelines.

But in the case of satellite television, the authorities faced a more subtle problem, and they recognized that in this case there was no way of stopping the satellite transmissions at the gates. The Minister for Information, Harmoko, put it this way:

> We appeal to all sections of the community who use the parabolas [satellite dishes] to strive to keep at arm's length broadcasts that may bring negative effects to us as a community, a people, and a nation.
>
> In facing this high technology, apart from the government's efforts to clamp down on its negative effects, the understanding of the community is indeed hoped for, so that we do not weaken our national resilience, because it is just not possible to escape the touch of this technology. (Menteri Penerangan 1988, 32–33)

But old habits die hard, and the department introduced regulations to control the use of satellite dishes. The general tenor of these regulations was defensive. Individuals were permitted to erect satellite dishes as long as they used locally manufactured antennae, registered them with local authorities, and tuned them only to Palapa. Local authorities in known TVRI "blankspots" were permitted to erect communal antennae at their own expense and run distribution cables to households as a way of improving the reception of TVRI. All installation had to be done by Directorate of Telecommunications personnel, and the antennae were not permitted to be tuned to any other satellite (Menteri Penerangan 1986; Menteri Pariwisata, Pos dan Telekomunikasi 1986).

The legislation was fundamentally flawed. It failed to acknowledge that even tuning to Palapa meant that viewers had access to Thai and Malaysian television because both used Palapa for their own national purposes. The government seemed to recognize this when it acknowledged that whether viewers watched other broadcasts was "a moral responsibility" (*Tempo,* 18 October 1986). The rules seemed to require that viewers develop a kind of moral squint and look away when foreign content appeared on screen. Beyond that, enforcement of the regulation was impractical. Did the government envisage that inspectors would move around eyeing the angle of people's antennae? Short of a complete ban on receiving devices, any control could only be illusory and partial.

The government's halfheartedness over legislating to control satellite reception can be attributed to five considerations. First, the equipment was expensive and mainly restricted to a sophisticated urban elite who the government believed would not be "corrupted" by the foreign broadcasts (*Kompas,* 13 February 1986). Second, policing was very difficult, as it involved intruding on individuals' leisure time, and it was very difficult to prove any offense unless someone was "caught in the act." Third, the technology had obvious benefits in extending the reach of TVRI into blankspot areas at no cost to the government (*Tempo,* 18 October 1986; *Mutiara* V August 1989). Fourth, it was acknowledged that satellite broadcasts provided access to foreign films and sporting events that TVRI could not supply and that this alternative was preferable to the circulation of underground videos. Fifth, international television, being public, was not considered as dangerous as video, for it was a public service and did not show pornography or illegally sourced tapes. TV3 programs, after all, were broadcast by a neighboring Muslim country.

The government demonstrated a greater acceptance and a more informed understanding of transnational satellite technology in its

1990 update of the 1986 regulations when individuals were authorized to erect and use satellite dishes for private use and tune them to whatever satellite broadcasts they wished. The restriction on local authorities' use of cable distribution from a communal antenna was, however, maintained. It was in this context of the pervasive influence of new television technologies such as video, spillover, and satellite television described above that the government made its decision to introduce commercial television.

Commercial Television: Reframing the Monopoly

Throughout the 1980s there were intermittent calls in the press for commercial television to be introduced to provide the public with an alternative service and to stimulate business turnover through commercial advertising (*Antara,* 19 January 1981; *Kompas,* 7 January, 10 January 1981; *Sinar Harapan,* 25 August 1984; *Prioritas,* 13 November 1986, *Suara Karya,* 27 November 1986; *Tempo,* 29 August 1987 67). There was, however, no sustained pressure for any deregulation or privatization of the industry, though Macintyre reports that a lively debate on the general issue of privatization of state enterprises was conducted during 1986/87 (1991). It came as something of a surprise, then, when the government legislated on 20 October 1987 to establish a pay TV service for Jakarta and environs (Menteri Penerangan #190A 1987). In practice this meant that the service would be available only to those who purchased a decoder for their television set. The decree authorized TVRI to license a third party to conduct the service on a day-to-day basis under terms and conditions to be decided between the two partners. The decree noted that the channel's programs would be permitted to carry advertising likely to promote national development. TVRI was authorized further to use whatever funds it received from the commercial channel for normal operational purposes.

A week later, on 28 October 1987, TVRI nominated Rajawali

Citra Televisi Indonesia (RCTI) as the provider of the first commercial television service in Indonesia. On 17 January 1990, TVRI came to a similar arrangement with Surya Citra Televisi (SCTV) to provide a pay TV service in Surabaya, Indonesia's second-most populous city. This arrangement was outside the terms of Ministerial Decree #190A (Menteri Penerangan 1987), which had authorized commercial television for Jakarta only. In July 1990, the department widened the provisions of the original decree in a major revision of the structure of the broadcast system.

Ministerial Decree #111 (Menteri Penerangan 1990) authorized two different categories of commercial services and stations. The first category comprised stations broadcasting general program material to a local audience. No more than one such broadcaster was permitted to operate in either the national capital (Jakarta) or provincial and regional capitals. They were not permitted to develop network services and were intended to provide television services exclusively to the local area. The second, specialist broadcaster category comprised a sole, commercial, educational broadcaster that was authorized to broadcast nationally. TVRI remained entitled to receive a contribution from commercial broadcasters according to conditions agreed to by each of the different parties.

It was not long, however, before Ministerial Decree #111 was revised, first in May 1992 and again in January 1993. In 1992 the mixed criteria of broadcast coverage (local, regional, national) plus program emphasis (educational, general) were set aside, and commercial providers were simply categorized in terms of their programming emphasis. Apart from the "general" and "educational" categories familiar from decree #111, an additional category of "special economic broadcaster" was created. This broadcaster was given the right to broadcast nationally and to use satellite and terrestrial links to transmit its programs. There was to be only one special economic broadcaster, and it was to be located in Jakarta (Menteri Penerangan 1992).

On 18 January 1993, Ministerial Decree #04A created an entirely different basis for structuring commercial television broadcasting. The criteria for categorizing broadcasters shifted once more, this time reverting to spatial considerations. The decree established two categories of broadcaster, one located in Jakarta, with a national broadcast coverage, and a second located in provincial or regional urban centers with a local broadcast range. A maximum of five national commercial channels was permitted, and there was a limit of no more than one local broadcaster in each of the various regional or provincial centers. National broadcasters were permitted to use Palapa and terrestrial link facilities and to establish a network of stations or branches to assist them. Local broadcasters, however, were restricted to local area transmission and could not use the satellite.

With these provisions, the decentralized structure established in decree #111 and more or less preserved in #84A was radically altered, and a highly centralized system of five national commercial broadcasters was established in Jakarta. The national broadcasters licensed as of March 1993 were PT Rajawali Citra Televisi Indonesia (RCTI), PT Cipta Televisi Pendidikan Indonesia (TPI), PT Indosiar Visual Mandiri, PT Cakrawala Andalas Televisi (ANTEVE), and PT Surya Citra Televisi (SCTV).

Shadow Language: Competition and the Television Sector

Minister of Information Harmoko's announcement in October 1987 that he had issued a license to establish a pay TV service for Jakarta and environs caught most commentators by surprise. No prior announcement about the introduction of commercial television had preceded the minister's announcement, nor had there been any call for tenders for licenses. Nevertheless, the minister's announcement was generally favorably received. Over the months leading up to RCTI's first broadcast, the introduction of commercial television was eagerly anticipated. Most of the commentary in the press framed the introduction of commercial television within a discourse of "competition" (*persaingan*), and as the number of approved commercial licenses grew, within a frame of competition and deregulation (*deregulasi*).

The framing of the debate in terms of (economic) competition caught my attention because it seemed to be an exaggeration. Competition between channels for audiences and advertisers is the name of the game where commercial providers vie with each other for market share. But RCTI did not present any economic threat to TVRI, which could not accept advertising. On the contrary, licensing arrangements meant additional income would flow to the cash-strapped public broadcaster. Beyond that, at the content level, TVRI's programming was comprehensive and included substantial local content. Its audience was national, and its broadcasts were free to air. RCTI, on the other hand, could accept advertising, but its broadcasts were restricted to the greater Jakarta area for just a few hours a day. Furthermore, it was available only to subscribers willing to pay for a signal decoder and a substantial (Rp 30,000) monthly rental charge. Given these circumstances, the emphasis on competition in press discussion of commercial television seemed to misunderstand the situation.

Many commentators have noted, however, that debate in the Indonesian press is very indirect and is written in "shadow language." Ariel Heryanto, for example, notes that senior editor and journalist Mochtar Lubis complained that it took a great labor to grasp meanings from the printed pages of the Indonesian press (Heryanto 1990, 294). Although the overt economic signification of the discourse of competition seemed premature and exaggerated in 1987, my argument is that in the debate over the introduction of commercial television, "competition" may be read as a site of challenge to the monopoly exercised by the state in "imagining the nation."

In *Imagined Communities* Benedict Anderson defines a nation as an imagined community that is (spatially) limited and sovereign (1991, 6). His eye is fixed largely on the moment of revolution in postcolonial states such as Indonesia. Once the moment of revolution is past, however, Anderson argues that the revolutionary nationalist regime tends to engage in "systematic, even Machiavellian, instilling of nationalist ideology through the mass media, the educational system, administrative regulations, and so forth" (1991, 114).

As I have described, during the 1980s the idea of the nation as imagined community, and TVRI's role in the official imagining of the nation, came under pressure. Electronic products and services, accessed in a variety of ways, made it obvious that national borders were electronically porous and that state authorities could not easily (if at all) seal off the national cultural space from contradictory cultural phenomena. These several sources of threat exposed, both to the regime and its citizens (to a greater and lesser degree), the *constructed* nature of the nation. For those whose business it is to manage the representation of national identity, other imaginings, insinuated into the national space produce "an anxiety to continuously construct and tighten national unity in the face of multiple narratives or competing interpretations of what constitutes the nation" (Robinson 1993, 167).

And if transnational flows of symbolic goods and services create anxieties for official nationalism, they also cast doubt on the continued theoretical adequacy of the modernist idea of the nation as a territorially limited, sovereign, imagined community. Without wanting to deny the groundedness of Indonesian viewers in a historically and culturally specific national cultural space, cross-border flows situate Indonesian audiences in a nonnational, virtual, global space, imaging events, people, and places beyond the national perimeter. The impossibility of regulating electronic transmissions erodes national sovereignty, and the diversity of programming blurs and may contest the hegemonic cultural constructs circulated by official nationalism. But the slip and slide of national constructs within a global flow of capital and cultural goods does not totally disable the explanatory power of nation, nationalism, and national identity. Nation and global flow figure as a palimpsest, each inflecting the other in a relationship that shifts between enthusiasm and reluctance over integration into the world economic system. The

Indonesian government's contradictory decisions over transnational television flows illustrate its recognition of the reality and value of the international trade in televisual products and services and its struggle to wrestle down global influences and maintain the cultural and spatial integrity of the nation.

To combat the largely unwanted, unasked for, but unstoppable infiltration of extranational cultural products, and to satisfy the equally irresistible pressure from politically well connected capitalists to profit from the trade, the Department of Information decided to open up television services and "acculturate" foreign influences, as Minister Harmoko later put it (Harmoko 1993). The department's decision carried a number of benefits for the government, but as we shall see, it inflected its acknowledgment of the reality of global flows with a long-held concern to control and shape the cultural identity of the nation. First, the decision satisfied pressure from well-connected capitalists to enter the television industry. It also went some way to meet the charge that the government's "Open Sky Policy," which permitted private citizens to own satellite dishes, was creating classes of information-rich and information-poor. It reasserted the spatial integrity of the nation by making the satellite dish, the means of transnational reception, an unnecessary extravagance at least for the Jakarta audience, who could now access high-quality, internationally sourced product on their own sets fitted with just a decoder. It reasserted control over the distribution of foreign cultural products by limiting broadcasts to the national capital, and it allowed the state to exercise influence over programs broadcast by requiring RCTI to submit all its programs for clearance by the Board of Censors prior to transmission. Finally, it reinforced indigenous values by requiring RCTI to boost local content.

But even so, these benefits hardly appear to have been compelling. Soesastro and Andrew Macintyre have both noted that Indonesia was pushed into deregulation more out of "economic necessity" than ideology (M. Hadi Soesastro 1989, 854; Macintyre 1994, 255). Certainly in the television sector, state authorities displayed little enthusiasm for sharing their territory with the private sector. In fact, many of the decisions made may be read as almost hostile to liberalization. The decision to establish a pay TV channel in Jakarta was at best a partial solution to the various pressures the government faced, and at worst, no solution at all.

For the Department of Information, deregulation of the television sector represented a potential loss of hegemonic power and influence. In press analyst Ariel Heryanto's words,

> The state [that is, the Department of Information] has purposefully monopolised radio [and television] news production all over the country, tightly controlled and constantly intimidated the press, invested an immense amount of capital in movie production, satellite installation, and [has] monopolised [the] television network. The mass media have proved to be the most important force of production, reproduction, and nurturing of some of the fundamental principles of legitimation of the state. (1990, 298)

No wonder then that deregulation of the television sector came hard to the Department of Information. Unlike deregulation in other sectors of the economy (Mari Pangestu and Ahmad Habir 1989), there was no deregulation package associated with television. This is understandable in the sense that there were no other players already in the game and, at that stage, no formal regulation of the sector. One might have expected an announcement of the government's intention to open up this new field, but there was no public announcement, no discussion, let alone celebration, of the government's intentions. It was a deal done quietly, grudgingly, through the back door.

Passing over an initial application from the Indonesian-Chinese-owned Rajawali Group, the license was granted only when Rajawali joined up with the Bimantara group headed by the president's son Bambang Trihatmodjo. Indeed, all the commercial television licenses have been issued to business leaders very close to the presidential family: the president's cousin Sudwikatmono is a major shareholder in SCTV, the president's daughter Siti Hardiyanti owns TPI, ANTEVE is owned by the well-favored *pribumi* (indigenous) Bakrie Group, and Indosiar Visual Mandiri (IVM or Indosiar) is owned by Liem Sioe Liong's Salim Group, which has been a major beneficiary of presidential patronage. Thus the deregulation of television was in no sense a *liberalization* of the sector. It is a case that illustrates Macintyre's point that patrimonialism is the norm in Indonesian business and is a case that illustrates the conflicting pressures national governments face in trying to accommodate the demands of international capitalism mediated through powerful indigenous elites (1994, 257).

The Department of Information's equivocal and interventionist approach to commercial television reflects a tension between economic and cultural nationalism and liberalization that has deep roots in Indonesian cultural history. Many observers have noted an anticapitalist ideology in Indonesia and have linked the position to bitter memories of colonial exploitation, fears of Indonesian-Chinese domination of the modern market economy, and more positively, values of the equitable distribution of wealth for the benefit of the whole community (Glassburner 1978; Liddle 1982; M. Hadi Soesastro 1989; Mackie 1971; McCawley 1982; Macintyre 1994; Milne 1991; Rice 1983; Robison 1986).

From the nationalist or nativist perspective, capitalism is regarded as a treacherous Western institution likely to victimize Indonesia in international competition. Articulation of the Indonesian economy with the international economy through liberalization and deregulation is, therefore, regarded with suspicion. Within the nation, the foreignness of capitalism and the fear of the economic influence of ethnic Chinese are conflated, reinforcing the Otherness of capitalism:

> The great majority of *pribumi* [indigenous] Indonesians fear that if market forces were allowed a free rein, substantial proportions of the Indonesian economy would fall under "foreign" control—either domestic foreigners (the non-*pribumi*) or international investors. This consideration has come to play such a major part in economic policy formulation in Indonesia that it is difficult to overstate its importance. (McCawley 1982, 107)

The Discourse of Competition

Competition and deregulation are therefore loaded signifiers in Indonesia because of their links with capitalist values and structures. In what follows, the discourse of competition surrounding the introduction of commercial television is traced through press comment from 1981 through 1995. For some commentators, the idea of competition in the television sector was greeted positively, while others, including high-level state officials, chose to deny and deflect the possibility that the master narrative of cooperative values and structures might be open to counter suggestion.

The discourse is inscribed across a range of issues such as the impact of competition on program quality, competition as limiting the state television monopoly, competition and its contribution to audiences' choices, and competition and its impact on the advertising industry. In some of these issues, the horizon is very clearly the national; in others it reaches out beyond national boundaries to acknowledge the global circulation of televisual products, which crucially underwrite the local commercial sector. Put another way, the discourse acknowledges a hierarchy of national and global competitive relations within which local schedules take their place.

Competition is constructed as a process productive of general communal benefit in the sense that program quality is expected to improve all round. Whereas in economic relations competition has historically been demonized in Indonesia for its contribution to "free fight liberalism," the "magic of the marketplace" (McVey 1992, 10) was given a positive value in the television sector for its potential to focus attention on audiences' needs and interests (*Suara Karya,* 6 May 1981; *Mutiara,* week 1, July 1990). The focus on the audience is constitutive of a two-way communicative relationship between broadcaster and audience. *Lack* of competition, on the other hand, is typically associated with a lack of creativity and a one-way, top-down communicative process wrapped up in its own priorities: "News broadcasts are more top down than bottom up, and in them, state affairs are mostly presented for community viewing, while information about the community—in this context meaning community aspirations—have hardly ever been addressed by TVRI" (*Bisnis Indonesia,* 25 June 1994).

Read as shadow language, the link made between competition and quality in cultural production gestures toward a desire for more responsive and more sensitive relations between the state and the community. A better quality of cultural life, it is implied, will be produced in circumstances in which those involved are pushed to inject energy and creativity into their cultural production.

From the earliest days, the introduction of commercial television was celebrated because of the increased choice the service provided. As media analyst Eduard Depari said, "The presence of these two audio visual media will make it possible for the community to think of alternatives. Choices between screenings from these two media will make it possible for the community to decide which program they wish to watch and which they will ignore" (*Suara Pembaruan,* 24 August 1990).

As the number of stations grew, and eager production teams pushed out the envelope of regulations constraining them in the production of news and current affairs, the acknowledgment of the value of the choices commercial television offered became increasingly frank. In some commentary, the language in favor of choice, of alternative perspectives, is mapped clear onto the face of the surface text as if the sun stood directly overhead and cast no shadow. In economic analyst Christianto Wibisono's words, for example, "RCTI will not only weaken the monopoly of TVRI, which is bureaucratic, PR-ish, monotonous, authoritarian and undemocratic. RCTI can create conditions for dialogue, discussion, free speech, [and] differences of opinion through its panels which have integrity, are popular, and will become vehicles for democracy" (*Tempo,* 12 March 1994).

What these writers signal is that in a deregulated media sector, what is imaged (imagined) on screen will differ systematically between TVRI and the other channels. The commercial sector will not simply provide different programs but by its very logic will encourage viewers to make choices, to choose consciously between a dominant official vision of national identity and other, more diverse counterimages.

What is at stake here is not simply that viewers will have a wider choice of programming but that viewers may choose not to become complicit in television's mediation of the national culture project. Audience resistance to TVRI's official voice was discussed in chapter 6. The commercial sector already exploits TVRI's vulnerability on this point. In 1990, for example, RCTI chose not to present a live relay of Pancasila Day but instead offered viewers the controversial Dutch-Indonesian movie *Max Havelaar* at the time TVRI went to air with the solemn ritual from Lubang Buaya, where the bodies of three generals and four aides were dumped following an abortive coup in 1965 (*Tempo*, 13 October 1990). On some occasions RCTI has also chosen to postpone the late news in favor of live broadcasts of European Soccer League games (*Tempo*, 13 October 1990).

The performance of diversity, the stock in trade of a competitive media sector, sits uncomfortably with the thrust of New Order politics, which has been to emphasize and manufacture consensus and convergence through corporatist structures and policies (Macintyre 1994). Competition between commercial channels and the state service systematically displays and performs the possibility of alternative imaginings, a possibility that TVRI is consistently at pains to efface. Program schedules in newspapers and magazines and the varied nightly lineup impel viewers to choose between the official "folklore of the regime" (Takashi Fujitani 1993, 101), and other, perhaps conflicting, even contradictory narratives. While TVRI's mission is determinedly and insistently developmental and political, the commercial channels are much more concerned with their audience appeal, reversing the top-down invention of tradition designed to create and maintain the obedience, loyalty, and cooperation of the national community. Of course, in encroaching on the space the state reserved for itself in the construction and invention of national identity, the commercial media also perform a political role, helping to construct a play of contested images of national identity.

Competition and Advertising

Advertising on television has been a sensitive issue in Indonesia since commercials were banned on the grounds that they contributed to consumerism in rural communities. Somewhat surprisingly, while the issue of consumerism has been a topic of press comment, in recent years the main focus in articles dealing with advertising has been speculation about likely revenues and the effect of competition on advertising across the television, radio, and print media (*Tempo,* 25 August 1990; *Prospek,* 19 January 1991; *Kompas,* 18 January 1992; *Jakarta Post,* 3 February 1993). When RCTI was permitted to broadcast free to air in 1990, the competition between the press and television for advertising became intense. By mid-1991, *Kompas* (8 May 1991) reported that the electronic media had captured 70 percent of the advertising budget. Television accounted for 60 percent of the budget and had contributed to a rise in advertising expenditure of 32 percent from 1990 to 1991.

The discourse of competition between sections of the media and the powerful position ascribed to television may also be read as an indictment of the *lack* of competition created by the government's allocation of licenses to favored clients. Articles that suggest that television will be highly profitable because of its access to advertising draw attention to the rent-seeking opportunities the new licenses made possible. Read this way, the shadow language of the profitability of television is first an implicit attack on the incomplete deregulation of the media and second a suspicion that official nationalism has simply been diverted from TVRI to a compliant commercial sector run by favored cronies.

Competition and the Loss of State Control

The Indonesian government has promoted and defended its decision to break up its television monopoly in press comments, seminars, interviews, and well-publicized launch ceremonies. But state authorities also appear to have had reservations about the initiative. The pattern of their decisions and policies in establishing the sector reveals a tension between support for economic liberalism as a way of solving an immediate problem and ambivalent, even negative attitudes toward competition and the threatened loss of state control. The state fears that deregulation of the sector will erode its influence in the development of the industry and in the reproduction of a specific social, economic, and cultural order. It is to these issues that I turn now.

If, as Soesastro has argued (1989, 854), it is not policy but necessity that has driven financial and industrial deregulation in Indonesia, then it is technological determinism that has pushed reluctant state authorities into deregulation of the television sector. Words such as "invasion" (*serbuan*), "attack" (*menerpa*), and "possession of our soul" (*merasuk*) signify authorities' feelings of vulnerability in the face of the technological superiority of international capitalism. The *Lensa* (1 May 1991) cartoon shown in figure 7.1 expresses many of these fears and anxiety over whether national culture and TVRI can resist the impact of *"globalisasi."*

Officials keen to support a cultural nationalist policy argue that as the international penetration cannot be resisted, it is better to domesticate the global by putting it in the hands of local providers. This position is clearly stated in the preamble to Ministerial Decree #84, 1992: "c. In accordance with these developments and to *balance* the overseas television broadcasts, it is necessary to open up the opportunity for television broadcasts by the private sector, which will broadcast programs particularly in the field of information concerning economic development, [programs] that are compatible with national needs and priorities" (Menteri Penerangan 1992, my emphasis).

It is this perception of technological vulnerability that has

Figure 7.1. The ogre arms tearing TVRI away to replace it with a bright new commercial TV set have "Foreign Culture" on them, and the body of the giant is inscribed with "Globalization." The sick TVRI rests on a rickety stand labeled "TV Technology," with a patched and torn money bag labeled "Capital" spilling money. The stand rests on the national territory "Bumi Nusantara." The figure in traditional Javanese costume at right holding onto TVRI is "National Culture," who is said to be "lacking nutrition" (*Lensa*, 1 May 1991).

pushed the Department of Information into the policy and regulatory compromises I described above. These display clearly the tension between a conservative state sector keen to maintain its hegemonic power and a commercial sector driven by the pressures of intrasector competition and the need to maximize market access. The Department of Information has attempted to exert control over the commercial sector since its inception. License conditions that allowed for a subvention to TVRI and regulations concerning program mix, broadcast reach, and the number of licenses all evidence a bureaucracy reluctant to let go of its monopoly role. But as the number of license holders has grown and commercial considerations have pushed the channels to compete with each other, the department's scope for influencing the sector has diminished. Much as we have seen in Australia concerning pay TV, the government has been forced into a piecemeal and haphazard regulation and reregulation of the sector (Kitley 1994a).

At the same time, it would be wrong to underestimate the department's power to act decisively when it considers its fundamental interests are at stake. When Minister Harmoko discovered in June 1994 that economic ministers had declared the media open to foreign investment and even majority shareholding, he went straight to the president and had the decision reversed (Hill 1994, 152). A few weeks later the department withdrew the licenses of the influential news magazines *Tempo* and *Editor* and the tabloid *DeTIK*. In 1995, SCTV was cowed into taking its very popular *Perspektif* off air after a series of controversial interviews with prominent journalists and intellectuals.

The department has also dragged its feet over the drafting of a broadcasting law. This can be understood as another example of the bureaucracy's desire to keep the upper hand in working with its thrusting protégés. Adverse judicial decisions in 1995 in cases appealing the bans against *Tempo* have no doubt contributed to the department's temporizing over codifying rights and obligations for the broadcast media. For while the regulatory environment is vague, there is much more room for the state to use its authority and power to keep the private sector in line. In a clientelist system, lack of specificity in media regulations affords all parties room to maneuver.

Competition as Cooperation

Rajawali Citra Televisi Indonesia ... is not TVRI's rival, rather it is a partner that will round out [TVRI's] programs to meet rising audience wishes. (Ishadi SK quoted in *Kompas*, 24 June 1988)

The introduction of commercial television in Indonesia does not represent competition for TVRI, nor, on the other hand, is TVRI a rival for commercial television. (Harmoko quoted in *Suara Karya*, 16 July 1990)

On the occasion of laying the foundation stone for the RCTI studio, the then director of national television services, Ishadi SK, emphasized that there was no competition between TVRI and the new channel. Indeed, the decision to launch the new channel on the occasion of TVRI's anniversary symbolically represented the fraternal relations between the two. Minister Harmoko noted that RCTI was not autonomous but was licensed as an activity of the TVRI Foundation (*Yayasan* TVRI), the incorporating body of TVRI itself. RCTI was not therefore a competitor so much as a member of the family, assisting the nation's development by performing a function that TVRI was not funded to perform. In line with article 33 in the constitution, RCTI could not be seen as taking over a strategic service properly under the control of the state, but rather as helping the state authority mount a service it lacked the means to establish. Harmoko noted further that RCTI would contribute part of its earnings to TVRI, underlining again the cooperative, family-type relations between the two broadcasters.

Harmoko's incorporation of RCTI under the TVRI Foundation maintained the practice of "control without ownership" in the deregulation of state enterprises, which Robert Rice considers a hallmark of the Soeharto regime (Rice 1983, 79). His remarks also foregrounded elements of the master narrative of the New Order regime. Ideas of cooperation and cooperative enterprise rather than out-and-out profit taking (a *Yayasan* [Foundation] is a non-profit institution), the invention of a family tradition, and a shared orientation are all emphasized. It is a denial that "free-fight liberalism" has been invited within the walls. The possibility of crass commercialism is denied, and so is the idea that RCTI represents any kind of rival to TVRI in its reach for audiences. The *Suara Karya* cartoon (28 July 1990) chose to represent the fiction of non-competitive media relations as an essentialized indigenous cultural trait—"Malay diplomacy," signified by the resigned shrug and comment of the little figure (the audience?) caught in between.

RCTI and later all the commercial channels were brought under the umbrella of the TVRI Foundation and represented as "extensions" of TVRI. The commercial channels, like the state service, were given an explicit cultural and political role: to "acculturate" the foreign sourced product in which Indonesian viewers have displayed such interest. The foundation structure is another example

Figure 7.2. On left, commercial channel SCTV; on right, TVRI's Surabaya (East Java) channel. Man on left: "We don't want to be in competition with you." Man on right: "We don't feel under pressure [of competition]" (*Suara Karya,* 28 July 1990).

of the New Order's strategy of facilitating state control through compliant corporatist organizations (Macintyre 1994, 252).

Another aspect of the denial of competition has been the consistent refusal to allow TVRI to accept advertising and compete with the commercial stations despite repeated calls for this to happen (*Suara Pembaruan,* 21 June 1987; *Tempo,* 29 August 1987; *Suara Pembaruan,* 24 August 1990). Prior to 1981, TVRI funded itself handsomely from advertising revenues. TVRI's continued exclusion from competitive relations needs to be explained in two ways. First, as noted, the Indonesian state has been "strikingly interventionist" across many areas of the economy (Macintyre 1994, 245). The Soeharto government has frequently intervened to manage industrial capacity and has closed off areas of investment if it considered capacity was sufficient (Rice 1983, 67). The government's recognition of the high levels of up-front investment in the television industry and its concern over potential levels of advertising revenue (*Republika,* 5 September 1994) explain in part TVRI's exclusion from competition. The patrimonial or clientelistic relations between the state and the five commercial operators add another dimension to the explanation. As Olle Tornquist points out, in reciprocation for broad political and economic support, a rentier state must ensure that its clients "do reasonably well" and have minimal motivation to move away and find other patrons (Tornquist 1990, 35). The minister's decision to limit the number of commercial licenses to five is a specific example of this general principle at work. TVRI's transmission capacity and national profile would make it a formidable rival to the other, barely established broadcasters. Keeping the strongly positioned TVRI out of competition with the other channels is consistent, then, with the dynamics of clientelist relations.

The second line of explanation, having less to do with political economy and more to do with processes of official nationalism, fills out our understanding of TVRI's role of *primus inter pares*. Positioning TVRI above the ruck of competition enunciates TVRI's nation-building role in a series of tropes central to the New Order imagining of the nation. First of all, its noncommercial role reasserts the anticapitalist tradition enshrined in article 33 of the 1945 constitution, foregrounding the fiction of cooperative arrangements in which the commercial channels are represented as working for the state as much as themselves. But perhaps most productively for the strategy of official nationalism, the exclusion of TVRI creates a binarism that can be mobilized and inflected to privilege a specific national cultural construct and counter the infiltration of the Other—namely, foreign-sourced cultural products and services.

As a noncommercial service, TVRI can be represented by state authorities as addressing the national "public," the nation people, rather than segments, niches, or target groups in particular markets. The rhetoric of public service broadcasting is mobilized to emphasize TVRI's disinterested relationship with its audience. TVRI addresses its audience as partners in national development rather than as a market for exploitation. As the Director General of Radio, Television, and film, Alex Leo Zulkarnain, put it, "If it's government, it has to be nonprofit" (conveniently forgetting nearly twenty years of profit taking by TVRI [*Tempo*, 21 July 1990]).

In a competitive industry, a public broadcaster represents one pole of an opposition between "private" and "public" spheres. TVRI displays the split that is the ground of the perceived problem of the penetration of the national culture space. As a way of dealing with the unsettling potential that the high-technology products of transnational capitalism have to promote differences, contradictory values, and alternative political processes, the complexity is reductively simplified to a polarization of "us and them." In this way, TVRI represents the indigenous against the foreign, the unitary and unifying construct of national identity against the potentially subversive and fragmenting effects of nonindigenous culture. Never was this more starkly displayed than on 28 January 1996, when Prime Minister Guterres of Portugal broadcast directly to the people of the contested territory of East Timor in their own language via AsiaSat 2 about their "wish for freedom" and "right to self-determination" (*Republika Online* WWW.REPUB-LIKA.CO.ID, 29 January 1996).

The Other that is feared is both the foreigner without and the foreigner within. Predictably, external contamination from scanty costumes, suggestive ("porno") scenes (in both American and Japanese movies), screen violence, recipes using taboo ingredients, and unfavorable commentary on internal political events have all caused alarm. But the internal disruption that a deregulated system may cause has been as much the site of official anxiety as these external influences. In 1986, the deputy head of the parliamentary commission that oversees media matters argued that commercial television would best be organized as a consortium, to minimize the possibility of one group monopolizing opinion. He went on to urge the government to be cautious about the development of regional stations. "We don't want to get to a point," he said, "where regional stations promote a spirit of narrow regionalism, a spirit of provincialism, on the pretext of broadcasting regional culture" (*Suara Karya*, 24 April 1986).

In 1994, long-term fears concerning the domination of the business sector by ethnic Chinese erupted into a very public row when Indosiar was accused of overlooking local talent and employing expatriate expertise from Hong Kong in crucial management and production roles (*Republika*, 7 September 1994). RCTI executives barely contained their concerns about Indosiar's programming and ethnic orientation in a meeting I attended in Jakarta in September 1995. At that meeting, it was said that Indosiar represented "unfair competition," which on probing seemed to be linked to the strength of the Salim Group itself, and to its links with Shaw Brothers TV-B in Hong Kong. Although the Indosiar issue was represented in the press as a legal and immigration matter, the shadow meanings of this dispute loomed densely behind the technical matters discussed. For the first time in the history of the media in Indonesia, the affiliation between Chinese capital and a local producer raised fears that a strategic cultural service would be managed and guided not only by non-*pribumi* interests from inside Indonesia but also by non-*pribumi* interests abroad. For some, Indosiar was simply a conduit, even an "agent" of unwelcome "foreign" (that is, Chinese) business and cultural influence (*Suara Karya,* 13 August 1994; *Republika,* 15 September 1994; 19 September 1994). I return to the Indosiar affair in chapter 9.

TVRI exploits the us-them binarism by parading its indigenous culture credentials, emphasizing that only about 20 percent of its programming is imported. On the commercial stations the local to imported ratio is inverted. Despite regulations requiring them to boost local programming, none of the channels, with the exception of TPI, has taken the requirement seriously (Kitley 1994b). Official reaction to the lack of compliance has been tolerant. Once again, clientelistic relations might explain the Department of Information's willingness to overlook noncompliance. But given the opprobrium imported product attracts from time to time, circulation of the Other within the nation keeps the us-them bogey and the fear of cultural disintegration ever present. Under these circumstances, TVRI's familiar if unexciting programming is culturally reassuring. TVRI's celebration of local production preserves the cultural integrity and clarity of the imagined national community. TVRI has underlined its role as circulator of official culture most obviously in the way it has reserved for itself the right to produce and circulate "hard news." Commercial channels are required to carry TVRI news and are forbidden from producing their own news and current affairs programs. In the sensitive area of domestic affairs and international relations, it is only TVRI's news producers who shape the official interpretation of national affairs. I explore this issue further in chapter 8.

These various strategies for dealing with competition and deregulation both represent and contain the appearance of the Other in the national culture space. Commercial channels circulate approved or domesticated "nationless" cultural product within guidelines. TVRI, by standing apart, asserts itself as a model of indigenous cultural values. TVRI's indigenism and acknowledged superiority in the television film (*sinetron*) genre (*Tempo,* 25

August 1990) may yet win back its audiences. But its seeming inability to move away from its didactic, instrumentalist nation-building role has meant that for most of the time the commercial channels' programs rate higher than TVRI's (Philip Rich, personal interview, 14 May 1993). The whole thrust of TVRI, for so long the sole channel for imagining the nation (more embracive than the print media Anderson described as so influential), has been displaced in the popular imagination by the commercial channels. The vigor and growth of the commercial sector parallels the way the private sector more generally has displaced and overtaken state enterprises in business and industry (Macintyre 1994, 254). While the print media emerged historically in complicity with nationalism, the whole logic of the new medium of commercial television is antithetical to such totalizing constructs as "nation." It searches for and attempts to create niches, audience categories, and market fractions within the national audience. Commercial channels appeal to and *differentiate* between individuals and groups. They do so at present by relying largely on imported programming. But whether access to global flows of television news, entertainment, and information and circulation of transnational cultural products within the nation might lead to the dismantling of the nation state is something I will touch on briefly in conclusion.

Nation, Global Flows, and Cultural Identity

Benedict Anderson (1991) has rightly emphasized the crucial role print capitalism, colonial institutions, and language played in constructing the imagined community of nationalist Indonesia. But as Schlesinger (1987) has argued, national culture is not produced ready-forged and timeless from radical processes such as revolution in postcolonial nations. Anderson's discussion of the revolutionary appropriation of official nationalism and "Machiavellian instilling of nationalist ideology" (1991, 163) does recognize the ongoingness of the construction of national identity but fails to emphasize the inevitability of shifts in the national construct. As Schlesinger says, a national culture is "continually redeveloped and the contours of national identity chronically redrawn" (Schlesinger 1987, 250). In the late twentieth century national cultural identity is constructed continuously through discourses that occupy the interstitial spaces between official constructs of national identity and a range of other, contradictory constructs advanced by interested factions, as Graeme Turner has argued in *Making It National* (1994).

The preceding argument has shown how television, a historically important means in the construction and circulation of official culture, became a site of cultural contestation. Government initiatives to open up and expand the sector provided an opportunity for a delicately articulated but necessarily muted discussion of ideas of Indonesian culture mediated through debate over the role of television, its ownership, its content, and the public's right of access to new and interesting international programs. While the dynamic and intrusive role of global flows of cultural goods and services is obvious, it is equally obvious that at least in the case of Indonesia, a powerful state may negotiate with international capitalists. The state may trade off some attenuation in the monological construct of national culture in return for a mixed bag of benefits: profits for favored local capitalists, access to high-technology services and facilities, a measure of control over the circulation of popular international televisual products within the national culture space, and a rearticulation of national culture and identity by way of an Othering binarism.

It is also clear that the discourse of competition mobilizes a view that welcomes the presence of international programming and the benefits of the "Open Sky Policy," not because it is hoped that access will result in the "retreat of the nation-state" (Hobsbawm 1990, 191), but because it is hoped it will contribute to a more open, more inclusive public debate on the idea of the nation, national culture, and identity. The idea of the nation that emerges from this is an imagined community but not necessarily a deep horizontal comradeship, and certainly not a homogenous community. The broadcast by Prime Minister Guterres, the fears over resurgent provincialism, and the high profile of ethnic Chinese on Indosiar all draw attention to the limits of the idea of the nation as a "deep horizontal comradeship" (Anderson 1991, 7), for the Indonesian nation has always already been constructed, fractured, and invaded since it was mapped over the territory appropriated by former colonial regimes.

The question of national sovereignty requires a finer analytic mesh than is often used when discussing the integration of nations into flows of international capital and goods. A distinction needs to be made between political and economic sovereignty. For most First and Third World nations today economic sovereignty is diffused across a whole range of supranational agreements, protocols, and organizations. But political sovereignty is far more assertively exercised at the national level, even though at times economic relations between nations may be manipulated as a means of achieving political objectives. The threat by Canada and the Netherlands to suspend aid funds to Indonesia following the massacre in Dili in 1991 is an example. But in that instance, Indonesia asserted its political independence by refusing any further aid from the Netherlands and disbanding the Inter-Governmental Group on Indonesia (IGGI), which managed multilateral aid to Indonesia.

Finally, the question of the way the spatiality of the nation figures in the construct of national culture and identity is problematic at a time when, as David Morley and Kevin Robbins say, "New media technologies and markets seem to make a mockery of borders and frontiers" (1995, 176). There is not space here to pursue this question in depth, but three illustrations that caution against an easy assumption of "collective alienation" (Castells 1983, 7) as an outcome of media flows may be useful.

Anderson's discussion of the cultural role of totalizing colonial institutions such as the map, the census, and the museum in Indonesia shows that the national space of Indonesia is a colonial artifact.

Various passages and phrases emphasize that the impulse of these institutions of power was essentially inward-looking. Map and census *separated* people and space from their surroundings to construct a congruent political, social, and cultural space. But whatever colonial motivations and processes might have been, the processes Anderson describes had both an inward and an outward impulse for those involved. This is well illustrated in the first few pages of Pramoedya Ananta Toer's novel (and here the title is surely significant) *This Earth of Mankind* (Pramoedya 1981). Pramoedya shows that while colonialism produced the national space, it simultaneously linked *inlanders* to worlds beyond the colonial nation—obviously to the metropolitan center, but to Europe and America as well. In the first few pages of the novel, the Javanese Minke speaks Dutch, Javanese, and French and muses on the modernizing power of zyncography and printing, which have brought him images of Princess Wilhemina, skyscrapers in America, and steam trains. These languages and images metonymically represent the enlarged world colonialism had delivered at least to educated Indonesians. And finally, since at least the fifteenth century, for millions of Muslims, the cultural space of Indonesia has been, and remains, inextricably linked with Mecca in Saudi Arabia and other centers of Islamic scholarship in the Middle East.

These three illustrations draw attention to the always already dispersed cultural space of Indonesia, suggesting that a representation of the sense of cultural space as *either* national *or* transnational ignores an extended history of complex transactions between the global and national. In the past the imagined cultural space has had relatively fixed coordinates. In the late twentieth century, however, the global trade in images moves within a featureless, virtual territory whose coordinates carry few if any of the associations of the traditional territory. The lived experience of every day and the emotional attachment many Indonesians feel toward *tanah air* (the land and waters) only recently liberated from colonial oppression and Japanese occupation make for strong attachments to territory, attachments global flows have little likelihood of quickly erasing. Indeed, if European and Latin American experience is any guide (Straubhaar 1991), the commercial channels may become the means for more assertive subnational programs, further reinforcing, but not in an unproblematic way, the continued salience of the spatial construct known as Indonesia.

Conclusion

In the space of just five years, under pressure from new television technologies and transnational capitalism, television in Indonesia has developed from a single-channel, government monopoly to a service that at the end of 1994 is poised to take off with five national commercial broadcasters and a public service channel. In chapter 2 I argued that there was a historical tension in broadcasting objectives and interests in Indonesia—with the needs of national integration and nation building at odds with a more populist, entertainment-oriented television culture. It may seem that with the changes introduced in 1987, the tension has been largely resolved, with two related but separate sectors addressing these different objectives. To a certain extent this is true, but the tension is still incipient. The commercial services are largely controlled by the state and have been established in a way that is intended to position them as a compliant adjunct to the political and cultural objectives of the government rather than an assertive, socially responsive broadcasting sector. TVRI has not let go its monopoly; it is just trying to manage it differently. In the chapters that follow, however, I will argue that the changes introduced in deregulating the sector have progressively disabled the scope the state has to manage its influence over the national culture project.

Chapter 8

COMMERCIAL TEVEVISON NEWS AND THE CULTURE OF DIVERSITY

News Broadcasts on Commercial Channels in Indonesia

TVRI NEWS BULLETINS IMAGE the territorial space of the nation state through a nested series of reports that link local, regional, and national events in an ever more inclusive spatial hierarchy. License conditions require the commercial channels to relay TVRI's news bulletins and forbid them from producing their own. Commercially disadvantaged by the government's news monopoly, the nongovernment channels have developed "soft" news and current affairs programs, which, while observing the letter of the regulation against news production, have enabled them to stake a claim as news providers. In this chapter I analyze news programs on TPI and RCTI and argue that government restrictions on the production of news can be interpreted as signifying a struggle over the roles, rights, and opportunities for social groups to participate in the framing of issues of public concern and to influence political process and decision making. I will also show that this contest over participation in the public sphere involves significantly different conceptions of political and cultural subjectivity.

The arrival of commercial television was hailed in the Indonesian press as an alternative that would improve the quality and content of TVRI and provide the community with alternative perspectives on matters of social and national interest (*Mutiara,* week 1, July 1990). The positive valorization of competition between public-sector and private-sector broadcasters and the possibility of increased public participation in political and social affairs mediated through television invokes the idea of the bourgeois public sphere, which promotes the open, rational exchange of ideas and commentary and the possibility of (indirect) influence on the political environment (Habermas 1989). It is not suggested, however, that the idealized bourgeois public sphere has particular explanatory or theoretical power in late-twentieth-century Indonesia. Critics have pointed out the essentially exclusive character of a *bourgeois* public sphere and have argued that the notion of a "counter public sphere" needs to be imagined to take account of interests not represented in the bourgeois public sphere (Negt and Kluge 1993). Beyond that, however, the Habermasian ideal presupposes forms of speech (discussion, debate) and print as the predominant modes of communication in the public sphere. The bourgeois public sphere is also predicated upon the assumption that public affairs are largely national and does not acknowledge the always already transnational character of national affairs in the postmodern world (Hansen 1993; Venturelli 1993).

In this discussion, the public sphere is thought of as a discursive space where in a wide variety of ways—such as debate and discussion in meetings; on radio, television, and the internet; in printed publications; and also through performance, exhibitions, representation, and lobbying, and public action such as street marches and demonstrations—social groups constitute and represent themselves as identities with a public face and project. From time to time, and for different periods of time, the concerns of various social groups may reach beyond their immediate project and raise "public issues" or matters that constituents believe concern a relatively large number of people, and about which they wish to influence public opinion and political decision making (Poole 1989). In the late twentieth century, public issues are just as likely to be transnational or global as national. Global concerns over environment, public health, human rights, and weapons testing are all examples of public issues that have mobilized coalitions of national and international groups. The contestation of public issues, mediated and performed in a variety of ways, will typically involve state actors as participants alongside social groups and occasionally prominent individuals.

The possibility that commercial television might contribute to the public sphere in Indonesia seems implausible at first glance. Television broadcasts for the most part are programmed and do not admit any degree of spontaneous interaction between producers and individuals. Television reflects production conditions and a process of communication quite unlike that envisaged between the free citizens of the public sphere. As a mass medium, television addresses an unknown, mass audience, and "the wealth objectified in social production appears so omnipotent that relationships between individuals fade into insignificance" (Negt and Kluge 1993, 99–100). Further, if, as Ariel Heryanto has argued, repressive state control and direct intervention into the press have forced it into contorted indirection in presentation of its point of view, it seems naive to claim that an open public sphere exists in Indonesia (1990). Former editor of the magazine *Jakarta Jakarta* Seno Gumira Ajidarma agrees, arguing that economic pressures have led to a "journalism of fear" and that competition has imposed self-censorship (Seno Gumira Ajidarma 1995, 24). But even if we accept that despite the bans and intimidation (in themselves signs of the conflictual and emancipatory role the press can play), the crippled press does in part constitute the public sphere, the government's decision to reserve the production and broadcast of television (and radio) news for itself seemingly rules out the possibility that television news broadcasts might contribute to any systematic contestation or alternative construct of what passes officially for "national news."

It is significant that in TVRI planning documents, news programs are always bracketed with "information" programs. Indeed

TVRI researcher J. B. Wahyudi has suggested that most of TVRI's 5 P.M. and 7 P.M. bulletins are best described as "information" as they are lacking in news values (Wahyudi 1985, 37). The bracketing of news with information signifies that news is understood as reportage or observation on political process, rather than commentary, analysis, or interpretation. News is attributed positivist truth values and represented by state authorities as informed, objective discourse that is not complicit with nor constitutive of political life. It is constructed as a separate, metadiscourse circulated by responsible authorities with the aim of giving citizens access to objective information that will facilitate their participation in and contribution to national development. As the chair of the Indonesian Journalists' Association put it, "[the Indonesian] press is not a 'watchdog' and should only criticise within the constraints of the Pancasila political system" (cited in Hill 1994, 47). Within this paradigm, any idea that television news might contribute to a systematic practice of commentary on or contestation of state priorities is beyond consideration. As the independent journalist Seno Ajidarma disarmingly puts it, "the assumption in Indonesia is that the media should naturally side with the government" (Seno Gumira Ajidarma 1995, 8). The sheer generality of the phrase "the assumption" and the loaded signifier "naturally" draw attention to a process Habermas calls the "refeudalization" of the public sphere, "where the rational-critical public is transformed into a mass, manipulated by pervasive authority" (Livingstone and Lunt 1994, 19).

It is not only politics-as-news that is denied to commercial channels. Any programming that specifically addresses political activity is considered to be beyond the brief of both commercial and state television. In 1992, prior to the national elections, RCTI announced that it would be willing to screen political commentary provided the responsible organizations were willing to pay. Information Minister Harmoko promptly advised that neither the state nor commercial media were permitted to engage in political debate. All radio and television were authorized to do, he said, was publicize details of the organization of the national campaign. Political debate and commentary should properly be conducted in seminars convened by the parties; it was not the function of the media (*Media Indonesia,* 31 January 1992).

Implicit in the (mis)representation of the role of the media as disinterested information giver is embedded a specific construction of the individual self in Indonesian political life. The minister's assertion about the "proper" place for political commentary denies the majority of Indonesian citizens the opportunity to learn about and reflect on political issues or formulate their own, private point of view. In the New Order, political participation is understood, organized, and managed as collective activity that must be pursued through corporatist organizations such as the huge, unrepresentative political parties and the state-sponsored "union of functional groups," Golkar. There is little scope for the articulation of individual opinion and little scope for small interest groups to publicize their views, as the hierarchical, corporatist structures suppress difference and diversity in favor of compromise and consensus. Totalizing myths of "traditional" collectivist structures and consensual practices are invoked to reinforce the representation of the Indonesian subject as a subject-in-community, not an autonomous political agent who has a need and a right to be well informed about matters of public interest and concern. Indeed the refusal of the media's role in fostering public participation in political activity is part of a more general policy of "depoliticization" introduced in 1975, which prevents citizens, particularly rural citizens, from engaging in political activity except at election times.

The Department of Information relied upon a similar corporatist strategy in incorporating the new commercial stations (alongside TVRI) as license holders under the TVRI Foundation rather than allowing owners to establish their businesses as limited liability companies. Minister Harmoko uses the fiction of the formal status of the commercial stations to argue that there is no rivalry between TVRI and the commercial channels. The channels are represented as members of the one team working together to serve the public, but with different responsibilities. Harmoko's view is that the commercial stations have been established to screen popular television entertainment such as international sports events and movies, which TVRI, with its limited financial resources, found it was unable to provide (*Suara Karya,* 16 July 1990). This argument allows the commercial channels to import high-rating popular entertainment, while TVRI goes on, doggedly but responsibly, delivering the news. Under this convenient division of labor, Harmoko argues that it is just not the commercial channels' job to produce news.

The commercial channels have pressured the government to relax the prohibition against the production of news bulletins by nonstate producers with mixed success. Their arguments have emphasized, like the press commentary, that it is valuable for the community to have access to alternative points of view. RCTI argued before a parliamentary commission on the role and function of commercial television in national development that its news programs were educational in that they contributed to the development of critical thinking (RCTI, 1989). Despite such submissions, Information Minister Harmoko has continued to insist that "hard news" (defined as whatever has happened within a twenty-four-hour time frame) is the exclusive preserve of TVRI but has allowed the commercial channels to develop a variety of news features, current affairs, and human interest programs.

In practice these concessions have meant that TVRI's news bulletins are challenged by a variety of information and (soft) news genres. RCTI's *Seputar Indonesia* (Around Indonesia) pays scant attention to the twenty-four-hour constraint and has moved its production and copy deadline closer and closer to its 6:30 P.M. time slot in order to maximize the timeliness of its bulletins. Thus the commercial channels have pried open the government's grip on news and have created a (limited) space for the discussion of national and international political and social issues. Programming strategies that schedule high-rating news programs such as RCTI's *Seputar Indonesia* immediately before the TVRI national news relay are used to keep viewers tuned to RCTI and naturalize the information role it hopes one day to be permitted to develop more fully.

But while the press and commercial television representatives appear united in their desire to have television play a role in the public sphere and advance the democratic process, commercial television's interest in the right to produce news is motivated as much, if not more, by commercial considerations than by political commitment. Peter Langlois, formerly station manager and news director at KCRA Sacramento and long-term senior adviser at RCTI, stated frankly that RCTI was keen to get permission for news production because it was RCTI's news that would differentiate it from its competition and attract and hold audiences for the nightly lineup (personal interview, 30 April 1993). The public relations manager at Indosiar was equally frank when he stated that Indosiar's planned news bulletins would focus on crime because "it would be easier to sell [to advertisers]" (*Republika Online*, 27 February 1996).

It is understandable, then, that on the commercial channels the viewer is addressed as a private, individual consumer and is typically offered (the illusion of) involvement in decision making about a variety of personal and family issues. On TVRI, however, the viewer is addressed not as an individual with specific needs and interests but as a public citizen-in-community whose needs and interests are believed to be satisfied by information *about* political activity rather than (mediated) involvement and participation in political process. While the commercial media might seem emancipatory and ascribe agency to the individual, it is illusory, for the subject is addressed by the commercial media as a consumer rather than as a citizen whose needs and interests extend beyond consumption to *involvement* in political activity. The development model adopted by TVRI, on the other hand, positions the subject not as an involved agent but rather as an observer of processes managed and conducted by elite and unrepresentative mass groups.

The different modes of address of the public and commercial

channels manifest a tension in the cultural construction of the ideal Indonesian subject. It seems that the mode of address of the commercial news and information programs has been influential in attracting audiences to those programs and away from TVRI. RCTI's *Seputar Indonesia* is popular with audiences because it is more concerned with everyday issues rather than bureaucracy and government. *Seputar Indonesia* news items often include actuality footage, unlike TVRI news, which is ceremonial and often looks as if it is produced from press releases. *Seputar Indonesia* items are more balanced because they give victims a chance to have their say, compared with TVRI items, which tend to present only high officials' or government members' side of a story. *Seputar Indonesia* news is more worldly, focusing on issues such as crime and slum clearance, unlike TVRI, which just reports news of development success (*Republika,* 8 October 1994). It is these qualities that prompted prominent economic analyst Christianto Wibisono to declare that RCTI may become a democratizing power far more effective than demonstrations or the reformist magazine *LSM,* let alone social and political organizations (*Tempo,* 12 March 1994).

The Letter of the Law: "Soft News" on Commercial Television

Despite the formal restrictions and recent heavy-handed government intervention into the print media's news and current affairs activities, commercial television stations have been imaginative in developing a variety of programs to get around the letter of the law restricting them from producing their own news programs. Usually described as "information programs," all stations now present dialogue, current affairs, news features, news magazines, forums, and even, in the case of TPI, an additional news bulletin, *Morning News* (*Berita Pagi*), which is produced out of agency material not included in the previous night's *Dunia Dalam Berita.* In February 1996 Indosiar announced that it would cooperate with press giant Gramedia and the production house Intermedia to produce a daily news bulletin featuring crime reporting (*Republika Online*, 27 February 1996).

The commercial channels are creative in nuancing their news programs in order to circumvent the strict requirement not to broadcast hard news, but they try all the while to produce "information" that is topical and up to the minute (*aktual dan segar*). In December 1991, for example, RCTI sent a crew to Manila for the Southeast Asia Games and reported on the events by profiling the athletes rather than restricting their coverage to reporting the races and results. The different production and distribution conditions of television and the print media also mean that from time to time television scoops the print media. In April 1993, for example, RCTI's *Seputar Indonesia* broadcast live footage of a major fire at the Pasaraya department store in Jakarta. Readers of papers such as *Kompas* were not able to read about the fire until the next day.

TPI's *Good Morning Indonesia*

If the content of the news programs produced by the commercial stations is analyzed, the expectation that television might contribute to a more open public sphere in Indonesia seems optimistic. An examination of TPI's news magazine *Selamat Pagi Indonesia* (Good Morning Indonesia) and RCTI's *Seputar Indonesia* over a "constructed week" (Jones and Carter 1959) for the month of April 1993 revealed that *Selamat Pagi Indonesia* is largely uncritical and rarely analytical in its coverage of social and (more rarely) national political events. The program's mode of address seems to imagine an audience of (mainly Muslim) women. Many items promote national development in a style very similar to the development programs of TVRI and tend to close off a diversity of viewer responses by highly directive introductory comments at the head of each item. High-level government figures such as ministers, directors general and secretaries of departments or directorates are often interviewed during the program, perpetuating the top-heavy, bureaucratic emphasis that audiences have resisted for so long in TVRI's news programming (*Bisnis Indonesia,* 25 June 1994).

A shifting construct of the Indonesian subject is inscribed in the program. Commercial segments address individual consumers, and the final segment, *"Sosok"* (figure, identity), profiles the achievements of prominent individuals such as popular entertainers, craft workers, the first female police general, and a rural cooperatives official. Aerobic exercise segments, however, always feature corporate groups of (mainly) women, all identically dressed, self-consciously performing a tightly choreographed routine (often to the same music day after day), which the group has obviously practiced for months. The exercise segments are a regular feature of the program and obviously provide an opportunity for organizations and workplaces to build staff relations by offering their exercise teams the goal of appearing on TPI. The groups are largely drawn from institutions closely associated with the government, such as *Dharma Wanita* (Public Servants' Wives) groups, the National Development Bank, and The Indonesian People's Bank.

Although the aerobic segment assumes individual viewers, there is no address to the person at home. The segment displays a group performance rather than demonstrating routines or exercises for individual viewers to follow. There is no attempt to speak to the viewer to encourage participation, nor are there any suggestions about the specific value of the routines. The displays are all performed outside in large spaces and do not invoke or seem to recognize the cramped spaces of most Indonesian's homes. The selection of corporate groups to perform the routines reinforces the normative subject-in-community, not the individual trying to work on fitness. This corporate mode of address contrasts strongly with the address of the commercials selling flu tablets, vitamins, shampoo, and the like. In these segments, the embodied individuals are addressed directly and their well-being and desires acknowledged and indulged. In brief, the bureaucratic style, the uncritical focus on development, and the reinforcement of the corporate ethos in social life in the information and news content of *Selamat Pagi Indonesia* is largely complicit in reinforcing the values of the dominant ideology of the New Order regime. The program offers little scope for any enlargement of the public sphere even granted the "soft" news values of the early morning news magazine genre.

RCTI's *Around Indonesia*

The high ratings of RCTI's live-to-air half-hour news features program *Seputar Indonesia* suggests that its production values sharply differentiate it from TVRI news bulletins. Since it was first introduced in late November 1989 as *Seputar Jakarta* (Around Jakarta), *Seputar Indonesia* has attracted and held on average 85 percent of the audience for the 6:30 P.M. time slot (Philip Rich, Survey Research Indonesia, personal interview, 2 April 1993). *Seputar Indonesia* has always presented itself as a news program. Chief editor Chrys Kelana told me that when he was recruited from *Kompas* to develop the program, he and senior executive Peter Gontha, who was determined to develop RCTI's "image" through *Seputar Indonesia*, studied CNN's news style as a model for *Seputar Indonesia* (personal interview, 19 April 1993). It was not long before *Seputar Indonesia* began to attract attention, and influential figures from outside Jakarta sought opportunities to appear on the program. Under these circumstances, the "Around Jakarta" scope of the program soon became restrictive, and it was opened up to national events and issues and renamed *Seputar Indonesia*.

Seputar Indonesia is not modeled on face-to-face communication but replicates the information dissemination role the newspaper has traditionally performed. Seated at the desk of a studio news set, the male and female anchors presenting the show jump straight into the business of the day as soon as the insistent ostinato of the signature tune has ended. With nothing more than a brisk "Good Evening," the anchors announce the nightly lineup of stories in rapid succession, prioritizing them as they are announced in the same lead story/less important stories/human interest/close structure that is practiced on TVRI and, of course, on Australian screens. The presentation is urgent, the feeling communicated is that there is a lot to get through and that it is important. At the same time, and in contrast to TVRI, the anchors are always named, and full credits are given to crews who file stories from the field. The news team presents itself as a team of individuals, as men and women who have a job to do and intend to do it well.

Seputar Indonesia content mixes international and national political stories, such as the visit of U.N. Special Envoy Amos Waco to East Timor, and the visit of American warships to Surabaya, with items that take up a wide variety of local issues such as the relocation of batik workers in Jakarta, telephone fraud in Bandung, the renovation of the ancient Beringharjo market in Yogyakarta, a fraudulent share certificate scandal on the Jakarta Stock Exchange, slum clearance, and local protest over the redevelopment of the burial site of the ancient Sundanese king Prabhu Siliwangi (1482–1521) as a golf course. Stories are always based on actuality footage, very often with a reporter on location reporting live. To date the practice of live crossing between the reporter in the field and the studio anchor has not been part of *Seputar Indonesia*'s style, no doubt because of the cost of satellite feeds. From time to time *Seputar Indonesia* includes ceremonial items such as the promotion of high-ranking officials in the program, but it usually manages to include informal comment from key figures involved to differentiate its coverage from the much more ceremonial style practiced by TVRI on such occasions.

Seputar Indonesia content is obviously highly accessible, and although the style of presentation is modeled on the CNN style of mass syndication of news to national and even global audiences, the structure of stories is highly developed and offers viewers many mediated opportunities to become involved in the issues and perhaps formulate their own points of view. Whenever practicable, *Seputar Indonesia* accesses relevant voices on camera and edits footage to create a narrative that draws attention to the range of interests involved in the issue. Thus, although the *Seputar Indonesia* style is "informational" and not "conversational" in the rather self-conscious manner of *Selamat Pagi Indonesia, Seputar Indonesia* stories offer viewers more opportunities for participation than *Selamat Pagi Indonesia*. *Seputar Indonesia* constructs a mediated space that acknowledges viewers as members of the national public, but also as private citizens, living in specific, named locations, with a rich array of interests, pressures, problems, desires, and attachments to local places and traditions. The embodied individuality of *Seputar Indonesia* viewers is reinforced in the three commercial breaks included in the program.

The popularity of *Seputar Indonesia,* a result of its acknowledgment of the complexity and situated subjectivity of its audience and its interest in investigating the effect of official policy on the community, has occasionally put it on a collision course with the government. It is difficult to obtain information on such sensitive matters, but I understand that a story that presented graphic shots of bulldozers breaking up the flimsy shelters of urban squatters as part of a government policy of slum clearance prompted State Secretary Moediono to warn RCTI that the close-ups "were unnecessarily graphic." Other complaints, generally forwarded by sections of the government most directly affected and rarely from the Department of Information, have been made over the unethical practice of showing the faces of prostitutes and AIDS victims on screen, over the championing of clove farmers' and traders' perspectives on a controversial clove marketing monopoly awarded to President Soeharto's son Tommy, and over the comments from a Democratic Party spokesperson about the composition of the commission established to inquire into the Dili massacre in 1991.

Soft News, the Indonesian Subject, and the Public Sphere

In concluding I review the subjectivity presupposed in the news and information programs described and draw some tentative conclusions about their discursive contribution to the public sphere in

Indonesia. We can begin with the names of the programs themselves. TVRI's *National News* addresses the audience as a national public, dispersed across a politically bounded space and held in an imposed synchronicity. Citizens are disembodied and without specific individual interests and desires. Other TVRI bulletins address citizens in reports in which the local, the sphere of immediate individual experience, is subordinated to the national space. Individuals who make up the national public are taken-for-granted participants in national development activities and are addressed as subjects in whose name national development is advanced. The actions, policies, and words of elite public figures are superior to those of members of the public whose voices rarely, if ever, are heard. The mode of address is informational and hierarchical, not conversational.

Selamat Pagi Indonesia, tracing its genealogy no doubt to the American Broadcasting Company's flagship *Good Morning America,* also declares its interest to be the mass audience of Indonesians. Unlike the TVRI bulletin, the title, a customary greeting, is conversational and recognizes the social and communicative potential in the dissemination of television programs. The conversational character of the title is carried into the style of presentation of the program's male and female "hosts," who are almost excessively courteous and take care to address viewers in their introductory remarks and story leads. The program set mimics a domestic living room, with a verandah opening onto a tropical garden. The title, domestic setting, and host couple all construct a semiotic space of comfortable domesticity and conversation. But the performance of conversation is stilted and ultimately illusory. Story leads are highly directive and frame items in a way that offers little room for consideration of alternatives. The screening of set pieces on development, and the frequent appearance of government figures overdetermine what is represented as a private discursive space with public priorities and interests and inhibit the potential for the conversation signaled in the title. In other words, *Selamat Pagi Indonesia* does not foreground critical analysis in its imagining of the Indonesian citizen but positions the subject as one who is more passive in the sphere of public affairs and favors consent with the dominant ideology.

Finally, the title of *Seputar Indonesia* invokes the national space and imagines an active subject ready to move within that space. "Around" (*Seputar*) signifies an interest not in contemplation of a geopolitical abstraction but in the exploration of the national space, of visiting and revisiting people and places throughout the country. The endlessness of "Around" opens up the lasting fascination of Indonesia, a named, familiar homeland of great diversity. *Seputar Indonesia* holds out the excitement of a journey and an opportunity to discover and talk about people and places. The signature graphics that introduce the program are a series of snapshots of sites throughout the archipelago, presented one after the other. But these are not memories, frozen in time. The landscape in the frame is manipulated electronically and changes while we watch, growing larger and closer until it is replaced with another image, which in turn takes its place, semiotically imaging the diverse and changing character of contemporary Indonesia.

In TVRI's *National News*, the national public is imagined negatively in relation to at least three aspects of the individual—the physicality of the body, individual economic interests, and the interiority of individual subjectivity, which is considered ultimately private. In contrast, the commercial mass media create an imaginary space of viewership and participation in which individual choice and freedom exist at the level of consumption. The specific, embodied needs and interests of consumers are recognized as potentially unlimited, and advertisers and producers work to generalize specific desires and create a mass market. In the TVRI news, Indonesian subjectivity is imagined as the public citizen whose interests are taken to be coincident with those of the elite who manage the nation-state in their name. In mass mediated commercial programs, the ideal subject is a viewer/consumer addressed as an embodied individual whose social, psychological, emotional, and economic interests are acknowledged and understood.

Selamat Pagi Indonesia acknowledges the individual and opens up the promise of mediated conversation, only to wrap it up and fold it along the familiar creases of the homilies and assumptions of the dominant ideology. *Seputar Indonesia,* in contrast, addresses its viewers in a style that at first glance seems to efface the individual and promote the concerned-citizen mode of address more familiar in TVRI bulletins. But unlike TVRI, *Seputar Indonesia* addresses the viewer as a decision maker, a subject who considers alternatives, who thinks things through. This is achieved in the way the program deliberately creates a discursive space within news stories. The *Seputar Indonesia* program opens up spaces of mediated participation and in this way models the critical norms of the bourgeois public sphere. *Seputar Indonesia*'s choice of stories also recognizes popular culture, foregrounding the everyday concerns of viewers rather than imposing upon them priorities that are not theirs.

Conclusion

There appears to be a contradiction in the commercial stations' enthusiasm to develop and publicize their own news programs, and on balance, a reluctance to use the news genre to create a space that mediates between society and the state. I have noted, however, that *Seputar Indonesia* has been more successful than *Selamat Pagi Indonesia* in encouraging the discursive participation of its audience in social and political commentary and criticism. Perhaps we can interpret this situation by simply noting that under the present restrictive regulatory environment and the intimidation of the print and electronic media, the commercial stations are prudently biding their time. Another, less sanguine view, following Tornquist, might be that their compliance is an outcome of the politically compromised position of the owners of the stations. As Tornquist argues, clients in a clientelistic system must pay their dues in return for the rent-seeking access they have been awarded (Tornquist 1990, 35).

But even if this were the case, it is not certain that these circumstances will continue. The logic of competition requires that stations do as much as they can to differentiate their product from others. Ironically, in the short term, this means that all the stations have to develop similar lineups. But once the lineup is in place, then the focus shifts to consideration of the appeal and perceived quality of the different channel's programs, and I have noted Peter Langlois's comments on the crucial role news can play in creating station image. Media researcher Ahmad Zaini Akbar is confident that the economics of commercial television will inevitably involve it in opening up the public sphere: As he says, "capital that depends for its accumulation on information must adopt a critical stance toward the dominant power and disseminate information that captures the aspirations of the community, for it is that which will maximize advertising" (*Bisnis Indonesia,* 25 June 1994).

This potentially emancipatory scenario describes exactly, however, the dilemma faced by the print media, and as David Hill and others have argued, the repressive power of the state has worked successfully against emancipatory journalism (Hill 1994; Ariel Heryanto 1990). In 1995 RCTI's network partner, SCTV, voluntarily canceled its popular interview program *Perspektif* because of the outspokenness of some of the personalities interviewed. Ironically, in a kind of "back to the future" strategy that has implications for the mediation of the public sphere in Indonesia, the presenter, Wimar Witoelar, took the show "on the road" and performed his interviews for enthusiastic crowds in large public venues such as sports grounds. And although these events were not canceled by authorities, Wimar's anchor role in an international television hook-up on the subject of APEC was canceled by SCTV at the last minute (Wimar Witoelar, e-mail correspondence, 27 February 1996). Even though what I might call Wimar Witoelar's Theater of Interview has caught public attention, the electronic media have far greater access to the public and are the preferred medium for information and entertainment. The communicative potential of television is obviously a concern for the government, and lies behind its reluctance to open up news broadcasts and create a space where government policy and the construction of national identity and culture may be debated. The very slow progress on drafting the broadcasting law reveals a preference for keeping the parameters of the role of commercial television in national political affairs as vague as possible for as long as possible, leaving the regime room to move. For as long as the government keeps a tight regulatory control over news in the licensing conditions of commercial broadcasters and demonstrates a resolve to act decisively when it believes its interests are threatened, the commercial channels have little leverage. On the other hand, the commercial stations have been conspicuously successful in lobbying for a more favorable commercial environment since they were first established under very restrictive regulations (Kitley 1994b). Given that record, it is likely that news programming will be deregulated, although the commercial channels may have to wait at least until after the national elections in 1997 (see Kitley 1999), and until the ratification of the broadcasting law, which at the time of writing, the president has yet to sign.

Chapter 9

REGULATING OWNERSHIP AND CONTROL

Deregulation and Reregulation

IN THIS CHAPTER I PRESENT case studies of three disputes concerned with the ownership and control of cultural services and facilities: the license fees affair; advertising, education, and children; and the foreign workers affair. These disputes developed as the state relinquished its monopoly over television broadcasting and opened up the sector to favored client capitalists. The process of deregulation, the commercialization of broadcasting, and the privatization of state roles provoked a public debate about television that displayed a tension between the construction of the audience as public, the audience as consumer, and the audience as active public citizen. As indicated in chapters 7 and 8, the commercialization of broadcasting was generally welcomed for the improved standards and diversity of programming it was expected to deliver. But there was also a recognition that the audience as consumer constructed by the commercial channels disempowered the audience, making it dependent on the commercial priorities of the commercial licensees. The debate over advertising on TPI projected the public's right to override commercial priorities in favor of public and educational values. The globalization of television also introduced a tension between government aspirations to maintain a national culture and commercial pressures to take advantage of the circulation of global cultural products and services. Some imported programming was perceived by members of the community and the government as incompatible with Indonesian cultural values. The presence of a team of foreign television producers working illegally in Jakarta embodied the problematic of the ownership of cultural production. The Indosiar affair was in part a reaction against the penetration of "foreign" culture into the production of domestic programming. The government's quick action to expel the team's disturbing presence displayed its interest in maintaining the national culture space in Indonesia.

The License Fees Affair

In late 1990, President Soeharto signed a decree (Presiden Republik Indonesia #40, 1990) that authorized the private company Mekatama Raya to collect annual television license fees (*iuran pesawat penerima televisi:* television set levy, dues, contribution) from all set owners on behalf of the TVRI Foundation (*Yayasan TVRI,* YTVRI). This authorization covered the period from 1991 to 2005. The president's son Sigit, his cousin Sudwikatmono, and Henry Pribadi, a businessman closely connected with Liem Sioe Liong, were principals in Mekatama Raya. The contract was awarded to Mekatama Raya without any public tender or prior announcement that YTVRI would no longer collect fees (*Jakarta Post,* 20 March 1992). In announcing the arrangements, Minister Harmoko advised that Mekatama Raya had promised to deliver substantially higher revenues to TVRI through a system of door-to-door collection. The company guaranteed to deposit Rp 90 billion with YTVRI in its first year of operation, a substantial increase over the Rp 63 billion deposited in 1990 by YTVRI's agent, the Directorate of Post and Telecommunications, which collected fees through its nationwide network of post offices.

The License Fees Affair involved citizens "from the villages to the Parliament" (*Tempo*, 28 March 1992) in face-to-face encounters, debate, and for some, public action, over something that affected their everyday lives and, more specifically, their monthly budgets. The affair turned the private domain of television reception into a public discourse focused on the sense of identity as citizens. The fees affair united citizens throughout Indonesia against a poorly conceived and executed privatization of part of TVRI, an institution that for nearly thirty years had been synonymous with national development and unity.

Mekatama Raya began collecting fees in April 1991. Almost from the beginning angry citizens complained about the company and its subcontractors. A confused Mataram viewer who tried to pay at the post office found that staff there could not answer her question: "So, now that paying has shifted, where should I pay? Has another collector been named?" (*Kompas*, 4 April 1991). And in Jakarta another disgruntled viewer confronted Mekatama Raya head office staff, saying, "How long do I have to wait at home for your collectors? Until they never arrive, come on! Who is to blame? I am a good citizen, you know" (*Kompas*, 4 April 1996).

Over the next twelve months newspapers ran complaint after complaint. Mekatama Raya collectors called twice. They intimidated householders as they made their rounds accompanied by police officers, provoking questions about the use of state facilities (police) by a private company. Collectors failed to arrive, depriving citizens of the opportunity to pay, and left them in confusion over their legal position. Collection offices were closed at times when they were advertised as being open. The long chain of subcontractors letting collection duties in the provinces to other subcontractors left the public uncertain as to the bona fides of collectors (*Kompas*, 9, 10, and 11 April 1991; *Kompas*, 11 June 1991; *Kompas*, 31 December 1991; *Suara Pembaruan*, 15 January 1992; *Media Indonesia*, 18 January 1992; *Bisnis Indonesia*, 4 March 1992; *Jakarta Post*, 12 March 1992).

For its part, Mekatama Raya advised members of Parliamentary Commission I that it had experienced problems collecting fees. As no sanction applied for the nonpayment of license fees, the company could rely only on licensees' good will for payment. Records of set ownership were often missing or inaccurate. The company estimated that it needed two years to recruit and train collection staff to work throughout Indonesia, but TVRI had pushed it to begin on 1 January 1991. TVRI also required Mekatama Raya to make regular deposits of revenue, even though the company had often not received payments from its regional subcontractors. Finally, petty corruption by local government officials who charged their own license fees often made it difficult for Mekatama Raya to collect official fees (Mekatama Raya 1991).

On 17 January 1992, Mekatama Raya announced a month's halt in collection of fees. It realized that it would fall short on meeting its target, and even after taking out bank loans to cover the shortfall, it found it was still Rp 7 billion below the target. Mekatama Raya claimed later that it lost Rp 50 billion in its fees venture (*Tempo,* 28 March 1992). On 5 February, Mekatama Raya abandoned its door-to-door strategy and fell back on simply urging citizens who had not paid to pay through nominated banks. On 1 February, the Department of Information announced that television license fees would rise by 100 percent, arguing that operational costs had risen, that fees had not risen for eleven years, and that there was a greater capacity to pay in the community (*Suara Pembaruan,* 2 February 1992). On 14 April, the Director General of Radio, Television, and Film announced that Mekatama Raya would cease collecting fees but that it would continue to act as a consultant to TVRI, advising on fees collection.

The abortive privatization of fees collection and the government's sudden decision to raise fees was felt right across the community, affecting everyone who owned a television set. While there had been a steady stream of letters from aggrieved viewers throughout 1991 over Mekatama Raya's practices, the sudden announcement of the rise in fees crystallized opposition to the company. A rash of angry denunciations of the company and the government followed in the press. The coincidence of the fee increase with Mekatama Raya's financial difficulties led the *Jakarta Post* (editorial, 20 March 1992) and John Nazar, a lawyer representing aggrieved citizens, to question whether the increase was meant to benefit TVRI or to provide a windfall benefit to the failed Mekatama Raya operation (*Jakarta Post,* 20 March 1992; *Warta Ekonomi,* 20 April 1992; *Suara Pembaruan,* 20 March 1992; *Tempo,* 28 March 1992).

Early in March 1992, a coalition of consumer advocates called on citizens to boycott the payment of fees, pending a clear official statement of the fee increase. This coalition consisted of leading nongovernment organizations—the Indonesian Foundation of Consumers' Organizations (*Yayasan Lembaga Konsumen Indonesia*) and the respected Foundation of Indonesian Legal Aid Institutions (*Yayasan Lembaga Bantuan Hukum Indonesia*), led by a former chair of the Consumers' Organizations. The committee they formed publicized grievances over the fees issue, urged a fees boycott, and lobbied members of Parliamentary Commission I. They gained the support of the Democratic Party faction. Unrelated to the committee's activities, lawyer John Pieter Nazar filed a class action in the Jakarta Administrative Court against the Minister for Information, challenging the legality of the increase in fees on behalf of himself and twenty-eight disgruntled viewers. An editorial in the *Jakarta Post* (20 March 1992) interpreted the Committee's call for the community to suspend fee payments as historic: "The call made by the committee ... for the public to 'suspend' payment constitutes ... the first such call for taking a stand on an issue made in the New Order period." The same newspaper referred to the committee's work again in April: "A number of citizens of considerable prominence even urged the public to "defer" payment of the television fees until the authorities had satisfactorily explained their policies—something that was tantamount to a call for civil disobedience" (*Jakarta Post,* 16 April 1992).

The depth of public feeling surrounding Mekatama Raya's tax

farming foray and the potential for the matter to become an election issue (*Pelita*, 20 March 1992; *Bisnis Indonesia*, 20 March 1992) prompted the Department of Information to act quickly. On 14 April 1992, it announced that Mekatama Raya would no longer collect fees and that in the future fees would be paid at post offices. While the department reversed its policy on the collection of fees, it did not reverse the fees increase. It was saddled with Mekatama Raya as an "expert consultant" for years afterward. In 1994, Minister Harmoko disclosed in a hearing before Parliamentary Commission I that the company had continued to receive 10 percent of TVRI fees revenue under the terms of the 1991 contract. Commission members argued that this was improper as Mekatama Raya was no longer involved in fees collection (*Media Indonesia*, 5 February 1994).

The Mekatama Raya affair was a case in which widespread public action, mediated through the press, spurred on by the formation of a high-profile lobby group, and supported by elite figures such as the Speaker of the Parliament, made a substantial impact on state television sector management. It is stretching credibility to suggest that the public in the guise of these high-profile activists "won" this issue. But it would also be simplistic to suggest that the affair was resolved in the government's favor. The affair drew public attention to a range of issues that state authorities had always preferred to manage privately. The coincidence of Mekatama Raya's mismanagement of fees collection with other major scandals was noted by the Speaker of the Parliament in his end-of-session address in March 1992 and drew attention to a lack of transparency and due process in television since deregulation.[1] Indeed, as the potential electoral backlash of the affair became more obvious, Minister Harmoko shifted in his support for Mekatama Raya over the course of the dispute and by late March voiced (muted) criticism of the company's mishandling of its contract (*Pelita*, 18 March 1992; *Suara Karya*, 23 March 1992; *Pelita*, 23 March 1992).

Mekatama Raya's failure to deliver higher revenue to TVRI also focused attention on the anomalous status and revenue situation of

TVRI which, unlike the commercial television stations, was forbidden to raise funds through advertising. The Mekatama Raya affair led to accusations that regulations denying advertising revenue to TVRI were more related to protecting privileges extended to Presidential family companies than to any coherent policy related to TVRI's status as a public broadcaster (*Kompas,* 3 February 1992; *Pelita,* 20 March 1992; Suharsono Hadikusumo, Letter, *Suara Pembaruan,* 16 July 1992).

The License Fees Affair politicized the television sector, damaging the government's credibility. As the extent of Mekatama Raya's incompetence became more obvious during 1992, a shadow language emerged challenging the government's role in the affair: the increase in fees had "burdened the community." The focus on the impact of the increase put the government's actions center stage but still permitted the impact of political patronage to be indirectly examined: "After working for more than a year, it has recently become evident that Mekatama has not been successful in fulfilling its mission.... But strangely, Mekatama Raya has not attracted sanctions of any kind. Just the opposite, the community is the one that has been burdened with carrying the rising operating costs" (*Pelita,* 10 March 1992; see also *Merdeka,* 26 February; *Pelita,* letter, 10 March; *Tempo,* 28 March; *Kompas,* 3 May; *Suara Pembaruan,* 21 June; *Suara Karya* 12 September 1992).

The privatization of fees collection and its fallout were represented as central to the government-citizen relationship. The government had not acted to protect the community. Quite the reverse; it had delivered the public up to harassment, even exploitation, and when Mekatama Raya had failed to deliver on its contract, the government appeared more interested in protecting the private company than redressing the harm that had been done (*Media Indonesia,* 14 February 1992; *Suara Pembaruan,* 20 and 28 March 1992; *Jakarta Post,* editorial, 20 March 1992; Ashadi Siregar 1995, 92–95). As member of Parliament Marzuki Darusman commented, "If we go back now to the old model for collecting fees, then you can say that there has been no benefit [from the privatization]" (*Merdeka,* 26 February 1992). Not only was there no benefit from the privatization of fees, but the government had conspicuously failed to fulfil its mission "to protect the poor from greedy capitalists"—a mission that Adam Schwarz argues has been part of government ideology in both the Sukarno and Soeharto periods (1994, 82).

The fees affair also led to questions and complaints about transparency, due process, and the management of public funds (*Pelita,* 10 March 1992; *Media Indonesia,* 18 March 1992; *Kompas,* 3 May 1992). The community projected its anger at the irresponsible way the government had permitted a private company, with minimal preparation and without any relevant experience, to take control of a complex public sector responsibility. Retaining the failed company as an adviser added insult to injury. The perception that the sector had been changed by deregulation was expressed by the Indonesian Front for the Defense of Human Rights: "Television has become a tool of propaganda for the government and strong businesses, rather than a means of communication for the public" (*Jakarta Post,* 19 March 1992).

Beyond representation in the press and electronic media, the affair created an embodied sense of citizenship and turned the audience into a public. The privatization of fees precipitated widespread social interaction and discussion of the role of television in daily life and the ownership and control of public facilities, and it asserted the public's right to be treated fairly. The Mekatama Raya affair also demonstrated that public advocates, speaking on behalf of citizens who believed that TVRI was "theirs" because they paid license fees (*Suara Pembaruan,* 24 August 1990), were prepared to pursue the issue and generate publicity over it. The strategic use of publicity, civil processes, and institutions and the deliberate use of lobbying and research have become a feature of disputation over aspects of the regulation of television since the Mekatama Raya affair. The License Fees Affair signaled that deregulation had established a complex mediascape that offered the political public more opportunities for influencing policy formulation than was ever the case before (see appendix I).

Advertising, Education, and Children

Given Indonesia's late introduction of advertising, television and its customary modes is creating new tensions and possibly new processes of community and government interaction, policy making, and cultural construction. With the deregulation of television, advertising became a site of considerable public discussion and agitation. What follows is to some degree speculative in the sense that data on television advertising and its role and character are greatly lacking in Indonesia. While Stuart Cunningham was able to draw on nearly thirty years of diverse "flagship national advertising" campaigns and substantial public documentation in his discussion of the cultural role and significance of advertising on Australian television, similar materials for the Indonesian case are lacking (Cunningham 1992a, chapter 3). The reasons for this are complex. Suffice to say the perceived "unworthiness" of advertising in promoting consumerist values, which led to its being banned in 1981, the absence of advertising from television for nearly ten years, and the lack of industry standards all contributed.

In April 1981 the key objections to television advertising were its perceived contribution to the spread of consumerism, particularly in rural communities and the Department of Information's desire to shift TVRI toward the role of a public broadcaster in the style of ABC (Australian Broadcasting Corporation) or BBC in recognition of the growing maturity of the Indonesian economy and system of governance. Whatever political pressures might have motivated the ban on ads, it was supported by data from Alfian and Chu's government-sponsored longitudinal field study reporting that television commercials had a "counter developmental potential" (1981, 97). The use of research in support of tighter control over television advertising has continued to the present. Interest groups intent on keeping TVRI free from ads or regulating advertising to lessen its negative impact have increasingly relied on empirical research to make their cases. But in 1990, when the government issued a license for an educational channel and agreed that it would be permitted to raise funds through advertising, opposition to what was proposed was argued in terms of principle and policy.

Since January 1991, *Televisi Pendidikan Indonesia* (Indonesian Educational Television, TPI) has embarked upon an ambitious program of providing educational programming to a national audience of school-age and adult viewers. Its idealism echoes the hopes of President Sukarno and Information Minister Maladi, who established TVRI in 1962. Maladi's early statements and Sukarno's first presidential decree concerning television both identified education as Indonesian television's prime goal. Former Director General of Radio, Television, and Film Soegito, argued that TVRI's early involvement with commercial sponsors, however, shifted its programming toward popular entertainment. It was never able to operate as a general, development-oriented broadcaster and deliver on its promise to become primarily an educational channel, despite the urgent need for such a service in a rapidly developing country (Sjamsoe Soegito, personal interview, 7 May 1993).

In 1990, in what some informants suggested was no more than sibling rivalry or "me too-ism," TPI lobbied the Department of Information for the right to broadcast nationally. RCTI and SCTV were granted licenses under provisions that restricted their broadcast range to the cities of Jakarta and Surabaya respectively. TPI argued that education was a national priority and that in supplying educational television, TPI was complementing the state's activities. It suggested further that educational programming, when compared with entertainment programming, lacked commercial appeal for advertisers and that a national market was a reasonable trade-off for the risks and high costs associated with developing an educational television channel.

TPI's arguments were persuasive. In August 1990 the Department of Information granted the company Cipta Lamtoro Gung Persada a national broadcast license. This gave TPI significant commercial advantages over RCTI and SCTV. With a national broadcast license, TPI gained access to a national advertising market. While the channel was designated as an educational broadcaster, formal educational programming was limited to 16.6 percent of total hours. The vague "nonformal" education segment was also set at 16.6 percent. That left 12.5 percent for news and information, 31.9 percent for entertainment, 20 percent for commercials, and 2.4 percent for continuity.

TPI also benefited from state patronage: studio facilities at TVRI were made available, and it piggybacked on TVRI's broadcast facilities and used TVRI staff and expertise. TPI was also authorized to work with the Center for Communication Technology (*Pusat Teknologi Komunikasi*), the Open University (*Universitas Terbuka*), and the Department of Education and Culture. In reciprocation for these substantial advantages, TPI was required to pay 20 percent of its advertising revenue to TVRI (notes of meeting, Parliamentary Commission I, 11 February 1993, 39). TPI covered the costs of updating and equipping a recording studio at the Center for Communication Technology and agreed to share production and development costs in making educational programs at the center. Similar arrangements were made with the Open University (Arief Sadiman, Dewi Patmo, personal interview, 18 May 1993; Awad, personal interview, 27 April 1993).

TPI's surprise entry into the commercial television scene with an ambitious educational mission was controversial. The promise of increased educational services was welcomed (*Suara Karya*, 2 February 1991), but most press comment was guarded or critical. When TPI's license was granted in August 1990, it announced it would begin broadcasting in January 1991—barely five months later. Educational television had been mooted for nearly thirty years, but delivery had proved to be an intractable problem. The pious idealism—Siti Hardiyanti told journalists that God had pushed her into this venture (*Editor*, 26 January 1991)—of a company with no television experience rushing onto screen with what seemed unrealistic haste was greeted with skepticism. There was a feeling that TPI's interest in television, despite its high moral tone, was superficial and no more than an indirect way of gaining a commercial advantage over rival commercial channels. There were also suggestions that the move into educational television was largely motivated by Siti Hardiyanti's political ambitions. Access to a national television service would help Siti Hardiyanti promote her social welfare and political programs such as the nationwide youth movement *Kirab Remaja* (confidential interviews, April and May 1993).

More serious conflict surfaced between TPI and the Departments of Education and Culture and Information. Minister for Education and Culture Fuad Hassan resented TPI's precipitous rush into educational broadcasting. He interpreted it as an intrusion into his department's field of responsibility and a grab for funds (*Tempo*, 2 March 1991). While appearing to endorse the TPI proposal, the minister suggested that nighttime broadcasts would suit students and teachers better, as very few schools were equipped with television receivers. Given that TVRI's facilities would not be available to TPI in the evenings, the minister's apparently supportive comments were understood as being critical of TPI's rush into education. The minister also noted that his department had no funds to supply sets to schools, as TPI seemed to expect (*Kompas*, 18 August 1990; *Suara Merdeka*, 19 January 1991; *Tempo*, 2 March 1991). And finally, Fuad's comment following TPI's inaugural broadcast that a "true teacher" would never wear a miniskirt reinforced the impression that the Department of Education and Culture did not consider that TPI took its educational aspirations seriously (*Kedaulatan Rakyat*, 27 January 1991).

The commercial character of TPI has been the focus of public criticism since the channel was first announced (LPPK and TPI 1992, 1). Most critics acknowledged and accepted that television was an expensive medium and that advertising revenue was crucial to TPI's existence despite the considerable advantages handed to it by the state. Siti Hardiyanti's claims that TPI commercials would be different from those of the other channels were, however, received with some skepticism (*Tempo*, 26 January 1991;

Suara Merdeka, 28 January 1991; *Suara Pembaruan,* 2 February 1991). At a seminar in Jakarta in January 1991, Siti Hardiyanti stated that commercials on TPI, like the formal educational programs, would have "educational characteristics." First, she noted that TPI would not accept advertisements for cigarettes or alcohol. She then gave two examples of what she meant by educational commercials. Advertisements for milk were acceptable, she said, because milk was a vital part of children's health. Second, in advertisements for products such as cars, the technology used in making the vehicle would be featured, not simply the brand name. Spokesperson Yoenarsih Nazar added that TPI would not screen commercials that relied upon gratuitous display of women's bodies (*Jawa Pos,* 21 January 1991).

These rather simplistic remarks came in for lighthearted and mocking comment from critics concerned about the influence of advertising on an educational channel (*Suara Pembaruan,* 2 and 4 February 1991; *Jawa Pos,* 21 January 1991). The generally derisory response to the claims about TPI's commercials provides further evidence of a general suspicion over TPI's motives in developing an educational service (*Merdeka,* 7 May 1994). More seriously, the objections to advertising on TPI made by consumer organizations, parliamentarians, prominent intellectual and cultural figures, and teachers and academics focused on a perceived tension between the principles and priorities of an educational broadcaster and TPI's commercial imperatives. The Semarang-based Consumer Development and Protection Institute put it this way: "TPI gives the impression of going in two directions. On one hand, TPI is a medium for public education, [which is] not profit-oriented, but on the other hand TPI can only develop if it is managed on a commercial television model that is profit-oriented." As a result of its ambivalent position, TPI does not have an opportunity to be managed as a broadcaster that is profit-oriented. For that reason, TPI is confronted with more problems than TVRI and the other commercial stations because of a clash between the two poles of its priorities as an educational medium that should be noncommercial and the priorities of a commercial broadcaster (LPPK and TPI 1992, 1).

Criticism about advertising itself focused on three familiar issues: the alleged vulnerability of children to advertising (*Berita Buana*, 20 January 1991; *Suara Merdeka*, 28 January 1991), the alleged harmfulness of television advertising (*Kedaulatan Rakyat*, 25 January 1991), and the potential conflict between educational and commercial values in programming (*Suara Pembaruan*, 2 August 1990; *Suara Merdeka*, 28 January 1991; *Suara Pembaruan*, 1 February 1991; *Suara Karya*, 2 February 1991; *Suara Pembaruan*, 4 February 1991). The besotted, smiling faces of the children and their mother in the *Suara Merdeka* cartoon shown in figure 9.1 certainly suggest that homework and educational programs will be hard pressed to match the entertainment values of advertising. It is also possible to identify a more general anticapitalism, anticonsumerism value stance behind the criticism of advertising on TPI. It is worth noting, however, that the concerns expressed about

Figure 9.1. The clown figure is holding up a banner labeled "Advertisement" (*Suara Merdeka*, 28 January 1991).

television advertising on TPI have also been key concerns in debates over television commercials and children in Australia, the United States, and the United Kingdom (Hodge 1992; Cunningham and Turner 1993; Comstock and Paik 1991, 191f; and Buckingham 1993, 242).

We might ask, then, whether TPI has presented a more "ethical" or responsible regimen of commercials than other channels. The consensus appears to be that it has not, though criticism has been more of an "in-principle" kind than a catalogue of specific objections (*Suara Pembaruan,* 2 and 4 February 1991; *Suara Karya,* 2 February 1991). The objection to advertising on TPI may, indeed, be part of a more general disquiet over what is seen as commercial intrusion into areas traditionally managed by the state (Robison 1993, 55–74). It may also represent, more narrowly, resentment at the seemingly ever-widening operations of powerful and politically privileged conglomerates and individuals.

My own analysis of weekday advertising on TPI in December 1991 and April–May 1993 provides no grounds for believing that TPI commercials are any more "educational" than commercials on other, noneducational channels.[2] In the one advertisement for cars in the sample, the technological values of the car were not referred to, but unsurprisingly, the brand was. In milk product advertisements, the brand name of the products was foregrounded, while nutritional information was secondary. All commercials, with the exception of some community service announcements, as we might expect, were more persuasive than informative.

While TPI commercials do not differ from commercials on noneducational channels, the overall advertising profile during its morning hours is not a relentless, hard-sell targeting of children. Most ads are not pitched to children. The implied audience is adults, and adults (mostly women) feature in commercials far more frequently than children. Even so, ads on TPI amount to nearly 11 percent of broadcast hours, about 2 percent more than ads on RCTI. In that sense, TPI is "more commercial" than RCTI.

Most ads in 1991 and 1993 advertised low-value products for personal and household use and were pitched at an adult audience with relatively low disposable income. Proprietary medicines and vitamins for children were the most frequently promoted products. In most cases the pitch was to parents. No ads inscribed appeals that instruct children to ask their parents for a particular product. No ads for toys or consumer items such as bicycles, sunglasses, or board games were screened. The only consumer durables that featured in ads were television sets—perhaps a way of developing a bigger market over the longer term, as was the practice in the United States in the early days of television (Comstock and Paik 1991, 189).

On RCTI, in contrast, consumer goods such as television sets, jeans, cigarettes, sound systems, computers, and food and drink products, were the most frequently advertised products (fig. 9.2). Ads on RCTI were not repeated nearly as frequently as on TPI. Production values on RCTI were advanced, with 15- and 30-second spots as standard. The representation of upmarket lifestyles was more pronounced on RCTI than TPI. Many ads, for example,

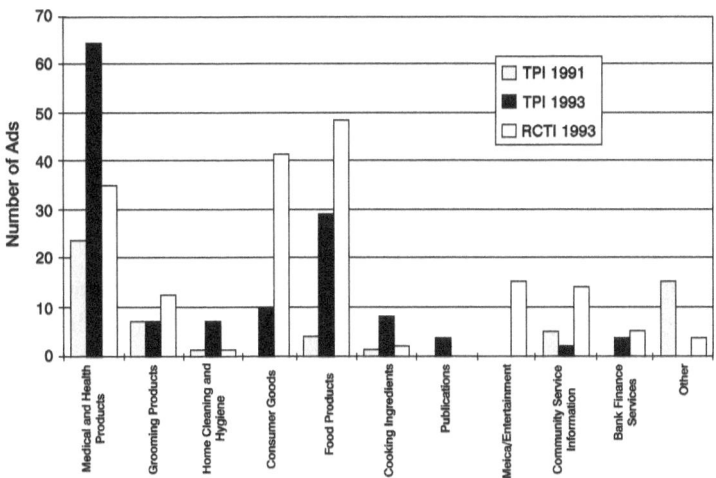

Figure 9.2. Ads for Categories of Goods and Services on TPI and RCTI, 1991 and 1993

used English-language narration to lend an "international" cachet to the goods and services advertised.

The criticism leveled against advertising on TPI was uncoordinated and ineffective and had no direct impact on TPI's advertising practices. It did, however, politicize advertising as an issue and raised public awareness of concerns that were taken up more deliberately by children's welfare and consumer organizations a few years later as the advertising pressure became more insistent with the establishment of three more commercial channels. From interviews I conducted, it appeared that four factors inhibited critics from pushing their complaints: (1) a general willingness to give the educational experiment a fair go, (2) the distracting territorial dispute between the Department of Education and Culture and the Department of Information, (3) TPI's legal right to screen ads, and (4) the powerful political connections of TPI's owner. The disquiet over the perceived conflict of interest died down without any specific action being taken to change TPI's reliance on advertising.

The debate over advertising on TPI projected an (indirect) public attack on the privatization of state functions and on the extension of state facilities and licenses to client capitalists. The publicity that surrounded this issue revealed a long-running dispute between the Department of Information and the Department of Education and Culture about which department should properly have control over educational broadcasting. But beyond that, the potential benefits to the community from a new educational broadcasting channel seemed to outweigh the perception that TPI would benefit from its favored treatment.

Since then, the antiadvertising lobby has become better organized, intellectually more coherent, and more forceful. In the mid-1990s, attitudes toward advertising on television are varied. There are those who argue in favor of advertising mainly for the benefits increased revenue would deliver to TVRI, which is perceived as low quality, under-resourced, and disadvantaged by the ban. A range of voices has urged this view upon the government, not least members of Parliament (*Bisnis Indonesia*, 24 September 1994). In part, the pressure to permit advertising on TVRI should be understood as a strategy to push for a change in the legal status of TVRI. For TVRI to raise revenue through selling advertising, it would be necessary to change TVRI's present noncommercial, foundation status and incorporate the national broadcaster as a commercial body (*Republika,* 2 November 1994). Those who argued for this change were primarily interested in making TVRI revenue and expenditure more transparent, removing the privileged status of the commercial stations by injecting more competition into the market, and improving the management, efficiency, and appeal of TVRI (*Jakarta Post,* 9 November 1992; *Bisnis Indonesia,* 24 August 1994; *Republika,* 12 April 1995).

Other voices, such as the Indonesian Medical Association (*Ikatan Dokter Indonesia*) and the Institute for Consumer Development and Protection, Semarang (*Lembaga Pembinaan dan Perlindungan Konsumen*), offered qualified support for advertising on television, including TVRI, but argued that the present lack of regulation of advertising was inadequate, even dangerous, and that a properly regulated industry, with a code of practice, should be developed (*Republika,* 17 May 1994; *Suara Karya,* editorial, 1 November 1994).

Understandably, the commercial channels support advertising on television but are opposed to the extension of advertising to TVRI. They argued first that TVRI had the benefit of three sources of income: an annual 12.5 percent share (20 percent in the case of TPI) of advertising income from the commercial channels themselves, license fees receipts, and an annual government budget allocation. Second, they asserted that advertising on TVRI was incompatible with TVRI's public broadcaster or national broadcaster status and role; third, that it would be unfair to allow advertising on the well-established TVRI at a time when the commercial stations were in the process of developing their broadcasting infrastructure; and fourth, that if TVRI were permitted to carry advertising, then the commercial licensees should no longer pay fees to TVRI and that TVRI should be treated as just another commercial broadcaster. There is a certain amount of bluff in this last suggestion, as a commercially oriented TVRI with its fully developed national broadcast reach would present a formidable challenge to the nascent commercial stations (*Republika,* 6 October 1994; *Jakarta Post,* 25 November 1994).

While these arguments can be dismissed as special pleading by the commercial stations, the arguments presented by consumer organizations in favor of tighter regulation of advertising are more convincing. The call for improved regulation has addressed a wide range of perceived negative impacts that are attributed to television advertising. Familiar arguments—that television commercials encourage consumerism, that they make false claims and "trick" young viewers, that they are often unethical, encourage bad eating habits, and take away a sense and time of play from children—have been argued by the three nongovernment organizations named below and by others (Kunkel and Roberts 1991; Hodge 1992; Frith and Biggins 1994). These arguments will not be expanded upon here as the focus of attention is on the dynamics of policy formation over advertising and television, rather than the validity or otherwise of the arguments.

Nongovernment organizations such as the Indonesian Consumers' Foundation (*Yayasan Lembaga Konsumen Indonesia*), the Institute for Consumer Development and Protection (*Yayasan Pembinaan dan Perlindungan Konsumen*), and the Indonesian Children's Welfare Foundation (*Yayasan Kesejahteraan Anak Indonesia,* YKAI) have conducted a long-term campaign against aspects of television advertising. Their strategy has been to use publicity, empirical research, and expert knowledge to press for policy change. They have convened seminars and conducted their own research into aspects of advertising. The Indonesian Children's Welfare Foundation worked with the research section of the Directorate of Radio, Television, and Film in one study and published its findings under joint names. These groups have argued for better regulation, for "advertising-free zones" during children's programming, and higher ethical standards. YKAI has also published a booklet addressed to parents (1994). The three organizations have also used the print media effectively in publicizing their positions.

The Department of Information has presented an unconvincing case for the continuation of the ban on advertising on TVRI. Until May 1996, Minister Harmoko and the former Director General Alex Leo Zulkarnain simply stated that "it wasn't time" for TVRI to screen ads (*Suara Karya*, 7 October 1994). The public broadcaster rhetoric that underpinned the 1981 decision to ban television advertising has not been raised, and the consumerism argument has been undermined by the government's preparedness to allow ads on TPI and the other commercial channels. The weakness in the government's advocacy of its own position was perplexing. On one level it was understandable. The consumerism argument was no longer convincing and for that reason there were grounds for authorizing ads on TVRI. But that position was not helped by statements that TVRI would screen ads, but not just yet. This equivocation undermined any authority for treating TVRI as a public broadcaster station. It left observers with the impression that the only thing really holding TVRI back was probably pressure from its potential rivals, the five commercial channels. It appeared that the government was reluctant or unable to make a decision that might adversely affect the advertising revenues of the commercial channels. Alex Leo Zulkarnain also argued that consumers had to look out for themselves, a remarkable shift from an official who spent most of his working life regulating television in the name of protecting the public (*Republika*, 16 January 1995).

In the draft broadcasting law, however, TVRI is permitted to raise funds by advertising and sponsorships (article 8, clause 3). In the official "clarification" (*Penjelasan*) attached to the draft bill, it is noted that advertising must be carefully produced because it has the potential to encourage consumerism. Advertising is justified for its information giving role, and because it can assist consumers make better informed choices about their purchases of goods and services (Republik Indonesia 1997 clarification re article 31, 23).

In the policy environment envisaged by the draft bill, advertising on television would be regulated by the industry itself within broad guidelines set out in the bill. The bill makes it illegal, for example, to screen ads that promote ideology, religion, and political position. Beyond that, advertising is handed over to the industry for self-regulation, although as for many other sections of the bill, there is a note that advertising will be subject to government regulations yet to be drafted.

To summarize, then, the press has been very influential in publicizing community concerns over advertising on television. The government has appeared indecisive and compromised. It has chosen to make the regulation of advertising an industry responsibility under very broad guidelines that do not include significant community representation. Despite its professed interest in using the broadcasting law as a way of protecting the vulnerable, the government has chosen not to regulate advertising itself and has not made any specific provisions concerning advertising and children in the draft broadcasting law. This issue will be discussed in more detail in chapter 10.

The Foreign Workers Affair

On 7 September 1994 the progovernment Muslim paper *Republika* drew attention to internal problems at Indosiar, the fifth commercial channel, which began broadcasting on 11 January 1995. The article reported complaints from Indonesian staff at Indosiar that their decision-making and production roles had been taken over by 150 expatriate (mainly) Chinese advisers from the Hong Kong television station TV-B. The Indonesian staff claimed that the foreign workers did not have the required work permits. The article also stated that the Hong Kong workers justified their right to direct Indonesian staff by claiming that TV-B held 40 percent of Indosiar shares. If this claim was correct, then TV-B was in breach of foreign investment regulations, for in June 1994 Minister Harmoko had obtained the president's agreement that the mass media were off-limits to foreign investment. *Republika* and other papers followed the Indosiar story day by day for nearly a month, until finally the Minister for Justice announced that the alleged offenders had all left the country (*Media Indonesia,* 28 September 1994).

Indosiar denied much of what was claimed. It admitted that there were expatriate advisers working at the station, but that there were only about forty of them. The station announced that its advisers were drawn from many countries and that they were all working with proper authorization. It rejected the claim that they were performing production or creative roles and said that they were all technical staff (*Republika,* 9 and 14 September 1994). Indosiar Director Handoko played down the presence of the foreign workers with a homely analogy. He said the foreigners were just like the top Sumatran cooks a new Padang restaurant in East Java might invite to help train local staff. Once the locals were up to it, he said, the "cooks" would be sent home (*Republika,* 12 September 1994). The story became a little muddied when the Human Resources Manager at Indosiar stated that there were indeed 150 foreign workers helping out and that they had been authorized, not by the Department of Manpower or Information, but by an agreement reached with the Coordinating Body for Foreign Investment (*Badan Koordinasi Penamanan Modal Asing*) (*Republika,* 9 September 1994).

While claims about the actual number of expatriate staff were tossed back and forth between government departments, the press, and the station for weeks, the general contours of the "Indosiar case" (*Republika,* 19 September 1994), as the affair became known, were simple enough. But the employment of foreign workers in the television sector, whether there were 150 or only 40 of them, resonated profoundly with deep-seated fears and resentments in Indonesia: "The fact that many community interests expressed strong critical reactions about the [overseas workers' artistic control over local production, and the dumping of scenarios] shows that these two issues have touched something very sensitive in the body of the nation" (*Republika,* 19 September 1994).

In simplest terms the Indosiar case concerned the superior competitive position of Indosiar and the fear that Indosiar might dominate or monopolize television production (*Merdeka*, 13 September 1994). The station was owned by the Salim group, the most powerful conglomerate in Indonesia (*Warta Ekonomi*, 24 April 1995), and was associated with the highly successful Shaw Brothers television operation based in Hong Kong. Shaw Brothers was reported to produce five thousand hours of product per year (*Republika*, 7 September 1994). There were claims that the TV-B staff had brought scenarios of eight hundred television dramas to Jakarta from Hong Kong and that it was their intention to translate the material into Indonesian and produce it locally (*Republika*, 14 September 1994). The expatriates were represented as super producers, capable of producing in three days what took Indonesian producers between four and seven days (*Republika*, 9 September 1994). Film Director and Member of Parliament Sophan Sophian was also concerned that the foreign workers at Indosiar were taking jobs away from local creative talent: "Indosiar produces all its own material. Their artists are tied up in contracts ... and they are not allowed to work for any other company. 'I am worried that Indosiar will throw the livelihood of production houses and artists in Indonesia into chaos,' said Sophan" (*Republika*, 13 September 1994).

But beyond concerns about market dominance, the illegal presence of the expatriate workers at Indosiar generated a public debate about cultural dominance and control of cultural facilities. It was acknowledged that television was a global industry and that for reasons of efficiency and cost international programming was attractive to all the commercial channels in Indonesia (*Republika*, 16 September 1994; *Kompas*, 18 September 1994; *Bisnis Indonesia*, 14 October 1994). What made the Indosiar case of particular concern was that the foreign workers were making decisions about the production of *domestic* programs:

> The Indosiar case is different.... It is obvious that the other commercial stations are also dominated by foreign programming. Yet

in the case of Indosiar, for some time the makers of the foreign programs have actually been in positions where they can direct production. If before commercial stations were like distributors, but with full discretion to choose imported programming, in the case of Indosiar, *local* programming material is in fact *produced by foreigners.* (*Republika,* 16 September 1994, my emphasis)

Some critics were concerned that under these circumstances, the influence of foreign producers was undetectable. Commentator Umar Natuna argued that as the Indonesian community was not used to information diversity, skills of information analysis were underdeveloped, and viewers were not always aware of the influence of television (*Merdeka,* 1 October 1994). Sophan Sophian argued that viewers may not be aware that what they were seeing had been put together by foreigners whose outlook and values were different from Indonesian values. The values inscribed in domestic programs directed by foreigners could promote "deviations" in community values, he said, and had the potential to promote conflict and weaken Indonesian culture (*Merdeka,* 13 September 1994). Journalist and writer Yudhistira Massardi was also concerned that foreign values and culture might be passed off on unsuspecting Indonesian viewers: "People get defensive when local cultural products are decided by foreigners.... People get defensive when foreign cultural values dressed up as Indonesian [values] are smuggled into a local format [*Sedangkan sikap penolakan terjadi tatkala ke dalam format budaya lokal hendak diselundupkan nilai nilai budaya asing yang dikemas dengan 'baju' Indonesia*]" (*Republika,* 19 September 1994).

In these articles discussing the cultural impact of the foreign workers and the wholesale packaging of Hong Kong scenarios, there is a suspicion that the Indosiar affair was a deliberate attempt to disrupt and take control of parts of Indonesian culture. The assertion was regularly repeated that a "strategic" sector was "dominated" by the foreign workers (*Republika,* 12 and 13 September 1994) and that their influence was "dangerous" (*Republika,* 12 September 1994). Media analyst Alwi Dahlan reinforced such ideas when he raised the question of TV-B's reported shareholding in Indosiar, and he asked rhetorically "what's behind Indosiar?" (*Republika*, 15 September 1994). Uncertainty surrounding the number of expatriates at Indosiar and questions about their legal status only reinforced the impression of a secretive, subversive presence (*Merdeka*, 1 October 1994). Journalist Akhmad Zaini Abar wrote, "It is feared that the foreign workers will become the source and center of decisions about the entry of foreign culture that conflicts with national culture and the culture of development of the Indonesian nation" (*Bisnis Indonesia*, 14 October 1994).

In other comment, the presence of the expatriate workers was interpreted as part of a process of cultural imperialism or colonization (*penjajahan budaya*) that would result in the domination of indigenous culture and the alienation of Indonesians from their own cultural values (*Republika*, 16 September 1994; *Merdeka*, 1 October 1994; *Bisnis Indonesia*, 14 October 1994). The concept of "colonization," with its powerful historical associations for Indonesians, connected an alleged loss of control and ownership of a key cultural facility to the historical conditions of occupation and rule that the colonial period imposed upon Indonesia.

A series of medical and military metaphors is scattered throughout the press comment on the Indosiar affair. They represent not only the fear that the colonized nation may be "attacked" (*kini bahkan kita disergap lagi oleh subversi budaya*) and subjugated but that it may be psychologically and culturally transformed by the presence and actions of the foreign workers (*Republika*, editorial, 16 September 1994). The cultural battle is represented as a secret war in which a "strategic" cultural sector is "subversively" "infiltrated by foreign cultural values" (*infiltrasi budaya [asing]*) (*Republika*, 13 and 16 September 1994; *Merdeka*, 1 October 1994).

Symptoms of psychological disturbance are present in *Republika*'s and *Media Indonesia*'s early reports on the affair, where indigenous Indonesian staff were described as "uneasy" (*resah*—on edge, restless, nervous) about the presence of the foreign workers (*Republika*, 7 and 9 September 1994; *Media Indonesia*, 13 September

1994). The representation of a body at risk is inscribed in expressions that refer to internal problems in the "body" of Indosiar (*Bisnis Indonesia,* 14 October 1994), the sensitivity of "the national body," and the nation "irradiated by foreign culture" (*mengidap radiasi budaya*) (*Republika,* 16 September 1994). Like contaminants, the agents of foreign culture that cause disorder in the national body must be "filtered" out lest all national institutions are penetrated (*Merdeka,* 13 and 21 September 1994; *Republika,* 19 September 1994). *Republika*'s editorial of 16 September 1994 raised fears for the "heart" of the national culture when it concluded by saying that the Indosiar situation took cultural imperialism beyond anything experienced previously: "Before, foreign values were present in actual foreign products, now these values are in the heart of local products [*Bila sebelumnya nilai-nilai asing hadir dalam wujud produk asing, kini nilai-nilai tersebut berada di jantung produk lokal*]" (*Republika,* 16 September 1994).

The MISS SARA guidelines, which constrain reporting on issues that may affect the peace and stability of Indonesian society, prevented Indosiar's critics from directly attributing their fears of cultural colonization to the ethnicity of the TV-B workers. Readers would have been in no doubt, however, that the Indosiar affair was largely concerned with the threat of economic and cultural domination by Chinese culture and business. References to expatriates from Hong Kong, the repetition of some workers' (Chinese) names, the description of the head of the Salim group, Liem Sioe Liong, as a "taipan," and Hong Kong as a *koloni kelentong*, a colony of Chinese peddlers, all foregrounded the Chinese ethnicity of the two conglomerates and the foreign workers involved. The resentment over Indosiar's resources and links to a powerful Chinese entertainment corporation, and the assertions of Indosiar's arrogance (Eduard Depari, *Republika,* 15 September 1994) all manifest what Hal Hill (cited in Schwarz 1994, 81) has called "the politics of envy" and hostility toward the Indonesian Chinese minority for its business success, alleged involvement in the Indonesian Communist Party, and the coup in 1965.

Government departments were cautious in their remarks on the Indosiar affair. Powerful and well-connected entrepreneurs were involved, and it was clear that if there was a large group of expatriates working illegally at Indosiar, then some parts of the bureaucracy had not done their job. Senior officials restricted themselves to promising to investigate the reports. The affair ended when the Minister for Justice announced simply that all unauthorized expatriate workers had left the country. Just how many foreign workers were involved was never clarified (*Media Indonesia*, 28 September 1994).

The government's prompt action in resolving the Indosiar affair served its own interests. It protected domestic television producers from direct transnational competition and reasserted the sovereignty of the national culture space. But the voices raised against cultural colonization were an implicit criticism of the deregulatory policy that the government had initiated. However exaggerated the claims of the effects of the foreign workers, the hyperbole registered an indirect but forceful protest that the government had exposed a major cultural resource to control by nonindigenous entrepreneurs and foreign capital. As in the License Fees Affair, critics of government policy were able to make a case that the government's management of the broadcasting sector since deregulation was most likely to benefit a few powerful entrepreneurs and not the general public. In this context the Indosiar affair can be interpreted as another example of the indirection that Indonesian economist Kwik Kian Gie finds characteristic of social criticism: "What Indonesians feel is often different from the terminology they use. When they criticise conglomerates they are really calling for social justice, fair competition and a more equitable distribution of wealth" (cited in Schwarz 1994, 99).

The military and medical metaphors that framed the Indosiar debate, however, indicate a deeper intensity of ethnic hostility than Kwik Kian Gie's comment suggests. The stridency that characterized the Indosiar affair may be attributed to what was seen as an unauthorized attempt to establish an offshoot of a foreign broadcaster on Indonesian territory, combined with deep-rooted resentment of the economic power of the Chinese community in Indonesia.

Conclusion

In this chapter I have discussed three debates led by nonstate actors such as the press, members of parliament, intellectuals, and nongovernment organizations. These debates have challenged the government on aspects of the control and management of television in a deregulated market. In each of the debates, the protagonists have intervened to protect what they perceive to be the public interest against the commercial priorities of the licensees and an exclusive political alliance between the government and client capitalists. In the next chapter the impact of nonstate actors on media policy is taken further in an examination of the drafting of the broadcasting law and concerns over sex and violence on children's television.

Chapter 10

REGULATING TELEVISION CONTENT AND POLICY

IN THE PREVIOUS CHAPTER I examined three controversies that were largely concerned with the politics of the control and ownership of television. In this chapter I focus on controversy over the *content* of television, the role of public discussion in effecting change in the formal regulation of television, and the link in Indonesia between the media and policy determination. The public controversies discussed here center on the lack of a broadcasting law and the amount and impact of sex and violence in (mainly imported) programs screened by commercial channels. These two issues became closely linked in late 1996 when the draft broadcasting law's silence on the regulation of children's programming and other matters of community concern stimulated an intense period of public advocacy in the press and parliament.

These events provide some insight into the nature of media and public policy interaction in Indonesia, particularly the role and influence of the press in Indonesian policy. In this discussion, I will draw on a model of media-policy relations from the United States and suggest that certain modifications of the model are necessary for it to have any heuristic value in Indonesian media culture. Second, the analysis provides insights into the way tensions related to deregulation of the television sector have an important impact on the construction and contestation of Indonesian cultural identity in the late New Order period. In an industrialized democracy, the events to be described would be regarded as unexceptional. But in an authoritarian state such as Indonesia, public intervention in government policy making is rarer and sometimes dangerous, especially when intervention may cut across the personal interests of powerful figures within the government or those closely connected to its functionaries. And finally, the analysis suggests that deregulation and the mechanism of public debate are contributing to a reconstitution of the idea of the citizen in Indonesia, proffering models of the active citizen and sovereign consumer alongside that of the "developmental" citizen of the New Order and the passive consumer of the deregulated, commercial television market.

The Broadcasting Law Debate

Unlike the license fees affair, which touched the hip pocket nerve of almost everyone who owned a television set, the debate over the government's slowness and apparent reluctance to finalize Indonesia's first broadcasting law involved a more restricted group of intellectuals. These included members of parliament, television licensees, and professionals in the advertising industry. Because of elite players' prime interest in the issue, the broadcasting law became a site of public debate from the beginning of the deregulation period. In reports of seminars and meetings and in "opinion roundups" (*Republika Online,* 16 October 1995) the press reported the view from those closely involved that the proposed legislation cut across a number of matters of general cultural importance, such as the uneven distribution of information, access to diverse sources of news, and the legislative role of the parliament (*Suara Pembaruan,* 10 October 1992; *Kompas,* 21 February 1993; *Prospek,* 27 February 1993).

The objectives of the broadcasting law are not specified in the draft. But summarizing scattered sections, the law is designed:

- To contribute to the development of a regime of general broadcasting (no religious, political, or other narrow interest group may establish a radio or television station)
- To be locally owned and controlled
- To foster local talent and programming over international product
- To foster and develop the mental outlook of the Indonesian community
- To consolidate the union and unity of the Indonesian people. (articles 3, 5, 9, 10, 24)

The debate on the broadcasting law is most conveniently discussed in terms of two phases of its development. The first phase, from 1987 to May 1996, covers the long period of drafting the law. The second phase of the debate began in May 1996 with the tabling of the draft law in the fourth sitting of the 1995/96 parliamentary term and continued until the revised law was ratified by the Parliament on 9 December 1996.[1]

Public discussion of the need for a broadcasting law in the years 1987 to 1992 was intermittent, amounting to little more than a few scattered comments, until 1993 when the issue began to attract more attention.[2] The main reasons for the protracted development of the legislation are as follows. First, in the early years of commercial television, when only one or two stations were on the air and broadcasts were restricted to Jakarta and Surabaya, the government had no particular motivation to develop legislation. In these years the Department of Information dealt individually with licensees. Second, governmental planning for a law was often interrupted. The former Director General of Radio, Television, and Film, the late Alex Leo Zulkarnain, admitted that in the early years of the development of the commercial television sector, government broadcasting policy was reactive. The government was frequently overtaken by developments in global electronic broadcasting and had little time to project a model of the broadcasting sector into the future. Alex Leo specifically noted problems with spillover, the popularity of satellite dishes, and the sudden deregulation of the sector as taking the department's attention away from forward planning (*Kompas Online*, 6 February 1996). The emphasis on control in the draft law, about which observers such as Abdul Muis have commented, suggests that the Department of Information was much clearer about what it did *not* want than what it did want for the broadcast sector (*Kompas*, 10 May 1996; *Suara Pembaruan*, 22 May 1996; *Kompas Online*, 3 June 1996; *Kompas*, 7 June 1996).

From 1993 to 1995 discussion on the broadcasting law featured much more frequently in the press. However, even here it remained abstract and unfocused in the absence of a draft text and any statement of intention from the department. The draft law was largely a bureaucratic concern as it moved through various levels of discussion until it was submitted to the State Secretariat, where it languished for nearly two years (*Kompas*, 10 May 1996). Apart from discussion of the draft with the National Broadcasting Council in 1994, there was no attempt to involve the public or media specialists in its drafting.

By 1994, however, the increased availability of commercial television programming created a different climate of controversy. There was a particular concern among children's welfare organizations over the apparent lack of regulation of violent and sexually explicit imported films considered incompatible with Indonesian cultural values. Frustrated by the delay in drafting the law, Member of Parliament Marwah Daud Ibrahim threatened that the Parliament would exercise its right to develop its own law if the government delayed any longer, saying that "the need for the broadcasting law is pressing. It is *urgent*. The community's attention to television issues and improvement of audiovisual broadcasting is very high. There have been many inputs to Parliament" (*Republika Online*, 13 September 1995; original emphasis).

Commercial television licensees were also impatient with the delay in preparing legislation. As I will show more fully in the next section of this chapter, the commercial stations were frequently the target of angry denunciation in the press for their inappropriate programming. The stations' defense, that the programs screened had all been passed by the government's own Film Censorship Institute (*Lembaga Sensor Film*), seemed only to underline the perception of disarray in the regulation of television broadcasting. The resignation of the respected former governor of East Java Mohammad Noer from the Board of SCTV over the station's screening of *Deadly Exposure,* after it had been banned by the Censorship Institute, significantly raised the profile of the debate (*Jakarta Post,* 28 February 1994).

Under attack from within and without, the commercial channels urged the government to introduce a broadcasting law that would deliver them more certainty over the import of films, programming standards, and the required proportion of local programming (*Suara Pembaruan,* 24 November 1994; *Republika,* 13 July 1995; *Kompas,* 8 May 1996). The commercial channels were also keen to speed up the government's legislation so that the question of TVRI's status could be resolved. Debate over whether TVRI should sell advertising time, led by high-profile speakers such as Alwi Dahlan, and opposed by the armed forces faction in Parliamentary Commission I, made commercial channels' forward planning uncertain (*Republika Online,* 9 June 1996; *Media Indonesia,* 11 June 1996). Thus, for different reasons, both the commercial licensees and the public had a common interest in lobbying government to speed up final drafting of the broadcasting law so it could be more widely debated.

On 6 May 1996 Information Minister Harmoko finally presented a draft broadcasting law (*Rancangan Undang-Undang Republik Indonesia Tentang Penyiaran*) to the Parliament for discussion and ratification. The law has come under intense scrutiny since it was tabled. According to Marwah Daud Ibrahim the draft has attracted more submissions from the public than any other law (*Kompas,* 12 September 1996). The debate has centered on matters of social and legal principle, scope and content, and the operation of the proposed law.

Social and Legal Principles and the Broadcasting Law

Adverting to the minister's phrase about "protecting the community" (*Republika Online,* 7 May 1996), the draft law was represented by critics such as Member of Parliament Marcel Beding (*Kompas,* 3 June 1996) and sociologist Azis Saleh (*Kompas,* 10 May 1996) as an authoritarian, "backward-looking" document that sought to preserve both the government's dominant position in the broadcast sector and its preference to keep global broadcasting at arm's length. To support their claims, these and other observers, such as communications scholar Budiyatna and prominent writer and journalist Goenawan Mohamad, pointed to the coordinating role preserved for TVRI (*Pasal* [article] 20); the requirement that commercial channels continue to relay official news bulletins and state announcements (article 34); and the prohibitions—first, against production houses producing news bulletins (article 27, *Ayat* [clause] 4); second, against sectional interest groups establishing broadcast stations (article 9, clause 3); third, against commercial broadcasters "receiving any help from foreign organizations" (article 12); fourth, against foreign broadcasters establishing themselves in Indonesia (article 19); and finally, against foreign investment in the commercial broadcast sector (article 10) (*Suara Pembaruan,* 22 May 1996; *Kompas,* 3 June 1996; *Warta Ekonomi,* 3 June 1996; *Kompas,* 7 and 11 June 1996).

The perception that the law was more intent on ownership and control issues than the imaginative development of broadcasting *content* was reinforced by spokespersons from the armed forces, the Indonesian Democratic Party, and the Development Unity Party parliamentary factions, whose members noted that twenty-two of the law's fifty-eight articles depended on the application of government regulations (*Peraturan Pemerintah*) that were not available for scrutiny (*Kompas,* 11 June 1996). In Indonesian law, regulations are drafted and promulgated on ministerial authority. Questions of compliance with government regulations are left to ministerial discretion, whereas it is up to the courts to rule on possible cases of infringements of laws (*Undang Undang*). Member of Parliament Marcel Beding objected to the reliance on government regulations and stated that the Parliament was being asked to sign a blank check (*Kompas*, 3 June 1996). Other observers argued that regulations should not go to the substantive content of the law but should be concerned only with administrative and technical matters (*Kompas*, 10 May 1996; *Antara*, 29 May 1996; *Kompas Online*, 11 June 1996). Member of Parliament and film director Sophan Sophian, taking up the issue of transparency and government accountability, was even more direct when he said that in his experience regulations were often a "dangerous ruse or trick," and for that reason, "In future, it is proper that in sounding out a new draft law, the government should specify at least the concept of the regulations so that the context [in which they will apply] and their relevance can be easily appreciated and understood. The Parliament should not be forced to accept a cat in a sack, and then later become just a rubber stamp" (*Kompas Online*, 11 June 1996).

In some newspaper articles, objections to the proposed role of government regulations in the regulation of broadcasting were linked to controversial ministerial bans imposed in 1994 on three high-profile publications: *Tempo*, *Editor*, and the tabloid *De Tik* (Hill 1994, 88). Marcel Beding made the point this way: "What I am concerned about is the kind of experience [we had] with the press law, namely the problem that the publishing permit and its cancellation were administered by government regulation. I hope the publication permit experience will not be repeated with broadcasting" (*Kompas*, 10 May 1996).

Echoing the arguments made in support of opening up the news sector, which I discussed in chapter 8, critics of the government's perceived preference for control pointed out that information was "not a boon or gift granted to the community by government" (*Suara Karya*, 24 May 1996; *Kompas*, 11 June 1996). Azis Saleh argued that restricting information was undesirable, as alternative sources of information allowed the community to be discriminating. Azis stated that people do not learn only from what is good but also from what is bad, and he deplored the policy that restricted information from overseas sources. Banning information from overseas, he said, was likely in the long run to be more worrying than screening it, as banned material frequently became fertile ground for gossip. He summed up his case against the government's prohibitionary zeal by quoting the proverb "If you are mad at a mouse, don't burn down the rice barn" (*Kompas,* 10 May 1996).

National representatives of the five officially recognized religions in Indonesia described the draft law as "very repressive" in a joint statement to parliamentary representatives of the Development Faction (*Suara Pembaruan,* 22 May 1996).[3] They challenged its legality, arguing that prohibiting sectional interests from establishing television stations contradicted articles 27 and 28 of the 1945 constitution, which endorsed freedom of the press, speech, and assembly and the equality of all citizens before the law (*Antara,* 29 May 1996).

Abdul Muis extended the debate, arguing that the even distribution of information and the freedom to access, use, and distribute information is a universal human right, regardless of the social, cultural, and political situation of a particular state (*Republika Online,* 15 May 1996; *Suara Karya,* 24 May 1996). He questioned why the proposed law should prohibit sectional interests from establishing television stations when the Press and Film Acts included no such provision, and he asked further why global broadcasters should have unfettered access to Indonesian viewers when indigenous broadcasters were not extended the same rights. Abdul Muis suggested further that the authoritarian provisions of the draft law were a hangover from colonial attitudes and law. This was most obvious, he said, in the sanctions against freedom of expression in political matters, especially in article 9, clause 3, which prevents sectional interests such as religious organizations, political parties, and other similar organizations from owning a television station (*Republika Online,* 6 June 1996).

In these discussions and demands there is an obvious family resemblance in the calls for transparency, accountability, and due process in contesting government decisions. Together they construct an emergent policy arena, an "arm's length" relation between executive government and broadcasting regulation, and they can be understood as public resistance to the government's persistence in trying to hold on to control of the sector despite its radical restructuring.

Scope and Content of the Broadcasting Law

Long before Minister Harmoko tabled the draft law in the Parliament, he stated that its significance lay not only in its regulation of the present national broadcasting system but also in the way it would address the future, given developments in global satellite broadcasts outside Indonesia. For Harmoko, "[the law] must anticipate these developments" (*Kompas,* 15 February 1996). The way the government chose to anticipate global communications has been a site of contention between the government, the industry, and media specialists. Speaking for the broadcasting sector, prominent advertising executive Fachry Mohamad, for example, indicated that the industry hoped the law would not be based on a spirit of *control* or restraint, but rather on a willingness to *progress* or facilitate national broadcasting. His advice to government was this: "Don't look on radio and TV as something dangerous that must be controlled. It will be all for nothing, because soon there will be broadcasts from Direct Broadcast Satellites that cannot possibly be resisted" (*Kompas,* 12 September 1996).

Media analyst Akhmad Zaini Abar has attempted to leaven the perceived power of the media in official circles, pointing out that the media is one among many social institutions and is not especially powerful as the "magic bullet" theory of the media suggests (McQuail 1994, 44). Akhmad argued that the government's wish to control electronic broadcasting and restrict diverse sources of information was related to two factors in the political economy of broadcasting in Indonesia. It was rooted first in the government's apprehension over the power of the electronic media both to influence and to shape public opinion, especially on political matters, and to effect profoundly social and cultural spheres. Second, and more controversially, Akhmad argued that the restrictions on new players in the television market were designed to maintain the competitive advantages of the client capitalists licensed to develop the industry (*Republika,* 19 June 1996).

Other media specialists such as Alwi Dahlan criticized the law for its introverted concern with national issues and argued that it conspicuously failed to be forward looking: "The present law is more concerned with issues of the past and the present. It does not adequately anticipate future developments.... Advances in information and communications technology are extraordinary. And [these advances] will continue" (*Republika Online,* 9 June 1996).

The director of Indonesia's satellite communications authority, Tjahjono Soerjodibroto, and the director of RCTI, Ralie Siregar, echoed Alwi Dahlan's point, saying that broadcasting is moving toward convergence and multimedia, and for that reason the broadcasting law must indeed anticipate future developments (*Kompas,* 12 September 1996). More specifically, media specialist Bachtiar Ali criticized the law for being out of touch, noting that it failed even to mention the role of computers or the internet in communications (*Antara,* 29 May 1996; *Jawa Pos,* 16 October 1996).

Debate over the implementation and administration of the proposed legislation proved equally assertive but was mainly restricted to technical matters (*Kompas,* 10 June 1996). Law and media specialist Abdul Muis was scathing in his comments on the government's lazy and inappropriate decision to lift sections from the press and film laws to regulate broadcasting, which, he argued, needed quite different treatment. Abdul Muis argued that the necessity to develop appropriate broadcasting legislation was evident in the frequent disputes over the censorship of films on television. He suggested that the sometimes unpopular decisions made by the Film Censorship Institute arose because the Institute was bound by criteria relevant to the screening of films in cinemas, criteria that were not suited to the different viewing conditions of television (*Suara Karya*, 24 May 1996).

Other criticism focused mainly on the lack of specificity in regulations covering advertising and whether commercial stations would be required to continue paying part of their advertising income to TVRI (*Suara Merdeka*, 23 May 1996; *Warta Ekonomi*, 3 June 1996; *Republika Online*, 9 June 1996). Finally, debate focused on the structure of the broadcasting system and the role of the new regulatory authorities proposed in the draft law. Article 41 requires that the "broadcasting profession" establish an Honorary Broadcast Ethics Council (*Dewan Kehormatan Kode Etik Siaran*) to monitor the application and observance of the industry's Code of Ethics. Article 44 establishes the National Broadcasting Board of Review (*Badan Pertimbangan Penyiaran Nasional*) to advise government. Discussion on these new bodies has focused mainly on the fact that their membership, role, and responsibilities are not described in the law (*Republika Online*, 5 May 1996 and 11 June 1996). At the time of writing these controversies were ongoing and are outside the scope of this study.

Sex, Violence, Children, and Television

Beyond these technical matters, debate on the draft law by Members of Parliament Marwah Daud Ibrahim, Abu Hasan Sazili, and Aisyah Aminy has noted that it does not address issues such as sex and violence, the provision of children's programming, advertising standards, and consumer issues, all of which have been an important focus in the public debate on television. Since May 1996 public advocates have publicized these popular concerns and have urged government to regulate television content through the broadcasting law.

The view that children are particularly susceptible to television programming that is graphically violent or that screens sexual imagery incompatible with community standards has been a major focus for research and discussion in the United States since 1920 and in many other countries since the end of the Second World War (Cunningham 1992a, 138). Relatively recently these concerns have also been the focus of a sustained public debate in Indonesia, a debate that has become more lively and more nuanced since the advent in 1993 of national television licenses.[4] Critics who write against sex and violence on Indonesian television frequently link undesirable content to the imported origin of the offending programs (usually simply described as "Western"). In blaming the "West," the critics overlook the violent scenes that are part of Japanese-produced cartoons such as RCTI's popular *The Knights of the Black Armor* (*Kasatria Baja Hitam*) and the more stylized violence of Hong Kong–produced kung fu movies that have been screened more frequently since 1994 on most channels (*Kompas*, 19 November 1995). Nevertheless, commercial television is perceived to be culturally threatening in the way it has put Indonesian viewers, especially children, at risk through increased exposure to "Western" programs that are violent and sexually inappropriate according to Indonesian community standards:

> Something that concerns us nowadays is that violent scenes in children's [television] films are more frequent.... Almost all children's films include violent scenes. But the context of the violence is only suitable for adult viewing.... Generally speaking, films that feature violence are imported films, most of which come from the United States.... These children's films are based on Western culture, which plays down the importance of the collective and rates aspects of individualism as more important. (*Bisnis Indonesia*, 17 March 1995)

> The Western films broadcast by a number of the commercial television stations are a factor in the rise of criminal action of late. If this is examined with full awareness, with sincerity and responsibility, commercial television programs in no small measure may ruin the morality of the community, especially the young segment.... Our sons and daughters are inclined to imitate the style of Western people whether in clothes, socializing, flirting, fighting, murder, or even rape. (*Suara Karya*, 13 January 1995)

The noted film director Slamet Rahardjo expressed concern over the sexual values inscribed in Western television series such as *Beverly Hills, 90210:* "Film series such as *Beverly Hills* systematically teach free sex and thus are much more dangerous than national films, which these days are attacked for their sexual and violent themes. The total number of *Beverly Hills* episodes numbers tens, hundreds of titles. If each week [*Beverly Hills, 90210*] is part of our young people's diet, won't that be dangerous?" (*Republika*, 24 January 1995).

Forceful demands for reregulation of television in a deregulated sector have put the government in a difficult position. These expressions of a cause-effect link between television programming and behavior are entirely consistent with the theory of developmental communication that underpins government media policy. For the government to argue against the link would involve contradicting a central tenet of development theory and Indonesian television policy, namely that the media are powerful and influential. The difficulty the government faces in determining an appropriate response to community demands for regulations that uphold idealized and essentialized Indonesian cultural values and in determining what might be appropriate intervention in the programming decisions of the commercial stations has become obvious in the government's lack of engagement in the debate over television regulation and in its equivocal position over the regulation of sex and violence. I explore this issue further below.

There are observers who take a broader, more nuanced look at the phenomenon of sex and violence on television. Indeed, academic Sri Lestari H. N. draws attention to two different perspectives in the community:

> Since television business spread in this country, there developed two views of the impact of television on the growth, development, and education of children. The first tends to be angry about the negative impact of television, especially its portrayal of elements of violence, sadism, evil, and the consumerist lifestyle. . . . The second comes across as optimistic [and believes that] television broadcasts are not able, of themselves, to influence directly the lifestyle of children. (*Bisnis Indonesia*, 25 April 1994)

Unsurprisingly, perhaps, the second view is endorsed by commercial licensees, even though this involves them in arguing against a central plank in the government regulator's logic, which is based on the perceived power of television. It is conflicts of this kind that inevitably "loosen the knot" that ties the government and private sector together:

> Television, or the mass media, in the opinion of the representatives of the five national commercial television stations, in general only operates as a *contributing factor* or *mediating factor* [in violent behavior]. Thus it is too simplistic to conclude that the media is the factor that ignites violence. Actually the fact is that there are many nonmedia variables that are more significant as causes of violence. (*Merdeka*, 25 April 1995, original emphasis)

In summary then, community concerns over television and children are that there is a lack of children's programming on Indonesian television, especially on commercial television, and that the programming that is available is often culturally unsuitable in its portrayal and presentation of violence, sexuality, and cultural values. Children are believed to watch too much television and to watch indiscriminately whatever is on screen. There is increasing concern that because of changing work practices, children's viewing is often unsupervised by parents or other adults.

The issue of children's television has been more keenly discussed, by a wider cross-section of the community, than any other single issue concerning television. As the *Republika* editorial of 16 January 1995, noted in its opening sentence, "For the umpteenth time, television programs are being discussed again." Children's television has been debated in innumerable seminars (see appendix I); it has been the subject of parliamentary lobbying, the impetus for the formation of the commercial television broadcasters' Forum for Communication and Coordination of Television (*Forum Komunikasi dan Koordinasi Televisi, FKKT*), and the subject of numerous press conferences, sustained press reporting and comment, and even theatrical performance (*Merdeka*, 6 May 1996).

The extracts from press discussions included above indicate a wide range of opinions on key issues and show that well-known arts, religious, media, community, and government voices have contributed to the debate. What is not obvious from these extracts, but is immediately obvious when the debate is tracked over a number of years, is that there is a reflexivity or self-awareness in the debate that has made discussion of children's television a true public debate in Indonesia. Opinions presented by an individual or an organization are taken up and explicitly addressed by others involved in the debate. In press reports and feature articles, in seminars and in specialist publications such as YLKI's *Consumer News (Warta Konsumen)*, the public debate on Indonesian television is recognized as being part of an international concern about children's television. Research from Australia, Malaysia, and the United States is cited and commented upon (*Merdeka*, 1 October 1994; *Republika*, 23 November 1994; *Kompas*, 11 and 17 December 1994; *Kompas*, 29 January 1995; *Suara Karya*, 30 April 1995; *Kompas*, 4 and 10 March 1996). Research from Indonesian consumer groups and other nongovernment organizations is also analyzed and the implications for domestic policy explored (*Kompas*, 29 January 1995; *Merdeka*, 26 April 1995; *Kompas*, 7 May 1995; *Kompas*, 24 August 1994).

Perhaps the best illustration of this is the discussion that erupted in April–June 1995 over research done by the Indonesian Children's Welfare Foundation (YKAI). In 1993 YKAI surveyed fifteen children's programs (195 episodes) shown on four television channels: TVRI, RCTI, SCTV, and TPI. Using the methodology of content analysis, YKAI counted the number of "prosocial" and "antisocial" scenes in the selected programs. YKAI released its results early in 1994, attracting a moderate amount of press interest. In 1995, the chair of YKAI was invited to speak at a seminar convened by TVRI on the topic of children's television. In her paper, the YKAI chair, Lily Rilantono, referred to the foundation's 1993 study. In a report of the seminar, the quality newspaper *Kompas* reported the speaker's comments in a front-page article as referring to all five commercial channels and as claiming that there was a causal link between antisocial scenes in children's programs and children's violent behavior (*Kompas,* 19 April 1995).

The commercial channels reacted swiftly and in concert. At a press conference convened by the commercial channels, Eduard Depari, a doctoral graduate in communication studies from an American university and public relations manager for RCTI, attacked the YKAI research design and findings and claimed that the commercial channels were being scapegoated over children's programming (*Merdeka,* 25 April 1995). The commercial channels compounded the error that *Kompas* had made by basing their comments on the *Kompas* report and not checking the original research. This enabled YKAI to respond immediately, noting that they had released the results in 1994, and that at the time, the commercial operators had not reacted so stridently. YKAI research director Guntarto noted further that YKAI had never claimed any causality and that its research was related to only three commercial channels, for at the time when the research was done, ANTEVE and Indosiar were not even on air (*Republika,* 26 April 1995).

What is worth noting about this storm in a teacup is that for a period of a few weeks it sustained public debate on issues such as children's programming, research methodologies, sample sizes, the definition of "prosocial" and "antisocial" scenes on television, and the role of parents in supervising children's viewing. YKAI came out of the incident well and was able to represent itself as a responsible, prudent organization whose voluntary and professional efforts were misrepresented by the commercial channels, probably for their own ends (Guntarto, research director, YKAI, personal communication, August 1996).

But this incident was unusual. More usually the reflexivity is inscribed as in these two quotations:

> Dr. Alwi Dahlan's declaration that about 50 to 60 million Indonesian children are "raised" by television is disturbing at the time when we are celebrating Children's Day. (*Republika,* 23 July 1994)
>
> According to a study by YKAI, in general, children watch 20 to 25 hours of television each week. They watch whatever is on the TV

screen. They don't care whether the program is for parents, adults, adolescents, or children. (*Kompas,* 24 August 1994)

I have traced the extensive publicity given to the view that a steady "diet" of violent and sexually permissive programs is hostile toward (an essentialized) Indonesian culture. Such programs are believed to cause criminal violence and sexually inappropriate behavior. I do not have scope here to assess the merit of the television effects paradigm. That has been discussed comprehensively in specialist monographs (see Cunningham 1992; McQuail 1994). My interest lies in describing and analyzing how the growing public concern over children and television has been articulated, displayed, and performed in the Indonesian public sphere. In this discussion my focus is on the role intellectuals, nongovernment organizations, the press, television operators, the government, and the parliament have played in the public debate on this issue and what the policy outcomes have been, or might be, in the regulation of television. As Virginia Nightingale observes, the effects tradition of research is implicated directly in the practical business of the regulation of television, as "the regulation and control of the media are highly political issues. That political struggle is about the right to control the means of media production" (Nightingale 1993, 291).

The Media-Policy Link in Indonesia

For all the community activity on children and television, there is a noticeable lack of specific suggestions for action in the extensive publicity. Few articles suggest, for example, that the broadcasting law should include sections on the classification of programs or that an advertisement-free children's program time should be established. Those that do make suggestions for action often vaguely recommend that the government do something. There have been a number of suggestions, mostly from individuals, for new, nongovernment regulatory bodies and codes of ethics (concerning advertising, programming, and broadcasting more generally) (*Merdeka,* 21 February 1994; *Suara Pembaruan,* 23 August 1994; *Merdeka,* 30 January 1995; *Bisnis Indonesia,* 21 February 1995; *Media Indonesia,* 13 July 1995; *Republika Online,* 22 November 1995; *Republika,* 4 September 1995).

Just why most of the participants in the debate tend not to follow through their popular advocacy by making specific recommendations in the press for policy or regulatory change is puzzling at first glance. William Liddle, for example, has included the press in a list of six "political variables" that he claims play significant and sometimes decisive roles in "inclining" authoritarian governments such as Indonesia's toward more egalitarian policies (1987, 128). Liddle notes specifically the role editorials, academics writing in the press, and "investigative reporting" may play in shaping policy under conditions of authoritarianism. Andrew Macintyre describes a similarly important role for the Indonesian press when he argues that "in the absence of other sources of open political debate, press commentary assumes particular importance in influencing the political agenda" (1991, 37). If this is so, then the commonly noted indirect style of press reporting and publicity in the Indonesian public sphere is of interest for what Robert Spitzer has described as "the underexamined connection between the media and public policy" (1993, 5). It is also of interest for what it suggests about processes of advocacy and policy agenda setting in Indonesian politics (McCombs and Shaw 1972; Rogers, Dearing, and Bregman 1993).

In an analysis of the link between the media and public policy making in the United States, Spitzer suggests that the media's policy impact may be investigated across three dimensions. These are, first, consideration of whether the media is active or passive in reporting a particular issue or conflict; second, the intention to effect policy through media activity; and third, the question of impact, where the question is "not whether the media has an impact, but how much, what kind, under what circumstances, and so on" (1993, 7–8).

But James Clifford and Vivek Dhareshwar have warned that

theory does not travel well, not in terms of space or translation, often overdetermining the results when it is applied in a context different from its origins (1989, v–vii). Spitzer's assumptions about media practice, his illustrations, and indeed the very dimensions of interaction he proposes are influenced by the adversarial culture of politics in the United States. As a consequence, these dimensions, particularly the first two, may not be useful in all analyses of media practice but may be salient only for particular journalism cultures and systems. While Indonesian editors and reporters are obviously active in initiating stories, the Woodward and Bernstein style of journalism, and the hard-hitting style of *60 Minutes,* which Spitzer cites as examples of "modern investigative journalism," are not part of contemporary Indonesian journalism. Second, as I have noted, the long-established American practice of seeking to influence government policy directly by making specific calls for legislative change is also not part of New Order–period journalism, which has developed a distinctively indirect style (Hill 1994). Active reporting intent on effecting policy change in the Indonesian environment will read differently from journalism in the United States or Australia, which actively and overtly seeks to influence the policy stream. Thus, if we were to attempt to analyze media-policy links in Indonesia using Spitzer's unmodified three-dimensional model of interaction, it is likely we would underestimate, or even miss, the impact of the media on policy making because of the different styles of journalism practiced in Indonesia. It may, however, be possible to rethink Spitzer's model, especially its implicit assumptions, and adapt it so that it more sensitively models Indonesian media and policy relations.

As far as the active/passive dimension is concerned, the potential for the press to investigate and initiate coverage of events and issues of public concern must be preserved without linking these activities to the a priori assumption that investigative journalism will necessarily involve confrontational or adversarial reporting. The press has been very active in reporting and publicizing the issue of sex and violence on television in Indonesia. The print media has given nongovernment organizations access and has publicized seminars devoted to the topic. More proactively, the press has given influential academics and intellectuals access to the media and has published feature articles and editorials on the issue. But these articles are not "hard-hitting" in the American sense, and many fall short of making *specific* recommendations for policy change.

In a close-grained study of capital controllers' relations with government in New Order Indonesia, Jeffrey Winters notes that a nonconfrontational style was the norm in public sector/private sector relations and that the convention was so strong that even World Bank representatives in Indonesia adapted their reporting, role, and procedures to avoid any public criticism of officials. As Winters says, "It usually takes the skills of a Cold War Kremlinologist to divine the bank's criticisms of Indonesian policy in its annual report" (Winters 1996, 148).

And in a detailed study of the public policy advocacy of nongovernment organizations (NGOs) in Indonesia, Philip Eldridge describes three frameworks that characterize NGO-government relations, all of which indicate a preference for the avoidance of *overt* conflict (1995, 35). He also identifies a more radical, activist tradition that is critical of the nonconfrontational stance of the established NGOs, but he suggests that this tradition represents more of "a resurgence of mass-based political action than a new stream of [NGOs]" (1995, 40). Most Indonesian NGOs explicitly disassociate themselves from macro-level politics and adopt nonconfrontational strategies in their dealings with the government. Eldridge attributes NGOs' practice of avoiding overt confrontation with the government to a desire to preserve their autonomy, to their micro-level rather than macro-level objectives, to the need to obtain government cooperation to achieve their objectives, to their lack of resources and capacity to operate at a national level, and to their members' lack of knowledge and lack of any feeling of involvement in national politics. He also notes that the values of conflict avoidance are "deeply rooted in many of Indonesia's cultural systems, most notably amongst the Javanese" (Eldridge 1995, 37).

Values of this kind undoubtedly influence NGOs and other community groups not to make specific recommendations to government for the regulation of sex and violence on children's television. The lack of specific, public suggestions for regulatory change should be understood as a well-established mode of interaction between government and the community and is not indicative of any lack of ideas nor lack of interest in influencing policy and achieving change. In the Indonesian context, NGOs' mode of influencing public policy is to present their case in the press and leave it at what in other media cultures might be described as public agenda setting. If this account of Indonesian NGOs' preferred mode of publicity is correct, it is then easier to account for the greater preparedness, always within Indonesian conventions of indirection, for *individual* critics, intellectuals, and reporters to make specific policy recommendations.

Much of what has been said about a distinctive, nonadversarial style of mainstream journalism in contemporary Indonesia applies equally to the way the second of Spitzer's dimensions, intentionality, is articulated in press articles. The intention to influence government policy is masked by indirection, and at times by absence, the mere presence and persistence of articles on the topic signaling to well-attuned readers that the public concern over sex and violence on television is a matter on which the public expects the government to act. To cite Winters again: "The approach the bank uses here is very specific to this place. The Indonesians are unwilling to be told what to do. We let the government ride out in front. We slowly and steadily push a set of policies, and in time they adopt them. They lead and we follow" (Winters 1996, 148).

Finally, regarding the question of impact, Spitzer notes that to "observe that reporting has an impact on policy is to state the obvious, because the very act of reporting implicates the media in the process, regardless of how or even whether it occurs" (1993, 8). Spitzer goes on to suggest that attention is better directed at the analysis of how much, what kind, and under what circumstances the media impacts policy. While an exploration of the conditions of media impact on Indonesian policy making would require a comprehensive study of its own, some tentative suggestions can be made toward a model of the dynamics of media policy interaction on the basis of the issue discussed above. I suggest that impact, in the sense of explicit policy response attuned to the public concerns, will be related to the following: (1) the national/local scope of the issues; (2) whether the policy issues largely affect what, for the sake of convenience, I will call the technological/financial/administrative dimension or the cultural/ideological dimension of social organization; (3) the perceived bearing of the issue on the prestige and authority of government and on its observance of due process; and (4) a judgment of the degree of likely benefit or hurt the proposed regulation would deliver to influential nongovernment stakeholders, particularly clients (see table 10.1).

The Media-Policy Link and the Draft Broadcasting Law

The quotations cited earlier in this chapter are clear evidence that the press has played a key role in publicizing the issue of sex and violence and children's television in Indonesia. It is through the print media that a vigorous, reflexive debate has been possible. The press has brought many diverse voices together in a public conversation that has extended over many years. The policy outcome of the mediation of the debate is, however, far less easily assessed. State authorities appear to have taken an equivocal stance. The draft broadcasting law, where community concerns over children's television might have been expected to be expressed, makes no specific provisions on the subject, and on those grounds, we might want to say that the attempt to influence policy has failed.

Despite the frequent invocation by community groups and individuals of cultural nationalist sentiments that reflect the government's own policies, and despite calls for government intervention to prevent the screening of unsuitable programs, there has been

Table 10.1
Variables Affecting Media Impact on Television Policy and Regulation

Event	Scope	Ownership and Control or Content	Bearing on Government Prestige	Impact on Interests of Nongovernment Stakeholders	Media Impact on Policy/Regulation
License fees	National	Ownership and control	When privatization went wrong, government prestige suffered, as it had authorized the change.	Major financial interests at stake. Minimized by government retaining Mekatama Raya as consultant.	Major impact. Privatization reversed.
Advertising	National	Content	No bearing.	Commercial operators dependent on advertising revenue.	No impact.

Table 10.1 (cont).

Event	Scope	Ownership and Control or Content	Bearing on Government Prestige	Impact on Interests of Nongovernment Stakeholders	Media Impact on Policy/Regulation
Foreign workers	National	Content	Presence of foreign workers suggested government incompetence. Range of government departments involved.	Repatriation of workers had minimal impact on Indosiar.	Major impact. Workers repatriated; workforce rules enforced.
Sex and violence	National	Content	No bearing.	Sex and violence rates well. Tight regulation would negatively impact client capitalists.	Minimal impact.

Table 10.1 (cont.)

Event	Scope	Ownership and Control or Content	Bearing on Government Prestige	Impact on Interests of Nongovernment Stakeholders	Media Impact on Policy/Regulation
Broadcasting law	National	Ownership and control and content	Initial phase, no bearing. As debate continued, government prestige involved as the broadcasting law was shown to be unimaginative and out of touch.	Complex, as the broadcasting law comprehensively affects all aspects of broadcasting.	Minimal impact at draft stage. As the press publicized public and parliamentary debate, the impact became more profound.

Scope: National government will only become involved in events that have national-level significance.

Ownership and control or content: Specifies whether the event was primarily concerned with ownership and control of television institutions or with program content.

Bearing on government prestige: Some events directly affect government prestige and reputation by drawing attention to the observance of proper process and the like.

Impact on interests of nongovernment stakeholders: This involves an assessment of the effect of the event on the financial interests of private-sector stakeholders.

Media impact on policy and regulation: Assessment of effect of publicity on policy process.

very little public comment by responsible officers in the Department of Information on the issue of children and television. There are some indications that the government is not convinced by the often simplistic arguments about the negative effects of sex and violence on television. It has given support to an industry- and community-managed regulatory regime, believing that self-regulation is more flexible and might better reflect community standards. Certainly Minister Harmoko appeared to endorse self-regulation when, at the height of the YKAI research controversy, he wholeheartedly supported the actions of parents in Yogyakarta who had decided to ban their children from watching television between 5 P.M. and 9 P.M. (*Republika*, 27 April 1995). At other times, when approached about violence on television, Harmoko has simply "requested" the commercial channels to be aware, vigilant, careful, and responsible and to exercise restraint in screening programs for both children and adults. The minister also warmly welcomed the commercial operators' initiative to establish the Forum for the Communication and Coordination of Television (FKKT) in May 1996, and he praised the forum's decision voluntarily to limit violent and sexually unacceptable films, and commercials and videoclips not in keeping with Indonesian cultural standards (*Kompas*, 2 May 1995; *Media Indonesia*, 3 May 1996). Finally, it is worth noting that the minister has never threatened sanctions against stations that screen inappropriate material.

The former Director General of Radio, Television, and Film has also supported self-regulation, saying that all parties in the community should be selective about what they watch. Alex Leo Zulkarnain pointed out that while the official censor is required to approve all material prior to screening, it is difficult to satisfy everyone, and that if a program is considered unsuitable, then viewers should just turn it off (*Media Indonesia*, 13 July 1995).

The government may also consider that a self-regulated industry is more in line with the market assumptions of a deregulated television sector. An alternative explanation, consistent with the dynamics of clientelistic relations between licensees and the government examined in chapter 7, is that the government is not anxious to intervene in commercial stations' programming, realizing that even an expanded regime of children's programming would not generate sufficient advertising revenue to make up for any substantial cutbacks to the high-rating but "unsuitable" programs. Akhmad Zaini Abar has noted that the group most sensitive to the new regulations is the commercial licensees. He observes that "for them it is very important that the draft broadcasting law reinforces their present position so that their business priorities preserve the status quo, which in this instance means continuing to grow rapidly" (*Republika,* 19 June 1996). It is obvious from press reports, Akhmad suggests, that "the commercial television entrepreneurs or operators have conspired to apply pressure so that they do not become the sector that is ruined by the introduction of the broadcasting law. They have convened various meetings and have lobbied politically, with the government, the parliament, and the press to get political support and to express their concerns" (*Republika,* 19 June 1996).

Considering the government's well-documented interventionist and highly directive role in education (Parker 1992) and cultural socialization through programs such as State Ideology courses (Morfit 1986), for example, its more laissez-faire approach toward the regulation of children's television in the draft broadcasting law is worth examination, for it reveals a tension, at least, if not some confusion, over the government's regulatory role in the television sector.

Minister Harmoko's comments on introducing the draft broadcasting law to the Parliament do not suggest that the government has shifted from its transmission model of the media as a powerful social and cultural influence, nor has it abandoned its paternalistic role and totalizing vision of the nation: "An important objective, which it is hoped will be achieved when this law is brought down, is to protect the community as an object of broadcasting. To be specific, the law aims to protect cultural values, the character and uniqueness of the nation, and the people from each attempt to fragment the union and unity of the nation" (*Republika Online*, 7 May 1996).

And noted above, the draft broadcasting law, as much by what is not said as by what is said, preserves direct government control over many aspects of television broadcasting, most notably news and access to foreign capital.

George Quinn's research on Harmoko's support for the very rapid growth in "Rural Mass Media Discussion Groups" (*Kelompok Pendengar, Pembaca dan Pirsawan*) organized by the Department of Information both for adults and, since 1994, for school students, also suggests that the government has not abandoned its interest in shaping audiences' perceptions and maintaining a focus on the government's development priorities. As Quinn puts it,

> Both the quiz show format and the *sumbangrasa* [debate] format seem to have been developed for the purpose of defining and consolidating a corpus of permissible topics for public discussion by villagers, as well as a politically safe, manageable structure for the conduct of these discussions. They emphasise the government as the ultimate source of authoritative information and as the final arbiter in matters of dispute. (Quinn 1996, 18)

On the other hand, the minister's comments in the House that he welcomed input on the regulation of sex and violence on television, and the unusual (in Indonesian legislation) provision in the draft law (article 46) that appears to formalize community input, gestures toward a more open, cooperative regulatory policy regime. But considering the time the government has had to put the law together, and considering that the debate over sex and violence was very high profile, the government's decision to wait until the law reached parliament to call for submissions does not seem credible and might simply be delaying tactics.

Speculation aside, what is clear is that the draft law failed to deliver on any specific measures connected with children's television and sex and violence on television. There were no suggestions about a scheduled children's program time nor any recommendations that a specified proportion of programming should be for children. There were no articles to regulate advertising during children's programs, nor were there any suggestions for a uniform classification system that might assist parents to select programs suitable for children.

The lack of attention to children's television, and related issues of the suitability and ethical standards of advertising in relation to child viewers, suggests that despite the intensive pressure from the community for legislative remedies, the government appears prepared to allow the television industry to regulate itself in this matter. While the government's decision may have been taken in the best interests of all parties, its silence on its intentions in the regulation of children's television left many in the community feeling very uncertain, even cynical. It stimulated further lobbying in the Parliament, which delayed ratification of the law and, ironically enough, challenged the Department of Information's authority as protector of the cultural values of the younger generation.

This account of the shifts in the minister and other officials' positions points to the increasing complexity of the media-policy environment since deregulation and under conditions of globalization. The minister's pragmatism—sometimes affirming magic bullet effects, sometimes subscribing to indirect media effects, sometimes legislating in a brute fashion, sometimes in favor of industry self-regulation—is obvious. It can be seen as political adroitness, which it is, but it can also be seen as an outcome of the complexity of the cultural and economic environment in which politicians and officials operate as they manage and promote different normative prescriptions for the media that are necessarily in conflict. This pragmatism of public officials intersects with processes of socialization of the idealized citizen. By promoting and withholding consumer sovereignty, responding and not responding to public concern, political figures indirectly contribute to and produce a more active citizen/audience. The responsiveness I have commented on, inconsistent and as pragmatically motivated as it undoubtedly is, is part of an emergent pattern of state and social relations that can be directly attributed to the increasingly complex policy environment that has developed since TVRI's monopoly position was dismantled.

But if the extensive publicity given to sex and violence on children's television failed to anchor regulation in government hands as at least some groups wanted, it influenced the commercial sector to take specific steps toward a regulatory regime that may partly satisfy community demands. On 2 May 1996 the commercial operators established the Forum for Communication and Coordination of Television (FKKT). This decision to club together and speak with one public voice is entirely consistent with the corporatist model of state-society relations that has developed under the New Order (Macintyre 1991, 26–31), and with the model that has been imposed on all other media such as the press, radio, and film. The forum's first public announcement was that the five commercial channels had voluntarily agreed to reduce screenings of violent and sexually inappropriate films. A few days later, the Censorship Institute convened a meeting with the forum to discuss revised criteria for the regulation of material "not in line with the culture of the Indonesian people" (*Republika,* 4 May 1996). The Minister of Education and Culture endorsed the forum's initiative and supported the move toward self-regulation in the industry, noting that in Japan self-regulation worked well (*Kompas,* 4 May 1996).

The establishment of the forum suits both the government and the licensees but is unlikely to advance the debate over the regulation of television. For the government, dealing with one representative body is easier than dealing with a range of divergent and possibly conflictual demands. If the government makes concessions over regulation, leaving matters of content to industry self-regulation, for example, then making concessions to a forum appears to be evenhanded rather than special treatment of favored clients. For the commercial operators, the forum is a vehicle that displays their interest in being seen to be responsible about issues of community concern. The forum is also a means through which they can advance their commercial interests without foregrounding the competitiveness of their relations, another illustration of the corporatist economic ideology discussed in chapter 7. The exclusiveness of the forum (membership is limited to television licensees) protects the licensees from having to deal directly with their critics, while at the same time it shows that they share the community concern about the regulation of television.

The standoff in the parliament over the draft broadcasting law suggests, however, that many in the community were not willing to leave regulation to a forum whose members have a poor record in responding to community inputs, a forum that has no charter and that narrowly represents the interests of the commercial operators with no provision for community representation. Community disquiet over the capacity of the commercial operators to regulate programming in anyone's interest apart from their own was well expressed by the prominent writer and former Director General of Radio, Television, and film, Umar Kayam: "Many bad television programs, though they are widely criticized, remain obstinately on screen. The most important thing for the operators are the advertisers, for as long as a film attracts plenty of ads, they don't care if it's good or not" (*Merdeka,* 8 August 1995).

The extensive publicity generated over children's television was also undoubtedly responsible for the unusual intensity of the debate in the House over the draft broadcasting law and the delay in its ratification. It is rare for draft bills to be so energetically debated and criticized. In the debate, the government was held to account for abandoning its duty of care to a vulnerable sector of the population in order to preserve the privileged position of a few well-connected entrepreneurs. One outcome of the debate could well be to influence the passage of the law, and perhaps change it even more radically. In this case then, community interests, through the mechanism of the public debate, have challenged the government's right to ignore, if not contradict, regulatory measures that have clear popular support.

Public Debate and the Indonesian Subject

By way of conclusion to this chapter, I want to speculate on what the mechanism of public debate implies for the construction of an Indonesian subject participating in that discourse. The equivocation in the government's position over the regulation of children's television points to the contested subjectivity of the idealized Indonesian subject. The ideal subject of the government's project, invoked in Harmoko's comments when introducing the law, is a citizen-in-development, a citizen mythologized and appealed to in terms of cultural abstractions. The discourses that inform this construction are the discourses of the revolutionary period and of the New Order, discourses that construct a disciplined, compliant citizen willing to set aside personal priorities to allow a place for the priorities of national development. The emergent, alternative construct of the viewer-as-consumer, constructed through opinion polls, audience surveys, and ratings surveys, is a different subject—a rational subject constructed through individualized preference and opinion.

For the first construct, the audience as public citizen in development, the viewer is positioned as a receptacle of an instructional, improving, didactic programming regime largely decided in the absence of any sustained or systematic dialogue with the audience. The audience as consumer construct is grounded in the knowledge of the situationally determined viewing habits, interests, tastes, and desires of the audience. This knowledge is then used to objectify the audience as consumer.

These two subject positions are boldly drawn and invoked by the government and the commercial sector in pursuit of their own political and economic interests. The controversies over both ownership and control and the content of television explored in this and the previous chapter suggest, however, that participants in the debates reject the simple dichotomy in being defined discursively as either citizens or consumers. The public discussion on television has shown that members of the public are interested in and value well-produced, varied, and entertaining programming, which a deregulated television sector can offer. At the same time community interest groups have demonstrated that they are willing to assert values and to publicize views that cut across the interests of both sectors. In Indonesia, where television mediated the development and cultural priorities of the state for nearly thirty years, it was perhaps unavoidable that with deregulation, a tension would develop between the audience constructs of the public and private sectors.

The public debate on television suggests that the polarization implied in the subject positions is overly simplistic and does not recognize the audience's complexity. The debate has challenged the governmental restriction on the diversity of information and programming and has argued that these restrictions have inhibited the development of the information and broadcasting sector. It has tackled the commercial channels for ignoring consumers' needs for ethical advertising practices and culturally sensitive programming. The public debate on television may be considered part of a broader process of the pursuit of public purposes outside the formal processes and apparatus of the state. Speaking at the "Open Skies" seminar, journalist and television presenter Wimar Witoelar suggested that a way out of this situation was for public-sector broadcasters to be less defensive and to understand that the process of deregulation inevitably produced diversity, but that alternative constructs should not necessarily be interpreted as a direct challenge to government authority. All sides in the debate needed to open themselves to dialogue: "A large gap exists between the public need for entertaining journalism and the jargon supplied by the broadcasting system in Indonesia. It is a mistake to interpret this need as political dissent. [The] public needs ... relief from propaganda" (Wimar Witoelar 1996, 2).

The debate over the reregulation of television has registered a concern that the deregulation of the television sector has precipitated a situation in which the meshed interests of the private commercial sector and the state sector have ignored or paid insufficient attention to a range of policy issues of general social and cultural concern. In the debate three conceptions of the Indonesian citizen have figured. The idea of the developmental citizen is a citizen whose highest priority is the national collective good. The citizen as sovereign consumer places satisfaction of private needs and values as the highest priority. The emergent, alternative construct of the viewer as consumer and participant in public debate and, occasionally, public action is mapped (accidentally and contingently) over the public-private divide. The third construct of the citizen is constructed through the apparatus of commercial research and marketing and through seminars and exchange of expert opinion, empirical research, and press dialogue. The active participant/consumer is idealized as a rational subject who has private interests and needs but who also values public discourse and is capable of making finely balanced judgments that respect evidence and acknowledge the interests of all parties involved. There is ample evidence that there are many in Indonesia who have adopted this subject position and that their energy has had a significant impact on the development of television policy and culture.

Chapter 11

CONCLUSIONS: THE CULTURAL POLITICS OF TELEVISION IN INDONESIA

THIS STUDY PRESENTS the first detailed account of television in Indonesia. I have discussed how and why television was established, analyzed some of its key institutional sites, and critically examined its textual characteristics and effects over the New Order period. I have examined changes in some of the early policy and institutional structures in the late 1980s and have described how these changes have affected programming, television's mediation of the national culture project, the scope for public intervention in the regulation of television, and the idea of the Indonesian nation and subject.

I have argued that Indonesian television is best understood as "the same but different" from television in Western democratic countries. The similarities are rooted in the adoption of television technology marketed worldwide in the 1950s and 1960s and in the way British, American, Japanese, and Australian technology, ideas, and training were shared with Indonesian broadcasters. There are similarities also in the utilization of television as a medium of popular entertainment and in the commercial sector's involvement with television as an advertising medium. It is also no coincidence that Indonesian television began by televising a major sporting spectacle. Berliners in 1936, Londoners in 1938, and New Yorkers in 1939 first experienced television with broadcasts of sporting events. In Australia it was the same. Indeed, Brian Johnston argues that sports "fathered" television in Australia (cited in Cunningham and Miller 1994, 65). Even in the 1990s in Indonesia, when RCTI first began, its live broadcasts of World Cup soccer were an important draw for audiences. It is no coincidence either that TVRI's trial broadcast was a national political ritual. Daniel Dayan and Elihu Katz argue that there is "a pre-natal link between television and political ceremony," citing the coronation of Queen Elizabeth II in England and the 1967 victory parade in Israel as events that inaugurated television in those two countries (1995, 170). Thus, although Louis Damais may have "winced" at the politicization of television in Indonesia in its earliest years (chapter 2), it was not so different from television elsewhere in the world.

Differences become more marked if we pay attention to the preoccupations of television in Indonesia and the distinctive form and content of some (though not all) domestic productions. Here again, the distinctiveness should not be exaggerated. As discussed in part 1, Indonesian television is best understood as guided by the theory of development communications, and in that way it is similar to television in "developing" countries such as China, India, and Malaysia. Although it was funded commercially until 1981, it was a state monopoly, and its goals were overwhelmingly normative and "developmental." Television's preoccupations from 1962 to 1989 were the promotion of national development, the construction of the national citizen, and the modeling and circulation of ideas of official national culture. These preoccupations have remained significant even after deregulation. Deregulation was in no sense a liberalization of the television sector, but is best understood as motivated by state authorities' interest in regulating the influx of foreign televisual services and programming, which became popular in the mid-1980s. The distinctive structure that positioned TVRI as a leader among equals reflected the government's desire to hold onto its political and cultural investment in the television sector even when all the signs indicated its previous monopoly had gone forever.

This study has been concerned with the cultural politics of television in Indonesia. There are relatively few extended studies of Indonesian popular culture available. Rarely do outsiders consider popular culture to be more than a gloss on national politics. However, as I have shown throughout this book, popular culture, represented here by television, is bound up in the production of political ideas and values and in the symbolic legitimation of government programs and policies. Much of this discussion has been devoted to TVRI—its structure, its programs, and its policies—and to how it has positioned itself in relation to the new channels. TVRI has been largely overlooked in discussions of contemporary Indonesian politics and culture. This lack of interest is regrettable, because as I have shown, since the launch of Palapa, TVRI has been arguably the most important means of mediating the political and cultural center's ideas of nation and national identity to the peripheries. Understood in this way, television cannot be separated from politics. The particular historical, political, and cultural circumstances in which television is meshed make Indonesian television distinctive while still having much in common with television in other countries.

I have argued that even though television in Indonesia cannot be understood as a wholly distinct form of cultural expression, modes of analysis and criticism of television must be sensitive to the political, economic, and cultural discourses in which it is situated. I have argued that popular culture is best understood not as a given set of texts or genres connected with a fixed set of meanings or class fractions, but as a field of contestation where signifying practices intersect with cultural policy, cultural criticism, and audience intentions. I have shown that a full appreciation of individual programs, and even flows of programs, depends on extending the frame of reference beyond the screen to the political and cultural discourses in which television plays a part, and to the everyday life of viewers. To show what television means to Indonesians, I have taken care to surface these discourses and show their range. I have cautioned, however, against any simple idea that the voices raised in debate over television can simply be categorized as "oppositional" or "left" or "right." The discussion of the Indosiar and license fees affairs, the debate over advertising on TPI, and the debate over television content showed that television is not a surface or purely textual phenomenon. It is complexly articulated with a range of historical tensions and political and cultural policy issues that attract interest and comment from advocates representing widely differing views. Following deregulation, for example, there are groups that would prefer the government to take charge again, and there are those who want more self-regulation. There are also those who support a deregulated industry and self-regulation but argue for transparency in licensing and privatization and responsible regulation of content and ownership.

Focus on the discourses and practices in which television is meshed has also revealed that the New Order's reliance on a transmission model of communication in the mediation of the national culture project has limited its effectiveness. The picture of the national culture project that emerges from this discussion is of a project that is modernist in its interests in mapping a unitary and unifying official culture over the great diversity of Indonesia, and hegemonic in the way it selects specific ideological principles and values and invents traditions. At times, the project attempts to privilege elements of Javanese culture as a model for social relations. But while state authorities may control what appears on national television screens (at least they did before satellite transmissions made control more difficult), they cannot control how viewers respond to particular programs, nor what people think and the meanings they attribute to particular programs. Even highly popular programs such as *Si Unyil* attracted criticism, with some young viewers complaining that the program gave insufficient attention to regional languages. Some adult viewers complained that Ogah and Ableh set a poor example, still others that the series was unentertaining and patronizing because it was too intent on improving children and publicizing government projects. Criticisms of TVRI news and of the *Keluarga Rahmat* series have also shown that state authorities' belief that television would unambiguously transmit preferred values and cultural constructs is ill-founded. In the language of reception theory, television texts are polysemic and do not transmit an unambiguous meaning, connotation, or objectively definable significance. The recent history of Indonesian television has also shown that television that is overly didactic, pays little attention to viewers' interests and needs, and promotes unitary culture and social conformity will be ignored or disparaged. Viewers will search out alternatives—whether in the form of video, spillover transmissions, or, for those who can afford it, satellite television. Since deregulation, commercial television has weakened the unifying power of the national culture project by providing visions of alternative social formations, different ways of living, and different values. One striking and almost bizarre example of this was the weekly schedule in which TVRI screened *Keluarga Rahmat,* with its theme of simple living, at the same time as RCTI screened the American program *Lifestyles of the Rich and Famous.*

I conclude further that the tension evident in the early days of television between development television and a more audience-centered, entertaining, and internationally informed service has not been resolved. It still haunts the present system, though it has not split it apart. Although increasingly assertive under conditions of intensifying competition, the commercial stations are captives of their patronage and position as supporters of the regime, rather than independent commercial producers. If the broadcasting law permits commercial stations to produce their own news broadcasts, restructures the sector, withdraws TVRI's privileged position, and allows a greater degree of industry self-regulation, then the long-term tension will likely disappear. TVRI will be left to perform its role as a government mouthpiece, and the commercial channels will be relieved of the burden of conforming to the values of a public broadcasting regime. If, on the other hand, TVRI is permitted to accept advertising and sponsorships, as seems likely, then the tension, although diminished, is likely to linger for as long as TVRI's national infrastructure delivers it advantages not presently enjoyed by the newer channels. These possibilities, however, reach beyond the time frame of this study and will be the subject of future research.

In part 2 of this book I have surveyed the impact of the global dispersal of new televisual technologies and products and looked at how this affected the role of television in mediating the national culture project. I concluded that these developments drew attention to and problematized the idea of the nation as a territorially limited, sovereign, imagined community.

The history of television in Indonesia illuminates questions of national identity and the production or the imagination of the nation, given state authorities' reliance on television in "nation building." National identity can be understood as a discursive field focused on concerns about international position and internal integration. After the launch of Palapa gave TVRI a national platform, it was drawn increasingly into a period of internal political and cultural consolidation. TVRI was relied upon to promote national development, socialize viewers into the national culture project, and encourage viewers to accept their position as citizens in development. From the early 1970s through to the mid-1980s the New Order state developed and circulated its symbolic repertoire most emphatically as a way of asserting its legitimacy. The "depoliticization" of politics was managed through the mechanism of forced amalgamation of existing political parties into two corporatist groupings in 1973, and the policy of the "Floating Mass," which barred the general population from political activity except during the five-yearly election campaigns. A new syllabus in moral education in Pancasila was introduced in the 1975 school curriculum, and compulsory national "P4" courses in Pancasila ideology were established. The *"azas tunggal"* legislation, which ensured that all mass-based organizations accepted Pancasila as their sole guiding principle, was proposed in 1982 and adopted in 1985. On TVRI, the proportion of domestic productions was boosted after the government's monopoly was secure and programming became more focused on the government's national development priorities.

In the mid-1980s Indonesia's external or geopolitical situation asserted itself more forcefully. The boom in international oil prices that had so abundantly financed New Order policies of import substitution and restricted foreign investment fell apart in 1984 through 1986. Falling oil and commodity prices, a global economic recession, and the declining value of the rupiah put the Indonesian economy under great pressure. These events opened up opportunities for more market-oriented macroeconomic policies and put Indonesia back on the path of export-oriented growth and increased foreign investment.

Indonesia's reintegration into the international economy coincided with the global development of transnational communications technologies, which created flows of televisual products and services beyond the daily control of governments. Where once television everywhere in the world had been largely a medium of national culture, in the mid-1980s through to the early 1990s it shifted decisively to become a globalized medium circulating product from both the First and Third Worlds. These developments challenged the national culture construct of Indonesia as a bordered, spatial unity. The intrusion of foreign cultural products and services, which met a mixed reception from viewers, eventually led the government to dismantle its television monopoly and to integrate the sector into the global system of exchange of products. The government attempted to modify the impact of foreign cultural products by domesticating the global—by granting licenses only to close friends of the regime, by urging stations to maximize local productions, and by putting TVRI in the position of leader. But as the number of channels grew and competition between them for audiences and advertising intensified, the idea of a united team of broadcasters seemed nostalgic and little more than wishful thinking by the government.

If deregulation had a major effect on Indonesia's economy and international relations, its effects were probably only directly appreciated by the business elite. It is likely, however, that deregulation of the television sector will have a more direct and comprehensive impact. A more definite conclusion will require research beyond the time frame of this book. The introduction of commercial television, with its high levels of imported programming in the early years and growing proportion of domestic production since, has significantly altered the cultural role of television. Whereas once TVRI was the sole television channel mediating official, national culture, it now sits alongside five other national channels that are increasingly differentiating fractions of the national audience and thus contributing to breaking up the unitary construct of official culture, which TVRI had represented for so long.

Parallel to this, and as a result of it, representation of the Indonesian subject, the way Indonesians see themselves in the world, has shifted. This is a complex process articulated across discourses in the public sphere concerned with ideas of national identity, national culture, and citizenship. The shift is attributable in part to the influence of increasingly diversified programming. These days television circulates a greater array of ways of living, ways of behaving, and representations of self than it ever did. But more important, I suggest, is the way the reorganization of the television sector has opened up the public sphere for increased participation and the performance of roles premised on ideas of personal agency and commitment to reform and policy development. Screen representations of the Indonesian subject thus articulate with political performance, setting up a complex exchange between imagined and realized subjectivities. I have drawn attention to the debates over television in the public sphere, noting the increasing number of seminars, press debates on television policy issues, and the way specialized knowledge and research have been utilized by advocates in publicizing and arguing for their views. The combination of shifting representations of idealized subjectivities and increased activity on cultural policy issues is likely to lead to the "gradual redefining of the most basic and subtle aspects of the relation between the government and the people" (Lull and Sun, cited in Berwanger 1995, 323). I have also noted the varied impact of public advocacy on television regulation, and I have argued that the link between publicity and changes in media policy is complex and must be understood in terms of the political economy of relations between stakeholders.

While state authorities have opened up the Indonesian economy and television to international markets, the political public has become more focused on the sphere which they can most directly influence—namely the local or domestic sphere. The discourse of nation and national identity tracks back and forth along the Möbius strip of nationhood, between ideas of internal coherence and external relations, between concern with what citizens believe they share together and concern with what separates Indonesia from other national communities. Assertions of cultural distinctiveness and the need to protect a unique cultural heritage entwine with expressions of relief that the system has opened up and that hegemonic constructs of identity are under scrutiny. The idealized self constructed in these discourses is now a fragmented subject mapped across national borders and hailed by ideas of belonging that reject exclusive association with a particular territory, preferring instead a sense of cultural identity informed by both national and transnational coordinates.

In making these conclusions, I do not want to exaggerate the political impact of developments in the television sector. What has been attributed to the cultural field does not amount to a major shift in cultural and political relations. The politicization of television is not "party political" as the street riots over government intervention in the Indonesian Democratic party were in 1996, nor as the trials over the banning of *Tempo* were, for example. I have been concerned with the mediation of culture and with viewers' varied reactions to programs, services, censorship, policies or the lack of policies on the regulation of content, and aspects of ownership and control of national cultural services. It is obvious that there has been and is resistance to many aspects of the government's management of the sector. It should not be exaggerated, but neither should it be underestimated. I have shown that at times television policy and changes have had the power to create alliances and prompt interest groups and social and cultural institutions to assert their will collectively.

For most people, however, television is *experienced* as a private, domestic activity. This is why I have been interested in tracing shifts in television's representation of what it means to be "Indonesian" at the end of 1990s. The totalizing and unitary concept of the viewer as "citizen-in-development" has fragmented into the viewer as sovereign consumer and the viewer as consumer and active citizen. Not that these are the only possible models of what it means to be "Indonesian." As Stuart Hall says, "identity is always an open, unfinished game—always under construction" (1993, 362). There certainly are other representations of the Indonesian subject. The idea of "world citizen," for example, informs Indonesian discourses of universal human rights, but this debate has not figured significantly on television to date. My focus on the shift from citizen-in-development to sovereign consumer to sovereign consumer/active citizen has derived from the way ideas of the subject have intersected and been formed by changes in the television sector.

Whether the structural changes introduced with deregulation and foreshadowed in the broadcasting law will emphasize the external face of nation building rather than internal integration is unclear. It is, after all, unlikely to be an either/or issue, but rather a matter of ethos and emphasis. Whether decreased emphasis on internal integration will shift television programming away from developmental priorities and ideas of a unitary and unified culture is something to be investigated further. As commercial channels develop their own news bulletins, it is likely that the ritualistic representation of a unified national community will come under challenge. I argued in chapter 8 that there were signs of this already on RCTI's *Seputar Indonesia*.

Under conditions of monopoly, there was obviously resistance to an unrelieved regime of improving, didactic programming, and audience interest in imported programming and video was high. But in the late 1990s state authorities may believe that after fifty years of independence, the battle for integration has been won, and it is now time to open up the sector.

But with the requirement in the broadcasting law that 70 percent of programming must be produced domestically, there will inevitably be increased attention on domestic issues. A key question is whether programming will be based on appeals to what are usually called "primordial" loyalties in the attempt to win audiences. Will domestic producers emphasize regional languages, ethnicity, and religion as a way of attracting viewers? There already are popular programs on TVRI and the commercial channels whose audience appeal derives from the representation of particularistic cultural associations. TVRI Yogyakarta's weekly program of the popular regional drama *kethropak* and the rural program *Bangun Desa* are broadcast in Javanese and have an enthusiastic following. And RCTI programs such as *Lenong Rumpi* and *Si Doel*, which represent Betawi culture through the Betawi dialect, have rated very well in Jakarta but much less so in the provinces. Programs that revert to easy assumptions about Indonesian identity are likely to be divisive and are unlikely to attract audiences beyond the subcultural group targeted. The challenge for Indonesian television (and cultural processes beyond it) is to reinvent Indonesia's motto, "They Are Many, They Are One" (*Bhinneka Tunggal Ika*), which under the New Order has authorized the imposition of a unitary culture rather than a respect for difference. The challenge for all channels will be to develop programs that explore ideas of identity beyond the hegemonic assumptions of the national culture project and beyond the idea of identity imagined simply at the level of ethnic, regional, or religious community. Such programs might imagine a subjectivity that empowers citizens to engage with pressing contemporary economic and political issues such as the unemployment of young people or the structural position of women. Further, will there be a move toward programs that begin to explore the history and politics of contemporary Indonesia, opening up the (probably inevitable) clash with official history and interpretation of political events?

The scope and content of domestic programming is therefore likely to become an important site of cultural and political struggle in the years ahead. The intense activity during the 1970s and early 1980s in political symbolism was directed toward heading off political activity rooted in and inspired by prenational sentiments. The imposition of the *azas tunggal* legislation, the MISS SARA convention, the creation of corporatist political parties and the depoliticization of politics were all intended to proscribe nonstate ideologies and guard against a revival of the overheated ideological debates of the Sukarno period that divided Indonesians along religious, ethnic, and regional lines.

Against this background, in the context of deregulation, the government's emphasis on noncompetitive relations among the commercial channels, the swift action taken over the Indosiar affair, and deregulation of the sector within an organizational structure that set TVRI apart in a coordinating role may be understood as an attempt to prevent commercial channels from fragmenting the sector by differentiation of the audience in terms of ideological affiliation or primordial sentiment. The broadcasting law proposes to dismantle the TVRI Foundation and take away its coordinating role. It does, however, bar religious and political groups from establishing television channels for their own purposes, and it severely restricts the use of regional languages on television. All licensees are expected to provide comprehensive television services that promote national union and unity. The law also requires both government and commercial operators to form two associations—one to oversee broadcasting and the second to promote professionalism in broadcasting. Coordination of the first association will be in the hands of government. The operation and powers the government may hold as coordinator of this body are unspecified at present. The desire to draw individual operators together into a representative body is, however, a familiar New

Order strategy and may be taken as evidence of a continuing interest in moderating aspects of competition that might threaten principles of national political and cultural consensus.

Just how the commercial channels will react to these constraints in the future will be important. It may be that in a culturally diverse nation, the idea of a television sector that pulls together, and that is rooted in, New Order ideas of political and religious secularism may be helpful in managing a peaceful transition as President Soeharto's period in office draws to an end. On the other hand, the highly restrictive policies and regulations that have framed cultural politics in the New Order may constrain the commercial objectives of commercial operators too tightly and work against the development of entertaining, socially responsive programming. In this case, both operators and viewers will become increasingly frustrated that the benefits of deregulation cannot be realized. Frustrations of this kind may introduce considerable strain between licensees and the government. Whether this tension will emerge, and just how it might be resolved, will, however, have to be the focus of future research.

New Areas for Research

At the time of writing, the broadcasting law lies on the table, awaiting the president's signature. There are indications that for the first time ever, the law will not be ratified and will either be sent back to Parliament for redrafting or will be scrapped and a new law drafted from scratch (Alex Leo Zulkarnain, telephone interview, 1 April 1997). Television in Indonesia is poised on the brink of major changes, as significant in its history as the launch of Palapa or the breakup of the state monopoly in 1989. This book has laid the groundwork for new research that will take the story of Indonesian television on from here. The history and character of regional television has yet to be written and would provide a very useful counterpoint to the focus on the center, which my argument has necessarily presented. Contemporary developments in television offer researchers a great variety of topics. In the policy field, the development of the broadcasting law is vital for understanding the cultural politics of television in Indonesia. The political economy of the booming production-house industry that has developed since deregulation is worthy of intensive study. It is likely that the industry will refract the tension between domestic values and the increasing globalization of television series and advertising, which has been part of the development of television culture in Indonesia since it began. The conflict over Indosiar's plan to make over hundreds of scenarios borrowed from Shaw Brothers in Hong Kong prefigured a debate over the construction and meaning of Indonesian culture, which is likely to become more pressing in the years ahead. Allied to this issue, research on the way the TVRI and the commercial channels imagine their audiences and satisfy the government's domestic production requirement will be an important contribution to understanding the symbolic culture of the regime that succeeds President Soeharto.

Appendixes

Appendix A

SIGNIFICANT DATES IN THE DEVELOPMENT OF INDONESIAN TELEVISION

Year	Date	Event
1952		Maladi first proposes development of TV to Cabinet; rejected as too expensive.
1959		Maladi proposes development of TV to Cabinet; accepted.
1961	16 July	Interim committee to plan development of TV met in Cipayung, W. Java.
	25 July	Ministerial Decree #20 formally establishes planning committee.
	23 Oct.	Sukarno's cable from Vienna advises Maladi to purchase TV equipment from NEC, Japan.
1962	17 Aug.	Trial broadcast of Independence Day anniversary.
	24 Aug.–12 Sept.	TVRI broadcast of Fourth Asian Games in Jakarta.
	13 Sept.–17 Sept.	TVRI off air.
	18 Sept.	TVRI resumes broadcasting.
	11 Oct.	First TVRI broadcast from Studio 1 at Senayan, Jakarta.
	24 Sept.	TVRI incorporated into the Spirit of Sukarno Foundation.

Year	Date	Event
	14 Nov.	TVRI Senayan station formally commissioned.
1963	1 Mar.	TVRI accepts advertising and sponsorships.
	20 Oct.	TVRI established as a foundation in its own right.
1965	17 Aug.	Yogyakarta station established by Directorate of Radio, Dept. of Information.
1966		TVRI "brought within the environment" of the Directorate General of Radio, Television, and Film, Dept. of Information.
1969	29 Sept.	Inauguration of satellite ground station at Jatiluhur, W. Java, by President Soeharto.
	10 Nov.	TVRI broadcasts launch of Apollo XII using Intelsat service for the first time.
1970	15 Aug.	Inauguration of TVRI Training Center in Yogyakarta.
	20 Dec.	Medan broadcasting station commissioned.
1972	7 Dec.	Ujung Pandang broadcasting station commissioned.
1973	22 Jan.	Balikpapan broadcasting station commissioned.
1974	31 Jan.	Palembang broadcasting station commissioned.
1975		TVRI confirmed as part of Directorate of Radio, Television, and Film, Dept. of Information.
1976	8 July	Palapa satellite launched from Kennedy Space Center.
	16 Aug.	Inauguration of Palapa satellite by President Soeharto.
1977	10 Mar.	Palapa A2 launched.
1978	3 Mar.	Surabaya broadcasting station commissioned.
	16 July	Denpasar broadcasting station commissioned.
	22 Dec.	Manado broadcasting station commissioned.
1978	22 Dec.	"World News" (Dunia Dalam Berita) broadcast begins.
1979	1 Sept.	TVRI Jakarta begins full-color broadcasting.

Year	Date	Event
1980	Jan.	President Soeharto announces advertising ban on TV.
	1 Apr.	TV ad ban comes into effect. TVRI employees absorbed into Dept. of Information.
1982	12 May	Mobile production units commissioned for nine provincial cities.
	24 Aug.	"English News" service begins.
1986	20 Aug.	Satellite dishes authorized for individual use; Indonesia initiates the "Open Skies Policy."
	24 Aug.	English News Service transmitted by terrestrial relay to TVRI Denpasar.
1987	11 Mar.	Bandung broadcasting station commissioned.
1987	20 Oct.	Ministerial Decree #190A, Dept. of Information authorizes commercial pay TV service; TVRI Foundation to have oversight of commercial operators.
	28 Oct.	RCTI nominated as pay TV licensee for Jakarta and environs.
1989	1 Apr.	TVRI Second Channel (Programa Dua) begins broadcasting to Jakarta and environs.
	24 Aug.	RCTI pay TV service begins in Jakarta.
	27 Sept.	Letter of agreement between SCTV and Dept. of Information authorizes SCTV as pay TV licensee for Surabaya and environs.
1990	17 Jan.	Agreement reached between SCTV and TVRI Foundation for pay TV service in Surabaya; SCTV originally known as Surabaya Centra Televisi, later as Surya Citra Televisi.
	1 Aug.	RCTI reaches agreement with TVRI Foundation to establish RCTI Bandung.
	16 Aug.	Agreement reached between TPI and TVRI Foundation for a national educational TV service.

Year	Date	Event
	24 July	Ministerial Decree #111 updates Decree #190A.
	24 Aug.	RCTI and SCTV begin free-to-air service.
	11 Dec.	Private company Mekatama Raya awarded contract to collect TV license fees.
1991	23 Jan.	Educational TV channel TPI on air.
	24 Jan.	"Morning News" (Berita Pagi) begins on TPI.
	1 May	RCTI Bandung begins broadcasting.
	1 July	RCTI authorized to use Palapa for domestic broadcasts.
1992	1 Jan.	RCTI and SCTV joined forces to broadcast to Jakarta, Bandung, Surabaya, and Denpasar.
	May	Ministerial Decree #84A updates #111.
	18 June	License for commercial TV broadcast awarded to PT Indosiar Visual Mandiri (IVM).
1993	18 Jan.	Ministerial Decree #04A updates #84A.
	28 Feb.	ANTEVE begins broadcasting.
1995	11 Jan.	Indosiar Visual Mandiri (Indosiar) begins broadcasting.
1996	June	Draft broadcasting law introduced into DPR for discussion.
	Dec.	Revised broadcasting law ratified by DPR, forwarded to President Soeharto.
1997	July	President Soeharto returns broadcasting law to DPR for further revision.
	29 Sept.	President Soeharto signs Broadcasting Law #24.

Appendix B

EXCHANGE RATES FOR THE INDONESIAN RUPIAH, U.S. DOLLAR, AND AUSTRALIAN DOLLAR, 1962–1996

Year	Rupiah	U.S. Dollar	Australian Dollar
1962	45–173	1.00	0.4482
1963	315–349	1.00	0.4499
1966	78	1.00	0.8980
1967	176	1.00	0.8921
1968	277	1.00	0.9009
1069	277	1.00	0.8945
1970	362.833	1.00	0.89286
1971	391.875	1.00	0.88267
1972	415.000	1.00	0.83870
1973	415.000	1.00	0.70350
1974	415.000	1.00	0.69667
1975	415.000	1.00	0.76387
1976	415.000	1.00	0.81828
1977	415.000	1.00	0.90183
1978	442.045	1.00	0.87366
1979	623.055	1.00	0.89464
1980	626.994	1.00	0.87824
1981	631.757	1.00	0.87022

Year	Rupiah	U.S. Dollar	Australian Dollar
1982	670	1.00	1.045
1983	990	1.00	1.095
1984	1,060	1.00	1.17
1985	1,650	1.00	—
1986	1,650	1.00	1.429
1987	1,650	1.00	1.387
1988	1,690	1.00	1.19
1989	1,785	1.00	1.28
1990	1,875	1.00	1.28
1991	1,977	1.00	1.27
1992	2,040	1.00	1.43
1993	2,110	1.00	1.50
1994	2,200	1.00	1.33
1995	2,290	1.00	1.35
1996	2,375	1.00	1.26

Table shows units of Indonesian and Australian currency valued against the U.S. dollar.

Sources: Asiaweek, various years; United Nations, *Statistical Yearbook.* 1965; 1974; EconData CD-ROM Database, World Bank Data Tables.

Appendix C

SI UNYIL EPISODES ANALYZED

1980/81
"Timun Mas" [Timun (girl's name) with a Radiant Face]
   Scenario: Animation. Adaptation of a Javanese folktale
   Director: Suyadi

1982/83
"Atu Belah" Part 1; "Atu Belah" Part 2. [The Split Boulder]
   Shooting Script: Kurnain Suhardiman
   Director: Endang Mindaryati

1984/85
"Hardiknas" [*Har*i Pendi*dik*an *Nas*ional—National Education Day]
   Shooting Script: Kurnain Suhardiman
   Director: Endang Mindaryati

1985/86
"Petinju Cilik" [The Little Boxer]
   Shooting Script: Kurnain Suhardiman
   Director: Agust Suprapto

"Hijrah" [The Migration of the Prophet]
   Shooting Script: Kurnain Suhardiman
   Director: Agust Suprapto

1986/87
"Pekan Manula" [Pekan *Man*usia *U*sia *La*njut—Elderly People's Week]
   Shooting Script: Kurnain Suhardiman
   Director: Agust Suprapto

"Saya Anak Indonesia" [I am an Indonesian Child/I am a Child of Indonesia]
   Shooting Script: Kurnain Suhardiman
   Director: Agust Suprapto

"Mengenang Hari Mulia" [Commemorating the Glorious Day of Independence]
   Shooting Script: Kurnain Suhardiman
   Director: Agust Suprapto

"Girah, Anak Juru Kunci" [Girah, the Caretaker's Daughter]
   Shooting Script: Kurnain Suhardiman
   Director: Agust Suprapto

1987/88
"Tua Muda Belajar Membaca" [Old and Young Learn to Read]
   Shooting Script: Kurnain Suhardiman
   Director: Agust Suprapto

1988/89
"Anak Masa Depan" [Child of the Future]
   Shooting Script: Kurnain Suhardiman
   Director: Agust Suprapto

1989/90
"Festival Kuda Lumping" [Festival of Horse Dances]
   Shooting Script: Kurnain Suhardiman
   Director: Agust Suprapto

1990/91
"Mana Yang Paling Bagus?" [Which One Is the Best?]
   Shooting Script: S. Yadi
   Director: Agust Suprapto

1991/92

"Kuli Tinta Ke Desa" [The Reporter (Ink laborer) Goes to the Village]
　Shooting Script: S. Yadi
　Director: Agust Suprapto

"Wartawan Kecil" [The Young Journalist]
　Shooting Script: S. Yadi
　Director: Agust Suprapto

"Perjalanan Kakek Abror" [Grandfather Abror's Journey]
　Shooting Script: S. Yadi
　Director: Agust Suprapto

"Uti Di Belantara" [Uti in the Deep Forest]
　Shooting Script: S. Yadi
　Director: Agust Suprapto

1992/93

"Uti Di Sarang Raksasa" [Uti in the Giant's Lair]
　Shooting Script: S. Yadi
　Director: Agust Suprapto

"Uti Terhindar Dari Maut" [Uti Escapes Death]
　Shooting Script: S. Yadi
　Director: Agust Suprapto

"Pelukis Wanita Masuk Desa" [The Women Painters Come to the Village]
　Shooting Script: S. Yadi
　Director: Agust Suprapto

"Sopan dan Ramah" [Polite and Friendly]
　Shooting Script: no credit
　Director: Agust Suprapto

"Bu Bariah Jadi Model" [Bu Bariah Becomes a Model]
　Shooting Script: S. Yadi
　Director: Agust Suprapto

Appendix D

THE FLOW OF *SI UNYIL* AND *RIA JENAKA*

TVRI Schedule 22 Dec 1991

08:00 My Indonesia
      Review of Events
      People and Events
      Series *Si Unyil*
      Family Skills
09:15 Cartoon: "The Mighty Orbots"
09:39 This Week's Album
10:39 Comedy: *Ria Jenaka*
10:56 Youth Forum
11:26 From Stadium to Stadium
12:26 News in Brief

TVRI Schedule 18 April 1993

07:00 Morning News
07:30 Health Forum
07:40 Film: "Alice in Wonderland"
08:30 Comedy: *Ria Jenaka*
08:45 Series: *Si Unyil*
09:05 People and Events
09:30 Entertainment
10:35 Youth Forum
10:55 Family Program
12:20 News

Appendix E

KELUARGA RAHMAT'S SETTING AND CHARACTERS

The series is set in a fictional Jakarta suburb. The urban locations and their relationship with other sections of the city are invoked in montage sequences under the title of each episode. Montages usually present the suburb as a green, relatively uncrowded, pleasant environment, almost an image of the country in the city. The sequences include images of prominent Jakarta landmarks such as the fountain at the northern end of Jalan Thamrin and the national monument in Freedom Square (Lapangan Merdeka).

Four families live within easy walking distance of each other in a housing complex in the suburb. In Jakarta a "complex" (*Kompleks*) is a housing development owned by a government department or private company. Employees are assigned housing according to their status. An employer may own a number of complexes within the city, some in elite areas, some in middle-range suburbs, and some in lower-value locations. The complex in *Keluarga Rahmat* appears to be a middle-level development built in the 1970s.

The Rahmat Family

Mr. ([Ba]Pak) Rahmat: Javanese. Fifty years. Muslim. Head of personnel in a government department.

Mrs. (Ibu) Rahmat: Javanese. Forty-eight years. Muslim. Teacher in a state junior high school.

Slamet: Twenty-seven years. First-born son. Graduate in forestry.

Wahyuni: Twenty-one years. Daughter. Student in Teachers College.

Nastiti: Seventeen years. Niece who lives with the family as a foster child. Junior high school graduate.

The Sadikin Family

Mr. Sadikin: Sundanese. Sixty-five years. Muslim. Retired army major.

Mrs. Sadikin: Sundanese. Sixty years. Muslim.

Mumun: Sundanese. Female. Thirty-six years. Muslim. Live-in maid.

The Tambayong Family

Mr. Wim Tambayong: Manadonese. Forty-five years. Christian. Medical aide.

Mrs. Tambayong: Batak (born Simanjuntak). Forty years. Christian. Midwife.

Pingkan: First-born daughter. Twenty years. University student (Indonesian literature).

Mutiara: Daughter. Eighteen years. Senior high school student.

The Subangun Family

Mr. Subangun: Javanese. Fifty years. Muslim. Head of transport section in a government department.

Mrs. Subangun: Javanese. Forty-five years. Muslim.
Pratomo: First-born son. Twenty-six years. University student (economics).
Dwi Lestari: Daughter. Twenty-five years. Married with children.
Tri Astuti: Daughter. Twenty-three years. Married with children.
Purnomo: Son. Twenty-one years. Law school drop out.
Untung: Son. Nineteen years. Senior high school student.
Dewi: Daughter. Sixteen years. Junior high school student.
Iwan: Son. Twelve years. Elementary school student.
Ninuk: Javanese. Female. Eighteen years. Live-in maid. Graduated elementary school.

(These details are a translation from the unpublished *Kerangka Cerita: Film Seri "Manusia Manusia KORPRI"* [Story Framework: Film Series "People of the Public Service"] n.p., n.d., kindly supplied to me by Fritz Schadt).

Appendix F

THE CORPUS OF *KELUARGA RAHMAT* EPISODES ANALYZED

Episode 1: "Ulang Tahun" [Birthday]. Setting: Jakarta. Writer: Tatiek Maliyati. Director: R. Subiyanto.

Episode 2: "Rumah Itu Masih Ada" [The House Is Still There for You]. Setting: Jakarta. Writer: Tatiek Maliyati. Director: R. Subiyanto.

Episode 3: "Sebuah Harmoni" [Harmony]. Setting: Jakarta. Writer Tatiek Maliyati. Director: Fritz Schadt.

Episode 4: "Sang Perkasa" [The Courageous One]. Setting: Jakarta. Writer: Tatiek Maliyati. Director: Fritz Schadt.

Episode 15: "Melepas Sang Perjaka" [Let the Young Man Go]. Setting: Jakarta. Writer Tatiek Maliyati. Director: Fritz Schadt.

Episode 16: "Warung Sepi Siang Ini" [The Stall Is Quiet This Afternoon]. Setting: Jakarta. Writer: Rayani. Director: Fritz Schadt.

Episode 17: "Air Tuba Dibalas Air Susu" [Good for Evil]. Setting: Jakarta. Writer: Taufik Iman. Director: Putu Wijaya.

Episode 19: "Mutiara Di Bunaken" [Mutiara in Bunaken]. Setting: Bunaken, Manado, North Sulawesi. Writer: Fritz Schadt. Director: Fritz Schadt.

Episode 27: "Loro Sae Selalu Dalam Hatiku" [Loro Sae (East Timor) Will Stay in My Heart Forever]. Setting: East Timor. Writer: Iskandar Nugroho and Fritz Schadt. Director: Fritz Schadt.

Episode 32: "Ketika Tuna Menghempas" [When the Tuna Are Tossed About]. Setting: Gorontalo, North Sulawesi. Writer: Fritz Schadt. Director: Fritz Schadt.

Episode 36: "Menyambut Hari Natal" [Christmas Celebration]. Setting: Jakarta. Writer: Johan Khalayan. Director: P. Ngian Hutagalung.

Episode 49: "Bila Wader Makan Manggar" [When the Fish Eat Coconut Blossoms]. Setting: Jakarta. Writer: Fritz Schadt. Director: Fritz Schadt.

Episode 52: "Kuncup Kuncup Bermekaran" [The Young Ones Blossom]. Writer: Tatiek Maliyati. Director: G. Novaris Ar.

Appendix G

RECORDING DATES DURING DECEMBER 1991

Sunday	22	29
Monday	16	30
Tuesday	17	31
Wednesday	04	11
Thursday	05	26
Friday	06	13
Saturday	07	14

Appendix H

CATEGORIES OF NEWS ITEMS

Seven different categories of ceremonial event were identified in the bulletins studied. These events were categorized as follows:

1. Report (*Laporan*): An event during which an individual or group presents a verbal report to a high-status actor who may or may not be accompanied by an assistant.
2. Speech (*Sambutan*): An event that involves the key actor featured in the item delivering a formal address to an audience. It is usually made clear in the news reader's introduction that the individual was invited expressly for the purpose of giving a speech.
3. Meeting (*Rapat*): A meeting event. This category refers to formal meetings where it is clear that there is a minority group of individuals in control of the conduct of the meeting and a larger audience group who submit to the direction of the organizers.
4. Visit (*Kunjungan*): Refers to a formally structured field survey or inspection. Characterized by the visit team actively moving in and around the location visited. Guidance provided by individuals from the field site.

The categorization of events as a "visit" or "meeting" followed closely the way the events were described in the news reports. On occasions it was difficult to assign a particular item to a single category, as some events displayed characteristics of more than one type. A minister might deliver a speech, for example, and also sign a foundation stone or commemorative plaque as part of the occasion. Under these circumstances the item was assigned to a single category according to which activity took the most time during the item.

5. Signing (Tanda Tangan): Refers to an occasion when a high-status individual signs a foundation stone, plaque, or book to commemorate the launching or official opening of a particular venture, such as an irrigation project or the connection of electricity to a group of villages.
6. Courtesy call: Refers to a formal visit by an individual or group with a high-status figure as a way of expressing mutual regard and acknowledgment of the power and influence of the person visited.
7. Award presentation (Penghargaan): The presentation of awards of different kinds in recognition of particular achievement or status.

Four other categories of items were identified:

1. Film report: As used here, the term refers to a news item distinguished by its extensive use of "actuality" or taped footage. Unlike the categories described above, film reports do not involve any structured occasion, but rather present descriptive coverage of topics such as the building of a dam, flooding, or an exchange visit by students.
2. Press conference: Refers to those occasions when a group of reporters conduct a question-and-answer session with one or more key actors. The press corps is shown on screen, and exchanges between reporters and key actors are visualized.
3. Vox pop: Recorded interviews with "people in the street."
4. TVRI: This category includes items that are studio announcements or studio commentary by TVRI personnel. The weather report is included in this category, and so is the first item of every bulletin, during which time a member of the news team reads the lead story headlines. Also included are public service announcements.

Appendix I

SEMINARS ON TELEVISION, 1993–1996

This list of formal discussions of television and related topics is drawn largely from press reports. It has not been possible to supply full details for each of the events listed because of gaps in the press record. The list makes no claim to be comprehensive and is biased toward events held in Jakarta, given the mainly national metropolitan newspapers consulted. This list is presented to give some impression of the way and the degree to which television issues have figured in the public sphere in recent years.

1996

11 Sept.: Seminar on Draft Broadcasting Law. Jakarta. (*Kompas*, 12 Sept. 1996).
18 July: Seminar on Narcotics, Sex, and Violence Among Young People. Department of Criminology, University of Indonesia, Jakarta.
17 July: Seminar on Women and Human Resources. Yogyakarta. Eighteen women's cooperative groups. (*Republika Online*, 20 July 1996).
26–28 June: Seminar—"Open Skies: Toward an Open Society? The Challenge of Broadcasting in Asia." Indonesian Institute for Press Studies, Alliance of Independent Journalists, International Federation of Journalists. Jakarta.

1 June: Seminar—"The Controversy Over the Draft Broadcasting Law." Institute for the Study of the Flow of Information. Jakarta. (*Kompas Online*, 3 June 1996).

29 May: Seminar [no title announced, but related to television]. Muhammadiyah. (*Antara*, 29 May 1996).

6 Apr.: Seminar—"TV Media." Gaja Madha University, Yogyakarta.

1995

9 Sept.: Seminar—"Developing Local Programming: Opportunities and Challenges." Jakarta. (*Republika Online*, 12 Sept. 1995).

25 Aug.: Seminar—"Women as Moral Managers in the Era of Globalization." (*Suara Karya*, 26 Aug. 1995).

21–27 July: Conference—International Film and Television Schools. Jakarta. (*Republika*, 14 July 1995).

28 May: Seminar on Children and Television. Yogyakarta. (*Kompas*, 27 May 1995).

12–17 Mar.: Summit Conference on Children and Television. (*Suara Karya*, 24 Aug. 1995).

21 Jan.: Seminar—"Television and National Identity." TPI and Pustekkom. (*Kompas*, 23 Jan. 1995).

18 Jan.: Seminar: "Diversity in the Indonesian Nation Now and the Possibility for its Development in the Future." (*Republika*, 21 Jan. 1995).

16 Jan.: Seminar—"Television and Radio in Indonesia." (*Kompas*, 29 Jan. 1995).

11 Jan.: Seminar—"The Impact of Television for Religious Life in Indonesia." Yayasan Addiniyah Attahiriyah. (*Suara Karya*, 13 June 1995).

(?)11 Jan.: Seminar—"Development of Television in the Asia Pacific." (*Kompas*, 29 Jan. 1995).

1994

(?)Dec.: "[TV] Production Houses in Indonesia."
8 Dec.: Seminar—"Development of Television in the Asia Pacific." (*Kompas*, 9 Dec. 1994).
7 Dec.: Seminar—"Boosting the Role and Function of TVRI and RI." DPR. (*Republika Online*, 8 Dec. 1994).
24 Sept.: Seminar—"The Impact of Television." Erasmus Huis, Jakarta.
(?)Aug.: Seminar—"Impact of Television on Children." (*Jakarta Post*, 25 Aug. 1994).
18 July: Seminar: "Creating Creativity in Children and Adults."
16 July: Seminar—"The Best Way for Children to Watch Television." (*Kompas*, 13 July 1994).
24 May: Seminar—"The Penetration of Overseas Television via Satellite Dishes." (*Merdeka*, 26 May 1994; *Kompas*, 14 May 1994).

1993

3 May: Seminar: "Opportunities and Challenge in the Media Business Approaching the Year 2000." Bimantara seminar. Jakarta.
1 Feb.: National Seminar on the Influence of Development in Communications Technology for the Mass Media Information Industry. Bandung. (*Merdeka*, 3 Feb. 1993).
12–13 Feb.: Seminar—"The Impact of Transnational Information Media on Education and Information regimes in Indonesian Villages." (*Kompas*, 13 Feb. 1993).
13 Feb.: Seminar—"Addressing the Impact of Electronic Media on School Children."

NOTES

CHAPTER 1

1. The Pancasila [Five Principles of State Ideology: belief in one supreme God, a just and civilized humanitarianism, Indonesian national unity, Indonesian democracy through consultation and consensus, and social justice for the entire Indonesian people] was formulated by Sukarno in 1945 and was included in the 1945 Constitution and its successors.

2. Of course Indonesia is not the only country where the political and business elite have close links to television. In the United States, for example, then Senator Lyndon Johnson was involved in television when his wife was granted a license in 1952 for a station in Austin, Texas. Johnson used his years of firsthand media management experience to further his own political interests when he later became president. Eric Barnouw claims that no president before Johnson had worked so hard to "cajole, control and neutralise the news media" (Barnouw 1977, 387). In Italy, the entrepreneur Silvio Berlusconi became wealthy through television and later used it very effectively to bolster political support during his term as Prime Minister. Public opposition to his dominance of the media helped bring about his fall from power in 1995 after only six months (Smith 1995, 341). But in Indonesia, the influence of the political and first family business elite is more undiluted in the sense that for almost thirty years TVRI was a state monopoly, and since deregulation, all the commercial licenses have been issued to President Soeharto's children, close relatives, or business partners.

3. In a somewhat surprising move, Ishadi joined TPI as Director of Operations in 1996 (*Kompas*, 27 March 1996).

CHAPTER 2

1. Maladi, born in Matesih, Solo, Central Java, in 1912, was Minister

for Information from 10 July 1959 to 6 March 1962. On 6 March 1962 he was appointed Minister for Sports and served from 1962 to 21 February 1966. In 1961 Maladi was Head of Radio Republic Indonesia (RRI) and head of the Organising Committee for the Fourth Asian Games (personal interview, 30 January 1992). Like many Javanese, Maladi has only one name. See also *Tempo* 1981, page 341.

2. The late Alex Leo Zulkarnain was involved in Indonesian television since he led the team of reporters at TVRI's first trial broadcast on 17 August 1962. Alex Leo was at different times Head of Station at Ujung Pandang, Head of News, TVRI Jakarta, Director of Television, and Director General of Radio, Television, and Film.

3. Sumartono explained that in the early phase of the Planning Committee's work, and in preparation for calling tenders for equipment, members had called on foreign embassies in Jakarta to discuss aspects of television systems in different countries.

4. Behind the scenes the whole Radio and Television Broadcasting Committee had become used to working under pressure. The main broadcast antenna on top of the newly constructed tower at Senayan was only hauled into place by hand under the "can-do" eye of (the late) engineer Rooseno at 4 A.M. on the opening day. The Japanese construction advisers had given up on determining a way of safely positioning the antenna with no mechanical lifting equipment (Sumartono, personal interview, 23 January 1992).

5. Statistics of the import and local manufacture of television sets for 1962–67 are entirely lacking. The Bureau of Statistics publication Industry Statistics does not list TV sets as a separate category of communication equipment until 1968. In 1968, 4,812 "television sets and parts thereof" were imported. In 1969, the figure had almost doubled to 8,716. In 1970, 12,931 sets were imported, 11,666 of them from Japan.

6. H. Mohamad Yamin was Minister for Information from 6 March 1962 until his death in October 1962.

7. The broadcasting law, ratified by Parliament in December 1996, altered TVRI's institutional status. It established TVRI as "an organic work unit," under the direction and responsibility of the Minister for Information. Under these arrangements, TVRI is permitted to raise funds from "selected advertising." At the time of writing, the broadcasting law has not been signed into law by President Soeharto.

8. The members of the presidential staff were H. Roeslan Abdulgani, Assistant Chief Minister with special responsibility for Information as Head of Staff; M. Arief, Director of TVRI as Secretary; Major General D. Suprayogi, Head of Presidential Staff of the Spirit of Sukarno Founda-

tion; R. Maladi, Minister for Sport; Soepardo, Assistant to the Minister for Education and Culture with responsibility for Elementary Education and Culture; Brigadier General Soemantri Hardjo Prakoso, Assistant to the Minister for Education with responsibility for Higher Education and Science; Colonel A. Manan, Assistant to the Minister for Religion; T. Yusuf Muda Dalam, Director of the Spirit of Sukarno Foundation (Presiden Republik Indonesia 1963b).

9. Major General (Air Force) Boediarjo was Minister for Information from 1968 until 1973.

10. Ali Murtopo was Minister for Information from 29 March 1978 until 15 March 1983.

11. This tendency culminated in the "Monoloyalty" principle of 1970, which required that all state employees be exclusively loyal to the state and government, and in the "Floating Mass" regulation of 1975, which quarantined rural constituencies from active involvement in politics except during elections.

12. I first saw Indonesian television in the small Central Javanese village of Babadan, Gedongkuning, near Yogyakarta in 1969. Every Friday night my host, (the late) Bambang Oetoro, would place his television set on the verandah so members of the village could watch. My only clear memories of the programs are of the *National News,* and in the Javanese setting, the surprisingly blond hair of Ilya Kuryakin in *The Man from U.N.C.L.E.*

13. The statisics in Alfian and Chu's (1981) table 2.1 are unreliable. The additions in a number of cases are incorrect. The figures cited for 1975/76 to 1977/78 seem more accurate than the subtotals cited for earlier years.

14. Emil Salim was Minister for Communications from 1973 until 1978. A Ph.D. graduate from the University of California–Berkeley, Emil Salim was a member of President Soeharto's Economic Advisory Team from 1966 until 1973 and Deputy Chair of the National Development Planning Board (*Bappenas*) from June 1968. Emil Salim was later Minister for Development and Environment (1978–83) and Minister for Population and Environment (1983–88).

Indonesia rejoined the United Nations in September 1966.

15. Barbara Hatley (1994, 239) implies that Palapa was launched as a result of "booming oil revenues," whereas my information shows that it was launched using commercial funding under difficult government financial circumstances.

16. Iskandar Alisjahbana, Dean of the Faculty of Engineering at the Institute of Technology (ITB), and later rector of the same institution.

Alisjahbana's inaugural lecture delivered on 16 September 1968, "Telecommunications for Education and National Development," dealt with the use of modern telecommunications in the field of education and national development and warned of the security implications of spillover and what he called "the revolution of rising frustration." Alisjahbana was a member of the organizing committee of the 1974 seminar convened by the Directorate General of Communications.

17. National elections were held in 1977 (Cribb 1992).

18. Iskandar Alisjahbana noted that when he had first proposed satellite communications for Indonesia, colleagues in the social sciences, influenced by Schumacher's work, had argued that his proposals simply played into the hands of international capitalism. He was accused of thinking only about hardware, about technocratic solutions to social problems (Iskandar Alisjahbana, personal interview, 19 April 1993).

19. Astrid Sunarti Susanto has had a long association with the development of communications in Indonesia. She was Dean of the Faculty of Journalism at Padjadjaran University from 1971 until 1975. In 1974 she was appointed head of the Information, Science, and Culture section in the National Development Planning Board. In 1990 she was appointed Professor in the School of Social Sciences and Politics at the University of Indonesia, Jakarta.

20. Mashuri was Minister for Information from 28 March 1973 until 28 March 1978.

21. Translation of *palapa* is problematic. The *Kamus Besar Bahasa Indonesia* (1990) [Large Indonesian Language Dictionary] translates palapa as "domestic satellite." Cribb (1992) indicates that the word might refer to a fruit, a spice, or sex. The newspaper *Merdeka* of 31 August 1976 translated the word into Indonesian as "*beristirahat*" (rest), suggesting that the Prime Minister, like Blake's Christian, would not cease fighting until the nation had been reunited. The *New Standard* on 14 August translated "palapa" as "fruit of success." The Directorate General of Posts and Telecommunications (Direktorat Jenderal Pos dan Telekomunikasi 1984, 36) provides the following translation and explanation of the significance of the oath: "lamun huwus kalah nusantara isun amukti palapa. lamun huwus kalah ring gurun, ring seran, tanjungpura, ring haru, ring pahang, dompo, ring bali, sunda, palembang, tumasik, samana isun amukti palapa. Yang artinya: Jika telah berhasil menyatukan Nusantara, saya baru akan beristirahat. Jika Gurun, Seran, Tanjungpura, Haru, Pahang, Dompo, Bali, Sunda, Palembang, dan Tumasik telah bersatu, baru saya akan beristirahat. 'Amukti Palapa' (Jawa Kuno) mempunyai arti sebagai berikut: Palapa ialah wohing gawe (Buah hasil karya). 'Amukti' berarti menikmati.

Namun demikian, istilah 'Amukti Palapa' berarti beristirahat. 'Sumpah Amukti Palapa' berarti, bahwa Mahapatih Gajah Mada tidak akan istirahat, sebelum Nusantara (Indonesia) bersatu." My translation of the Indonesian passage is as follows: "Which means: When I have unified the archipelago, only then I will rest. When Gurun, Seran, Tanjungpura, Haru, Pahang, Dompo, Bali, Sunda, Palembang, and Tumasik are united, only then will I rest. 'Amukti Palapa' (ancient Javanese) has the following meaning: Palapa is the fruit of one's labors. 'Amukti' means to enjoy. Therefore it follows that 'Amukti Palapa' means rest. 'Sumpah Amukti Palapa' means that Prime Minister Gajah Mada will not rest until Indonesia is united." The oath itself is not consistently reproduced. The Directorate of Television 1984 publication *Televisi Republik Indonesia* (Televisi Republik Indonesia 1984, 35) presents the following text: "lamun huwus kalah nusantara isun amukti palapa. lamun kalah ring gurun, ring seram, tanjungpura, ring huru, ring pahang, dompo, ring bali, sunda, palembang, tumasuk, samana isun amukti palapa."

22. When I commented to Astrid Susanto that the Japanese had been involved in the establishment of television in 1962, she commented, "Of course, Dewi [Sukarno] was Japanese."

23. Informants suggested that the cool response from the Directorate of Posts and Telecommunications over the Department of Information's proposal in the 1980s to develop a Direct Broadcast Satellite (DBS) system was in part resentment over the department involving itself in matters that were "not its business." See also Republik Indonesia (1974), where the section on telecommunications mentions the development of a communications satellite that will assist television and educational services, but there is no mention of a satellite in the section on Information and Communications. Similarly, in the Third Five-Year Plan, the section on telecommunications (pages 203–6) notes the launch of Palapa I and II [sic] and the scheduled launch of Palapa III and IV [sic]. The use of Palapa for the distribution of television is explicitly noted. These details are not mentioned in the Information and Communications section. The only reference (section 25, page 23) to Palapa is a comment about the need to develop additional earth stations in anticipation of Palapa III and IV [sic] (Republik Indonesia 1979).

24. Sjamsoe Soegito related that he had had various meetings with colleagues in the Department of Education when he was Director General of Radio, Television, and Film, but these meetings had not produced any results (personal interview, May 1993).

25. "Malari" is an abbreviation for "*malapetaka Januari 15*," or "the January 15 disaster."

26. I am grateful to Ariel Heryanto for his helpful suggestions in the interpretation of this cartoon.

27. If this exchange did take place, it is likely that Soeharto was signaling his intentions. As head of the TVRI Foundation he would have been aware that advertising was very profitable.

28. The only other source that links Sudharmono to these events is Arswendo Atmowiloto (1986, 79), who quotes Sudharmono's remarks on advertising on television made in an address to the *Dewan Perwakilan Rakyat* (DPR, or House of People's Representatives) in early February 1981. Krishna Sen (1994, 65) notes that it was Sudharmono who appointed Gufron Dwipayana as Head of the State Film Centre. Sen describes Dwipayana as "the chief presidential image-builder." It was Dwipayana who developed the *Si Unyil* series and the *Keluarga Rahmat* series, which I describe in chapters 4 and 5.

CHAPTER 3

1. Note that the further inflection of the audience as *active* citizen/consumers which I develop in chapters 9 and 10 reflects the increasing involvement of the audience in television affairs *after* 1991.

2. As I have shown, funding public broadcasting from license fees or government appropriations exclusively is relatively uncommon. We can best understand Subrata's remark as signaling a desire to separate public affairs from private sector constraints.

3. I am grateful to Ariel Heryanto for pointing out that it was Radio Republik Indonesia (RRI) that first popularized the use of *Saudara* as a form of address in the mass media.

4. Benedict Anderson discusses Johnny Hidayat's work in "Cartoons and Monuments: The Evolution of Political Communication under the New Order" (Anderson 1978).

5. All commercial channels were authorized to broadcast nationally in Ministerial Decree 04 A, 1993 (Menteri Penerangan 1993).

CHAPTER 4

1. P4 is an abbreviation for **P**edoman **P**enghayatan dan **P**engamalan **P**ancasila.

2. Now "Perum Produksi Film Negara." "Perum" [Perusahaan Umum] signifies that PPFN is a state-owned company.

3. Gufron Dwipayana was a journalist and former member of President's Soeharto's personal staff. Suyadi described him as "a great favorite of the president" (personal interview, 5 May 1993). "Pak Dipo," as he was known, was appointed head of PPFN by State Secretary Sudharmono (later vice president) when he was Acting Minister for Information in 1981. Under Pak Dipo, who Krishna Sen describes as "the chief presidential image-builder," "PPFN was committed to big-budget feature films about the head of state" (Sen 1994, 66).

4. I was unable to gain access to the early episodes of the series. With PPFN's help a selection of episodes produced in 1981 were made available from the National Archive. I discovered that episodes produced from 1979/80 to 1984/85 were shot on 35mm film. Costs of transferring these episodes onto videotape were beyond my research budget. PPFN was reluctant to project the original 35mm print because of its archival significance.

5. Kong was taken out of the series in the late '80s. He was deleted from the program as Indonesia's official relations with the People's Republic of China began to improve after many years of stand-off following Indonesian allegations that communist China was implicated in the coup of 1965. It was believed that Kong was prejudicial to harmonious relations with the Chinese. Kong's appearance was anachronistic, his slit eyes, long moustaches, pigtail, and dark blue clothing more in keeping with the Indonesian Chinese of the nineteenth century than contemporary Indonesia. His sing-song accent, poor Indonesian, and the nonverbal expressive gestures he characteristically used were also heavy-handed, making Kong an altogether unsympathetic representation of a Chinese. Kong was not replaced with a more sympathetic character ("Petinju Cilik" and Suyadi, personal interview, 5 May 1993).

6. The ninety-minute film was titled *Si Unyil Jadi Manusia* and was produced by PPFN in 1981. Scenario by Kurnain Suhardiman. Bambang Utoyo, the voice for Unyil in the television series, played Unyil in the film. Artistic director Suyadi played "Pak Raden." "Pak Ogah," perhaps best described in Australian idiom as "the bludger" (freeloader) character in the series, developed fortuitously out of the film. The voice actor Hamid, who contributed to the postproduction of the film, had a face that Suyadi found irresistible, and he made a puppet in his likeness. Kurnain Suhardiman loved the puppet face and decided to develop a character around Hamid's voice and the new puppet. It was in this way that Ogah, one of the most interesting and controversial characters in the series, was born.

7. In Williams's original formulation the concept of "flow" was restricted to the sequence of programming during one evening's viewing.

There is no real justification for restricting the time frame of the concept in this way. Channels invariably orient viewers to programs scheduled for later in the week, just as they lead viewers to anticipate programs scheduled later on the same day. In linking flow with intertextual relations of content across time and genre I am following Fiske (1987).

8. *Ria Jenaka* is hard to translate as the two words of the title have similar meanings in English. Translated literally, the title would be something like *Cheerful [and] Funny*. Compounded, the two terms intensify the sense of fun.

9. "Suka Maju" is a trope that has a life beyond the *Si Unyil* series. Lynette Parker notes that elementary school textbooks in Bali in 1981 and 1989 referred to a model student and citizen, Budi, and his family and friends. They lived in a model village, "Suka Maju," which Parker translates as the "Village of Like-to-Progress" (Parker 1992, 52–53).

10. Inpres: **Ins**truksi **Pres**ident (Presidential Instruction). Schools in Indonesia may benefit from funds allocated by a particular presidential directive.

11. There are some episodes that extend over two or more weeks, but these are exceptional. The episodes that form the basis of the analysis in this chapter derive from three sources: (1) recordings of three episodes made off air in Jakarta in 1991 and 1993; (2) eight episodes produced between 1981 and 1990 supplied to me by Suyadi from his private collection; (3) eleven episodes produced between 1982 and 1993 selected at random in consultation with PPFN. Written scenarios for an additional fifteen episodes were also made available by Suyadi. These scenarios have not been used in this analysis. Details of episodes studied are provided in appendix C. This selection of episodes is not necessarily representative of the twelve years of the *Si Unyil* series. The notion of representativeness, drawn from statistical discourse, asserts a putative relationship of likeness or typicality between parts and episodes and a whole (all episodes), which is problematic in the study of television texts. Representativeness assumes a determinate position of meaning outside of the texts that can act as a standard or criterion for typicality. To claim that this episode is, or is not, like all (or the majority) of other episodes assumes agreement on what those episodes have in common. But each and every episode is textually unique first because of its distinctive pattern of signification and second because any assessment of its significance or meaning will be a product of interaction between the text and individual viewers.

12. Sitcoms screened by TVRI before the advent of *Si Unyil* include *Hogan's Heroes* (in 1980), *Swiss Family Robinson* (in 1979), *Mr. Ed* (in 1978), and *I Dream of Jeannie* (in 1974/76).

13. Examples of folktales and legends presented include "Timun Mas"

and "Ayu Berubah Rupa" (Java); "Atu Belah" (Sumatra) and "Raksasa Mengejar Apen" (unknown provenance). "Uti Di Belantara" and "Uti Di Sarang Raksasa" by Agust Suprapto are written in the style of traditional "monster stories." "Girah, Anak Juru Kunci" concerns children's fears of the *sundel bolong*, a mysterious spirit creature in the form of an attractive young woman. The *sundel bolong* has a large hole in her back, which she covers with her long hair (Danandjaja 1984). Episodes that celebrate folk culture include "Panjat Pinang," which shows children climbing a greasy palm for prizes tied at the top, and "Arak Arakan Sisinarang," which features a young boy's circumcision procession.

14. It deserves more than a brief comment, of course, but a more comprehensive discussion is beyond the scope of this chapter. See Saya Shiraishi 1995 and 1997.

15. "Unyil" is not a common Indonesian name. Suyadi informed me that it was a generic name (Everyboy?), invented to sound like an Indonesian name but impossible to associate with any particular ethnic group or region. *Pos Kota* (13 September 1981), quoting Kurnain Suhardiman, traces Unyil to a character in a comic strip published in the magazine *Sudut Remaja* in the 1950s. It is not clear whether Kurnain was responsible for creating Unyil in that publication. His name is simply mentioned as a contributor along with "Ayip Rosidi and others." *Hai* (#28 1981), again quoting Kurnain, claims he named the comic strip character after a favorite nephew.

16. Suyadi (personal interview, 5 May 1993) used the English word *gang* when describing the relations between the village children. In my description, I have chosen to use the more neutral *group*, as it more accurately represents the relations between the characters. The groups are not rigidly structured and are not inscribed as rivals. Unyil frequently interacts with members of the other group. The word *gang*, with its more rigid adversarial connotations, seems inappropriate under these conditions.

17. Pak Raden usually introduces himself to visitors with barely managed modesty as "Raden Mas Singomenggolo Jalmowono." The name, drawn out in a low purring tone of self-congratulation signifies in the Raden Mas, Javanese aristocratic status. "Singomenggolo" carries equally illustrious associations, signifying a man who is a leader, a lion among men. But the final element pricks the bubble, as it signifies a man who lives in the forest, an orangutan in other words! Having said his name, Pak Raden usually goes on to say, "But if that's too much of a mouthful, call me Pak Raden for short." Once again Pak Raden's pretended modesty carries a sting in its tail. The combination of "Pak" (Indonesian) with "Raden" (Javanese) is ludicrous, as inappropriate as saying something like "Call me Mr. Your Majesty."

18. Ableh and Enyeng ("Nyeng") are different characters but both play straight man to Ogah. Ableh was written out of the series in 1990 because the character was believed to be "counterproductive" (*kurang mendidik*) (*Pos Film*, 30 December 1990). Nyeng is not as stupid as Ableh, but he is otherwise much the same as his predecessor. Nyeng parodies Ogah's lack of status by invariably referring to him as "Boss" (*sic*).

19. **Sistem K[e]amanan Ling**kungan—local environment security system. Usually staffed on a rotational basis by adult males.

20. Siegel notes that in Java, it is only when children have acquired the ability to speak High Javanese that they find a place in Javanese adult society. Until they are integrated into Javanese society, children are described as "not yet Javanese." As such, they are not imagined to be part of any other ethnic group but rather as "animalish" (Siegel 1986, 18). Ogah and Ableh, unnaturally fixed at the child stage, have a disturbing otherness, which I have expressed in the spider metaphor. See also the quotation from Geertz (1960, 247) above.

21. MISS SARA stands for Menghasut, Insinuasi, Sensasi, Spekulasi (MISS) and Suku, Agama, Ras, Aliran (SARA) and refers "to anything deemed seditious, insinuating, sensational, speculative or likely to antagonise ethnic, religious, racial or class tensions" (Hill 1994, 45).

22. The game is a device for choosing who is to be "in," rather like the "eenie meenie minee mo" Australian children use for the same purpose. The full text of the Indonesian rhyme is "Om Pim Pah, Alaya Om Gambreng; 'Pok Minah Pake Baju Rombeng" (Ratna Sulastin Chalmers, personal communication, September 1993).

23. Rujak petis is a kind of fresh fruit salad spiced with chili and fermented shrimp paste. It is a specialty of Surabaya and Madura. The character Ibu Bariah is a woman from the island of Madura.

24. Bu Bariah's speech is Indonesian, spoken with a Madurese accent, with (Surabaya) Javanese words and phrases inserted in place of Indonesian elements: "Gah, aduh *awake* saya *peno* tulungi *opo-o*. Ini lho, saya dapat surat, tapi saya nggak bisa baca. Tolong ya Gah, dibacakan (Surabaya Javanese words are italicized). In line with Madurese morphology, Bu Bariah creates her own compound words by taking the second syllable of a word and making it the first syllable of the original word: ca-baca, yu-ayu, kep-cakep (*sic*).

25. TVRI announcers are encouraged to speak in a "standard" accent that neutralizes any association with places such as Java, Madura, or Jakarta (Wahyudi 1985).

26. These comments are summarized from Department of Informa-

tion Regional Offices unpublished reports written in response to a 1989 PPFN survey on *Si Unyil*. Comments cited summarized from respondents in Maluku, Irian Jaya, and Sulawesi Utara.

27. Soetatmo Soeriokoesomo cited in Saya Shiraishi 1997, 84.

CHAPTER 5

1. The idea of a second channel for Jakarta had been around for a long time—at least since advertising was banned on TVRI. However, Minister Harmoko's decree authorizing commercial television in October 1987 (Menteri Penerangan 1987) signaled the imminent competition TVRI would face and spurred it to develop a channel that would meet the Jakarta audience's demand for an alternative service (Ishadi, personal interview, 17 May 1993).

2. Hans Antlov (1995, 129) confirms the gendered character of the private/public spheres in a rural community in West Java.

3. Fritz Schadt, director of *Keluarga Rahmat*, is a second-generation Indonesian. His great-grandfather was an expatriate German pioneer planter in North Sumatra.

4. Early production documents have the series titled *Manusia Korpri* (People of the Public Service). Iskandar Nugroho, "Pratomo" in the series, confirmed that President Soeharto had proposed the series to Gufron Dwipayana. He also reported that the State Secretariat had assisted production of the series with the loan of a high-quality camera and archival film resources for some historical segments (telephone interview, 2 February 1995).

5. In 1986 an article by the Australian journalist David Jenkins (*Sydney Morning Herald*, 10 April 1986) concerning the wealth of the Indonesian presidential family precipitated a diplomatic rift between Indonesia and Australia. Rebecca Gilling, star of the serial *Return to Eden*, which was very popular throughout Indonesia, was invited to Jakarta as part of the Australian embassy's cultural program. Rebecca Gilling's visit was widely covered in the local press, and Indonesian journalists considered Ambassador Bill Morrison's "glamor diplomacy" to be a shrewd way of healing the rift between the two countries.

6. The expression, literally translated as "poison answered with mother's milk," is a popular saying that has something of the meaning of "turning the other cheek," but it goes beyond that in the sense that *air tuba*, a poison made from pounded roots and usually prepared to kill fish, is opposed to the life-giving qualities of mother's milk (*air susu*).

7. The government-backed federation of anticommunist social organizations, Golkar, is sometimes referred to as "The Greater Golkar Family." Hamlets and neighborhoods in Indonesia are organized into *Rukun Warga* and *Rukun Tetangga* respectively. These are "communal organizations acknowledged and founded by the government to maintain and perpetuate the values of Indonesian social life, which is based on mutual assistance (*kegotongroyongan*) and familyism (*kekeluargaan*)" (Home Affairs Regulation #7/1983 cited in Sullivan 1992, 175).

8. The fan letters were provided by Fritz Schadt. In 1993 Fritz could find only thirty-two letters in PPFN files. He kindly allowed me to copy them all. Follow-up calls chasing more letters from TVRI and PPFN in 1994 failed to turn up any more letters. I contacted "Nastiti" asking for letters, but she was unable to find any. Only twenty-four of the thirty-two letters were dated. The majority (17) of dated letters were written in June–September 1989. Eleven authors were males, and eighteen were females. The letters were received from Sumatra (4), Java (14), Bali (2), Sulawesi (1), Irian Jaya (2), Malaysia (1), and Singapore (2). The remainder are of unknown origin. Ien Ang's well-known study of *Dallas* (1985) was based on her "symptomatic reading" of forty-two letters, some a few lines in length, others up to ten pages. The letters I had access to were all one to two pages long. Some were closely typed; others were handwritten.

9. The title translates literally as "The House Is Still There." The final scene of the episode, where Purnomo's father walks off, saying, "the house is still there," leaving Purnomo at the Rahmat's house, makes it clear that the title is more than a comment about the house. I have tried to express this in my translation "The House Is Still There for You."

10. The title literally translated is "When [*Wader*] Fish Eat the Stem of the Coconut Blossom," a popular saying that expresses a kind of "pigs might fly" impossibility.

11. Transmigration is a government-sponsored program of internal migration designed to relieve pressure in areas of high population density. Transmigrants are transported at government expense to specially prepared sites, given land, housing, and some agricultural supplies for a year or so. In recent years, transmigration sites have been equipped with communal satellite dishes to improve reception of TVRI and other channels.

12. "Bila Wader" was screened as the forty-ninth episode in the fifty-two-episode series.

13. Hari Raya Galungan is a ten-day religious celebration in the 210-day Balinese *Pawukon* cycle.

CHAPTER 6

1. In Indonesia the Guided Democracy regime and the New Order both distanced themselves from Western "liberal democracy," preferring to talk of "Pancasila democracy." The fourth principle of the Pancasila requires the state to abide by Indonesian-style democracy, a phrase that essentially refers to processes of consultation and consensus.

2. TVRI does not collect ratings data for TVRI news programs. Systematic surveys of audience response to TVRI programs are almost completely lacking.

3. The "calendar effects" of including Christmas day and New Year's day were taken account of by rejecting any constructed week that contained either day during the sampling process. See appendix G.

4. "Development activities" were defined in Alfian and Chu (1981, 89) as follows: "Development activities include stories about construction projects, factories and other industrial complexes, transportation, agriculture, produce transport and marketing, mineral exploration, tourism, and labour issues."

5. An individual was described as playing a "key role" if he or she had main responsibility for the resolution of a particular event that was the main focus or topic of the news item. In an item concerning a bridge-opening ceremony, for example, the event is resolved by an individual performing some symbolic act of "opening" the bridge. It is usually the case that the individual who performs the key role is also the person of highest status featured in the news item.

6. The article, "A Cultural Approach to Communication," first appeared in *Communication* 2, no. 2 (1975) and was reprinted in Carey 1989.

7. These topics (agricultural practices, flooding, and pollution) were discussed in film reports during the two-week period.

8. The *Nagarakertagama* records that the king traveled not at the head of his entourage but at the center, a practice that has been interpreted as signifying the pivotal role and status of the king (Gesick 1983).

9. These remarks apply to the "older styles" of *wayang* performance. Sears notes that in the innovative *wayang padat*, "if one of the rules of a conventional wayang says that all wayang stories must begin and end in a court, wayang padat no longer feels the need to abide by this rule" (1996, 251). On TVRI, intertextual allusions are located in the older style of wayang, which is unambiguous in the inscription of power and authority.

Newer wayang forms such as the innovative Rebo Legi perform "a subtle struggle between the unseen authority at the performance—the Jakarta government—and the visible authority of the individual puppeteers" (Sears 1996, 244) and do not encode the meanings a development-oriented government endorses.

10. Turner uses this form of the Latin when he introduces the term for the first time. He uses *"communitas"* thereafter. My understanding of *comitatus* is that it signifies ideas of attending, accompanying, and following, none of which seem appropriate. *"Communitas"* means community, society, fellowship, and the sense of community in feeling, which carries the main thrust of Turner's argument (Lewis and Short 1933).

11. Although Turner introduces the concept of *communitas* in the context of analysis of the liminal phase of rites of passage in preindustrial societies, he suggests later that it is not only in societies of that kind nor only in rites of passage that *communitas* is expressed culturally, but that "the collective dimensions, communitas and structure, are to be found at all stages and levels of culture and society" (Turner 1969, 113; see also 107, 109, and Turner 1977, 36).

12. The editor of RCTI's *Seputar Indonesia* told me frankly that he and his news team (most of whom were drawn from a print media background) studied CNN as a model for news production (Chrys Kelana, personal interview, 22 April 1993).

13. The change was made from 1 April 1993.

CHAPTER 9

1. The unprecedented expression of public discontent over the privatization of fees collection and Mekatama Raya's incompetence can be linked to a public scandal over the awarding of a monopoly early in 1991 to President Soeharto's youngest son, Hutomo Mandala Putra (Tommy), for the purchase and resale of cloves to the cigarette industry. This concession failed within a year amid criticism from the Speaker of the Parliament and the Secretary General of Golkar (*Tempo,* 28 March 1992). At the same time, another of President Soeharto's children, Siti Hardiyanti Rukmana (Tutut), was granted a television license to establish the first national (commercial) educational television channel. Communications specialists were skeptical over the inexperienced Tutut's entry into this specialized field, and television critic Eduard Depari expressed concern over the potential for conflict between educational and commercial priorities in channel management (*Tempo,* 11 August 1990; *Kompas,* 19 Sep-

tember 1990; *Kompas,* 20 November 1990; *Suara Pembaruan,* 19 August 1990; Kitley 1994b).

2. All advertisements screened on TPI on 16 December 1991 and 1 and 12 April 1993 were timed and classified into eleven categories (see fig. 9.2). Comparative data for advertising on RCTI was obtained for 8 April 1993.

16 December 1991: TPI start-up 5:30 A.M., close 1:30 P.M. Total: 8 hours broadcast. Ads represented 3.125 percent of broadcast hours.

1 April 1993: TPI start-up 5:30 A.M., close 1:30 P.M. Total: 8 hours broadcast. Ads represented 10.83 percent of broadcast hours.

8 April 1993: RCTI start-up 12 noon, close 2 A.M. Total: 14 hours broadcast. Ads represented 8.75 percent of broadcast hours.

CHAPTER 10

1. At the time of writing the broadcasting law has not been signed by President Soeharto. Until it is signed by the president, it does not become law.

2. The draft broadcasting law covers radio and television broadcasting. The law is couched in general terms, but more attention is given to regulating television than radio.

3. The Department of Religion recognizes Islam, Buddhism, Hinduism, Christianity, and Confucianism as official religions. "Belief systems" are acknowledged but have a subordinate status.

4. Debate over sex and violence in the media has a long history in Indonesia. Until recently, however, the concerns focused mainly on the cinema. The advent of five, national free-to-air television services has intensified the debate since 1993, as children are perceived to be more at risk than ever before.

WORKS CITED

Abeyasekere, Susan. 1987. *Jakarta: A History*. Singapore: Oxford University Press.
Acciaioli, Greg. 1985. "Culture as Art: From Practice to Spectacle in Indonesia." *Canberra Anthropology* 8 (1–2): 148–72.
Agassi, Judith B. 1969. *Mass Media in Indonesia*. Cambridge: Massachusetts Institute of Technology, Center for International Studies.
Aiko Kurasawa. 1987. "Propaganda Media on Java Under the Japanese, 1942–1945." *Indonesia* 44: 59–116.
Alfian and Godwin C. Chu, eds. 1981. *Satellite Television in Indonesia*. Jakarta: LEKNAS/LIPI; and Honolulu: East West Center.
Allen, Robert C. 1983. "On Reading Soaps: A Semiotic Primer." In *Regarding Television: Critical Approaches, An Anthology*, ed. E. Ann Kaplan. Los Angeles: University Publications of America.
———. 1985. *Speaking of Soap Operas*. Chapel Hill: University of North Carolina Press.
———, ed. 1995. *To Be Continued: Soap Operas Around the World*. London: Routledge.
Alwi Dahlan. 1981. "Indonesian Experience in Satellite Communication: Analysis of Policy-Making and Implementation Problems in Rural Development Communication Programs." Unpublished seminar paper, Seminar on Communication Policy for Rural Development, 2–8 March. Faculty of Journalism and Mass Communication, Thammasat University, Thailand.
Amrih Widodo. 1995. "The Stages of the State: Arts of the People and Rites of Hegemonization." *Review of Indonesian and Malay Affairs* 29 (1–2): 1–35.
Anderson, Benedict. 1991. *Imagined Communities: Reflections on the Origin and Spread of Nationalism*. Rev. ed. London: Verso.
Anderson, Benedict R. O'G. 1972. "The Idea of Power in Javanese Culture." In *Culture and Politics in Indonesia*, ed. Claire Holt. Ithaca, N.Y.: Cornell University Press.

———. 1978. "Cartoons and Monuments: The Evolution of Political Communication Under the New Order." In *Political Power and Communications in Indonesia,* ed. Karl D. Jackson and Lucien W. Pye. Berkeley: University of California Press.

———. 1987. "The State and Minorities in Indonesia." *Southeast Asian Tribal Groups and Ethnic Minorities: Prospects for the Eighties and Beyond.* Cultural Survival Report 22. Cambridge, Mass.: Cultural Survival. Proceedings of a conference held at Harvard University, October 1984.

———. 1990. "Sembah-Sumpah: The Politics of Language and Javanese Culture." In *Language and Power: Exploring Political Cultures in Indonesia.* Ithaca, N.Y.: Cornell University Press.

Anderson, Michael H. 1980. "Transnational Advertising and Politics: The Case of Indonesia." *Asian Survey* 20 (12): 1253–70.

Ang, Ien. 1985. *Watching Dallas: Soap Opera and the Melodramatic Imagination.* Trans. Della Couling. London: Methuen.

———. 1991. *Desperately Seeking the Audience.* London: Routledge.

———. 1996. *Living Room Wars: Rethinking Media Audiences for a Postmodern World.* London: Routledge.

Antlov, Hans. 1995. *Exemplary Centre, Administrative Periphery: Rural Leadership and the New Order in Java.* Richmond, Surrey: Curzon Press.

Ariel Heryanto. 1990. "Introduction: The Cultural Aspect of State and Society." In *State and Civil Society in Indonesia,* ed. Arief Budiman. Clayton, Vic: Centre for Southeast Asian Studies, Monash University.

Arswendo Atmowiloto. 1986. *Telaah Tentang Televisi* [Research Concerning Television]. Jakarta: Gramedia.

Ashadi Siregar. 1995. *Sketsa Sketsa Media Massa* [Sketches on the Mass Media]. Yogyakarta, Indonesia: Yayasan Bentang Budaya.

Astrid Susanto. 1978. "The Mass Communications System in Indonesia." In *Political Power and Communications in Indonesia,* ed. Karl D. Jackson and Lucian W. Pye. Berkeley: University of California Press.

Australian Broadcasting Tribunal. 1991. *Kidz TV: An Enquiry into Children's and Preschool Children's Television Standards.* 2 vols. Sydney: Australian Broadcasting Tribunal.

Babcock, Barbara, ed. 1978. *The Reversible World: Symbolic Inversion in Art and Society.* Ithaca, N.Y.: Cornell University Press.

Barnouw, Eric. 1977. *Tube of Plenty: The Evolution of American Television.* London: Oxford University Press.

Barthes, Roland. 1988. "Introduction to the Structural Analysis of Narratives." In *The Semiotic Challenge*. Trans. Richard Howard. Oxford: Basil Blackwell.

Becker, A. E. 1979. "Text-Building, Epistemology, and Aesthetics in Javanese Shadow Theatre." In *The Imagination of Reality*, ed. A. L. Becker and A. A. Yengoyan. Norwood, N.J.: Ablex.

Benda, Harry J. 1967. "Louis Charles Damais." *Indonesia* 3: 217–21.

Bernstein, Basil. 1971. *Class, Codes, and Control: Theoretical Studies Towards a Sociology of Language*. Vol. 1. London: Routledge and Kegan Paul.

Berwanger, Dietrich. 1995. "The Third World." In *Television: An International History*, ed. Anthony Smith. Oxford: Oxford University Press.

Bird, S. Elizabeth, and Robert W. Dardenne. 1988. "Myth, Chronicle, and Story: Exploring the Narrative Qualities of News." In *Media, Myths, and Narratives: Television and the Press*, ed. James W. Carey. Newbury Park, Calif.: Sage.

Boediardjo. 1972. "Sambutan Menteri Penerangan" [A Word from the Minister for Information]. In *Televisi Di Indonesia 1962–72* [Television in Indonesia]. Jakarta: Direktorat Televisi, Departemen Penerangan.

Booth, Anne. 1992. Introduction to *The Oil Boom and After: Indonesian Economic Policy and Performance in the Soeharto Era*, ed. Anne Booth. Singapore: Oxford University Press.

Bourchier, David. 1990. "Crime, Law and State Authority in Indonesia." In *State and Civil Society in Indonesia*, ed. Arief Budiman. Clayton, Vic.: Centre of Southeast Asian Studies, Monash University.

Bourdieu, Pierre. 1980. "The Aristocracy of Culture." In *Media, Culture, and Society* 2 (3): 225–54.

Boyd, Douglas A., Joseph D. Straubhaar, and John A. Lent. 1989. *Videocassette Recorders in the Third World*. London: Longman.

Brunsdon, Charlotte. 1983. "Crossroads: Notes on Soap Opera." In *Regarding Television: Critical Approaches—an Anthology*, ed. E. Anne Kaplan. Los Angeles: University Publications of America.

———. 1984. "Writing about Soap Opera." In *Television Mythologies: Stars, Shows, and Signs*, ed. Len Masterman. London: Comedia/MK Media Press.

Buckingham, David. 1993. *Children Talking Television: The Making of Television Literacy*. London: Falmer Press.

Buxton, David. 1990. *From "The Avengers" to "Miami Vice": Form and Ideology in Television Series*. Manchester, England: Manchester University Press.

Cannadine, D., and J. Price, eds. 1986. *Rituals of Royalty: Power and Cere-

monial in Traditional Society. Cambridge: Cambridge University Press.

Carey, James W. 1989. *Communication as Culture: Essays on Media and Society*. New York: Routledge.

Castells, Manuel. 1983. "Crisis, Planning and the Quality of Life: Managing the New Historical Relationships between Space and Society." *Environment and Planning D: Space and Society* 1 (1).

Chu, Godwin C., and Alfian. 1980. "Programming for Development in Indonesia." *Journal of Communication Research* 30 (4): 50–57.

Chu, Godwin C., Alfian, and Wilbur Schramm. 1991. *Social Impact of Satellite Television in Rural Indonesia*. Singapore: Asian Mass Communication Research and Information Centre.

Clifford, James. 1988. *The Predicament of Culture*. Cambridge: Harvard University Press.

Clifford, James, and Vivek Dhareshwar, eds. 1989. *Traveling Theories: Traveling Theorists*. Santa Cruz: Center for Cultural Studies, Oakes College, University of California.

Clifford, James, and George E. Marcus, eds. 1986. *Writing Culture: The Poetics and Politics of Ethnography*. Berkeley: University of California Press.

Comstock, George, and Haejung Paik. 1991. *Television and the American Child*. New York: Academic Press.

Cranny-Francis, Anne. 1988. "The Moving Image: Film and Television." In *Communication and Culture,* ed. Gunter Kress. Sydney: New South Wales University Press.

Crawford, Andrew. 1967. "The Djakarta Daily Press." Ph.D. diss., Syracuse University.

Cribb, Robert. 1992. *Historical Dictionary of Indonesia*. Metuchen, N.J.: Scarecrow Press.

Cunningham, Stuart. 1991. "Cultural Studies from the Viewpoint of Cultural Policy." *Meanjin* 50 (2–3): 423–36.

———. 1992a. *Framing Culture: Criticism and Policy in Australia*. North Sydney: Allen and Unwin.

———. 1992b. "The Cultural Policy Debate Revisited." *Meanjin* 51 (3): 533–43.

———. 1992c. "The Unworthy Discourse? Advertising and National Culture." In *Framing Culture: Criticism and Policy in Australia*. North Sydney: Allen and Unwin.

Cunningham, Stuart, and Elizabeth Jacka. 1996. *Australian Television and International Mediascapes*. Cambridge: Cambridge University Press.

Cunningham, Stuart, and Toby Miller. 1994. *Contemporary Australian Television*. Sydney: University of New South Wales Press.
Cunningham, Stuart, and Graeme Turner, eds. 1993. *The Media in Australia: Industries, Texts, Audiences*. St. Leonards, New South Wales: Allen and Unwin.
Danandjaja, James. 1984. *Folklor Indonesia: Ilmu Gosip, Dongeng, Dan Lain Lain* [Indonesian Folklore: The Science of Gossip, Legend, and the Like]. Jakarta: Grafiti Pers.
Dayan, Daniel, and Elihu Katz. 1987. "Performing Media Events." In *Impacts and Influences: Essays on Media Power in the Twentieth Century*, ed. James Curran, Anthony Smith, and Pauline Wingate. London: Methuen.
———. 1995. "Political Ceremony and Instant History." In *Television: An International History*, ed. Anthony Smith. Oxford: Oxford University Press.
Departemen Penerangan. 1989/90. "Laporan Penelitian: Kebutuhan Khalayak Akan Program Radio dan Televisi di Indonesia" [Research Report: Radio and Television Audience Needs in Indonesia]. Unpublished typescript. Jakarta: Badan Penelitian dan Pengembangan Penerangan, Bekerjasama dengan Japan International Cooperation Agency (JICA) [Research and Development Organisation in collaboration with the Japan International Cooperation Agency].
Dewan Perwakilan Rakyat (DPR-RI). 1991. "Catatan Rapat Sementara Komisi I [Draft Notes of a Meeting of (Parliamentary) Commission I]. Unpublished typescript. 28 January 1991.
———. 1993. "Catatan Rapat Sementara, Komisi I" [Draft Notes of a Meeting of (Parliamentary) Commission I]. Unpublished typescript. 11 Feb. 1993.
Directorate General of Posts and Telecommunications. 1983. *History of Posts and Telecommunications in Indonesia*. 5 vols. Jakarta: Directorate General of Posts and Telecommunications, Department of Transport, Communications, and Tourism.
Direktorat Jenderal Pos dan Telekomunikasi Departemen Pariwisata, Pos dan Telekomunikasi. 1984. *Megenang Sewindu SKSD Palapa* [Recollections After Eight Years of the Domestic Communications Satellite System Palapa]. Jakarta: Direktorat Jenderal Pos dan Telekomunikasi Departemen Pariwisata, Pos dan Telekomunikasi.
———. 1985. *Tokoh Tokoh Sejarah Perjuangan dan Pembangun Pos dan Telekomunikasi di Indonesia* [Identities in the History, Struggle, and

Development of Posts and Telecommunications in Indonesia]. Jakarta: Departemen Pariwisata, Pos dan Telekomunikasi.

Direktorat Radio, Televisi dan Film. 1983. *Televisi Republik Indonesia*. Jakarta: Direktorat Radio Televisi dan Film.

———. 1984. *Televisi Republik Indonesia*. Jakarta: Direktorat Radio Televisi dan Film.

Direktorat Televisi. 1972. *Televisi Di Indonesia: TVRI 1962–1972* [Television in Indonesia, 1962–1972]. Jakarta: Direktorat Televisi.

———. 1987. *25 Tahun TVRI 1962–1987* [Twenty-five Years of Indonesian National Television, 1962–1987]. Jakarta: Direktorat Televisi.

Dove, Michael R., ed. 1988. *The Real and Imagined Role of Culture in Development: Case Studies From Indonesia*. Honolulu: University of Hawaii Press.

Drake, Christine. 1989. *National Integration in Indonesia: Patterns and Policies*. Honolulu: University of Hawaii Press.

Dumont, Louis. 1970. *Homo Hierarchicus*. Chicago: University of Chicago Press.

East Asian Executive Reports. 1991. "China, Thailand, Indonesia Among Countries Criticized for Inadequate Protection of Intellectual Property." *East Asian Executive Reports* 13 (3): 8, 18–21.

Eaton, M. 1978/79. "Television Situation Comedy." *Screen* 19 (4): 61–89.

Eldridge, Philip J. 1995. *Non-government Organisations and Democratic Participation in Indonesia*. Kuala Lumpur: Oxford University Press.

Elliot, Philip. 1982. "Press Performance as Political Ritual." In *Mass Communication Review Yearbook*, ed. D. C. Whitney, E. Wartella, and S. Windhal. Beverly Hills: Sage.

Ericson, Richard V., Patricia M. Baranek, and Janet B. L. Chan. 1991. *Representing Order: Crime, Law, and Justice in the News Media*. Milton Keynes, England: Open University Press.

Errington, Shelley. 1983. "The Place of Regalia in Luwu." In *Centers, Symbols, and Hierarchies: Essays on the Classical States of Southeast Asia,* ed. Lorraine Gesick. New Haven, Conn.: Yale University Southeast Asia Studies.

Feith, Herbert. 1962. *The Decline of Constitutional Democracy in Indonesia*. Ithaca, N.Y.: Cornell University Press.

———. 1963. "Indonesia's Political Symbols and Their Wielders." *World Politics* 16: 79–97.

Feuer, Jane. 1986. "Narrative Form in American Network Television." In *High Theory/Low Culture: Analysing Popular Television and Film,* ed. Colin MacCabe. New York: St. Martin's.

———. 1995. *Seeing Through the Eighties: Television and Reaganism*. Durham: Duke University Press.

Fisher, Lyn, and Michael Leigh. 1988. "Australia-Asia Media Relations." Conference paper presented at the ANZAAS Centenary Congress, 18 May, University of Sydney.

Fiske, John. 1987. *Television Culture*. New York: Routledge.

Fiske, John, and John Hartley. 1978. *Reading Television*. London: Methuen.

Fitzgerald, Stephen. 1997. *Is Australia an Asian Country?* St. Leonards: Allen and Unwin.

Foulcher, Keith. 1990. "The Construction of an Indonesian National Culture: Patterns of Hegemony and Resistance." In *State and Civil Society in Indonesia*, ed. Arief Budiman. Clayton: Centre of Southeast Asian Studies, Monash University.

Frith, Stephen, and Barbara Biggins, eds. 1994. *Children and Advertising: A Fair Game?* Sydney: New College Institute for Values Research, University of New South Wales.

Frow, John. 1992. "The Concept of the Popular." *New Formations* 18: 25–38.

Ganley, G., and O. Ganley. 1986. *The Political Implications of the Global Spread of Videocassette Recorders and Videocassette Programming*. Cambridge, Mass.: Program on Information Resources Policy, Harvard University.

Garin Nugroho. 1995. *Kekuasaan dan Hiburan* [Power and Entertainment]. Yogyakarta, Indonesia: Benteng.

Geertz, Clifford. 1960. *The Religion of Java*. Chicago: University of Chicago Press.

———. 1963. *Agricultural Involution: The Process of Ecological Change in Indonesia*. Berkeley: University of California Press.

———. 1968. *Islam Observed*. New Haven, Conn.: Yale University Press.

———. 1980. *Negara: The Theatre State in Nineteenth Century Bali*. Princeton, N.J.: Princeton University Press.

———. 1990. "'Popular Art' and the Javanese Tradition." *Indonesia* 50: 77–94.

Geraghty, Christine. 1991. *Women and Soap Opera: A Study of Prime-Time Soaps*. Cambridge, U.K.: Polity Press.

Gesick, Lorraine, ed. 1983. *Centers, Symbols, and Hierarchies: Essays on the Classical States of Southeast Asia*. New Haven, Conn.: Yale University Southeast Asia Studies.

Gitlin, Todd. 1983. *Inside Prime Time*. New York: Pantheon Books.

Glasgow Media Group. 1976. *Bad News*. London: Routledge and Kegan Paul.

———. 1980. *More Bad News*. London: Routledge and Kegan Paul.

———. 1982. *Really Bad News*. London: Writers and Readers.

Glassburner, Bruce. 1971. "Economic Policy Making in Indonesia, 1950–1957." In *The Economy of Indonesia: Selected Readings,* ed. Bruce Glassburner. Ithaca, N.Y.: Cornell University Press. 70–98.

———. 1978. "Political Economy and the Soeharto Regime." *Bulletin of Indonesian Economic Studies* 14 (3): 24–51.

Gluckman, Max. 1965. *Custom and Conflict in Africa.* Glencoe, Ill.: Free Press.

Graves, Sherryl Browne. 1996. "Diversity on Television." In *Tuning in to Young Viewers: Social Science Perspectives on Television,* ed. Tannis M. MacBeth. Thousand Oaks, Calif.: Sage Publications.

Griffin, Michael. 1992. "Looking at TV News: Strategies for Research." *Communication* 13: 121–41.

Gripsrud, Jostein. 1995. *The Dynasty Years: Hollywood Television and Critical Media Studies.* London: Routledge.

Guiness, Patrick. 1986. *Harmony and Hierarchy in a Javanese Kampung.* Singapore: Oxford University Press.

Habermas, Jurgen. 1989. *The Structural Transformation of the Public Sphere: An Enquiry into a Category of Bourgeois Society.* Trans. T. Burger and F. Lawrence. Cambridge: Polity Press.

Hall, Stuart. 1980. "Encoding/decoding." In *Culture, Media, Language,* ed. Stuart Hall, D. Hobson, A. Lowe and P. Willis. London: Hutchinson.

———. 1993. "Culture, Community, Nation." *Cultural Studies* 7 (3): 349–63.

Hall, Stuart, Bob Lumley, and Gregor McLennan. 1978. "Politics and Ideology: Gramsci." In *On Ideology.* London: Hutchinson.

Hallin, Daniel C. 1992. "Sound Bite News: Television Coverage of Elections, 1968–88." *Journal of Communication* 42 (2): 5–23.

Hansen, Miriam. 1993. "Unstable Mixtures, Dilated Spheres: Negt and Kluge's The Public Sphere and Experience, Twenty Years Later." *Public Culture* 5: 179–212.

Harmoko. 1993. Opening Address, Seminar on "Opportunities and Challenges in the Media Business Approaching the Year 2000." *Jakarta,* 3 May.

Hartley, John. 1982. *Understanding News.* London: Methuen.

———. 1987. "Invisible Fictions: Television Audiences, Paedocracy, Pleasure." *Textual Practice* 1 (2): 121–38.

Hatley, Barbara. 1990. "Theatre as Cultural Resistance in Contemporary Indonesia." In *State and Civil Society in Indonesia,* ed. Arief Budiman. Clayton, Vic.: Centre for Southeast Asian Studies, Monash University.

———. 1994. "Cultural Expression." In *Indonesia's New Order: The*

Dynamics of Socio-economic Transformation, ed. Hal Hill. Honolulu: University of Hawaii Press.

Heider, Karl. 1991. *Indonesian Cinema: National Culture on Screen*. Honolulu: University of Hawaii Press.

Heidt, E. U. 1984. *Television in Singapore: An Analysis of a Week's Viewing*. Singapore: Institute of Southeast Asian Studies.

Hidetoshi, Kato. 1995. "Japan." In *Television: An International History*, ed. Anthony Smith. Oxford: Oxford University Press.

Higgins, Benjamin. 1990. "Thought and Action: Indonesian Economic Studies and Policies in the 1950s." *Bulletin of Indonesian Economic Studies* 26 (1): 37–47.

Hill, David T. 1994. *The Press in New Order Indonesia*. Nedlands: University of Western Australia Press.

Hill, David T., and Krishna Sen. 1999. *Media Culture Politics in New Order Indonesia*. Melbourne: Oxford University Press.

Hirst, Martin. 1995. "The Coming Republic: Citizenship and the Public Sphere in Post-colonial Australia." *Australian Journal of Communication* 22 (3):13–39.

Hobsbawn, E. J. 1990. *Nations and Nationalism Since 1780: Programme, Myth, Reality*. 2nd ed. Cambridge: Cambridge University Press.

Hobsbawn, Eric, and Terence Ranger, eds. 1983. *The Invention of Tradition*. Cambridge: Cambridge University Press.

Hodge, Bob. 1992. "Is There a Case for Regulating Children's TV?" *Media Information Australia* 65: 70–75.

Holt, Claire. 1967. *Art in Indonesia*. Ithaca, N.Y.: Cornell University Press.

Hooker, Virginia, ed. 1993. *Culture and Society in New Order Indonesia*. Kuala Lumpur: Oxford University Press.

Hoover, Stewart M. 1988. "Television Myth and Ritual: The Role of Substantive Meaning and Spatiality." In *Media, Myths, and Narratives: Television and the Press*, ed. James W. Carey. Newbury Park: Sage.

Hugo, G. J., et al. 1987. *The Demographic Dimension in Indonesian Development*. Singapore: Oxford University Press.

Hurst, John. 1987. "A Clash of Cultures: Indonesia and the Australian Media." *Australian Quarterly* 59 (3–4): 345–56.

Isaac, Graeme. 1992. "The Indonesian Film and Television Industries: Prospects for Australian Collaboration." Unpublished report prepared for the Australia-Indonesia Institute, Canberra.

Ishadi, S. K. 1984. "Indonesian Television, Journalistic Training—Needs and Problems." Unpublished conference paper, Conference of Journalism Training in Asia. Manila, Philippines, 6–11 January.

Jenkins, David. 1987. "The Australian Media and the Region." *Australian Journalism Review* 9 (1–2): 545–59.

Jones, Robert L., and Roy E. Carter Jr. 1959. "Some Procedures for Estimating 'News Hole' in Content Analysis." *Public Opinion Quarterly* 3: 399–403.

Kahin, George McTurnan. 1952. *Nationalism and Revolution in Indonesia*. Ithaca, N.Y.: Cornell University Press.

Kitley, Philip. 1992. "Tahun Bertambah, Zaman Berubah: Television and Its Audiences in Indonesia." *Review of Indonesian and Malay Affairs* 26: 71–109.

———. 1994a. "Fine Tuning Control: Commercial Television in Indonesia." *Continuum* 8 (2): 103–23.

———. 1994b. "The Indonesian Market for Educational Television." *Media Information Australia* 73: 97–103.

———. 1999. "Above the Law? The Political Economy of Regulating Broadcasting in Indonesia." *Indonesian Law and Administration Review* 5.1: 51–72.

Kunkel, Dale, and Donald Roberts. 1991. "Young Minds and Marketplace Values: Issues in Children's Television Advertising." *Journal of Social Issues* 47 (1): 57–72.

Lane, Max. 1991. *"Openness," Political Discontent, and Succession in Indonesia: Political Developments in Indonesia, 1989–91*. Nathan, Queensland: Centre for the Study of Australia-Asia Relations, Griffith University.

Larsen, Peter, ed. 1990. *Import/Export: International Flow of Television Fiction* (Report and Papers on Mass Communication, #104). Paris: UNESCO.

Lears, Jackson T. J. 1985. "The Concept of Cultural Hegemony: Problems and Possibilities." *American Historical Review* 90: 567–93.

Leigh, Barbara. 1991. "Making the Indonesian State: The Role of School Texts." *Review of Indonesian and Malay Affairs* 25 (1): 17–43.

Lembaga Ekonomi Kemasyarakatan Nasional (LEKNAS)/Lembaga Ilmu [ILMU] Pengetahuan Indonesia (LIPI). 1980. *TVRI Iklan Televisi* [Television Commercials on Indonesian National Television]. Jakarta: Direktorat Televisi.

Lembaga Pembinaan dan Perlindungan Konsumen (LPPK) [Consumer Development and Protection Institute] and Televisi Pendidikan Indonesia (TPI). 1992. "Summary Report. Research into the TPI Audience in Central Java." Unpublished typescript. Semarang, Indonesia.

Lewis, Charlton T., and Charles Short. 1933. *A Latin Dictionary*. Oxford: Clarendon Press.

Liddle, R. William. 1982. "The Politics of Ekonomi Pancasila: Some

Reflections on a Recent Debate." *Bulletin of Indonesian Economic Studies* 18 (1): 96–101.

———. 1987. "The Politics of Shared Growth: Some Indonesian Cases." *Comparative Politics* 19 (2): 127–46.

Lindsey, Timothy C. 1993. "Concrete Ideology: Taste, Tradition, and the Javanese Past in New Order Public Space." In *Culture and Society in New Order Indonesia*, ed. Virginia Matheson Hooker. Kuala Lumpur: Oxford University Press.

Livingstone, Sonia, and Peter Lunt. 1994. *Talk on Television: Audience Participation and Public Debate*. London: Routledge.

Lopez, Ana M. 1995. "Our Welcomed Guests: Telenovelas in Latin America." In *To Be Continued: Soap Operas Around the World*, ed. Robert C. Allen. London: Routledge.

Lull, James, and Se-Wen Sun. 1988. "Agent of Modernization: Television and Urban Chinese Families." In *World Families Watch Television*, ed. James Lull. Beverly Hills: Sage.

M. Hadi Soesastro. 1989. "The Political Economy of Deregulation in Indonesia." *Asian Survey* 29 (9): 853–69.

Macintyre, Andrew. 1991. *Business and Politics in Indonesia*. St. Leonards: Allen and Unwin.

———. 1994. "Power, Prosperity, and Patrimonialism: Business and Government in Indonesia." In *Business and Government in Industrialising Asia*, ed. Andrew Macintyre. St. Leonards: Allen and Unwin.

Mackie, J. A. C. 1971. "The Indonesian Economy, 1950–1963." In *The Economy of Indonesia: Selected Readings*, ed. Bruce Glassburner. Ithaca, N.Y.: Cornell University Press. 16–69.

Mackie, Jamie, and Andrew Macintyre. 1994. "Politics." In *Indonesia's New Order: The Dynamics of Socio-economic Transformation*, ed. Hal Hill. Honolulu: University of Hawaii Press.

Majelis Permusyawaratan Rakyat (MPR). 1960. *Ketetapan No. II Majelis Permusyawaratan Rakyat Sementara* (MPRS) [Decision No. II of the Interim People's Advisory Assembly]. Lampiran A Bab I pasal 18: "Tentang Pembangunan Siaran Televisi" [Attachment A, Part I Article 18 Concerning the Development of Television].

Marcel Beding. 1996. "Broadcasting and Change." Unpublished paper presented at the conference "Open Skies: Towards an Open Society? The Challenge of Broadcasting in Asia." Jakarta, 26–28 June.

Mari Pangestu and Ahmad D. Habir. 1989. "Trends and Prospects in Privatization and Deregulation in Indonesia." *ASEAN Economic Bulletin* 5 (3): 224–41.

Martin-Barbero, Jesus. 1993. *Communication, Culture, and Hegemony:*

From Media to Mediations. Trans. Elizabeth Fox and Robert A. White. London: Sage Publications.

McCawley, Peter. 1982. "The Economics of *Ekonomi Pancasila*." *Bulletin of Indonesian Economic Studies* 18.1: 102–9.

McCombs, Maxwell E., and Donald L. Shaw. 1972. "The Agenda-Setting Function of Mass Media." *Public Opinion Quarterly* 36: 176–85.

McQuail, Denis. 1986. "Commercialization." In *New Media Politics: Comparative Perspectives in Western Europe,* ed. Denis McQuail and Karen Siune. London: Sage Publications.

———. 1994. *Mass Communication Theory: An Introduction.* 3d ed. London: Sage Publications.

McVey, Ruth. 1992. "The Materialization of the Southeast Asian Entrepreneur." In *Southeast Asian Capitalists,* ed. Ruth McVey. Ithaca, N.Y.: Southeast Asia Program, Cornell University.

Mekatama Raya. 1991. "Penjelasan P.T. Mekatama Raya Sebagai Pelaksana Pemungutan Iuran Televisi Di Muka Sidang Komisi I/DPR Pada Tanggal 3 Oktober 1991" [Statement of Position to Parliamentary Commission I from Mekatama Raya Pty. Ltd., Collector of Television License Fees, 3 October 1991]. Unpublished typescript.

Menteri Penerangan R.I. 1988. "Jawaban Penjelasan Menteri Penerangan R.I. Atas Pertanyaan Pertanyaan Komisi I DRR-RI Dalam Rapat Kerja 18 Juli 1988." Unpublished typescript. Jakarta: Departemen Penerangan.

Milne, R. S. 1991. "The Politics of Privatisation in the ASEAN States." *ASEAN Economic Bulletin* 7 (3): 322–34.

Modleski, Tania. 1984. *Loving with a Vengenence: Mass-Produced Fantasies for Women.* New York: Methuen.

Moertono. 1968. *State and Statecraft in Old Java: A Study of the Late Mataram Period, 16th to 19th Century.* Ithaca, N.Y.: Cornell Modern Indonesia Project.

Moran, Albert. 1993. *Moran's Guide to Australian TV Series.* North Ryde, New South Wales: Australian Film Television and Radio School.

———. 1996. "National Broadcasting and Cultural Identity: New Zealand Television and *Shortland Street.*" *Continuum* 10 (1): 168–86.

Morfit, Michael. 1986. "Pancasila Orthodoxy." In *Central Government and Local Development in Indonesia,* ed. Colin MacAndrews. Singapore: Oxford University Press.

Morley, David. 1992. *Television, Audiences, and Cultural Studies.* London: Routledge.

Morley, David, and Kevin Robins. 1995. *Spaces of Identity: Global Media, Electronic Landscapes, and Cultural Boundaries.* London: Routledge.

Muhammad Yamin. 1959. *Naskah Persiapan Undang-Undang Dasar 1945*. Vol. 1. Jakarta: Siguntang.
Murdock, Graham, and Peter Golding. 1989. "Information Poverty and Political Inequality: Citizenship in the Age of Privatized Communications." *Journal of Communication* 39 (3): 180–95.
Murray, Alison J. 1991. *No Money, No Honey: A Study of Street Traders and Prostitutes in Jakarta*. Singapore: Oxford University Press.
Neale, S., and Frank Krutnik. 1990. *Popular Film and Television Comedy*. London: Routledge.
Neale, Stephen. 1981. "Genre and Cinema." In *Popular Television and Film*, ed. Tony Bennett et al. London: British Film Institute.
Negt, Oskar, and Alexander Kluge. 1993. *Public Sphere and Experience: Toward an Analysis of the Bourgeois and Proletarian Public Sphere*. Trans. Peter Labanyi, Jamie Owen Daniel, and Assenka Oksiloff. Minneapolis: University of Minnesota Press.
Newcomb, H., and R. Alley. 1983. *Television: The Producer's Medium*. New York: Oxford University Press.
Nightingale, Virginia. 1993. "The Vulnerable Audience: Effects Traditions." In *The Media in Australia: Industries, Texts, Audiences*, ed. Stuart Cunningham and Graeme Turner. St. Leonards: Allen and Unwin.
———. 1996. *Studying Audiences: The Shock of the Real*. London: Routledge.
O'Regan, Tom. 1992. "Some Reflections on the Policy Moment." *Meanjin* 51 (3): 517–32.
———. 1993. "(Mis)Taking Policy: Notes on the Cultural Policy Debate." In *Australian Cultural Studies: A Reader*, ed. John Frow and Meaghan Morris. St. Leonards: Allen and Unwin.
Parker, Lynette. 1992. "The Creation of Indonesian Citizens in Balinese Primary Schools." *Review of Indonesian and Malay Affairs* 26 (1): 42–70.
Patterson, John. 1987. "The Price of Dam Development in Central Java." *Inside Indonesia* 13 (December): 7–10.
Peacock, James. 1968. *Rites of Modernization: Symbolic and Social Aspects of Indonesian Proletarian Drama*. Chicago: University of Chicago Press.
Perum Produksi Film Negara (PPFN) (State Film Production Center). 1987. "Desain Produksi." [Production Design]. Unpublished mimeograph, 28 January.
———. 1989. "Bahan Untuk Pers. Serial Sinetron: Keluarga Rahmat" [Press Release on the Television Serial: *Keluarga Rahmat*]. Unpublished mimeograph, 20 April.

———. 1989. "Sinopsis Sinopsis" [Synopses]. Unpublished mimeograph, 19 December.

———. n.d. "Kerangka Cerita: Film Seri 'Manusia Manusia KORPRI.'" (Story Plan: Film Series "KORPRI People").

Poole, Ross. 1989. "Public Spheres." In *Australian Communications and the Public Sphere,* ed. Helen Wilson. South Melbourne: MacMillan.

Pramodedya Ananta Toer. 1981. *This Earth of Mankind.* Translated Max Lane. Ringwood, Vic.: Penguin.

Quinn, George. 1996. *"Kelompencapir:* Indonesia's Rural Mass Media Discussion Groups." Unpublished paper presented at Asian Studies Association of Australia Conference, Melbourne, La Trobe University, 8–11 July.

Ramage, Douglas E. 1994. "Pancasila Discourse in Soeharto's Late New Order." In *Democracy in Indonesia, 1950s and 1990s,* ed. David Bourchier and John Legge. Clayton: Centre for Southeast Asian Studies, Monash University.

———. 1995. *Politics in Indonesia.* London: Routledge.

RCTI. 1989. "Makalah RCTI Untuk Dengar Pendapat DPR—Komisi I" [RCTI Submission to Parliamentary Commission I Hearing]. Jakarta: RCTI. 17 February. Unpublished typescript.

Reeve, David. 1985. *Golkar of Indonesia: An Alternative to the Party System.* Singapore: Oxford University Press.

Reid, Anthony, ed. 1983. *Slavery, Bondage, and Dependency in Southeast Asia.* New York: St. Martin's.

Rendra, W. S. 1979. *The Struggle of the Naga Tribe.* Trans. Max Lane. St. Lucia, Australia: University of Queensland Press.

Republik Indonesia. 1997. *Rancangan Undang Undang Republik Indonesia Tentang Penyiaran.*

———. *Rencana Pembangunan Lima Tahun Kedua 1974/75–1978/79* [REPELITA II, Second Five-Year Development Plan]. Jakarta: Departemen Penerangan.

———. *Rencana Pembangunan Lima Tahun Ketiga 1979/80–1983/84* [REPELITA III, Third Five-Year Development Plan]. Jakarta: Departemen Penerangan.

———. *Rencana Pembangunan Lima Tahun Keempat 1984/85–1988/89* [REPELITA IV, Fourth Five-Year Development Plan]. Jakarta: Departemen Penerangan.

———. *Rencana Pembangunan Lima Tahun Kelima 1989/90–1993/94* [REPELITA V, Fifth Five-Year Development Plan]. Jakarta: Departemen Penerangan.

Rice, Robert C. 1983. "The Origins of Basic Economic Ideas and Their Impact on 'New Order' Policies." *Bulletin of Indonesian Economic Studies* 19 (2): 60–82.

Robinson, Michael. 1993. "Enduring Anxieties: Cultural Nationalism and Modern East Asia." In *Cultural Nationalism in East Asia: Representations and Identity,* ed. Harumi Befu. Berkeley: Institute of East Asian Studies, University of California.

Robison, Richard. 1986. *Indonesia: The Rise of Capital*. North Sydney: Allen and Unwin.

———. 1993. "Indonesia: Tensions in State and Regime." In *Southeast Asia in the 1990's: Authoritarianism, Democracy, and Capitalism,* ed. Kevin Hewison, Richard Robison, and Gary Rodan. St. Leonards: Allen and Unwin.

Rogers, E. M., and Antola, L. 1985. "Telenovelas: A Latin American Success Story." *Journal of Communication* 35: 24–35.

Rogers, Everett M., James W. Dearing, and Dorine Bregman. 1993. "The Anatomy of Agenda-Setting Research." *Journal of Communication* 43 (2): 68–84.

Salim Said. 1991. *Shadows on the Silver Screen: A Social History of Indonesian Film,* ed. John H. McGlynn and Janet P. Boileau. Trans. Toenggoel P. Siagian. Jakarta: Lontar Foundation.

Saraswati Sunindyo. 1993. "Gender Discourse on Television." In *Culture and Society in New Order Indonesia,* ed. Virginia Matheson Hooker. Kuala Lumpur: Oxford University Press.

Saya Shiraishi. 1995. "Children's Stories and the State in New Order Indonesia." In *Children and the Politics of Culture,* ed. Sharon Stephens. Princeton, N.J.: Princeton University Press.

———. 1997. *Young Heroes: The Indonesian Family in Politics*. Ithaca, N.Y.: Southeast Asia Program Publications, Cornell University Press.

Schadt, Fritz. 1988. "Catatan Untuk Para Penulis Skenario: Struktur Skenario/Episode Serial 'Sinetronik'" [Notes for Scenario Writers: Scenario and Episode Structure in Television Serials]. Unpublished mimeograph, Jakarta, 4 February.

Schechner, Richard. 1993. "Wayang Kulit in the Colonial Margin." In *The Future of Ritual: Writings on Culture and Performance*. London: Routledge.

Schlesinger, Philip. 1991. "Media, the Political Order, and National Identity." *Media, Culture, and Society* 13 (1): 297–308.

Schlesinger, Philip. 1987. "On National Identity: Some Conceptions and Misconceptions Criticized." *Social Science Information* 26 (2): 219–64.

Schulte Nordholt, Henk. 1991. *State, Village, and Ritual in Bali: A Historical Perspective*. Amsterdam: VU University Press.

Schwarz, Adam. 1994. *A Nation in Waiting: Indonesia in the 1990s*. St. Leonards: Allen and Unwin.

Sears, Laurie J. 1996. *Shadows of Empire: Colonial Discourse and Javanese Tales*. Durham, N.C.: Duke University Press.

Sediono M. P. Tjondronegoro. 1984. *Social Organization and Planned Development in Rural Java*. Singapore: Oxford University Press.

Sen, Krishna. 1994. *Indonesian Cinema: Framing the New Order*. London: Zed Books.

Seno Gumira Ajidarma. 1995. *Eyewitness: Protest Stories from Indonesia*. Trans. Jan Lingard. Potts Point, Sydney: Imprint.

Siegel, James T. 1986. *Solo in the New Order: Language and Hierarchy in an Indonesian City*. Princeton, N.J.: Princeton University Press.

Siune, Karen. 1986. "Broadcasting, Point of Departure." *Mass Media Politics: Comparative Perspectives in Western Europe*. London: Sage Publications.

Smith, Anthony. 1995. *Television: An International History*. Oxford: Oxford University Press.

Smith, Anthony D. 1991. *National Identity*. London: Penguin.

Soeharto. 1982. "Speech of the President of the Republic of Indonesia at the Opening of the TVRI Production Centre, 24 August, 1982." TVRI. 1983. *Televisi Republik Indonesia*. Jakarta: Direktorat Televisi.

———. 1985. *Amanat Kenegaraan: Kumpulan Pidato Kenegaraan di Depan Sidang Dewan Perwakilan Rakyat* [State Addresses: Collected State Addresses Made Before the Indonesian Parliament]. 4 vols. Jakarta: Inti Idayu Press.

Soemartono, T. J., nd. "Sejarah Televisi Republik Indonesia Masa Panca Roba 1962–63" [The History of Indonesian National Television at a Time of Uncertainty, 1962–63]. Unpublished typescript.

———. 1991. "Televisi R.I. 24 Agustus 1962–24 Agustus 1991." *Lensa* (July–Aug.): 33–37.

Spitzer, Robert, ed. 1993. *Media and Public Policy*. Westport, Conn.: Praeger.

Stallybrass, Peter, and Allon White. 1986. *The Politics and Poetics of Transgression*. Ithaca, N.Y.: Cornell University Press.

Stanley. 1994. *Seputar Kedung Ombo* [Concerning Kedung Ombo]. Jakarta: Elsam.

Straubhaar, Joseph D. 1991. "Beyond Media Imperialism: Assymetrical Interdependence and Cultural Proximity." *Critical Studies in Mass Communication* 8: 39–59.

Stronach, Bruce. 1989. "Japanese Television." In *Handbook of Japanese Popular Culture,* ed. Richard Gid Powers and Hidetoshi Kato, 127–65. New York: Greenwood Press.
Sullivan, John. 1992. *Local Government and Community in Java: An Urban Case Study.* Singapore: Oxford University Press.
Sullivan, Norma. 1991. "Gender and Politics in Indonesia." In *Why Gender Matters in Southeast Asian Politics,* ed. Maila Stivens. Monash Papers on Southeast Asia, No. 23. Clayton, Vic.: Centre for Southeast Asian Studies, Monash University.
Sumartono, T. J. 1991. "Mengenang 30 Tahun Yang Lalu TVRI Dalam Kandungan Kota Jakarta" [Recollections of Indonesian National Television Thirty Years Ago in Jakarta]. *Lensa* (July–August): 27–37.
Sumita Tobing. 1991. "Development Journalism in Indonesia: Content Analysis of Government Television News." Ph.D. diss., Ohio State University.
Supomo, Raden. 1959. Speech given 31 May 1945. *Naskah Persiapan Undang-Undang Dasar 1945* [Documents of the Drafting of the 1945 Constitution]. Vol. 1. Ed. H. Muhammad Yamin. Jakarta: Siguntang.
Survey Research Indonesia (SRI). 1992. "News Tracking, All Demographics, August–December, 1992." Unpublished computer printout.
Takashi Fujitani. 1993. "Inventing, Forgetting, and Remembering: Toward a Historical Ethnography of the Nation-State." In *Cultural Nationalism in East Asia: Representation and Identity,* ed. Harumi Befu. Berkeley: Institute of East Asian Studies, University of California.
Tambiah, S. 1985. "A Reformulation of Geertz's Conception of the Theater State." In *Culture, Thought and Action, An Anthropological Perspective.* Cambridge, Mass.: Harvard University Press.
Teeuw, Andries. 1979. *Modern Indonesian Literature.* 2 vols. The Hague: Martinus Nijhoff.
Televisi Republik Indonesia (TVRI). 1983. *Televisi Republik Indonesia* [Indonesian National Television]. Jakarta: Direktorat Televisi Departemen Penerangan.
———. 1984. *Televisi Republik Indonesia* [Indonesian National Television]. Jakarta: Direktorat Televisi Departemen Penerangan.
Tempo. 1981. *Apa Dan Siapa: Sejumlah Orang Indonesia 1981–1982.* Jakarta: Grafiti Pers.
Teruo Sekimoto. 1990. "State Ritual and the Village: An Indonesian Case Study." In *Reading Southeast Asia: Translation of Contemporary*

Japanese Scholarship on Southeast Asia. Ithaca, N.Y.: Southeast Asia Program, Cornell University.

Tornquist, Olle. 1990. "Rent Capitalism, State, and Democracy." In *State and Civil Society in Indonesia,* ed. Arief Budiman. Clayton, Vic.: Centre of Southeast Asian Studies, Monash University.

Tulloch, John. 1990. *Television Drama: Agency, Audience, and Myth.* London: Routledge.

Tulloch, John, and Albert Moran. 1986. *A Country Practice:* "Quality Soap." Sydney: Currency Press.

Turner, Graeme. 1994. *Making It National: Nationalism and Australian Popular Culture.* St. Leonards: Allen and Unwin.

Turner, Victor. 1969. *The Ritual Process: Structure and Anti-Structure.* Harmondsworth: Penguin Books.

———. 1977. "Variations on a Theme of Liminality." In *Secular Ritual,* ed. Sally F. Moore and Barbara G. Myerhoff. Amsterdam: van Gorcum.

United Nations. 1965. *Statistical Yearbook.* New York: United Nations.

———. 1974. *Statistical Yearbook.* New York: United Nations.

van Klinken, Helene. 1991. "The Kedung Ombo Court Cases." *Inside Indonesia* 26 (March): 17–19.

Venturelli, Shalini. 1993. "The Imagined Transnational Public Sphere in the European Community's Broadcast Philosophy: Implications for Democracy." *European Journal of Communication* 8: 491–518.

Veven Sp. Wardhana. 1995. *Budaya Massa Dan Pergeseran Masyarakat* [Mass Culture and the Displacement of the Community]. Yogyakarta, Indonesia: Yayasan Bentang Budaya.

Wahyudi, J. B. 1985. *Jurnalistik Televisi: Tentang dan Sekitar Siaran Berita TVRI* [Television Journalism: Concerning TVRI News Broadcasts]. Bandung, Indonesia: Alumni.

Wawan Kuswandi. 1996. *Komunikasi Massa: Sebuah Analisis Media Televisi* [Mass Communication: An Analysis of Television]. Jakarta: Rineka Cipta.

White, Allon. 1982. "Pigs and Pierrots: The Politics of Transgression in Modern Fiction." *Raritan* 2 (2): 51–70.

Wild, Colin. 1987. "Indonesia: A Nation and Its Broadcasters." *Indonesia Circle* 43: 15–40.

———. 1991. "The Radio Midwife: Some Thoughts on the Role of Broadcasting during the Indonesian Struggle for Independence." *Indonesia Circle* 55: 34–42.

Williams, Raymond. 1974. *Television: Technology and Cultural Form.* Glasgow: Fontana/Collins.

———. 1976. *Communications*. Harmondsworth, England: Penguin Books.
———. 1977–78. "Realism, Naturalism and Their Alternatives." *Cine-Tracts* 1 (3): 61–74.
Wimar Witoelar. 1996. "Lessons from *Perspektif*." Unpublished paper presented at the seminar "Open Skies: Towards an Open Society, The Challenge of Broadcasting in Asia." Jakarta, 26–28 June.
———. 1996. Internet. apakabar@clark.net. 27 Feb. 1996.
Winters, Jeffrey A. 1996. *Power in Motion: Capital Mobility and the Indonesian State*. Ithaca, N.Y.: Cornell University Press.
Yayasan Kesejahteraan Anak Indonesia (YKAI). 1994. *Bagaimana Menonton Televisi Yang Pas Untuk Anak Anak?* [What is the Appropriate Way for Children to Watch Television?]. Jakarta: YKAI.

INDONESIAN LEGISLATION CITED

Direktur Jenderal Radio, Telvisi Film. 1975. *Surat Keputusan #11 Tentang Ketentuan Siaran Periklanan TV-RI*. Jakarta: Departemen Penerangan.

Majelis Permusyawaratan Rakyat (MPR). 1960. *Ketetapan No. II Majelis Permusyawaratan Rakyat Sementara* (MPRS). Lampiran A Bab I pasal 18: "Tentang Pembangunan Siaran Televisi."

Menteri Negara Sekretaris Negara RI. 1996. *Rancangan Undang-Undang Republik Indonesia Tentang Penyiaran*. Jakarta: Sekretaris Negara.

Menteri Pariwisata, Pos dan Telekomunikasi. 1986. *Keputusan Menteri #49 Tentang Antena Parabola Penerima Siaran Televisi*.

Menteri Penerangan [Minister of Information]. 1961. *Surat Keputusan #20 Tentang Panitia Persiapan Televisi Di Indonesia*. Jakarta: Departemen Penerangan.

———. 1966. *Surat Keputusan #107 Tentang Pembentukan Direktorat Televisi di Bawah Direktor Jenderal Radio Televisi Film*. Jakarta: Departemen Penerangan.

———. 1975. *Surat Keputusan #55B Tentang Susunan Organisasi dan Tata Kerja Departemen Penerangan RI*. Jakarta: Departemen Penerangan.

———. 1981. *Surat Keputusan #30 Tentang Peniadaan Siaran Niaga/Siaran Iklan dalam Acara Acara Siaran TVRI*. Jakarta: Departemen Penerangan.

———. 1986. *Surat Keputusan #167B Tentang Penyelenggaraan Siaran Televisi di Indonesia*. Jakarta: Departemen Penerangan.

———. 1987. *Surat Keputusan #190A Tentang Siaran Saluran Terbatas Televisi RI*. Jakarta: Departemen Penerangan.

———. 1990. *Surat Keputusan #111 Tentang Penyiaran di Indonesia*. Jakarta: Departemen Penerangan.

———. 1992. *Surat Keputusan #84A Tentang Perubahan Ketentuan Pasal 7 dan Pasal 14 111/Kep/Menpen/1990 Tentang Penyiaran Televisi di Indonesia*. Jakarta: Departemen Penerangan.

———. 1993. *Surat Keputusan #04A Tentang Perubahan Ketentuan Pasal-Pasal 7, 14, 16, 19 dan 20 Keputusan Menteri Penerangan R.I. Nomor 111/Kep/Menpen/1990 Tentang Penyiaran Televisi di Indonesia Sebagaimana Telah Diubah Dengan Surat Keputusan Menteri Penerangan RI Nomor 84 A/Kep/Menpen/1992.* Jakarta: Departemen Penerangan.

Presiden Republik Indonesia. 1963a. *Keputusan #27 Tentang Peraturan Penggunaan Televisi RI Yayasan Gelora Bung Karno.* Jakarta: Sekretariat Negara.

———. 1963b. *Keputusan #215 Tentang Pembentukan Jajasan Televisi Republik Indonesia.* Jakarta: Sekretariat Negara.

———. 1963c. *Keputusan #217 Tentang Mengangkat Anggota Direksi Yayasan TVRI.* Jakarta: Sekretariat Negara.

———. 1980. *Peraturan Pemerintah #37 Tentang Pengangkatan Pegawai Yayasan Televisi Republik Indonesia Menjadi Pegawai Negeri Sipil.* Jakarta: Sekretariat Negara.

———. 1990. *Keputusan Presiden #40 Tentang Pemungutan Iuran Pesawat Penerima Televisi.* Jakarta: Sekretariat Negara.

INDEX

advertising, 90, 93, 110, 215, 216, 227, 235, 241
   ban on, 15, 63–72, 78, 85, 89, 112, 276
   on commercial channels, 224, 306, 324, 330, 343
   and development, 84, 224, 276
   "educational advertising," 108, 280, 282
   industry, 65, 232
   on TVRI, 77, 84
advertising, education and children affair, 268, 276–88
Alex Leo Zulkarnain, 26, 38, 104, 242, 287, 298, 321, 370 n. 2
Alfian and Godwin Chu, 4, 11, 41, 48, 66, 181, 185, 276
Ali Murtopo, 36, 67, 81
Anderson, Benedict
   cone of light metaphor, 82
   imagined community, 148, 188, 209, 210, 227, 247
   monuments of power, 5
   power in Javanese society, 81, 84, 205, 206
   role of media in national community, 228, 245
Ang, Ien, 74, 150
ANTEVE, 226, 349
Ariel Heryanto, 83, 227, 230, 252
Arswendo Atmowiloto, 10, 11, 43, 78, 186, 202
Asian Games, Fourth, 21, 22, 26, 28, 31
Astrid Susanto, 55, 56
audience, 15, 17, 33, 46, 64, 68, 73–111, 146
   as childlike, 83
   as consumer, 99, 216, 268, 327, 339
   as family, 82, 113
   as global citizens, 99
   as market, 216
   as nation, 79, 146
   as public citizens, 85, 90, 268, 275, 327
audience discourses
   commercial, 99
   critical, 89, 93, 100, 101
   journalistic, 93
   official, 79, 91
azas tunggal legislation. *See* unifying principle legislation

Bahasa Indonesia. *See* Indonesian language
Berita Malam. *See under* news
broadcasting law, 238, 267, 287, 288, 295, 296–329, 334, 339, 340, 342, 343
broadcasting, public television, 75, 77, 78, 89, 94, 105, 109, 111, 147, 242, 251, 276, 285, 287, 334
Boediarjo, 36, 80

Centre for Strategic and Information Studies (CSIS), 10
children's television. *See* television, children's
civil society, 17
commercial television, 74, 75, 76, 77, 78, 94, 96, 97, 99, 100, 101, 103, 111, 215–49, 307
Communist party, Indonesian, 25
communitas, 207, 208, 209, 210, 212
competition, 232–44
cultural studies, 12, 13

decoding/encoding, 187, 200, 205, 211
Department of Education and Culture, 63, 278, 279, 284, 373 n. 24

407

Department of Information, 180, 244, 262, 271, 273, 276, 284, 324
  attitude to advertising, 69, 276, 287
  cultural policies and television, 68, 323, 324
  involvement with Palapa, 63
  relationship with telecommunications institutions, 55, 56, 373 n. 23
  relationship with TVRI, 33, 34, 35, 36, 37
  television development policies, 56, 221, 229, 230, 231, 238, 254, 276, 277, 298, 299
deregulation, 3, 14, 73, 232, 295, 331
  Department of Information's attitude, 236, 244, 299, 321
  effects:
    cultural perceptions of, 94, 105, 231, 232, 328
    on domestic programs, 103
    on idea of the subject, 297
    on industry organization, 239, 243, 273, 294, 333, 336–37, 339, 342
    on public sphere activity, 17, 108, 268, 275
  reasons for, 224, 229, 230
development communication
  assumptions of, 308
  development content in news, 186, 263
  development content in *wayang*, 381 n. 9
  development goals in *Selamat Pagi Indonesia*, 258, 259
  goals of, 178
  relation to programming, 41
  television's role in national development, 372 n. 16
  TVRI's development goals, 115, 270, 277, 328, 335, 336
  TVRI exemplifies, 256, 331, 334
Directorate General of Radio Television and Film, 34
Dunia Dalam Berita. See World News *under* news

Eduard Depari, 86, 88, 90, 108, 143, 233, 311

Emil Salim, 48, 49, 50, 51, 52, 54

familyism, 83, 126, 146–77
fieldwork, 7, 8
flow, programming, 8, 114, 120, 143, 190, 191, 332
foreign workers affair, 268, 288–95

Geertz, Clifford, 201, 202, 203, 206
globalization, 14, 191, 236, 237, 268, 324, 336, 343
gotong royong, 5, 6, 118, 130
Guided Democracy, 5, 201

Harmoko
  attitude toward competition, 239, 254
  attitude toward foreign investment, 238, 288
  attitude toward self-regulation, 321
  comments on satellite dishes, 222
  on cultural effects of television, 322, 327
  issues license for Pay TV, 226
  news policy, 255
  policy on advertising on TVRI, 287
  policy on political debate on television, 253
  on satellite television, 229, 304
  support for mass media discussion groups, 323
  support for Mekatama Raya, 269, 273
Hartley, John, 73, 83, 192

ideological project, 16, 112–45, 146–77
imagined community, 14, 17, 148, 188, 209, 227, 228, 242, 244, 247, 335
Indonesian Children's Welfare Foundation, 286, 310–11
Indonesian language, 135, 137, 138, 139
Intelsat, 27, 45, 48, 49, 179, 221
Ishadi SK, 10, 220, 239
iuran televisi. See license fee
IVM, 226, 288–95, 349

Javanization, 130

kekeluargaan. See familyism

408   Index

Keluarga Rahmat, 8, 9, 16, 83, 114, 126, 146–77

license fee, 76, 78, 269, 271, 275
license fees affair, 268, 269–75, 294

Maladi, 21, 23, 24, 25, 26, 30, 33, 34, 41, 277, 369 n. 1
Malari, 64, 373n 25, 67, 81
mass media, 11, 33, 42, 43, 115, 288
MISS SARA, 132, 171, 293, 341, 378 n. 21
Mochtar Lubis, 65, 227

national culture project
 definition, 3
 development as central, 186
 management of, 249
 television's role in, 112, 190, 234, 330, 334, 335, 340
 unitary construct of, 130, 132, 133, 174, 215, 333
national development
 advertising and, 84, 224
 content on television, 121, 182, 202, 206, 381 n. 4
 discourses of, 114, 144, 148, 168, 174, 187, 201, 204, 205, 207, 209, 210, 242, 253, 263
 ethos, 113, 115, 122, 218, 292
 goals, 84, 87
 as nation building, 80, 161
 shaping society for, 81, 145, 323, 327
 television's role in, 64, 88, 110, 121, 180, 193, 197, 211, 217, 234, 236, 255, 257, 331, 339
New Order
 affiliation with, 42, 315
 cultural policy, 4, 12, 15, 38, 81, 215, 234, 240, 260
 culture, 163, 176, 201, 203, 206, 327, 333, 335, 340, 342
 government, 3, 5, 21, 122, 193, 201, 260, 272, 297, 314, 330
 industrial and political policy, 241, 254, 260, 325, 336
news, 178–212
 commercial channel news, 250–67

national news, 8, 14, 16, 17, 178, 191, 208, 209, 212
news as ceremony, 179, 185, 186, 189, 191, 208, 211, 257, 261
news as ritual, 16, 186, 187, 188, 193, 209, 210, 339
soft news, 17, 181, 250, 255, 257, 260, 262
Western-style news, 178
World News, 27, 100, 179, 191, 199, 206, 257

P4, *Pedoman Penghayatan dan Pengamalan Pancasila*, 115, 116, 335, 474 n. 1
paedocracy, 83, 89, 106, 113, 114, 123, 128, 129
Palapa
 effects of deployment, 15, 38, 46–48, 55, 57, 60, 62, 63, 64, 81, 84, 85, 91, 212, 222, 223, 226, 332, 335
 launch, 54, 56, 342
 meaning of *"palapa,"* 54, 82, 372 n. 21
 Palapa and the cone of light, 81–82
 support for deployment, 49, 51–52, 54, 62
 use by neighbors, 2, 91, 212
Pancasila, 5, 6, 41, 44, 88, 90, 100, 113, 115, 140, 172, 234, 253, 335, 369 n. 1
parabola. *See* satellite dish
parliament (*Dewan Perwakilan Rakyat* DPR), 18, 196
parody, 129, 130, 131
Pay TV, 94, 224, 226
Pembangunan. *See* national development
pemirsa, 83, 97
persatuan dan kesatuan. *See* unity and union
PFN (*Pusat Perfilman Negara*). *See* State Film Centre
PKI (*Partai Komunis Indonesia*). *See* Communist party, Indonesian
Play School, 116
PPFN (*Perum Produksi Film Negara*). *See* State Film Centre
private sphere, 146–77, 242, 270
privatization, 268, 270, 271, 274, 275, 284
Programa Dua. *See* Second Channel

Index 409

public access television, 56
public sphere, 2, 17, 146–77, 242, 252, 328, 329
   bourgeois or Habermasian, 250, 251, 253, 256, 258, 260, 262, 265, 266, 270, 312, 337
   transnational, 2, 3, 251

Radio, Indonesian National. *See Radio Republik Indonesia* (RRI)
Radio Republik Indonesia (RRI), 23, 25, 26, 30, 34, 41–42, 49
Ramage, 5, 6
RCTI, 226, 349
Return to Eden, 151, 379 n. 5
   ritual form in news, 186, 187, 188, 195, 198, 200
   meeting form, 195
   report form, 194
   speech form, 196
   visit form, 197
RTF (*Direktorat Jenderal Radio, Televisi dan Film*). *See* Department of Information

satellite dish, 91, 92, 96, 211, 212, 221–24, 229, 298
Schadt, Fritz, 8, 147–51, 154, 157, 159–61, 166, 169
SCTV, 226, 349
Second Channel (*Programa dua*), 146, 151, 180, 181, 379 n. 1
Selamat Pagi Indonesia, 258–60, 263, 265
self, Indonesian, 13, 254, 338
Sen, Krishna, 148, 156, 163
sender-message-receiver model, 116, 211, 322
Seputar Indonesia, 181, 255, 257, 258, 260–62, 265
serial, 150, 170
series, 170, 171
Sesame Street, 116, 144
sex and violence in programming, 306–12, 317, 321, 323, 325
shadow language, 227, 235, 274
Si Unyil, 8, 15, 112–45
sinetron, 104, 244
sitcom (situation comedy), 124, 125, 126, 170
Siti Hardiyanti Rukmana, 10, 278, 279, 280
soap opera, 8, 9, 16, 83, 114, 146–77
Soehardjono, 49
Soeharto, 10, 45, 94, 342, 343
   intervention in television programming, 9, 64, 66, 89, 148, 149, 163, 176
   involvement in television development, 49, 54, 64, 267, 269, 275
   mass media policy, 42, 89, 206
spillover transmission, 220–21, 334
Spirit of Sukarno Foundation (*Jajasan Gelora Bung Karno*), 22, 34
State Film Centre, 9, 22, 26, 118, 119, 143, 147, 148, 149, 153, 155
subject, Indonesian
   child, 112, 113, 123
   contested, 14, 17, 142, 250, 256, 257, 259, 262–65, 297, 327–29, 337
   dependent, 125
   idealized, 16, 116, 117, 123, 130, 139, 143, 254, 330
   inadequate, 126, 137, 145
Sukarno, 30, 49, 275
   cultural policy, 5, 6, 13, 25, 51, 103, 201, 277
   Guided Democracy period, 5, 341
   involvement in television development, 22, 23, 28, 34
   mass media policy, 24
Sumartono Tjitrosidojo, 26, 30, 33, 34
Sumita Tobing, 186
Suprayogi, 33, 34

Takdir Alisjahbana, 4
televisi umum. *See* public access television
television, children's, 113, 286, 295, 306–12, 317, 323, 324, 325, 326, 327
TPI, 226, 277–85, 349
transmission model of communication, 42, 86, 322, 333
transnational, 2, 27, 72, 147, 150, 151, 154, 175, 215, 216, 248, 252, 338
TVRI, 22–72, 347
   Televisi Republik Indonesia Jajasan Gelora Bung Karno, 22

TVRI Foundation, 36, 239, 240, 254, 269, 341
TVRI Yogyakarta, 8

unifying principle legislation, 6, 335, 341
unity and union, 53, 80, 215, 242, 298, 333, 339, 340, 341

video, 91, 215, 217–20, 222, 223, 334

Yayasan Kesejahteraan Anak Indonesia (YKAI). *See* Indonesian Children's Welfare Foundation
Yayasan Televisi Republik Indonesia (YTVRI). *See* TVRI (Televisi Republik Indonesia)

www.ingramcontent.com/pod-product-compliance
Lightning Source LLC
Chambersburg PA
CBHW031228290426
44109CB00012B/203